THE CAM|
THE LITERATU.

This *Companion* provides a comprehensive introduction to one of the most vibrant and expansive traditions in world literature. The American West occupies a unique place in the global imagination, and the literature it produced transcends the category of "region" in theme and form. Written by prominent international scholars, the essays cover a diverse group of key texts and authors, including major figures in the Native American, Hispanic, Asian American, and African American movements. Treatments range from environmental and ecopoetic to transnational and transcultural, reflecting the richness of the field. This volume places the literature in deep historical context and features a chronology and bibliography for further reading. It will be an essential guide for students of literature of the American West and of American literature generally.

STEVEN FRYE is a professor of English at California State University, Bakersfield. He is president of the Cormac McCarthy Society, editor of *The Cambridge Companion to Cormac McCarthy*, and author of *Understanding Cormac McCarthy* and *Understanding Larry McMurtry*.

*A complete list of books in the series is at the back of this book.*

THE CAMBRIDGE
COMPANION TO

# THE LITERATURE OF THE
# AMERICAN WEST

THE CAMBRIDGE
COMPANION TO
# THE LITERATURE
OF THE
AMERICAN WEST

EDITED BY
STEVEN FRYE
*California State University, Bakersfield*

CAMBRIDGE
UNIVERSITY PRESS

# CAMBRIDGE
## UNIVERSITY PRESS

32 Avenue of the Americas, New York NY 10013-2473, USA

Cambridge University Press is part of the University of Cambridge.

It furthers the University's mission by disseminating knowledge in the pursuit of
education, learning, and research at the highest international levels of excellence.

www.cambridge.org
Information on this title: www.cambridge.org/9781107479272

© Cambridge University Press 2016

First published 2016

Printed in the United States of America by Sheridan Books, Inc.

*A catalog record for this publication is available from the British Library.*

*Library of Congress Cataloging in Publication Data*
Names: Frye, Steven, editor.
Title: The Cambridge companion to the literature of the American West /
edited by Steven Frye.
Description: New York: Cambridge University Press, 2016. |
Series: Cambridge companions to literature |
Includes bibliographical references and index.
Identifiers: LCCN 2015042948 | ISBN 9781107095373 (hardback) |
ISBN 9781107479272 (paperback)
Subjects: LCSH: American literature – West (U.S.) – History
and criticism. West (U.S.) – In literature. |
BISAC: LITERARY CRITICISM / American / General.
Classification: LCC PS271.C36 2016 | DDC 810.9/3278–dc23
LC record available at http://lccn.loc.gov/2015042948

ISBN 978-1-107-09537-3 Hardback
ISBN 978-1-107-47927-2 Paperback

# CONTENTS

# CONTENTS

# FIGURES

# CONTRIBUTORS

JOHN DUDLEY is an associate dean in the College of Arts & Sciences and a professor of English at the University of South Dakota. He is the author of *A Man's Game: Masculinity and the Anti-aesthetics of American Literary Naturalism*, as well as several articles on naturalism, African American literature, and Western American literature. His most recent publications include chapters in *The Cambridge Companion to Cormac McCarthy* and *Dirty Words in Deadwood: Literature and the Postwestern*. His current projects include a book-length study of African American literature and culture between 1890 and 1928, with an emphasis on the role of music, technology, and material culture in developing notions of racial identity.

STEVEN FRYE is a professor of English at California State University, Bakersfield and president of the Cormac McCarthy Society. He is the author of *Historiography and Narrative Design in the American Romance: A Study of Four Authors*, *Understanding Cormac McCarthy*, and *Understanding Larry McMurtry*. He is the editor of *The Cambridge Companion to Cormac McCarthy*, *Critical Insights: The Poetry of Edgar Allan Poe*, and *Critical Insights: The Tales of Edgar Allan Poe*. He is also the author of numerous articles on Cormac McCarthy, Herman Melville, and other writers in the American Romance tradition.

ERIC GARDNER is a professor of English at Saginaw Valley State University. His *Unexpected Places: Relocating Nineteenth-Century African American Literature* won the Research Society for American Periodicals Book Award and was a *Choice* "Outstanding Academic Title" in 2010. His second monograph, *Black Print Unbound: The Christian Recorder, African American Literature, and Periodical Culture*, was drafted with the support of a fellowship from the National Endowment for the Humanities and explores the early years of the African Methodist Episcopal Church's weekly newspaper. Gardner has also edited three volumes, and his shorter work has appeared in venues ranging from *American Literary History* to *PMLA*.

M. CARMEN GOMEZ-GALISTEO holds a BA in English with honors and a PhD (sobresaliente cum laude) in American studies, both from the Universidad de Alcalá (Madrid, Spain). She is the author of *The Wind Is Never Gone: Sequels, Parodies and Rewritings of Gone With the Wind* and *Early Visions and Representations of America: Álvar Núñez Cabeza de Vaca's* Naufragios *and William Bradford's* Of Plymouth Plantation. She currently teaches at UNED (Universidad Nacional de Educación a Distancia) in Madrid.

CATHRYN HALVERSON is an associate professor of American literature at the University of Copenhagen, Denmark and the author of *Maverick Autobiographies: Women Writers and the American West* and *Playing House in the American West: Western Women's Life Narratives.* Her present book project is a study of the *Atlantic Monthly* and Western women's life writing.

SUSAN KOLLIN is a professor of English at Montana State University, where she teaches courses on Western fiction and film, transnational American literature, and environmental humanities. She is the author of *Captivating Westerns: The Middle East in the American West*, and the editor of *A History of Western American Literature* (Cambridge University Press, 2015). She is also a former Fulbright Scholar at the American University in Cairo.

PIERRE LAGAYETTE is Emeritus Professor of American Studies at the University of Paris-Sorbonne, where he taught graduate seminars on the American West and contemporary American history and literature. He is also the founder and director of the Center for Western America and Asia-Pacific Studies at Paris-Sorbonne and has been a visiting scholar at Stanford University. He is the author of *The American West: Reality and Myths, Strategies of Difference in Modern Poetry: Case Studies in Poetic Composition, Major Landmarks in American History, A Short History of American Literature, Contemporary United States, A Bilingual Guide,* and *Executive Empire: The American Presidency from F.D. Roosevelt to G.W. Bush.* He has also been a contributor to the *Cambridge Companion to Cormac McCarthy,* edited by Steven Frye.

LEE CLARK MITCHELL is Holmes Professor of Belles-Lettres at Princeton University. His recent essays have focused on Cormac McCarthy, the Coen brothers, Henry James, and noir fiction. His books include *Witnesses to a Vanishing America: The Nineteenth-Century Response, Determined Fictions: American Literary Naturalism, The Photograph and the American Indian,* and *Westerns: Making the Man in Fiction and Film.* Currently, he is completing a book on close reading in modernist American novels.

NICHOLAS MONK is an associate professor at the University of Warwick, specializing in twentieth-century American fiction, and director of the University's Institute for Advanced Teaching and Learning. His monograph on Cormac McCarthy will be published in 2016. He is also the editor of *Intertextual and Interdisciplinary Approaches to Cormac McCarthy*, to which he contributed the introduction and an essay titled "Versions of the *Seeleroman*: Cormac McCarthy and Leslie Silko." He teaches the MA module, "Literatures of the American Southwest," as well as modules on identity, drama, and performance. A coauthored piece "Letting the Dead Come Out to Dance: An Embodied and Spatial Approach to Teaching Early Modern Drama" appears in *Performing Early Modern Drama Today*, from Cambridge University Press. His other principal research interest is interdisciplinary and collaborative pedagogy – he is the lead author of *Open-Space Learning: A Transdisciplinary Pedagogy*.

MARGUERITE NGUYEN is an assistant professor of English at Wesleyan University, where she teaches and researches American and Asian American literature. Her publications have appeared in *Minnesota Review* and *Asian Americans in Dixie: Race and Migration in the South*, and a coedited special issue of *MELUS* titled "Refugee Culture: Forty Years after the Vietnam War" is forthcoming. Her current book project, *Games with Time: Vietnam, U.S. Empire, and American Literature*, examines Vietnamese-American literary connections from the nineteenth century onward to understand how U.S. empire has depended on managing competing notions of time. A second project is under way on Asian American racialization in New Orleans culture, with an emphasis on the relationship between literary form, local discourses of race, and Pacific routes of migration.

LINDA RADER OVERMAN is an adjunct professor of English at California State University, Northridge. She holds a PhD in creative writing from Lancaster University (United Kingdom) and a master of fine arts in creative writing from California State University, Chico. Her debut novel, *Letters Between Us*, was selected as a finalist in the 2008 National Best Books Awards, in the category of Fiction & Lit: Chick Lit/Women's Lit. Her work has appeared in many anthologies.

STACEY PEEBLES is director of film studies and an associate professor of English at Centre College in Danville, Kentucky. She is the author of *Welcome to the Suck: Narrating the American Soldier's Experience in Iraq* and the editor of *Violence in Literature* as well as a forthcoming book on Cormac McCarthy and performance. She is the editor of *The Cormac McCarthy Journal* and the author of a number of articles on McCarthy's work and the representation of war in literature and film.

RAFAEL PÉREZ-TORRES is a professor of English at University of California, Los Angeles. He has published numerous articles on Chicano/a literature and culture, postmodernism, multiculturalism, and contemporary American literature in *Cultural Critique*, *American Literary History*, *Genre*, *Aztlán*, and *American Literature*, as well as in numerous edited collections. He served as co-curator for the art exhibit "Just Another Poster? Chicano Graphic Arts in California," and he sits on several editorial boards. He is the author of three books: *Mestizaje: Critical*

*Uses of Race in Chicano Culture*; *To Alcatraz, Death Row, and Back: Memories of an East L.A. Outlaw* written with Ernest B. López; and *Movements in Chicano Poetry: Against Myths, Against Margins*. His current work addresses the role of modernity and modernization in the shaping of Chicano culture.

ROBERT THACKER is Charles A. Dana Professor of Canadian Studies and English at St. Lawrence University. Among his publications are *The Great Prairie Fact and Literary Imagination* and *Alice Munro: Writing Her Lives*; four coedited critical volumes, two on comparing the Canada-U.S. Wests and two on Willa Cather. He is now at work on another volume of *Cather Studies* and a collection of essays on Munro by various hands. Forthcoming in 2016 is Thacker's *Reading Alice Munro, 1973–2013*, a selection of his essays on the 2013 Nobel Laureate.

GIOIA WOODS is an associate professor of humanities and President's Distinguished Teaching Fellow in Northern Arizona University's Department of Comparative Cultural Studies. She is the author of the Western Writer's Series monograph *Gary Paul Nabhan* and the coeditor of *Western Subjects: Autobiographical Writing in the North American West*. She was president of the Western Literature Association in 2010 and continues research and publishing in Western American literature and culture, and ecological criticism. Her current project is a cultural biography of City Lights Bookstore and Press.

DANIEL WORDEN is an associate professor of English at the University of New Mexico. He is the author of *Masculine Style: The American West and Literary Modernism*, which received the Thomas J. Lyon Book Award in Western American Literary and Cultural Studies. He is also the coeditor of *Oil Culture* and the editor of *The Comics of Joe Sacco: Journalism in a Visual World*.

| | |
|---|---|
| AD 500 | Anasazi (ancestral Pueblo) culture widespread in Four Corners area. Approximately five hundred specialized small tribes are living in California. |
| 500–1400 | Hohokam culture brings large areas in southern Arizona under irrigation. |
| 950+ | Mesa Verde cliff dwellings constructed. |
| 950–1300 | Chaco culture emerges in New Mexico; includes 125 planned towns. |
| 1000 | Pueblo and Hopi villages active in their present locations. |
| ca. 1150 | Oraibi (Arizona) established. |
| 1220–1400 | Navahos arrive in the Southwest from the north. |
| 1276–1299 | Severe drought in the Southwest. |
| 1528 | Álvar Núñez Cabeza de Vaca shipwrecked on Gulf Coast; begins eight-year journey to Mexico. |
| 1540 | Francisco Vásquez de Coronado begins an exploration from Arizona; over the next two years, travels as far northeast as Kansas. One of his officers, Don Garcia Lopez de Cardenas, takes a trip with twelve other men and sees the Grand Canyon. They are the first Europeans to do so. |
| 1598 | Juan de Oñate colonizes northern Mexico. |
| 1609–1610 | Santa Fe founded; "Palace of the Governors" built. |
| 1680 | Pueblo Indians revolt and drive the Spanish from New Mexico. |

| | |
|---|---|
| 1692 | Don Diego de Vargas reconquers New Mexico. |
| 1769 | Father Junípero Serra founds mission at San Diego; in the next thirteen years, he establishes nine of the twenty-one Franciscan missions in California. |
| 1774–1776 | Juan Batista de Anza leads colonizing parties from Mexico to the San Francisco Bay area. |
| 1776 | Fathers Dominguez and Escalante travel much of Colorado and Utah. |
| 1783 | Treaty of Paris concludes Revolutionary War, sets United States at Mississippi River. |
| 1803 | Thomas Jefferson buys Louisiana Territory from France, doubling the size of the United States. |
| 1804–1806 | Lewis and Clark cross the Louisiana Territory and go on to the mouth of the Columbia River; they return with information about the West. Their *Journals* become an American classic. |
| 1805–1807 | Zebulon Pike explores Colorado and New Mexico. |
| 1810–1812 | J. J. Astor sends a party overland to the Pacific to gain control of the Western fur market. The expedition fails in its main purpose. Returning, "Astorian" Robert Stuart crosses through South Pass in Wyoming, documented in *On the Oregon Trail: Robert Stuart's Journey of Discovery*. |
| 1819 | Naturalist Thomas Nuttall makes a solo journey up the Arkansas River drainage onto the plains; describes the trip in *A Journal of Travels into the Arkansas Territory, During the Year 1819*. |
| 1821 | Mexico gains independence; assumes control of the Southwest. |
| 1824 | Jedediah Smith, Jim Bridger, and other trappers cross South Pass, enter Great Basin, and discover the Great Salt Lake. Mountain-man era begins. |
| 1826–1827 | Jedediah Smith accomplishes immense explorations through Great Basin, California, and Oregon. Records these trips in his journal, *The Southwest Expedition of Jedediah S. Smith: His Personal Account of the Journey to California, 1826–1827*. |

1832      Washington Irving tours a portion of Oklahoma; describes journey in *A Tour on the Prairies* (1835). Capt. Benjamin Bonneville, on leave from the U.S. Army, begins three years' stay in the West as a mountain man; keeps a detailed journal used by Washington Irving for *The Adventures of Capt. Bonneville U.S.A* (1837). Painter George Catlin tours the West. In *Letters and Notes on the Manners, Customs, and Condition of the North American Indians* (1841), suggests a huge "nation's park," covering much of the High Plains, in which Indians and wildlife would be left undisturbed.

1834      Mountain man Joe Walker leads a group across Great Basin to California; he sees Yosemite Valley, the first Euro-American to do so.

1835      Washington Irving meets J. J. Astor; working from Astor's documents, writes *Astoria* (1836).

1836      Washington Irving meets Capt. Benjamin Bonneville, buys his journal, and writes *The Adventures of Capt. Bonneville U.S.A.* (1837), the first account of the Western fur trade.

1839      John K. Townsend, *Narrative of a Journey across the Rocky Mountains, to the Columbia River, and a Visit to the Sandwich Islands, Chili, & c.*

1841      Last mountain-man rendezvous.

1842–1844      John Charles Fremont surveys the West for the government; writes *Report of the Exploring Expedition to the Rocky Mountains in the Year 1842, and to Oregon and North California in the Years 1843–44* (1845).

1845      Journalist John L. O'Sullivan coins the phrase "Manifest Destiny."

1846      Francis Parkman takes post-college tour into eastern Wyoming; writes *The Oregon Trail* (1849).

             Thousands of immigrants travel the Oregon and California Trails; Donner Party becomes trapped by Sierra Nevada snows.

1846–1848      Mexican-American War. Treaty of Guadalupe Hidalgo transfers control of the Southwest to the United States.

1847      Mormons cross from Nebraska to Salt Lake City.

1848–1849      Discovery of gold at Sutter's Mill on the American River inspires fortune hunters and others to enter California.

1850      California becomes a state.

1852      Approximately one hundred thousand prospectors and miners are at work in the foothills of the Sierra Nevada.

1853      Gadsden Purchase sets border with Mexico along its present lines.

1854      John Rollin Ridge, *The Life and Adventures of Joaquin Murieta, the Celebrated California Bandit,* the first novel published by a Native American (Cherokee).

1857      Mountain Meadows Massacre in southwest Utah; Mormon settlers, with Piute accomplices, kill somewhere between 90 and 115 members of a wagon train bound for California.

1858–1860      Gold rushes in Nevada, Colorado, and Idaho add to the Western population. San Francisco becomes the West's first literary center.

1860      House of Beadle and Adams, New York, begins publication of popular fiction with frontier and Western themes.

1861      Telegraph connects Eastern and Western United States

1862      Homestead Act precipitates Western settlement.

1864      The "Colorado Volunteers" destroy a village of Cheyenne Indians at Sand Creek.

     President Lincoln sets aside Yosemite Valley as a protected reserve.

     Majority of Navaho tribe is captured in Arizona and taken to New Mexico, where they are held until 1868.

1867      Appointment of General Philip Sheridan as commander of the Department of the Missouri signals increased militarization of U.S. policy toward Western Indians.

1868      Lieutenant Colonel George A. Custer leads the 7th Cavalry in massacre of a Cheyenne village on the Washita River in Oklahoma.

The *Overland Monthly* begins publication in San Francisco, under editorship of Bret Harte.

1869    "Golden Spike" driven at Promontory, Utah, completing the transcontinental railroad.

John Muir's first summer in the Sierra Nevada.

John Wesley Powell and party descend the Green and Colorado Rivers, make the last "discoveries" of a mountain range (the Henry Mountains) and river (the Escalante) in the continental United States.

1872    Clarence King, *Mountaineering in the Sierra Nevada.*

Mark Twain, *Roughing It.*

Yellowstone National Park created; world's first reserve of its kind.

1874    Barbed wire patented; "open range" days numbered.

George A. Custer, *My Life on the Plains.*

John Wesley Powell, *The Exploration of the Colorado River and Its Tributaries.*

1876    George A. Custer leads 7th Cavalry into disaster near Little Bighorn River, Montana.

1881    Helen Hunt Jackson, *A Century of Dishonor,* exposé of Indian policy.

1882    Clarence Dutton, *Tertiary History of the Grand Cañon District.*

1883    Sarah Winnemucca (Northern Piute), *Life among the Piutes.*

1884    Last significant shipment of buffalo hides from the Plains.

1887    Five hundred forty-one buffalo remain alive in the United States; of these, an estimated eighty-five are living in the wild.

1890    Ghost Dance takes place, followed by the massacre of Indian village at Wounded Knee, South Dakota, conducted by the 7th Cavalry; 102 Lakota men, 44 women, and 18 children are killed.

Yosemite National Park is created, as suggested by John Muir.

U.S. Census Bureau declares frontier closed.

Mormon leader Wilford Woodruff issues manifesto against polygamy; in succeeding decades, Mormon society becomes increasingly "mainstream."

1891 Hamlin Garland, *Main-Travelled Roads.*
President Harrison creates Forest Reserves.

1893 Frederick Jackson Turner promulgates "frontier thesis."

1894 John Muir, *The Mountains of California.*

1897 Klondike Gold Rush

1899 Frank Norris, *McTeague.*

1900 First motor vehicle reaches south rim of the Grand Canyon.

1902 Owen Wister, *The Virginian.*
Newlands Act establishes Bureau of Reclamation, inaugurating era of large, federally sponsored water projects that will affect much of the West.

1903 Mary Austin, *The Land of Little Rain.*
Jack London, *The Call of the Wild.*

1904–1907 Reuben G. Thwaites, ed., *Early Western Travels,* a thirty-two-volume set of narratives by explorers and early travelers.

1905 Los Angeles voters approve bonds for an aqueduct that will supply the city by taking the Owens River, 250 miles north.

1906 Much of San Francisco destroyed by earthquake and fire.

1911 Enos Mills, *The Spell of the Rockies.*

1912 Zane Grey, *Riders of the Purple Sage*
John Muir, *The Yosemite.*

1913 Congress authorizes reservoir in Hetch Hetchy, within Yosemite National Park.
Willa Cather, *O Pioneers!*

1915 Rocky Mountain National Park established.
Taos Society of Artists founded.

1916 National Park Service created.

Jeanette Rankin of Montana becomes the first woman elected to Congress.

Federal Aid Highway Act authorizes government road subsidies; federal highway building will have a major effect on the West.

1918     Willa Cather, *My Antonia*.

1920     Sinclair Lewis, *Main Street*.

1922     Willa Cather, *One of Ours* (Pulitzer Prize, 1923).

Colorado River Compact apportions that stream's flow among Wyoming, Colorado, Utah, New Mexico, Nevada, Arizona, and California; clarifies federal government's role in Western natural resource development.

1923–1924     Teapot Dome oil scandal.

1924     Mary Austin, *The Land of Journeys' Ending*.

1925     Willa Cather, *The Professor's House*.
Dorothy Scarborough, *The Wind*.
Robinson Jeffers, *Rian Stallion, Tamar, and Other Poems*.

1927     Ole Rølvaag, *Giants in the Earth*.
Mourning Dove [Okanogan], *Co-ge-we-a*, the first novel by an Indian woman.
Harvey Fergusson, *Wolf Song*.

1929     Oliver LaFarge, *Laughing Boy*.

1930s     Depression era enlarges federal presence in the West. In per capita assistance received through the New Deal, fourteen Western states lead the nation. Farm support and work relief programs contribute significantly to Western sustenance.

1931     Vardis Fisher, *Dark Bridwell*.

1932     Mary Austin, *Earth Horizon*.
Black Elk, *Black Elk Speaks*.
Bernard DeVoto, *Mark Twain's America*.
Vardis Fisher, *In Tragic Life*.

1933     *The Lone Ranger* debuts on station WXYZ, Detroit.

| | |
|---|---|
| 1934 | Thomas Hornsby Ferril, *Westering*. |
| | Taylor Grazing Act sets aside public domain for federal management, not for sale to the public. |
| 1935 | H. L. Davis, *Honey in the Horn*. |
| | Frank Waters, *The Wild Earth's Nobility*. |
| 1936 | D'Arcy McNickle [Cree/Irish], *The Surrounded*. |
| | Boulder Dam completed, largest federal project to date. |
| 1937 | John Steinbeck, *Of Mice and Men*. |
| 1939 | John Steinbeck, *The Grapes of Wrath*. |
| | Vardis Fisher, *Children of God*. |
| | Franklin Walker, *San Francisco Literary Frontier*. |
| | Nathanael West, *The Day of the Locust*. |
| 1940 | Walter Van Tilburg Clark, *The Ox-Bow Incident*. |
| 1941 | Entrance of United States into World War II. By 1943, the federal government has become the largest single employer in the West. |
| | Maurine Whipple, *The Giant Joshua*. |
| 1942 | One hundred ten thousand Americans of Japanese descent are removed from the West Coast and placed in camps. |
| | Frank Waters, *The Man Who Killed the Deer*. |
| 1943 | Wallace Stegner, *The Big Rock Candy Mountain*. |
| 1943–1945 | Atomic bombs are developed in a secret project at Los Alamos, New Mexico. |
| 1944 | Adloph Murie, *The Wolves of Mount McKinley*. |
| 1945 | Walter Van Tilberg Clark, *The City of Trembling Leaves*. |
| 1947 | A. B. Guthrie Jr., *The Big Sky*. |
| | Bernard DeVoto, *Across the Wide Missouri*. |
| 1949 | Jack Schaefer, *Shane*. |
| | A. B. Guthrie Jr., *The Way West*. |
| | Walter Van Tilberg Clark, *The Track of the Cat*. |
| 1950s | Military presence in the West and defense industries leads to increasing dependence of the area on Cold War spending. |

| | |
|---|---|
| 1950 | Frank Waters, *Masked Gods*.<br>Harvey Fergusson, *Grant of Kingdom*. |
| 1952 | Walter Prescott Webb, *The Great Frontier*. |
| 1954 | Frederick Manfred, *Lord Grizzly*.<br>Joseph Wood Krutch, *The Voice of the Desert*. |
| 1955 | Poetry reading at the Six Gallery in San Francisco inaugurates the "Beat Generation." |
| 1956 | Wright Morris, *The Field of Vision*. |
| 1957 | John Okada, *No-No Boy*. |
| 1958 | First ascent of Yosemite's El Capitan. |
| 1960s–1990s | Flourishing electronics and aerospace industries, along with growing Pacific trade, solidify the West's economic strength. |
| 1960 | John Graves, *Goodbye to a River*.<br>Vardis Fisher, *Orphans in Gethsemane*. |
| 1962 | John Steinbeck wins Nobel Prize for Literature.<br>California becomes the most populous state.<br>William Stafford, *Traveling through the Dark*.<br>Theodora Kroeber, *Ishi in Two Worlds*.<br>César Chávez organizes National Farm Workers Organization. |
| 1963 | Frank Waters, *Book of the Hopi*. |
| 1965 | Luis Valdez organizes El Teatro Campesino in support of César Chávez and the California farm workers.<br>Vardis Fisher, *Mountain Man*. |
| 1966 | Frank Waters, *The Woman at Otowi Crossing*.<br>Theodore Roethke, *The Collected Poems of Theodore Roethke*.<br>Larry McMurtry, *The Last Picture Show*. |
| 1967 | Gary Snyder, *The Black Country*. |
| 1968 | Edward Abbey, *Desert Solitaire*.<br>Leslie Fiedler, *The Return of the Vanishing American*. |

N. Scott Momaday, *House Made of Dawn*.

Larry McMurtry, *In a Narrow Grave*.

1969       Gary Snyder, *Earth House Hold*.

Wallace Stegner, *The Sound of Mountain Water*.

N. Scott Momaday, *The Way to Rainy Mountain*.

Indians occupy Alcatraz in protest against federal policies.

1970       John G. Cawelti, *The Six-Gun Mystique*.

1971       Wallace Stegner, *Angle of Repose*.

Frank Waters, *Pike's Peak*.

1972       Rudolfo Anaya, *Bless Me, Ultima*.

1974       Gary Snyder, *Turtle Island*.

John Nichols, *The Milagro Beanfield War*.

James Welch, *Winter in the Blood*.

Ann Zwinger, *Run, River, Run*.

1975       Edward Abbey, *The Monkey Wrench Gang*.

1976       Wallace Stegner, *The Spectator Bird*.

David Wagoner, *Collected Poems*.

Norman Maclean, *A River Runs Through It*.

1977       William Stafford, *Stories That Could Be True: New and Collected Poems*.

Gary Soto, *The Elements of San Joaquin*.

Leslie Silko, *Ceremony*.

Howard Lamar, ed., *Reader's Encyclopedia of the American West*.

Frederick Manfred, *Green Earth*.

Richard Hugo, *31 Letters and 13 Dreams*.

1978       Luis Valdez, *Zoot Suit*.

Barry Lopez, *Of Wolves and Men*.

1979       Wallace Stegner, *Recapitulation*.

1980       Sam Shepherd, *True West*.

1981       Frank Waters, *Mountain Dialogues*.

John Okadu, *No-No Boy*

1983     Gerard Haslam, *Hawk Flights: Visions of the West.*
Raymond Carver, *Cathedral.*

1984     Louise Erdrich, *Love Medicine.*
Sandra Cisneros, *The House on Mango Street.*

1985     Cormac McCarthy, *Blood Meridian.*
Donald Worster, *Rivers of Empire: Water, Aridity, and the Growth of the American West.*
Marc Reisner, *Cadillac Desert.*
Ursula LaGuin, *Always Coming Home.*
Larry McMurtry, *Lonesome Dove.*
Gretel Ehrlich, *The Solace of Open Spaces*

1986     James Welch, *Fools Crow.*
Barry Lopez, *Arctic Dreams.*
Louis L'Amour, *Last of the Breed.*

1987     Patricia Nelson Limerick, *Legacy of Conquest.*
Western Literature Association, *A Literary History of the American West.*
William Kittredge, *Owning It All.*
Charles Bowden, *Frog Mountain Blues.*
Vera Norwood and Janice Monk, *The Desert Is No Lady.*

1989     John Haines, *The Stars, the Snow, the Fire.*
Amy Tan, *The Joy Luck Club.*
Richard Nelson, *The Island Within.*
Maxine Hong Kingston, *The Woman Warrior.*

1990     William DeBuys, *River of Traps.*
Gary Snyder, *The Practice of the Wild.*
Linda Hogan, *Mean Spirit.*
James Welch, *The Indian Lawyer.*
Gerald Haslam, *The Other California: The Great Central Valley in Life and Letters.*
Douglas Peacock, *Grizzly Years.*

| | |
|---|---|
| 1991 | Terry Tempest Williams, *Refuge.* |
| | Rick Bass, *Winter.* |
| | Leslie Silko, *Almanac of the Dead.* |
| | Charles Bowden, *Desierto.* |
| 1992 | First captivity-bred California condors are released into the wild. |
| | James Galvin, *The Meadow.* |
| | William Kittredge, *Hole in the Sky.* |
| | Rick Bass, *The Ninemile Wolves.* |
| | Jane Tompkins, *West of Everything: The Inner Life of Westerners.* |
| | Wallace Stegner, *Where the Bluebird Sings to the Lemonade Springs: Living and Writing in the West.* |
| | Cormac McCarthy *All the Pretty Horses.* |
| 1993 | Linda Hogan, *The Book of Medicines.* |
| | C. L. Rawlins, *Sky's Witness.* |
| 1994 | Cormac McCarthy, *The Crossing.* |
| | Gerald Haslam, *Condor Dreams.* |
| | James Welch, *Killing Custer.* |
| 1995 | Wolves are reestablished in Yellowstone National Park. |
| | Ann Zwinger, *Downcanyon: A Naturalist Explores the Colorado River through the Grand Canyon.* |
| | Linda Hogan, *Dwellings: Reflections on the Natural World.* |
| | Rick Bass, *In the Loyal Mountains.* |
| | Maria Helena Viramontes, *Under the Feet of Jesus.* |
| 1996 | Gary Snyder, *Mountains and Rivers Without End.* |
| | Jack Turner, *The Abstract Wild.* |
| | Rick Bass, *The Book of Yaak.* |
| 1997 | Rick Bass, *The Sky, the Stars, the Wilderness.* |
| | Nora Okja Keller, *Comfort Woman.* |
| 1998 | Cormac McCarthy, *Cities of the Plain.* |
| | Western Literature Association, *Updating the American West.* |

| | |
|---|---|
| 2001 | Terrorist attacks on the World Trade Center and the Pentagon initiate the post-9/11 era. |
| | United States invades Afghanistan in search of Osama Bin Laden and to displace the Taliban. |
| 2003 | United States invades Iraq to displace Saddam Hussain. |
| | Dao Strom, *Grass Roof, Tin Roof*. |
| 2007 | Maria Helena Viramontes, *Their Dogs Came With Them*. |
| 2012 | Record drought begins in the western United States, primarily California. |

# ACKNOWLEDGMENTS

A heartfelt thanks to all the colleagues, friends, and family members who have helped bring this volume to fruition. I would first like to express appreciation to the contributors, all of whom wrote their essays with supreme dedication and good will, with a deep commitment to the field of the literature of the American West. The many tasks involved in bringing an edited collection to print are quite challenging, and the advice and support of numerous colleagues, named and unnamed, have been indispensable. I would like to thank the editorial team at Cambridge University Press, particularly Ray Ryan and Caitlyn Gallagher, for their attention to detail and tremendous effort. My special appreciation goes to Susan Kollin, whose insight into the proposal helped reshape the volume's conceptual structure. Thanks to Stacey Peebles for her wise advice along the way, and appreciation too for the steadfast collegiality and friendship of Eric Carl Link, Greg Trine, and Andy Troup. A special thank you to Curt Asher and Christy Gavin at the Walter W. Stiern Library at California State University, Bakersfield. Their efforts in assisting with research were invaluable. As always, thank you to my parents, Ed and Joann Frye, and to my sister, Laura Myers, for their lifelong support. And particular acknowledgment to my lovely wife, Kristin, who for more than twenty-five years has taken the time to listen and care. Special appreciation goes to my daughter, Melissa, who served as editorial assistant and was always ready with the necessary words of encouragement, empathy, and insight. Finally to my son, Thomas, now away at college, who as I worked was usually in the background playing music. As I think of this collection, I will faithfully conjure in my memory the sweet sound of his strings.

# I

STEVEN FRYE

# Introduction

The American West has always been a locale both physically real and ideologically substantial, with a distinctive topography and a history the contours of which have no recorded precedent. From the colonial period forward, the region has helped to define the European as well as the American imagination. The lines of demarcation have perpetually changed. The "West" started as a boundary region beginning only a few miles inland from the East Coast. In early British and French explorer narratives, the lush, mysterious, foreboding, and ultimately sublime wilderness attracted adventurers with an almost intoxicating force. Certainly, the aspirations of these men and the monarchs who commissioned them were largely material, but written reflections reveal deeper, more indefinable motives. Even their drive for acquisition took much energy from what F. Scott Fitzgerald so eloquently defined as "the incomparable milk of wonder." In pondering the regions west of the first settlements, the early Puritans thought of the unsettled land in typological terms, as a dark "wilderness" of spiritual trial and transformation. Later fiction writers like James Fenimore Cooper, Robert Montgomery Bird, and William Gilmore Simms imagined the West as the source ground for a quintessential American story: the frontier narrative, which has become perhaps the most dominant Western world mythology since the Renaissance. In literature, film, pictorial art, and photography, stories of the frontier and the American West have been exported successfully throughout the world, and they have been received with enthusiasm from Western Europe, into Asia, through the Middle East, to India. This interest has led to a tradition of Western writing and an identifiable regional literature – the literature of the American West.

British, French, and other northern European settlers transformed their experiences into stories, and the West as an idea was initially conceived in terms of an East/West trajectory. The "West," always a word frequently used, was alternatively described as both "wilderness" and "frontier," and the geographical line that distinguished the region moved from the coast, into the

Alleghenies, past them to the Great Plains and the Rocky Mountains, to the "Pastures of Plenty" in California's Great Central Valley, and further to the cliffs and surf-bound jutting rocks of Big Sur. Colonial writers ranging from John Smith, Samuel de Champlain, William Bradford, J. Hector St. John de Crevecoeur, and later Thomas Jefferson explored the shaping influence of Western lands on human identity. The expansion of the new nation westward in the nineteenth century fueled this mythic trajectory of mind, captured perhaps most vividly in Walt Whitman's celebratory poem of Manifest Destiny, "Passage to India." In the late nineteenth century, this East-to-West pattern of historical movement led to the most dominant historiographic understanding, which was articulated by Frederick Jackson Turner in "The Significance of the Frontier in American History" (1893). Reflecting on what he saw as the closing of the American frontier, which he dubiously defined as an unsettled, open, unoccupied space, Turner argued that the frontier and the movement westward was the defining motive of American historical development. His consideration was valid to the extent that it recognized something collective and universal in the American imaginary, a ubiquitous idea of American cultural identity that found and still finds expression in frontier mythology. However, clouded by a Eurocentric bias somewhat typical of the nineteenth century, Turner articulated an incomplete history, and in doing so offered a false narrative, one that motivated more than a half-century of American historiographic practice. In fact, the region now understood as the American West was never empty, having been occupied by numerous groups of indigenous peoples. Its settlement was circular rather than linear, beginning with Spanish colonization and continuing with a series of migrations including Asian immigrants, former African American slaves, Hispanic migrants from various locations in a series of waves, and a constant reconfiguration of Native American cultural identities. All of these cultures and peoples produced the literature of the American West.

As is often the case when a literature is explored in regional terms, a number of issues form the complex thematic texture in Western writing. Topography is central. The themes of perpetual migration and transience, settlement, familial displacement, cultural hybridization and identity formation, resource scarcity and competition, aridity and the concomitant environmental concerns – all of these inform the "New Western Writers," now a rather conventional and rather reductive term used to describe authors, poets, and playwrights roughly of the mid-twentieth century. Political conflict dovetails with these concerns, as the inevitable competition that emerges between distinct groups, some powerful and some disenfranchised, becomes a tangible force in the creation of cities and communities, as well as industrial and agrarian infrastructure. The history and literature of the

American West takes shape from these very tangible realities, but as scholars have continued to explore the region and its writing, new lines of inquiry and new layers of understanding have more recently emerged. These include transnational American studies, borderlands criticism, and ethnicity studies, as well as eco-criticism and environmental justice studies. The relative youth of Western cities makes them a primary focus of study, and the role California and other states have played in the formation of the New Left, often in cities ranging from Los Angeles to San Francisco, and Portland to Seattle, have served to inform if not redefine the contours of public discourse and public policy nationwide.

Transnational and transcultural considerations call attention to the circular nature of the West's colonial history, recalling truths already known but often ignored. In a flash of historical time, the American West was a magnet for a plethora of cultures, religions, languages, economies, and continually dynamic trans-hemispheric linkages. In the early nineteenth century, President Andrew Jackson, who hailed from Kentucky, self-identified as a "Westerner," and in doing so he meant to evoke a range of mythic associations: the frontier, visionary expansionism, egalitarian democracy, the rejuvenating power of violence, and the primacy of the individual. As the boundary shifted, so the range of peoples and cultures that redefined the American West multiplied. Many of the Native Americans who preceded the Spanish conquest were quickly lost to history (although fortunately their lives and cultures are preserved in part in early European explorer narratives), as distinct but hybrid plains cultures emerged – the Sioux, the Comanche, the Apache, and the Kiowa – who built societies and modes of living around the horse. This hybridization is in many ways the grand pattern of Western identity considered in a transnational and transcultural context, as native people reconstituted their own regional cultures, drawing an essential aspect of their sustaining identity from the European settler, while maintaining with stubborn force their own sense of self. In the nineteenth century, these tensions inform the diasporic experiences of migrants from the East certainly, but also from discrete groups like the Mormons and those not frequently enough considered in the linear conception of westward expansion. These included mixed-race Latin peoples, displaced Native Americans, Chinese and Japanese immigrants, African Americans moving during the postbellum period from the slave states, and peoples of various backgrounds displaced by the affirmative materialist dream of an industrial revolution that for them had become a nightmare. It is a process of cultural displacement, migration, blending, and hybridization that continued throughout the twentieth century and into the present time. This remapping of the West, which preserves but enriches the regional and geographic model with concepts of movement that can be charted along ethnic, economic, and cultural lines, has led to a more complete understanding of the American West as a locus point for an international imaginary. One might note the striking visual representation of this cultural complexity at the conclusion of Sergio Leone's *Once Upon a Time in the West*. The film begins in a train station, as three outlaws wait to murder the man who will become the film's mysterious but sympathetic protagonist. After the dark fairy tale reaches its conclusion, the iconic image of the train (which appears with evocative frequency throughout the film) emerges again, as a former prostitute provides water to the rail workers who gather around her. Ennio Morricone's score lifts to a crescendo and the camera pans to group of workers – white men, Mexicans, African Americans, others with shrouded faces implying an infinitude of ethnic identities – and the panoply of cultures and peoples merge around perhaps the most evocative symbols of nineteenth-century America, the Western town and the train.

In a contemporary context, the national mood immediately following the defeat of Germany and Japan in World War II was highly vulnerable, and this anxiety is perhaps expressed in the seemingly desperate attempt to retain and reaffirm an American mythology centered still in the premodern rural West. Western films in the 1950s and 1960s demonstrate this sensibility and, interestingly, popular Western television series in the 1960s such as *Bonanza*, *The Big Valley*, and *High Chaparral* are thinly veiled capitalist allegories in which the hero is the Captain of Industry (the rancher) and the villainous antagonist is frequently the indigent poor man who resents the hero's "legitimately" earned success. Running parallel to this allegory is the social reality it embodies in figurative terms. The West that dominates is no longer the rural but the urban and suburban. The Western hero's analog lives certainly on the East Coast, but he has moved to Los Angeles, San Francisco, Portland, and Seattle. In these postwar years, an economic expansion of unprecedented scale occurs. A defense industry focused on the space age locates itself primarily in Southern California, agricultural economies expand, the petroleum industry grows and flourishes, particularly in Texas and California, leading to one of the greatest migrations in American history, initially from East to West, but later from countries around the world. Cities expand and suburbs flourish. Vast Western spaces remained, but people lived primarily in sprawling coastal and semi-coastal regions in vast numbers, and in this context, the social fabric changed. The primacy of extended families faded as nuclear families relocated, and the insularity of the nuclear family was stressed and complicated by the civil rights movement and a rapid reconsideration of gender roles that contributed to or at least ran parallel with rising divorce rates and new familial arrangements. A significant migration of peoples from the Far East and Middle East occurred as a result of international conflicts and employment opportunities in the new Western economy. Transience, that central reality in the Western experience, was yet again the leitmotif of the postwar West. A mini-mall built in 1950, complete with a supermarket, a movie theater, and a drugstore, decorated with colors and landscapes of the space age, was razed and leveled in 1975. In its place came the new and expanded supermarket, a ten-screen movie theater, a video store, a vegetarian eatery, all draped in the light brown stucco that conformed to earthquake code. Perpetual change and impermanence was the outer projection of the social sphere, as city people struggled to constitute identities – marriages, friendships, political alliances, religious affiliations – in a new urbanized and suburbanized West. This experience of the postwar West and what has come to be called the "post-West" is explored by a host of authors.

Essential to the study of the literature of the American West, a field of inquiry emerged inevitably from a powerful if not distinctively American preoccupation. That school or paradigm has been alternately called eco-criticism, eco-poetics, environmental literary criticism, and green cultural studies. There are traceable linkages between this contemporary critical movement and the history of American nature writing, and these relationships cannot be ignored or underemphasized. Spanish explorers such as Álvar Núñez Cabeza de Vaca and Bartolome de la Casas wrote narratives of natural encounter that present American lands in spiritualized, sublime, and often deeply reverential terms. In a reinterpretation of their own experience through biblical typology, colonial Puritans in the Plymouth and Massachusetts Bay Colonies envisioned nature as both wilderness and garden, investing and imbuing it with a deep sense of the sacred. From coast to coast, the earliest settlers and colonists, most religious to varying degrees, defined their relationship with the land spiritually, and contemporary notions of "preservation" were alive in the concept of stewardship, a sense that "ownership" in a conventional sense was an untenable and spiritually bankrupt conception, the seed ground for corruption and religious declension. By no means did these colonists possess a modern environmental sensibility, but the true source of exploitation came from the avaricious material interests that traveled with them in greater numbers on the same transport ships. Thus was initiated an historical tension between the forces of environmental responsibility – a respect for and even a reverence for nature and the natural world – and a powerful legion of interests that saw nature as a thing to mine and exploit for material gain. This tension finds its expression in the work of American transcendentalists such as Ralph Waldo Emerson and Henry David Thoreau, who are resonating voices speaking in militant response to the extremes of the Industrial Revolution. Throughout the late nineteenth century and even today, their ideas inform the *zeitgeist* of American environmentalist conception, and it is worth remembering that the national park system as well as the civil rights movement can be directly traced to these nineteenth-century critics of culture and history.

Given the role that nature and the environment have played in the work of many Western authors, it is inevitable that eco-critical considerations would become an important avenue of scholarly endeavor in the field. The notion of region itself invites these approaches because eco-poetics and environmental literary criticism often begins at a fundamentally ontological level, as it inquires into the very meaning of place as a category of understanding. For Western writers and the eco-critics who explore them, nature becomes a physical reality to understand and a perceptual reality in the minds of travelers, settlers, and, in the end, readers. Important and yet quite common questions emerge: In a naturalistic context, what defines our relationship to the land? In what way are we "kin" to it and stewards of its material resources? In the context of its mystery, in what way may we cultivate an experience in nature that transcends the physical? Environmental literature and criticism is varied in its assumption about the nature of these essential relationships, ranging from Marxist-inflected inquiries into the role that literature has played, ideologically, in creating a superstructure supporting exploration and expansion, to historical considerations of the tension between "civilization" as an ideal and "nature" as a sustaining force, to a more contemporary inquiry into the relationship of words and things, between writing and American lands.

Thus, the study of Western American literature has a long history, with a diverse array of authors and genres represented. Critics have explored this distinctive literature for decades from a number of critical perspectives motivated by an evolving set of historiographic assumptions, and recent critical paradigms have served to enrich this field of inquiry and open spaces for a range of new and important realms of understanding. Long-held preoccupations motivated by the unique nature of the Western American experience also deserve continued inquiry, interests that serve to blend the regional and the universal: the human propensity to unspeakable violence, rapacious greed and the will to power, metaphysics and questions related to the existence of God, and the ever-present, malleable, contested, but perennially evocative notion of the "American Dream."

# 2

## M. CARMEN GOMEZ-GALISTEO

# Transnational Wests: the literature of Spanish exploration

For centuries, the West remained a scarcely known region only very few dared to venture into, which helped to perpetuate its mystery at the same time that it enhanced its attraction. Traces of the presence of the Spaniards, the first Europeans to set foot in the West, can still be found in a number of ways, most visibly in place-names but also in religious, economic, and legal practices as well as in literature (Bolton xlvii–xlviii). As it happened in other territories that would, in time, become part of what now is the United States of America, the first texts produced in the West were written not in English but in Spanish. These were authored by Spanish conquistadors so as to register their exploits. Geographical and ethnological descriptions occupied much space in their writings, but so did their expectations about what was to be found. In their minds, these territories were the setting for legends and myths.

By the time the Spaniards turned their attention to North America, the Spanish conquest and colonization of the Americas had already been under way for several decades. Despite the gold and silver found in New Spain and Peru, the disappointment and frustration at not finding the mythical places that the Spaniards had expected to discover in the New World drove them to explore territories further north. In the minds of the Spaniards, the failure to locate El Dorado, the Seven Cities of Cibola, Calafa Island, the Fountain of Eternal Youth, and other equally magnificent places only meant that they would have to be more extensively searched for. There was absolutely no doubt in their minds that they would eventually come across cities made of solid gold or an island where pearls abounded. After all, had Hernán Cortés not encountered a civilization so wealthy and glorious that he had exacted an enormous ransom from its ruler? Surely, wealth surpassing that already acquired lay waiting to be claimed, free for the taking, as multiple eyewitnesses hinted at and writers promised.

The fact that little was known with certainty about these territories was no deterrent, for folk beliefs, legends, and the dreams of those who had already been to other American possessions made up for the lack of reliable information (Allen 41–43; Gomez-Galisteo, *Early Visions* 53). In the light of the lack of authoritative sources of information and the discovery of phenomena that contradicted previous sources of knowledge such as the Bible or classical works, the influence of the spirit of adventure the *novelas de caballería* (knight stories) conveyed should not be overlooked or underestimated. An example of this is the fact that California was named after the setting of one of these novels, *Las sergas de Esplandián* (1510) by Garci Rodríguez de Montalvo (Buelna Serrano, Lucino Gutiérrez Herrera, and Ávila Sandoval 354–355).

Fueled by these dreams, the Spaniards enthusiastically undertook the conquest of North America. Expeditions typically followed one of two possible courses – either a full-fledged expedition from Spain (or other Spanish colonial territories) or an *entrada* from a nearby Spanish settlement. In contrast to the careful and time-consuming preparations of an expedition, an *entrada* consisted of a smaller number of conquistadors sent to explore, claim possession of the lands discovered in the name of the Crown, and assess the financial prospects of the area before returning to Spanish territory to report on their findings. Then, if the profitability of the project was deemed worthy, a more organized and better-equipped expedition would be sent. In contrast to the bourgeoning Spanish cities established in the first discovered territories, the settlements in North America "were the northern outposts of Northern Spain, maintained chiefly to uphold the country against foreign intruders and against the centers of Spanish colonial civilization" (Bolton xlv).

Amazed by their findings and wishing to have their deeds properly recorded (more often than not also exaggerated in the process to boost their own importance), Spanish conquistadors, more than newcomers of any other nationality, felt compelled to put their discoveries, thoughts, and impressions in writing (Iglesia 525). As it happened, the narratives, poetry, and drama that the conquistadors wrote in Spanish constitute the first pieces of North American literature – in spite of having often been overlooked in favor of texts written in English about Virginia and New England several decades later. The first text dealing with the West is *The Account* (alternatively known as *La Relación* or *Naufragios*, first published in 1542) by Álvar Núñez Cabeza de Vaca. This work is the chronicle of the nearly decade-long wanderings of three conquistadors (its author, Andrés Dorantes, and Alonso del Castillo) and Estebanico, a Muslim slave. They were members of the ill-fated expedition of Pánfilo de Narváez, the only survivors out of the six hundred who had sailed from Sanlúcar de Barrameda, Spain in June 1527. They would not return to Spanish territory until 1536, when they were found by troops from New Spain (present-day Mexico) and taken to Mexico City to report to the viceroy. During the years in between, the four survivors had been wandering throughout the Southwest, living among several Native American groups. Cabeza de Vaca penned *The Account*, the written testimony of their experiences, upon his return to Spain as part of his petition to Charles I for a royal pension and other honors. Cabeza de Vaca sought these as a reward in return for what he saw as a most valuable contribution to the advancement of the Spanish presence in America, if only from a literary point of view, as will be explained later in this chapter.

Cabeza de Vaca's work originally followed the formal structure of the *relación* (account) and, to denote this, its original title is *La relacion que dio Aluar nunez cabeça de vaca de lo acaescido en las Indias en la armada donde yua por gouernador Panphilo de Narbaez desde el año de veynte y siete hasta el año de treynta y seys quo bolvio a Seuilla con tres de su compañia* [*The account that Álvar Núñez Cabeza de Vaca gave of what happened in the Indies in the navy where Pánfilo de Narváez was governor from the year 27 to the year 36 when he returned to Seville with three of his company*]. However, Cabeza de Vaca's text soon departed from the rigid conventions of the genre and from the royal instructions regarding official writings that conquistadors were given (Borrero Barrera). The formality of the official report vanishes to instead express the physical and mental anguish of the survivors' trials (Pupo-Walker 279). The exact data and detailed descriptions expected in a report are replaced by imprecision, as Cabeza de Vaca ignores his exact whereabouts, a state of uncertainty matched by his doubts and distress at being in unchartered territory. To this was added his acculturation to the several Native American groups he lived with, adopting a number of roles (go-between, trader, healer [Wade; Gomez-Galisteo, "Subverting Gender Roles"]), further contributing to his confusion (Borrero Barrera). Instead of the official chronicle he was expected to submit as treasurer of the expedition, he created a highly original text that included elements of the *relación* as well as of other colonial texts such as the letter to the king and the *crónica de Indias* (*Chronicle of Indies*) or natural histories, romances of chivalry, the picaresque novel, moral novels, and the pastoral (Bravo-Villasante 8–9), making the resulting work different from existing discourse types (Mignolo quoted in Borrero Barrera). Furthermore, in narrating the miracles and supernatural occurrences that he claimed to have witnessed in the Southwest, his account at times reads like an adventure story, closer to works such as *John Mandeville's Travels* or *The Travels of Marco Polo*.

The vision of the West that Cabeza de Vaca transmitted would become, over the years, deeply ingrained in the popular imagination. He created an image of the West that to a large extent persists today – the West as an extraordinary place, where man fights for survival against an alien and extremely dangerous environment. Moreover, it is also peopled by Native Americans, who threatened the Europeans' survival but also made them redefine and reconceptualize their own identity. With its emphasis on the miraculous and almost incredible occurrences that happened to them, Cabeza de Vaca's text acquires a literary quality reminiscent of adventure tales. Some of these novel-like elements are probably the product of the writer's imagination and written with the sole purpose of holding readers' attention (different from the aim of the work as a whole, which is to bear testimony to his heroism and reflect well on his character with an eye on being granted royal prerogatives) and owed much to the literary taste of contemporary readers (Maura 220; Pupo-Walker 84). To name but one, a fictional episode is the pirate attack on the ship in which Cabeza de Vaca returned to Spain, which would have not been out of place in the Byzantine novels that were popular readings then (Pupo-Walker 84). *The Account* also contains elements from the *novelas de caballería*, a very favored reading in Spain at the time even though it was already out of fashion in Europe, or the picaresque novel, a typical Spanish genre.

Lost, drifting, with no certainty about his exact location, sometimes enslaved by the Native Americans, at other times regarded as a healer and a miracle-maker, Cabeza de Vaca could conquer neither these territories nor these peoples. His only contribution to the Spanish conquest was his recollections in the form of his book, as he had failed to take possession of new lands: "no me quedó lugar para hacer más servicio de éste, que es traer a Vuestra Majestad relación de lo que en diez años que por muchas y muy extrañas tierras que anduve perdido y en cueros, pudiese saber y ver" (Cabeza de Vaca 4).[1] Nevertheless, his writings served him well enough for his purposes for, even though the next expedition to Florida was assigned to Hernando de Soto, much to Cabeza de Vaca's chagrin, Cabeza de Vaca got the post of *Adelantado* [governor] of Río de la Plata, present-day Argentina. Yet with *The Account* he failed to achieve historical credibility. The emphasis on God having chosen him to carry out important deeds that permeates all his work played against him, as did his recurrent self-portrayal as a hero, and his emphasis on the similarities between his own situation and Jesus Christ's (Maura 45, 134).

That he wrote during the colonial period has not been an obstacle to Cabeza de Vaca being regarded as a forerunner of Chicano literature or even as the first Chicano writer. For Bruce-Novoa, *The Account* should be read as a "founding as well as a fundamental text of Chicano literature and culture" (quoted in Silva). Cabeza de Vaca, like Chicanos, was thoroughly changed by his experiences, which in turn made his return fraught because of his new identity and sensibility. His plight in the West and his ambiguous feelings about America, alternatively seeing it as a bleak wasteland and a paradise-to-be, have been viewed as characteristic of Chicanos too. Other points in common between Chicanos and Cabeza de Vaca that have made this identification of the latter as a Chicano possible are the following: feelings of displacement and dislocation; problems of defining one's own identity, no longer being the same person one used to be, but without having fully assimilated to the new culture; and isolation and alienation (Bruce-Novoa). Cabeza de Vaca's struggle to convey American realities in the Spanish novel is a process similar to the bilingualism of Chicano literature (Flores). In *The Account* we are witness to how "the immigrant ceased to be a foreigner and was never able to return to his place of origin" (Bruce-Novoa quoted in Shields and Nelson 103), a recurrent theme in early Chicano literature.[2]

Cabeza de Vaca and his three companions' arrival in New Spain caused a stir of interest – not only because hopes of ever learning the fate of the expedition had by then died out, but also because of the riches they reported having seen. What is more, because of their rather vague directions, they were suspected of having omitted accurate and exact details about the region's wealth so as to return on their own for their sole benefit and prevent others from finding it. As Hidalgo de Elvas, participant in the De Soto expedition, accusingly wrote, "he [Cabeza de Vaca] and another ... had sworn not to divulge certain things which they had seen, lest someone might beg the government in advance of them, for which he had come to Spain; nevertheless, he gave them to understand that it was the richest country in the world."

The promising testimony of Cabeza de Vaca prompted Viceroy Antonio de Mendoza to take immediate action to secure these territories for the Crown. Thus, he commissioned Friar Marcos of Nice, guided by Estebanico, to assess the region's prospects in 1539. This choice was not casual – Estebanico had already been there while Friar Marcos was considered an expert explorer on the strength of his previous participation in the expeditions of Francisco Pizarro and Hernando de Soto. In spite of being an eyewitness able to obtain firsthand information, Friar Marcos' perception was misleadingly influenced by Cabeza de Vaca and his companions' testimonies as well as by the *novelas de caballería* and legends circulating at the time. One of these misapprehensions was the Seven Cities of Cibola, according to which, fleeing from the Muslim invasion of the Iberian Peninsula in the eighth century, seven bishops had abandoned their sees, taking with them their cities' treasuries. Later, they were reported to have founded seven cities. The legend originally located these seven cities on an island in the Atlantic

Ocean, but, having failed to find it, explorers subsequently assumed that the bishops' destination was further westward.

In the course of the expedition, Estebanico, sent ahead to scour, was killed by Native Americans in the Zuñi town of Hawikuh. Friar Marcos himself never reached this town, just saw it from afar, while standing on top of a nearby *mesa*. Nevertheless, he was convinced that he could make out a city larger than Mexico City and whose houses were made of silver, gold, and turquoise. He believed it to be, without a doubt, one of the Seven Cities and he would claim as much in his account, *Relación del descubrimiento de las Siete Ciudades* [*Account of the Discovery of the Seven Cities*] (1539). This work further contributed to cement the image of the West as a land of fortune and riches beyond imagination. Even though his account contained little factual information but many promises, it was responsible for a renewed interest. Despite his tall tales, he earned the trust of the viceroy, who paid so much credibility to his story that he immediately organized a new expedition to the area. Led by Francisco Vázquez de Coronado, the expedition set off on April 22, 1540, with Friar Marcos as its guide. The promised Golden City, Hawikuh, was taken on July 7, 1540, only for the explorers to discover that it was an impoverished settlement. Absolutely no trace of the wealth that Friar Marcos had claimed to have seen from afar could be found. Coronado, to prevent Friar Marcos being physically harmed, sent him back to New Spain ahead of the rest of the expedition.

Entering these unexplored territories of the West was a perilous affair and numerous dangers awaited. Two Franciscan friars, Agustín Rodríguez and Francisco López, ventured into New Mexico as members of the 1581–1582 expedition commanded by Francisco Rodríguez Chamuscado but got lost. A new expedition was sent the following year to learn about their whereabouts, an expedition in which Antonio de Espejo took part. This was the first adventure exploring for Espejo, the wealthy owner of a cattle ranch in New Spain. His stated intention was that he had "entered those lands with a pious purpose," and was moved by a "desire of serving the Lord and augmenting our Holy Catholic Faith, and of increasing at the same time the realms of the royal crown" (quoted in Mecham), very conveniently omitting that the expedition also gave him the opportunity to run away from his legal problems.

The expedition party, consisting of fifteen soldiers, two Franciscan friars, Native American servants, interpreters, and 115 horses and mules (Mecham), set off on November 10, 1582. Insistent reports from the Piros Native Americans claimed that the friars had been murdered, but Espejo would not consider returning to New Spain until these rumors had been confirmed, and, more important, until they had discovered something valuable to show for their expedition. Even once the veracity of the rumors had been confirmed, Espejo went on to Arizona to explore the existence of the mines the Native Americans had told him about. Espejo would later claim that he did so, despite the accompanying friars' opposition, as "I deemed this a good opportunity to serve his Majesty by visiting and discovering those lands so new and so remote, in order to give a report of them to his Majesty with no expense to him in their discovery. I therefore determined to continue as long as my strength would permit" (quoted in Mecham). The expedition finally returned on September 10, 1583.

Following their return, Espejo wrote an account "to report to his Majesty that he may order what is best for the exploration, and pacification of those provinces, and for the service of God our Lord and the increase of His Holy Catholic Faith" (quoted in Mecham). This work, *The Account of the Journey to the Provinces and Settlements of New Mexico, 1583*, was full of exaggerations and placed special emphasis on the natives' willingness to be converted. On the strength of his experience and what he expected to find, Espejo volunteered to pay himself for a new expedition of five hundred colonists and twenty-four Franciscans to settle down in the discovered territories. However, despite his keenness, in 1595 it was Juan de Oñate who was appointed governor of New Mexico, *Adelantado*, and captain-general instead; Espejo's legal problems probably played a role in his being snubbed (Mecham).

Oñate, known as "the last conquistador," belonged to a prestigious family of conquistadors. His father, Cristóbal de Oñate, was the founder of Zacatecas, where he had established a successful mining business. Juan de Oñate had married Isabel de Tolosa Cortés de Moctezuma, the granddaughter of Hernán Cortés by his Aztec wife, who was therefore the great-granddaughter of Aztec emperor Moctezuma. The expedition (1595–1601) consisted of soldiers and four hundred prospective settlers with their families. Oñate founded the province of Santa Fe de Nuevo Mexico and soon became known for his strictness. In October 1598, the Acoma refused to give the Spaniards the supplies and victuals they demanded but with which the natives could not possibly part, lest they risked starvation. In the ensuing conflict, thirteen Spaniards were killed, including Juan de Zaldívar, Oñate's nephew. In retaliation, in what became known as the Acoma Massacre, eight hundred Native Americans were killed and five hundred more were enslaved. Additionally, all the surviving Acoma men older than twenty-five years old had their left feet amputated.

Oñate led an expedition to Great Plains with 130 Spanish soldiers, 130 native soldiers, twelve Franciscans, and servants, guided by the only survivor of the 1593 Humaña and Leyva expedition and another one in October 1604 to the lower Colorado River, becoming the only European who had been in that area after Hernando de Alarcón and Melchor Díaz's 1540 expedition and before Eusebio Francisco Kino's 1701 expedition. Other than its geographical dimension, the Oñate expedition also left an important mark in literature. Two of Oñate's soldiers authored the first epic poem and the first dramatic play of the West. The first poet in the West, Gaspar Pérez de Villagrá (also known as Gaspar de Villagrá), makes an atypical conquistador in that he was born in New Spain, not in Spain, and that his formal education (he read law in Salamanca [Martín-Rodríguez, *Gaspar de Villagrá* 24]) surpassed that of most conquistadors, which explains why his only known work was an epic poem instead of the more usual letter or report addressed to the king. Because of his having been born in America, his understanding of the colonies and the metropolis is, therefore, different from that of the first-generation conquistadors and shows a transatlantic sensibility (Martín Rodríguez, *Gaspar de Villagrá* 25). If conquistadors, upon encountering the West and its peoples, had to renegotiate their identity, as happened for Cabeza de Vaca, for Villagrá, the referent to compare these newly found territories to was not solely his parents' native Spain, where he had pursued his university studies, but also New Spain.

Villagrá was a captain in Oñate's expedition to New Mexico, which would be the subject matter of his *Historia de la Nueva México*. He devoted the first part of his work to an ethnographic survey of the region before turning to the epic in Canto XXII (Martín-Rodríguez, *Gaspar de Villagrá* 26). The work is structured in three sections; the first offers the historical background, the second recounts the exploration of the territories, and the third chronicles the resistance of the Native American inhabitants, the Acoma Pueblo, until they were defeated. Villagrá put an end to his work at this point, so as not to write of the terrible punishments Oñate inflicted on the survivors (Martín-Rodríguez, "Aquí fue Troia" 150–151). Because of its epic character, Villagrá's *Historia* has been often compared to Alonso Ercilla's poem *La Araucana*, which chronicles the Spanish conquest of Chile. However, the brutality of Oñate's repression has at times tainted the *Historia*'s literary standing, and, for example, Rabasa reads Villagrá's work as "an aesthetic of colonial violence" (quoted in Shields and Nelson 106).

Villagrá's decision to end his poem after the Acoma Massacre is evidence, once more, of the failure of conventional literary genres to convey some of the events happening in America. If the *crónica de Indias*, with its strict adherence to formal rules and its formulaic character, did not allow Cabeza de Vaca the freedom to express his more incredible exploits, the brutality of the conquest of the West and the subjugation of the natives could not be easily accommodated into epic poetry. That Villagrá decided to narrate this episode in a historical chronicle he never wrote is testimony of the shortcomings of language and the inability of the existing writing genres to broach the incomprehensible nature of America in the eyes of the Spaniards. Whereas *The Account* earned Cabeza de Vaca a new post in America (although his second American experience ended in failure and disgrace), this was a far cry from Villagrá's subsequent fate. He was sentenced to banishment because of his persecution, following Oñate's orders, of four deserters and because the riches of New Mexico he had promised to the viceroy of New Spain by letter proved false (Martín-Rodríguez, "Aquí fue Troia" 143). This shows that, at this point, after numerous misleading reports that had overestimated the potential material rewards of the West and had led to costly expeditions that inevitably ended in failure, not everything could be written about America. Unrealistic expectations were no longer allowed and those who dared to be too enthusiastic about these new territories were to be punished.

Despite Villagrá's pioneering position in North American poetry, his contribution remained mostly unknown. The timing of the publication of his work (1610) did not favor him – other issues were by then more pressing than the American conquest, and the epic character of the *Historia* was too elevated for readers who were celebrating the ironic portrayal of heroism of Cervantes' *Don Quixote* (first part published in 1605) (Martín-Rodríguez, "Aquí fue Troia" 139). Despite the pioneering position that Villagrá enjoyed as the first poet in the West, it would take several centuries until the aesthetic value of his work was appreciated. Mostly, Villagrá's *Historia* met adverse criticism (Martín-Rodríguez, *Gaspar de Villagrá* 23), and not until the twenty-first century was its literary value vindicated. Now, because of Villagrá's identification as a Chicano (in his case, this affiliation is easier than Cabeza de Vaca's, as Villagrá was born in present-day Mexico), his *Historia* is often regarded as the only Chicano epic poem (Martín-Rodríguez, "Reading Gaspar de Villagrá" 1337).

The other participant in Oñate's expedition to leave a literary imprint was Captain Marcos Farfán de los Godos. His only play known to exist, *Los Moros* (also known as *Moros y Cristianos* [*Muslims and Christians*]), first performed on April 30, 1598, was the first dramatic production ever to take place in the West. In the play, the Native Americans (called *los moros* or the Muslims, following the misidentification of them with the Muslim population who had lived in Spain from 711 to 1492), are urged to speedily convert to Catholicism to be saved. More often than not, the literature of the West, as already mentioned, intended to describe (accurately or not) the region with the goal of securing material rewards and recognition for the writer. Official agendas aside, the foremost goal in conquistadors' minds was a materialistic and down-to-earth one – to get rich as quickly and easily as possible. "We came here to serve God, also to get rich" (quoted in

Morison xvi), as conquistador in New Spain Bernal Díaz del Castillo wrote. Accordingly, those works by conquistadors tended to emphasize the prosperity to be gained from the colonial enterprise. However, sometimes there was a didactic and from their point of view idealistic goal too – the conversion of the natives. Actually, the officially sanctioned aim of the conquest of the Americas was the conversion of the souls of the Native Americans to Christianity, obeying Queen Isabella's explicit wishes. With this goal in mind, Franciscan friars usually accompanied the exploring and conquering expeditions, and this was the aim of Farfán de los Godos' play.

From a literary point of view, the discovery chronicles are at times repetitive, echoing the same wonder expressed ever since America was first discovered. So similar are accounts at times, so alike the metaphors and similes used to convey the newness of America and the wonder it provoked, that it has led to speculation as to whether authors were actually copying from one another or if this close resemblance was rather a by-product of the failure of language to express such novel ideas and concepts (Shields 356). Historically, these writings gave weight to the Spanish claim on those territories north of Río Grande; anthropologically, they created a new cultural identity. A distinctive New Mexican identity, different from both the Mexican and the American ones, is rooted in the writings of the Spanish conquistadors who first set foot in this region.

Writers' descriptions of America were inevitably colored by their own expectations as well as by the stories circulating about the New World. Moreover, their need to validate the worth of their testimonies made them exaggerate what they had seen – as well as what they hoped to find. Consequently, an underlying characteristic in all these texts is their authors' insistence on credibility. Aware of being the first people to describe these territories and knowing that some of the events narrated were hard to believe, they appealed to the authority of being eyewitnesses. Previous sources that may lend them credibility were unavailable to them, as what they saw in America often went contrary to the information contained in authoritative books such as the Bible or the writings of classical authors (reintroduced during the Renaissance). Some of these new writers, being young soldiers, more often than not lacked the formal education that could render them the erudition and appeal to authority necessary to give them historical credibility (Gomez-Galisteo, *Early Visions* 23–25).

Through their writings, conquistadors painted a picture of America as a special place where miracles, extraordinary occurrences, and wonderful opportunities could happen, an idea that, along with the seventeenth-century Puritan concept of the city upon the hill, would crystallize in the American Dream. Subsequent Spanish expeditions to the area would try to come to terms with the incommensurability of the West. Nevertheless, despite their attempts to offer a detailed picture of the area (from both a descriptive and a cartographical point of view), the West remained mostly unknown and would continue haunting the imagination of several generations of writers to come. Beyond their importance in crafting a lasting image of the West, these writers are also vital in their role as forerunners of Chicano literature. A problem for the acceptance of Chicano literature was that it seemed to have emerged spontaneously (Flores), without any previous literary tradition preceding and enriching it. Cabeza de Vaca's experience, as well as those writings by Spanish conquistadors, supplied Chicanos with a past of their own, in opposition to the "Anglo" story of Jamestown and the *Mayflower*, as "for Chicanos/as the challenge of dislodging the preeminence of a Puritan experience is the challenge of rewriting history" (Aranda 59–60).

Because of their sugarcoated vision of the West, Miller has called *The Account* and Friar Marcos of Nice's *Relación* the first tourist brochures of the Southwest (96). Villagrá's sentence for having exaggerated the riches of the region is indicative that invention in the West had ended for the Spaniards. Yet, despite the obvious exaggerations, it is useful to bear in mind that, at a time when little was known about the West, these narratives were often taken at face value and given enough credibility to launch new expeditions to the area solely on the strength of these accounts.[3] These stories would have a lasting influence in creating the image of the West that later writers challenged or partially reproduced. The West would continue to be described as a mysterious place, where the tall tales that conquistadors narrated were but the first ones told about this region. In the West, reality and myth are often indistinguishable. Even centuries later, in the eighteenth century, the West remained for British colonists "a physical fact of great if unknown magnitude" (Smith 6). Lewis and Clark's expedition would come to relive old legends, once more presenting the West as a mythical place full of possibilities and easy fortunes, just as the Spaniards had done centuries earlier.

## Notes

1  "I had no chance to serve in a way other than this, which is to bring Your Majesty an account of what I was able to learn and see in the ten years during which I was lost and naked in many and very strange lands" (translation mine).

2  In addition to being considered a forerunner of Chicano literature, *The Account* has also been identified as a precursor of the South American novel (Gandini 33).

3  As important as what these texts did claim was what they did not include, for there were mere persistent suspicions that authors had chosen to omit vital information so as to preserve these treasures for themselves.

# Works Cited

Allen, John L. "Lands of Myth, Waters of Wonder: The Place of the Imagination in the History of Geographical Exploration." In David Lowenthal and Martyn J. Bowden (eds.) *Geographies of the Mind: Essays in Historical Geosophy in Honor of John Kirtland Wright.* New York: Oxford University Press, 1976. 41–61. Print.

Aranda, José F., Jr. *When We Arrive: A New Literary History of Mexican America.* Tucson: University of Arizona Press, 2002. Print.

Bolton, Herbert E. (ed.) *The Spanish Borderlands: A Chronicle of Old Florida and the Southwest.* 1921. Albuquerque: University of New Mexico Press, 1966. Print.

Borrero Barrera, Mª José. "Las *Crónicas de indias* como documento informativo: Los *Naufragios* de Álvar Núñez Cabeza de Vaca." *Revista electrónica de estudios filológicos.* No. 7 (2004). Web. Oct. 23, 2006. www.um.es/tonosdigital/znum7/estudios/bfuncion.htm.

Bravo-Villasante, Carmen. *La maravilla de América: Los cronistas de Indias.* Madrid: Ediciones Cultura Hispánica, 1985. Print.

Bruce-Novoa, Juan. "Álvar Nuñez Cabeza de Vaca – Author Page." *Heath Anthology of American Literature.* 5th edition. 2005. Web. Sept. 22, 2015. http://college.hmco.com/english/lauter/heath/4e/students/author_pages/colonial/devaca_al.html.

Buelna Serrano, Elvira, Lucino Gutiérrez Herrera, and Santiago Ávila Sandoval. "Imaginario y realidad en la exploración de América Septentrional." *Análisis económico.* Vol. XXIV, no. 57 (2009): 331–358. Print.

Cabeza de Vaca, Álvar Núñez. *Naufragios.* 1542. N. p.: El Aleph, 2000. Print.

Flores, Arturo. "Etnia, cultura y sociedad: apuntes sobre el origen y desarrollo de la novela chicana." *Estudios Filológicos.* No. 32 (1997): 123–136. Web. July 19, 2014. www.scielo.cl/scielo.php?pid=S0071-17131997003200011&script=sci_arttext.

Gandini, María Juliana. "Fuerzas locales, espacios atlánticos, horizontes globales: Álvar Núñez Cabeza de Vaca conectando mundos." *Traversea.* Vol. 3 (2013): 32–47. Print.

Gomez-Galisteo, M. Carmen. *Early Visions and Representations of America: Álvar Núñez Cabeza de Vaca's Naufragios and William Bradford's Of Plymouth Plantation.* New York, London, New Delhi, and Sydney: Bloomsbury, 2013. Print.

"Subverting Gender Roles in the Sixteenth Century: Cabeza de Vaca, the Conquistador Who Became a Native American Woman." In Sandra Slater and Fay A. Yarbrough (eds.) *Gender and Sexuality in Indigenous North America, 1400–1850.* Columbia: The University of South Carolina Press, 2011. 11–29. Print.

Hidalgo de Elvas. *True Relation of the Vicissitudes that Attended the Gobernor Don Hernando De Soto and Some Nobles of Portugal in the Discovery of the Province of Florida Now Just Given by a Fidalgo of Elvas Viewed by the Lord Inquisitor.* Edward Gaylord Bourne (ed.) [Translated by Buckingham Smith] New York: Allerton Book Company, 1922. Mirror of a Transcription by Dr. Jon Muller. Web. Oct. 16, 2008. www.floridahistory.com/elvas1.html.

Iglesia, Ramón. "Two Articles on the Same Topic: Bernal Díaz del Castillo and Popularism in Spanish Historiography and Bernal Díaz del Castillo's Criticisms of the *History of the Conquest of Mexico*, by Francisco López de Gomara." *The Hispanic American Historical Review.* Vol. 20, no. 4 (1940): 517–550. Print.

Martín-Rodríguez, Manuel M. "'Aquí fue Troia nobles caualleros': Tradición clásica y otros intertextos en la *Historia de la Nveva Mexico* de Gaspar de Villagrá." *Silva: Estudios de Humanismo y Tradición Clásica.* No. 4 (2005): 139–208. Print.

Gaspar de Villagrá: *Legista, soldado y poeta.* León, Spain: Servicio de Publicaciones de la Universidad de León, 2009. Print.

"Reading Gaspar de Villagrá (in the Seventeenth Century)." In *Cien años de lealtad. En honor a Luis Leal. One Hundred Years of Loyalty. In Honor of Luis Leal.* In Sara Poot Herrera, Francisco A. Lomelí, and María Herrera-Sobek (eds.) Vol. 2. Mexico City: University of California, Santa Barbara, UC-Mexicanistas, Universidad Nacional Autónoma de México, Instituto Tecnológico de Monterrey, Universidad del Claustro de Sor Juana, 2007. 1337–1346. Print.

Maura, Juan Francisco (ed.). *Naufragios.* By Álvar Núñez Cabeza de Vaca. 2nd edition. Madrid: Cátedra, 1996. Print.

Mecham, J. Lloyd, "Antonio De Espejo and His Journey to New Mexico." *Southwestern Historical Quarterly Online.* Vol. 30, no. 2, 114–138. Web. Nov. 14, 2006. www.tsha.utexas.edu/publications/journals/shq/online/vo30/n2/article_4_print.html.

Miller, John C. "Literatura latina de los Estados Unidos." *Cuadernos de literatura.* Vol. 1, no. 2 (1995): 95–104. Print.

Morison, Samuel Eliot. "New Light Wanted on the Old Colony." *The William and Mary Quarterly.* Vol. 15, no. 3 (1958): 359–364. Print.

Pupo-Walker, Enrique (ed.) *Los Naufragios.* By Álvar Núñez Cabeza de Vaca. Madrid: Editorial Castalia, 1992. Print.

Rabasa, José. "Aesthetics of Colonial Violence: The Massacre of Acoma in Gaspar de Villagrá's *Historia de la Nueva México.*" *College Literature.* Vol. 20, no. 3 (1993): 96–114. Print.

Shields, E. Thomson, Jr. "The Genres of Exploration and Conquest Literatures." In Susan Castillo and Ivy Schweitzer (eds.) *A Companion to the Literatures of Colonial America.* Malden, MA, Oxford, and Carlton, Australia: Blackwell, 2005. 353–368. Print.

Shields, E. Thomson Jr., and Dana D. Nelson. "Colonial Spanish Writings." In Carla Mulford (ed.) *Teaching the Literatures of Early America.* New York: The Modern Language Association of America, 1999. 97–111. Print.

Silva, Alan J. "Conquest, Conversion, and the Hybrid Self in Cabeza de Vaca's *Relación.*" *Post Identity.* Vol. 2, no. 1 (1999). Web. Nov. 25, 2013. http://quod.lib.umich.edu/p/postid/pid9999.0002.106?rgn=main;view=fulltext.

Smith, Henry Nash. *Virgin Land: The American West as Symbol and Myth.* 1950. Revised edition, 1970. Cambridge, MA and London: Harvard University Press, 1978. Print.

Wade, Mariah. "Go-Between: The Roles of Native American Women and Álvar Núñez Cabeza de Vaca in Southern Texas in the Sixteenth Century." *The Journal of American Folklore.* Vol. 112, no. 445 (1999): 332–342. Print.

# 3

JOHN DUDLEY

# Western folk traditions: from colonization to Mark Twain and the San Francisco Circle

The earliest Euro-American writings about the American West involve travel narratives, memoirs, letters, and journals, including those of Lewis and Clark, as well as a subsequent infusion of literary works in the 1830s, such as Calvin Colton's, *Tour of the American Lakes, and among the Indians* (1833); James Hall, *Sketches of History, Life, and Manners in the West* (1834); Amos Parker, *Trip to the West and Texas* (1835); and Caroline Kirkland, *A New Home, Who'll Follow?* (1839). To a large extent, these texts follow established generic conventions and reflect the perspectives of educated, privileged Easterners providing their impressions of personal experience intertwined with the geographic features of the Western territories. Even exceptions to this rule, such as the accounts of the enlisted men from the Lewis and Clark expedition, James Ohio Pattie's *Personal Narrative* (1831), and Kit Carson's autobiography (1858), each of which purported to offer unvarnished accounts of adventure and exploration, were filtered through a conventionally "literary" editorial process. In this context, particularly after the acceleration of emigration following the discovery of gold at Sutter's Mill in 1848, a demand emerged for more folk-based accounts of Western expansion.

If Mark Twain's early writing seemed to fill this need for folkloric voices, it also represented the culmination of influences and impulses evident in the work of the so-called Southwestern Humorists, the rise of the "Sagebrush School" in Nevada and California, and the cultural turn toward folklore and ethnography that arose in the mid-nineteenth century. The circle of writers based in San Francisco in the 1850s and 1860s, which included Twain, along with Bret Harte, Prentice Mulford, Charles Warren Stoddard, and others, drew heavily on the diverse stories that accompanied the wave of immigration in the wake of the Gold Rush in fashioning a distinctive regional literature, one that would inform subsequent Western writers as well as a broader American literary culture. Given the lack of any English-language history in the region, to a large extent these writers and their contemporaries *invented* a coherent folk tradition out of the distinct and disparate sources they encountered. Accompanying the rapid influx of wealth and population was the development of a publishing industry and literary culture, fostered by the *Sacramento Daily Union* and literary journals such as *The Golden Era* and Harte's *Overland Monthly*. As Michael Kowalewski notes, "As early as 1850, some fifty printers worked in San Francisco, and the city boasted that by the mid-1850s it published more newspapers than London (many in languages other than English)" (210). Along with this vibrant local publishing scene, the literary journals of the East, eager to feed their readers' curiosity about the West, sought authentic Western voices for their pages.

The increasing emphasis on authenticity is central to the literary and popular culture of the nineteenth century in general, and to Western American literature in particular. In his study of the literature of the American West, Nathaniel Lewis unpacks the layers of performance behind Twain's desire for authenticity and cites Twain's own claim, in a letter, that "I don't care anything about being humorous, or poetical, or eloquent, or anything of that kind – the end & aim of my ambition is to be authentic – is to be considered authentic" (*Letters, Volume 2* 189).[1] As Twain reveals, authenticity does not necessarily involve a direct correlation with objective truth, but is rather an inevitable by-product of representation. The verifiable facts of history do not authenticate a work of literature; instead, the repetition of stories – particularly in a nonliterary context – authenticates the experiences and circumstances the stories themselves describe. As Neil Campbell claims, the American West is "a simulation reproducing images conforming to some already defined, but possibly non-existent, sense of Westness" (130). If our current understanding of the region stipulates the area west of the 98th meridian, defined by maps but also by the aridity of the climate and specific geographic qualities, the characteristics we associate with the West predate the period of settlement that took up much of the later nineteenth century. In the overtly folk-derived literature from the early period of expansion in the nineteenth century, we find evidence of the instability within the paradigm of authenticity, this "sense of Westness" that reverberates throughout Western American literature.

As Twain and his contemporaries understood, the authentication of a text ultimately lies in its ability to meet the expectations of an audience. In an 1873 sketch for *Overland Monthly* titled "Justifiable Fiction," Prentice Mulford confesses to lying to his British hosts when they expect to hear violent tales of the frontier: "I saw now so vividly how great had been my neglect to have lived full sixteen years in the roughest, wildest, most lawless camps in California, without killing at least one man.... I now mourned neglected opportunities." He exaggerates, invents violent episodes, and misrepresents actual events in order to meet the demands of his audience, "hungry for a mean of wild, western, bloody fiction" (40). Such was the "truth" that readers expected to hear, whether in a London parlor or the pages of the *Atlantic Monthly*, and the "justifiable fiction" that constituted the emergent folklore of the American West served as a powerful antidote to the encroaching anxieties of modernity.

In its celebration of "the folk," regional writing in the nineteenth century reveals formal, cultural, and ideological patterns related to the national program of Western expansion, which occurred alongside the development of the scholarly study of human societies and cultures, typified by the founding of the American Folklore Society in 1888. Regina Bendix, in a history of folklore studies, situates the emergence of interest in American folklore in the nineteenth century, and argues that "the search for authenticity is fundamentally an emotional and moral quest": "Folklore has long served as a vehicle in the search for the authentic, satisfying a longing for an escape from modernity. The ideal folk community, envisioned as pure and free from civilization's evils, was a metaphor for everything that was not modern" (7). The demographic, political, and economic transformations that accompanied the ideology of Manifest Destiny spawned a fascination with the folk cultures of the earliest Euro-American explorers, adventurers, and "pioneers," many of whom offered little in the way of documentation of their stories and practices, and who represented a diverse swath of ethnicities, nationalities, and beliefs. As Ernest Gellner notes, nationalist ideology "claims to defend folk culture even while in fact it is forging a high culture; it claims to protect an old folk society while in fact helping to build up an anonymous mass society" (124). In the United States, the development of literary regionalism played an enormous role in this process of defining and codifying a folk tradition tied to regional distinctions, but unified by national identity. This movement emerged in the era of national reconciliation following the Civil War, but its roots were in the antebellum West.

The cultural work of folk literature and its claim to "indigenous" status can be tied to the attempt to supplant, appropriate, or erase native peoples and traditions, as well as the Spanish cultural legacy throughout the Southwest, which over hundreds of years had informed countless ballads, pageants, plays, and other texts. An example of such a text is "Los Comanches," a popular folk play from New Mexico, written in the late eighteenth century, and performed throughout the region to the present day. Although ostensibly a record of the hostilities between the Comanche nation and Spanish colonial forces, the play draws on dramatic representations from "Moors and Christians'" reenactments of the Spanish "reconquista" of the Iberian peninsula.[2] Published during the Gold Rush period, John Rollin Ridge's novel, *The Life and Adventures of Joaquin Murieta* (1854), involves multiple levels of cultural performance and appropriation. Ridge, or Yellow Bird, a member of the Cherokee nation who emigrated from Georgia to California, provides a narrative for a high-profile California outlaw who was captured and killed in 1853, and his novel's success helped establish the dime novel genre and contributed to the folklore surrounding his Mexican protagonist. Although the Spanish traditions of the far West would continue to inform popular literature and culture, as with the immense notoriety of Helen Hunt Jackson's *Ramona* (1885), the Anglo-American folk tradition that displaced and elided Native American and Spanish narratives would ultimately define what came to be known as the literature of the American West.

By many accounts, the acknowledgment of regionalism as a literary phenomenon can be traced to the publication of Bret Harte's "The Luck of Roaring Camp" in 1868. Harte's short story established the formal characteristics of regional literature, including an ironic distance from its characters, a detailed depiction of vernacular speech and customs, and the pull of sentimentality and nostalgia. At the same time, it consolidated key elements of Western literature, representing the folklore and customs of the newly colonized territory, and simultaneously reinforcing and debunking the mythology of the West. In its attention to ethnographic detail and reflection of vernacular speech and customs, the work embodies the "seeming of reality" that Twain calls for in his well-known attack on the Romantic tradition, "Fenimore Cooper's Literary Offences" (12). Notwithstanding its allegiance with realism, however, the story that Harte conveys is fantastic and unabashedly sentimental, in the style of an overheard parable or folktale. The story, set in a primitive mining camp in 1850, describes the birth and tragic death of "Thomas Luck," an orphaned infant whose mother, the disreputable "Cherokee Sal," dies in childbirth. Raised by "Stumpy," "Kentuck," and the other "roughs" of Roaring Camp, the child prospers in "the invigorating climate" and under the collective nursing of the hardened miners (Harte 9). His fortuitous presence and the "flush times" of the miners' claims also trigger loftier aspirations for the nascent town: "With the prosperity of the camp came a desire for further improvement. It was proposed to build a hotel in the following spring, and to invite one or two decent families to reside there for the sake of 'The Luck' – who might perhaps profit by female companionship" (16–17). These hopes are dashed when a flash flood sweeps through the camp, and the child's lifeless body is found in the arms of the dying Kentuck, who says, "tell the boys I've got the Luck with me now," after which "the strong man, clinging to the frail babe as a drowning man is said to cling to a straw, drifted away into the shadowy river that flows forever to the unknown sea" (18).

Harte's story reflects the inherent antinomies of Western writing: within a homosocial world of hardened and violent men, with frequent reference to their unvarnished language, there persists a haunting and unrequited impulse toward domesticity and civilization associated with the feminized East. Set in the recent past, the story captures an already lost world, and the competing discourses of ethnography and sentimentality can be connected with its self-conscious attachment to folklore. As Stephanie Foote argues, "Regionalism, by definition, concentrated on regions that were spatially remote from its largely urban, middle-class readers. But regional writing's focus on places that were geographically remote tends to translate into an understanding of those regions as *temporally* remote, too. Regional writing, then, seems to be about not only the folk ways of people inhabiting remote geographic places, but also, and more crucially, about fast-disappearing folk ways" (27). The nostalgic impulse in Harte's writing, which introduced Eastern readers to a West that was already gone, reflects the broader effort to create a binding cultural memory of an Anglo-American folk past within the colonized spaces of the West. As with later regionalism, this effort also elides the presence of other folk cultures, in this case those from both the many indigenous nations of the American continent and the earlier wave of Spanish colonization.

While Harte's writing captures the vernacular speech patterns found in the mining camps, gambling halls, and saloons of the Western territories, his authorial stance, in stories such as "The Luck of Roaring Camp" and "The Outcasts of Poker Flat," remains that of the intellectual outsider. As with earlier travel narratives and journals as well as more recent accounts of the gold and silver mining camps, including the published letters by Louise Clappe (writing as "Dame Shirley"), the authority and authenticity of his tales rely on their content and the author's own firsthand experience within an exotic, violent, and disappearing locale. Harte's language in these stories, like that of his poetry, belongs to a broader nineteenth-century literary tradition, as does that of other members of the San Francisco Circle, such as Ina Coolbrith, the first poet laureate of California. Much Western writing, however, documents the fuller integration of a vernacular narrative voice, and finds its authenticity as much through the manner of telling as through the story that it tells. It might be said, in reference to Cooper's Leatherstocking series as well as such dime novels as Edward S. Ellis's *Seth Jones* (1860), that the first mythological "West" was located in upstate New York – across the original frontier, or geopolitical border. In terms of the development of so-called frontier humor and an Anglo-American folk consciousness, however, the first West was the South. Just as Samuel Clemens moved west to become Mark Twain, so did the folktales of the antebellum South transmute in the deserts and mountains of Nevada and California. Twain's honing of his story-telling persona reflects the range of his Western experiences, as well as the influence of earlier writers on his development.

The most well-documented antecedents to Twain and the "Sagebrush School" of writers who followed the gold and silver mining booms of the 1850s were the humorists of the "Old Southwest," including Augustus Baldwin Longstreet, George Washington Harris, and Thomas Bang Thorpe. Such works as Longstreet's *Georgia Scenes* (1835) and Thorpe's "The Big Bear of Arkansas" (1841) established the use of humor, exaggeration, and the "tall tale" in depicting the regional culture of the American South as it pushed across the western frontier. Also relevant to the emergence of vernacular storytelling was the tremendous popularity of authorized and unauthorized accounts of the life of Davy Crockett that celebrated the plainspoken wit of folklore, even as they reinforced the mythology of its hero. In a typical example of Southwestern humor, a framing device gives way to a vernacular narrator, whose story, often rendered in dialect, comprises the focus of the text and offers a combination of naïve good nature, malapropisms, and genuine insight.

A Western variant on such narratives was introduced by Alonzo Delano, whose "Pen-Knife Sketches," written under the pseudonym "Old Block," translated the dynamics of Southwestern humor to the far West. First published serially in 1850, the sketches contrasted the narrator's grandiose notions with occasional bracketed interjections by his penknife – the actual writing tool itself frequently objecting to its owner's elaborate language and ideas. For instance, when "Old Block" refers to the "the slow pace of his weary steed," he is interrupted: "[Pen-Knife: Pshaw! Why don't you say mule – it was a mule of the meanest kind]" (*Pen-Knife Sketches* 3). The authorial persona of "Old Block" was itself a variant on the aristocratic Southern gentleman who typically framed the stories of Longstreet et al., and the sketches' overt sentimentality and enthusiasm for the fast-developing culture of California, although sometimes deflated by his penknife's jibes, promoted Delano's literary celebrity among both Western and Eastern audiences. As Henry Wonham notes in *Mark Twain and the Art of the Tall Tale*, "When they appeared in 1853, Delano's *Pen-Knife Sketches* helped to popularize a style of humor that came to be associated with California and the West, a style that hinged on the contrast between exaggeratedly romantic images of western life and equally exaggerated accounts of abject poverty and hardship on the frontier" (91).

Delano also published under his own name, notably in his memoir of his journey from Illinois to California, *Life on the Plains and among the*

*Diggings* (1854), and a play, *A Live Woman in the Mines* (1857). A key distinction within his comic sketches is "Old Block's" focus on the emergent culture of the emigrants, rather than the specific hardships of individuals: "At this moment there are over two hundred thousand full grown men and women in California, who came from a distant land, each one of whom has an interesting tale of individual adventure to tell. What a volume it would form if collected. Two hundred thousand tales, more truthful, more exciting than even fiction itself" ("The Mountain Village" 1). While the realist impulses in Delano's work reveal the darker side of a tenuous and dangerous life, his sketches adhere to an optimism about the larger goals of colonization. Indeed, Delano's sketches offer an overdetermined representation of the "double-voiced discourse" Mikhail Bakhtin identified as a key characteristic of "comic, ironic or parodic discourse" (324), and the "heteroglossia" inherent in frontier humor informs Twain's masterful narrative unification of these voices within his own authorial persona, which emerges in his early stories and comes to fruition with the 1872 publication of *Roughing It*.

Twain's innovative adaptation of folk sources and techniques, including the tradition of tall tales and boasts, emphasis on vernacular wordplay, and the perfection of the "deadpan style" of storytelling, contributed to his first major literary triumph, "Jim Smiley and His Jumping Frog." Allegedly based on a story overheard in a saloon, the story was first published in the *New York Saturday Press* in 1865, and reprinted in 1867 as "The Celebrated Jumping Frog of Calaveras County," the title story of Twain's first book. Clearly indebted to the "Old Southwest" tradition, and resembling a number of tales from both white and African American sources, the story first introduces an impatient narrator, a worldly outsider much like the traditional Southern gentleman in Longstreet's stories. The narrator reports an unlikely anecdote about an inveterate gambler who is conned by a stranger when he tries to stake a wager on the jumping abilities of his frog. The story within the story is told by "good-natured, garrulous old Simon Wheeler," who "had an expression of winning gentleness and simplicity upon his tranquil countenance" (*Early Tales and Sketches, Volume 2* 282). Twain highlights the differences in apparent class and education between the frame narrator and Wheeler, and the narrator never suspects that the joke might be on him. Critics peeling back the layers of storytelling and deception have disagreed about whether Wheeler or the narrator proves more authoritative, but as Kenneth Lynn observes, "it is the vernacular, not the polite style, which teaches the lesson" (146), whatever that lesson might be.

In *Roughing It*, Twain incorporates a range of material, including his own experiences as a reporter in Virginia City and San Francisco, the gossip and sensational news he read, gathered, and wrote, and the myriad stories, lies, boasts, and legends he heard from the disparate characters gathered to find their fortune on the Comstock Lode in Nevada. More important for his career, he synthesizes a mode of storytelling, combining elements of the various character types from literary and folk sources – the innocent rube, the confidence man, the detached gentleman – into a single voice that would define his work and its far-reaching influence. In his "Prefatory," Twain writes, "This book is merely a personal narrative, and not a pretentious history or a philosophical dissertation. It is a record of several years of variegated vagabondizing, and its object is rather to help the resting reader while away an idle hour than afflict him with metaphysics, or goad him with science" (xxxi). His narrative voice hilariously combines ornate pomposity, braggadocio, and vernacular self-effacement:

> Yes, take it all around, there is quite a good deal of information in the book. I regret this very much; but really it could not be helped: information appears to stew out of me naturally, like the precious ottar of roses out of the otter. Sometimes it has seemed to me that I would give worlds if I could retain my facts; but it cannot be. The more I caulk up the sources, and the tighter I get, the more I leak wisdom. (xxxi)

The humor in Twain's persona comes from the juxtaposition of high and low sources, the unification of the earnest blowhard and the plainspoken skeptic, as represented in Delano's sketches by the author and his penknife.

If *Roughing It* is defined by its innovative incorporation of folk speech, it is also a book about hearing, retelling, and inventing stories, and more specifically about the importance of the West in creating a new, uniquely American mode of storytelling. Lee Clark Mitchell argues that "The West seems far more distinctive in *Roughing It* than in earlier narratives by Lewis and Clark, Irving and Parkman, and it does so because it emphasizes a language, not a landscape" (69). While the narrative chronicles the emergence of Twain's "authentic" voice, it also highlights the potential dangers of misrepresentation. As Nicolas Witschi says of Twain, "He was as interested in questioning the interplay of truth, value, and representation as he was in defending it" (32).

The many embedded stories in *Roughing It* consistently reinforce the challenge of assigning meaning to language. One example is the episode involving Buck Fanshaw's funeral, in which Buck's loyal friend Scotty Briggs approaches a "new fledgling from an eastern theological seminary" about delivering a eulogy (*Roughing It* 309). Both men speak in their respective jargons, full of allusion and metaphor, and divided by both class and regional affiliation. When the minister says, "I am the shepherd in charge of the flock whose fold is next door," Scotty is confused, and his own extended metaphor on gambling is equally lost on the minister: "You ruther hold over me, pard. I reckon I can't call that hand. Ante and pass the buck" (310–311). Both high and low discourse are revealed as closed systems, inscrutable from the outside. Another episode, introduced with some fanfare as Jim Blaine's story of the old ram, is a rambling and incomprehensible soliloquy that ends with a drunken Jim Blaine falling asleep. Twain writes:

> I learned then that Jim Blaine's peculiarity was that whenever he reached a certain stage of intoxication, no human power could keep him from setting out, with impressive unction, to tell about a wonderful adventure which he had once had with his grandfather's old ram – and the mention of the ram in the first sentence was as far as any man had ever heard him get, concerning it. He always maundered off, interminably, from one thing to another, till his whisky got the best of him and he fell asleep. What the thing was that happened to him and his grandfather's old ram is a dark mystery to this day, for nobody has ever yet found out. (367)

Here, the vernacular triumphs again; the joke is on Twain, but it is also on his readers. We are at the mercy of his intoxicated storyteller, and any attempt at interpretation must fail, not because of the inscrutability of its content, but because of the complete absence of content altogether.

The focus on empty wordplay in Twain's work calls attention to another literary form popular with early Western writers: the hoax. A satirical variant on the boasting tradition of Southwestern humor, the literary hoax situated the author as confidence man, and readers were either in on the joke or became the object of its satire. Twain and his friend Dan De Quille (the pen name of William Wright) perfected the art of the hoax in the pages of the *Virginia City Territorial Enterprise* and the *San Francisco Golden Era*, and along with other writers, such as J. Ross Browne, "produced satires and burlesques" of the colorful characters drawn to the Comstock Lode (Blodgett 44). Among Twain's more famous hoaxes was an 1862 item for the *Virginia City Territorial Enterprise* titled "Petrified Man," in which Twain claimed that a "stony mummy" had been found "in the mountains south of the Gravelly Ford" (*Early Tales and Sketches, Volume 1* 158–159). The satirical targets of Twain's hoax included a cultural fascination with scientific curiosities, the gullibility of the reading public, and the questionable journalistic standards of the day. Indeed, although some newspapers reported Twain's story as a hoax, several others simply reprinted the item as news. De Quille himself, no doubt inspired by Twain, followed suit with his articles "The Wonder of the Age, a Silver Man" (1865) and "The Traveling Stones of Pahranagat Valley" (1867), both of which reflected an understanding of the most recent debates in contemporary geology and paleontology.

De Quille's and Twain's hoaxes reveal a skepticism about science and scientific discourse that addresses the rationalism of the nineteenth century and the role of science and technology in westward expansion.[3] An early example of such humor came from George Horatio Derby, who, as John Squibob and John Phoenix, wrote a series of humorous sketches for the *San Diego Herald* in the 1850s. Derby was an unlikely author. After graduating from West Point with George McClellan, George Pickett, and Thomas ("Stonewall") Jackson, Derby worked as an army engineer in California, producing several accounts of surveying expeditions before his untimely death in 1861, although he gained considerable national notoriety with the publication of *Phoenixiana; or Sketches and Burlesques* (1855) and a posthumous collection, *The Squibob Papers* (1865). The first collection included the comically inaccurate "Lectures on Astronomy" and "A New System of English Grammar," but the most celebrated Squibob/Phoenix prank occurred when he facetiously commandeered the *Herald* during its editor's brief absence in 1853, announcing a realignment of its political sympathies from Democratic to Whig, and warning voters to avoid supporting candidates who tried to win them over "by furnishing you with whisky, gratis, and credit at his little shop": "Drink his whisky, by all means, if you like it, and he invites you, but make him no pledges" (Derby 123).

Derby's simultaneous investment in both the national project on colonization and the good-natured lampooning of both scholarly and political discourse highlights the double-voiced nature of popular and folk-based writing in this period. Neil Schmitz, linking the tall tales of Southwestern humor to Jacksonian skepticism about the symbolic function of paper money, claims that "tall talk, the pursuit of a lie under difficulties, is in some sense a commentary on this lie, a magnification of an already inflated tale" (479). If earlier folkloric texts such as Thorpe's "The Big Bear of Arkansas" speak to the "lie" of financial speculation, the boasts and tall tales of the far West simultaneously displace and magnify the lies behind its conquest: broken treaties, exaggerated claims of resources and prosperity, and the relentless boosterism that attracted settlers westward throughout the nineteenth century. Even before the California Gold Rush inaugurated the era of large-scale settlement, the American West demonstrated the complexities inherent in what Mary Louise Pratt has called "contact zones": "social spaces where disparate cultures meet, clash, and grapple with each other, often in highly asymmetrical relations of domination and subordination – like colonialism, slavery, or their aftermaths as they are lived out across the globe today" (4). In the wake of American expansion, however, the deployment of folk humor to contain the violence of colonial conquest suggests the role of these writers in constructing the complex and paradoxical authenticity that continues to define Western writing.

## Notes

1 See also Nathaniel Lewis, *Unsettling the Literary West*, 70.
2 For the play's text and history, see Enrique Lamadrid, *Hermanitos Comanchitos: Indo-Hispano Rituals of Captivity and Redemption*.
3 See Judith Yaross Lee, "(Pseudo-) Scientific Humor" and Lynda Walsh, *Sins against Science: The Scientific Media Hoaxes of Poe, Twain, and Others*.

## Works Cited

Bakhtin, Mikhail. *Discourse in the Novel*. Caryl Emerson and Michael Holquist, trans. Austin: University of Texas Press, 1981.
Bendix, Regina. *In Search of Authenticity: The Formation of Folklore Studies*. Madison: University of Wisconsin Press, 1997.
Blodgett, Peter J. "Worlds of Wonder and Ambition: Gold Rush California and the Culture of Mining Bonanzas in the North American West." In Nicolas S. Witchsi (ed.) *A Companion to the Literature and Culture of the American West*. Malden, MA: Wiley Blackwell, 2014. 29–47.
Campbell, Neil. *The Cultures of the American New West*. Chicago: Fitzroy Dearborn Publishers, 2000.
Delano, Alonzo. "The Mountain Village." *Sacramento Daily Union*, Sept. 14, 1853. *Pen-Knife Sketches, or Chips Off the Old Block*. Sacramento, CA: Union Office, 1853.
Derby, George Horatio [John Phoenix]. *Phoenixiana, Or Sketches and Burlesques*. New York: D. Appleton and Company, 1855.
Foote, Stephanie. "The Cultural Work of American Regionalism." In Charles Crow (ed.) *A Companion to the Regional Literatures of America*. Malden, MA: Blackwell, 2003. 25–41.
Gellner, Ernest. *Nations and Nationalism*. Ithaca, NY: Cornell University Press, 1983.
Harte, Bret. *The Luck of Roaring Camp and Other Sketches*. Boston, MA: Houghton Mifflin, 1869.
Kowalewski, Michael. "Romancing the Gold Rush: The Literature of the California Frontier." *California History*. Vol. 79, no. 2 (2000): 204–225.
Lamadrid, Enrique. *Hermanitos Comanchitos: Indo-Hispano Rituals of Captivity and Redemption*. Albuquerque: University of New Mexico Press, 2003.
Lee, Judith Yaross. "(Pseudo-) Scientific Humor." In Robert J. Scholnick (ed.) *American Literature and Science*. Lexington: University Press of Kentucky, 1992. 128–156.
Lewis, Nathaniel. *Unsettling the Literary West: Authenticity and Authorship*. Lincoln: University of Nebraska Press, 2003.
Lynn, Kenneth S. *Mark Twain and Southwestern Humor*. Boston, MA: Little, Brown, 1959.
Mitchell, Lee Clark. "Verbally Roughing It: The West of Words." *Nineteenth-Century Literature*. Vol. 44, no. 1 (1989): 67–92.

Mulford, Prentice. "Justifiable Fiction." *Overland Monthly and Out West Magazine.* Vol. 11, no. 1 (1873): 39–42.

Pratt, Mary Louise. *Imperial Eyes: Travel Writing and Transculturation.* New York: Routledge, 1992.

Schmitz, Neil. "Tall Tale, Tall Talk: Pursuing the Lie in Jacksonian Literature." *American Literature.* Vol. 48, no. 4 (1977): 471–491.

Twain, Mark. *Early Tales and Sketches, Volume 1, 1851–1864.* Berkeley: University of California Press, 1979.

*Early Tales and Sketches, Volume 2, 1864–1865.* Berkeley: University of California Press, 1981.

"Fenimore Cooper's Literary Offences." *The North American Review.* Vol. 161, no. 464 (1895): 1–12.

*Mark Twain's Letters, Volume 2: 1867–1868.* Edgard Marquess Branch and Robert H. Hirst (eds.). Berkeley: University of California Press, 2000.

*Roughing It.* Berkeley: University of California Press, 1995.

Walsh, Lynda. *Sins against Science: The Scientific Media Hoaxes of Poe, Twain, and Others.* Albany, State University of New York Press, 2006.

Witschi, Nicolas. *Traces of Gold: California's Natural Resources and the Claim to Realism in Western American Literature.* Tuscaloosa: University of Alabama Press, 2002.

Wonham, Henry B. *Mark Twain and the Art of the Tall Tale.* New York: Oxford University Press, 1993.

# 4

DANIEL WORDEN

# Settlement, promise, and catastrophe in the middle regions

John Gast's 1872 painting *American Progress*, which George Crofutt made into a chromolithograph in 1873 for wide distribution to the public, captures the force of Manifest Destiny as an ideology in the late nineteenth-century United States (see Figure 4.1). The image features an angelic female figure draping telegraph wire across the Western plains and carrying a common school textbook. The telegraph wire and the textbook signify the twinned progress of technology and public education as markers of the American settlement of the frontier. The allegorical image also contains a historical narrative, as the already industrialized East in the image, with its bridges, cities, and railroads, shifts into waves of frontier settlement – the yeoman farmer, the stagecoach, the Pony Express rider, the homesteader, minders, ranchers, and, ultimately, Native Americans, the bear, and the buffalo. This conflation of indigenous peoples with animals is but one of the markers of Manifest Destiny and its rationalization of displacement and violence. In *American Progress*'s allegory, as divinely sanctioned civilization progresses westward, indigenous peoples and nature recede, making way for frontier adventure, resource extraction, agriculture, and, eventually, urban development.

This process of settlement often connotes the development of an exceptionally American individualism that emerges through an engagement with indigenous practices. In his famous 1893 essay "The Significance of the Frontier in American History," Frederick Jackson Turner developed an account of how the distinctly American individual emerges through the synthesis of European and Native American cultures:

> The frontier is the line of most rapid and effective Americanization. The wilderness masters the colonist. It finds him a European in dress, industries, tools, modes of travel, and thought. It takes him from the railroad car and puts him in the birch canoe. It strips off the garments of civilization and arrays him in the hunting shirt and the moccasin. It puts him in the log cabin of the Cherokee and Iroquois and runs an Indian palisade around him. Before long he has gone to planting Indian corn and plowing with a sharp stick; he shouts

Figure 4.1 George Crofutt, chromolithograph of John Gast's *American Progress*, ca. 1873. Prints and Photographs Division, Library of Congress.

the war cry and takes the scalp in orthodox Indian fashion. In short, at the frontier the environment is at first too strong for the man.... Little by little he transforms the wilderness, but the outcome is not the old Europe.... The fact is, that here is a new product that is American. (Turner 20)

Notably, in both Turner's and *American Progress*'s presentation of Manifest Destiny, settlement is accomplished and American identity is achieved by men, although the "spirit" of civilization is often cast as feminine. This gendered logic – civilization as a feminizing impulse, settlement as a masculine pursuit – structures much of Western American literature and culture. From visual and historical texts about Manifest Destiny, to novels about homesteading and gunfights, masculine exertion at the frontier makes the West available for domestic life.

*American Progress*'s representation of the smooth and inevitable settlement of the American West resonates throughout Western American literature and culture, and while some Western fiction, like Owen Wister's *The Virginian* (1902), celebrates the taming of the frontier, other Western fiction expresses more ambivalence about the "legacy of conquest" that has gone into the making of the American West today.[1] This chapter will survey the ways that Western writers have addressed Manifest Destiny, Western settlement, and the violence that accompanied those histories. All in all, Western American writers have made visible the legacy of conquest in the West, increasingly characterizing the process idealized in *American Progress* as an uneven, violent, and difficult series of historical events, events that still resonate in American culture today.

In what follows, this chapter addresses three of the major ways that westward settlement's promises and catastrophes have been represented in twentieth-century literature and culture. First, I will discuss how homesteading and immigration have been represented in major works of Western American literature. Then, I will take up the ways that nationalism operates in the American West through representations of African American and Chicano military service. I conclude with the uneven geographies of settlement in the American West, from reservations and farms to cities and ghost towns. The promises and catastrophes of westward settlement resonate in all writing about the region, and in our contemporary moment, writers, artists, and the public continue to struggle with the legacy of conquest that has left its mark on Western land, borders, and ways of life.

## Homesteading, immigration, and agriculture

There is a long and understudied tradition of women's writing about the American West and settlement, and renewed scholarly interest in this tradition has substantially revised the received origin stories of Western American literature, which often center exclusively on men's writings about the frontier and neglect popular women's writings about settlement. As Nina Baym notes in her study of the largely marginalized tradition of nineteenth-century and early twentieth-century American women's writing about the West:

> By the 1890s, when the census declared the frontier closed, pioneer associations had begun to collect and solicit memoirs and histories. Elderly pioneers put down their memories; the younger generation celebrated their parents' and grandparents' achievements; historians and historical novelists went to work full-bore. As the Old West became a fading memory, the New Woman – independent, town-dwelling, professionally employed, tentatively sexual – enters the scene. She turns out to exemplify the New West, to be the reason for all that pioneering, the future realized. (Baym 11)

These pioneer texts were preceded by works like Eliza Farnham's *Life in Prairie Land* (1846) and Caroline Kirkland's *Western Clearings* (1845), as well as even earlier texts like Mary Rowlandson's *A True History of the Captivity and Restoration of Mrs. Mary Rowlandson* (1682), the best known captivity narrative. This long history of women's writing about the West both confirms the civilizing mission of westward settlement, and offers a sometimes distinctly different vision of gender roles in the American West.[2]

Trading nostalgia for homesteading, Laura Ingalls Wilder's *Little House in the Big Woods* (1932), the first of the eight *Little House* novels to be published during her lifetime, is set in 1860s Wisconsin. The novel centers on a family and details their day-to-day life as pioneers. The father hunts, the mother cooks and maintains the home, and the novel's focal point, Laura, the middle sister in the family, helps out however she can around the house. Vividly detailing the family's means of sustenance – they store food for winter, feast on bear meat and maple syrup, and churn butter – the novel paints a pleasant portrait of life in the wilderness. While much of the novel concerns housework and food, violence is also present through-out the text, often figured through dangerous animals such as wolves and panthers. Moreover, the novel details how ubiquitous and necessary guns are to life in the West: "The gun was always loaded, and always above the door so that Pa could get it quickly and easily, any time he needed a gun" (Wilder 51–52). The novel interestingly concludes by making clear that the homesteading past is still present. At the novel's conclusion, Pa plays "Auld Lang Syne" on his fiddle. Laura then asks:

> "What are the days of auld lang syne, Pa?"
> "They are the days of a long time ago, Laura," Pa said. "Go to sleep now."
> But Laura lay awake a little while, listening to Pa's fiddle softly playing and to the lonely sound of the wind in the Big Woods. She looked at Pa sitting on the bench by the hearth, the fire-light gleaming on his brown hair and glisten-ing on the honey-brown fiddle. She looked at Ma, gently rocking and knitting.
> She thought to herself, "This is now."
> She was glad that the cosy house, and Pa and Ma and the fire-light and the music, were now. They could not be forgotten, she thought, because now is now. It can never be a long time ago. (Wilder 237–238)

*Little House in the Big Woods* concludes by establishing the homesteading past as the present, as the immediate context in which Americans in the twentieth century should view themselves. The simple life of settlement, in Wilder's novel, is the life that we should all aspire to, a moment in American history that is imagined as less complicated, even if it is also constituted by violence.

Similar to Wilder's nostalgic treatment of homesteading as the past that Americans in the mid-twentieth century should view as their immediate context, Willa Cather's *My Ántonia* casts homesteading immigrants from Scandinavia as the ideal American settler. In the novel, set in Nebraska, Midwestern agriculture is represented as an heroic, nation-building under-taking. The Midwestern cornfields "would be one of the great economic facts, like the wheat crop of Russia, which underlie all the activities of men, in peace or war" (Cather 104). This is reinforced later in the novel, as the novel's narrator, Jim Burden, and the novel's heroine, Ántonia Shimerda, watch the sunset: "On some upland farm, a plough had been left standing in the field. The sun was sinking just behind it. Magnified across the distance by the horizontal light, it stood out against the sun, was exactly contained within the circle of the disk; the handles, the tongue, the share – black against the molten red. There it was, heroic in size, a picture writing on the sun" (Cather 183). The plough signals the dominance and even the beauty of agriculture in the West, as it takes over the landscape.

In *My Ántonia*, though, this idyllic representation of the Nebraskan prairie is complicated by scenes of violence. For example, Ántonia tells a story about "what happened up in the Norwegian settlement last summer ... We were at the Iversons, and I was driving one of the grain wagons" (Cather 133). As she is working with Ole Iverson, a "tramp" approaches them and asks if he can work the threshing machine: "the tramp got on the machine. He cut bands all right for a few minutes, and then ... he waved his hand to me and jumped head-first right into the threshing machine after the wheat" (Cather 134). This death remains inexplicable to Ántonia, whose work ethic and ties to the land determine her idealized role in the novel, as the pioneer spirit embodied. What strikes *My Ántonia*'s narrator as the plenitude of the modern United States is also, in contrast, represented as alienating, isolating, and inexplicably violent.

Both Edna Ferber's novel *Cimarron* (1929) and Lynn Riggs's play *Green Grow the Lilacs* (1930) dramatize Oklahoma's shift from a territory to statehood in the early twentieth century. In *Cimarron*, Yancey and Sabra Cravat move to the novel's eponymous, fictional town. The husband, Yancey, refuses to stay in the developing town, leaving to move ever westward, while his wife, Sabra, remains in town, manages the town's newspaper, and becomes a centerpiece in the social, political, and commercial life of Oklahoma. The novel concludes with the Oklahoma oil boom of the 1920s, a return to the frontier society that Sabra Cravat had tried to civilize with her newspaper and women's social groups:

> Oil. Nothing else mattered. Oklahoma, the dry, the wind-swept, the burning, was a sea of hidden oil. The red prairies, pricked, ran black and slimy with it. The work of years was undone in a day. The sunbonnets shrank back, aghast. Compared to that which now took place in the early days following the [Land Run of 1889] were idyllic.... Again the gambling tent, the six-shooter, the roaring saloon, the dance hall, the harlot. Men fought, stole, killed, died for a piece of ground beneath whose arid surface lay who knew what wealth of fluid richness. (Ferber 258–259)

The return of the nineteenth-century frontier spirit to twentieth-century Oklahoma is occasioned by the oil boom, a signal in the novel of the continued persistence of the Wild West into the modern United States. Sabra Cravat goes on to represent Oklahoma in the U.S. Congress, while her husband, who long ago abandoned his wife and children, is memorialized as the model for a state-commissioned "statue of the Spirit of the Oklahoma Pioneer ... an heroic figure of Yancey Cravat stepping forward with that light graceful stride in the high-heeled Texas star boots, the skirts of the Prince Albert billowing behind with the vigor of his movements, the sombrero atop the great menacing buffalo head, one beautiful hand resting lightly on the weapon in his two-gun holster. Behind him ... stumbled the weary, blanketed figure of an Indian" (Ferber 310). While Yancey is absent for most of the novel and the work of settlement is undertaken by his wife, Sabra, the masculine frontier hero is nonetheless projected as the symbolic representative of the West, a figure who comes to connote equality and meritocracy.

Best known because it was adapted into the Rodgers and Hammerstein musical *Oklahoma!* (1943), *Green Grow the Lilacs* also dramatizes the shift from the frontier to the domestic, as the play's main character, Curly, decides that he will give up his cowboy lifestyle and settle down. In his final speech in the play, before he is taken to stand trial for the accidental murder of the play's antagonist, Jeeter Fry (in the musical *Oklahoma!*, the character's name is changed to Jud), Curly remarks: "Oh, I got to learn to be a farmer, I see that! Quit a-thinkin' about dehornin' and brandin' and th'owin' the rope, and start in to git my hands blistered a new way! Oh, things is changin' right and left! Buy up mowin' machines, cut down the prairies! Shoe yer horses, drag them plows under the sod! They gonna make a state outa this, they gonna put it in the Union! Country a-changin', got to change with it! Bring up a pair of boys, new stock, to keep up 'th the way things is goin' in this here crazy country!" (Riggs 157). Curly's commitment to change resonates with the pattern of westward settlement established in late nineteenth-century treatments of American history and Manifest Destiny. As civilization progresses, the cowboy and the Wild West give way to modern domesticity and industry. In *Green Grow the Lilacs*, the cowboy becomes the farmer, and in *Cimarron*, the frontier town becomes a seat of the mid-century oil industry.

## Race, the military, and nationalism

Although homesteading, agriculture, and the development of towns and industry in the West represent major narrative strands in Western American literature about settlement, military service, racial meritocracy, and national belonging resonate, as well as another mode in which Western settlement is narrated. This section of the chapter will focus on the Buffalo Soldiers National Museum in Houston, Texas, and Américo Paredes's novel *George Washington Gómez* (1990), both of which represent military service and nationalism as modes of integrating African American and Chicano subjects, respectively, into the project of Western settlement.[3]

Founded in 2000 by Paul J. Matthews, a veteran of the Vietnam War, the Buffalo Soldiers National Museum in Houston, Texas chronicles African American military involvement from the Revolutionary War to the present. The museum focuses on its namesake, the Buffalo Soldiers, the regiments sent after the Civil War to the frontier to subdue Native Americans and Mexican revolutionaries, hunt down outlaws, and protect railroad workers. The museum's mission statement reads: "The primary objectives of the [Buffalo Soldiers National Museum] are to educate, preserve, promote and perpetuate the history and outstanding contributions of the Buffalo Soldiers toward the development and defense of the United States of America" (Buffalo Soldiers). The museum features a collection of farm tools used during slavery – rusty claws for picking pecans, old wooden buckets for washing, sacks for holding cotton. Moving from tools associated with slavery, the museum then displays many drawings and models of the Buffalo Soldiers on the frontier in Western cavalry garb, and relics – uniforms, medals, hats, patches, and insignia – from the Buffalo Soldier regiments in the two World Wars and beyond. The six African American army units, created in 1866, were the 9th and 10th Cavalries and the 38th through 41st Infantries, now the 24th and 25th infantry regiments. Military involvement, as narrated by the museum, is liberating; the guided tour moves from slavery to emancipation and military participation. Emancipation brings about the possibility for participation in the national project as a citizen, which means, in the museum, involvement in the expansion and defense of national territory. The museum features a portrait of Cathy Williams, the only female Buffalo Soldier, adding a hint of gender liberation to military participation, reaching beyond its predominantly male focus. The Buffalo Soldiers are portrayed as better citizens than most for their efficiency and ferocity in battle as well as the sacrifices made while living out on the frontier territories, away from home and civilization.

On a guided tour, museum founder Paul J. Matthews explains that the "Buffalo Soldiers" name was given to the 9th Cavalry by the Cheyenne because of the soldiers' fighting ability; the cavalry apparently fought as violently as a cornered buffalo. On the museum's Web site, alternate explanations are given for the name: "Some attribute it to the Indians likening the short curly hair of the black troopers to that of the buffalo. Another possibility for the nickname was the heavy buffalo robes the soldiers wore on winter campaigns" (Buffalo Soldiers). These alternate descriptions do not highlight noble battle, but instead deal with a racial marker – kinky hair – or the killing and eventual near extinction of the buffalo on the Western frontier. The "Buffalo Soldiers" moniker, then, has a dual meaning – both a sign of American individualism and exertion, and a reminder of the persistence of racial hierarchies and violence during westward settlement.

The West remains imaginary in the museum; while one sees artifacts from slavery and the wars of the twentieth century, one only sees models and drawings of the Buffalo Soldiers. The frontier – and the soldiers' participation in its annexation, settlement, and incorporation – remains the product of imagination. The West becomes an imaginary site not of actual historical struggle but instead of national belonging. By becoming national subjects through military exertion in the American West, the Buffalo Soldiers cross over from history into mythology, sharing in Manifest Destiny's vision of an American identity's emergence in the frontier.

The lore surrounding the Buffalo Soldiers partakes of the mythology surrounding the nineteenth-century American West. As Barbara Will charts in her essay "The Nervous Origins of the American Western," the late nineteenth-century American West became a site for masculine recuperation, a region where men could regain their lost virility and strength, removed from the feminizing effects of urban life and middle-class office jobs. Focusing on Owen Wister's prescribed trips to the frontier, trips that would result in Wister's influential Western novel *The Virginian*, Will finds an American imperialist logic behind Wister's heroic cowboy, the Virginian, who "offers himself up as both the model of balanced modern masculinity and the auspicious symbol of a strenuous expansionist ideology at the turn of the century" (Will 310). This narrative of regaining a vanished masculinity applies to men employed in white-collar professions, and therefore was exclusively a narrative of white empowerment through frontier tourism. This discourse surrounding remasculinization and the frontier was closely bound to nationalism, particularly through Theodore Roosevelt. In *The Anarchy of Empire in the Making of U.S. Culture*, Amy Kaplan argues that the logic of the West as the place where one regains masculinity as well as a national heritage, or even masculinity as national heritage, is broadened in the 1890s and the twentieth century to justify territorial expansion as a nostalgic return: "American imperialism reclaimed and galvanized the meaning of the West as the site of origins. The quintessential twentieth-century symbol of American nationhood – the lone self-reliant cowboy on the frontier – has endured parasitically by feeding on new outposts of the American empire" (Kaplan 120). This parasitic relation figures any new territories as a return to "the embodied American man" (Kaplan 120). With this structure of linking masculinity to nationalism and imperialism in mind, it is tempting to read the Buffalo Soldiers National Museum as yet another national romance; the historical conditions of African American soldiers in the Southwestern territories might be considered secondary to the narrative of national participation.

The Buffalo Soldiers National Museum can be seen, then, as yet another participant in American nationalism, relying on appeals to the abstract at the expense of the legacies of violence, genocide, and acquisition that also characterize westward settlement. By mythologizing the Buffalo Soldiers, the museum can be seen as controlling history, or, in Benedict Anderson's words, the museum "aspires to create, under its control, a human landscape of perfect visibility" (Anderson 185). However, the Buffalo Soldiers National Museum, although partaking in this nationalist project, also envisions a mode of alternate nationalism. By making clear the legacy of African American soldiers and, more broadly, African American settlers and workers in the American West, the museum contests the whitewashed narrative of westward settlement so prominent in American popular culture, from Owen Wister's *The Virginian* to the midcentury Western genre film and paperback. The museum supports a nationalism, but one that must be recognized as holding a complex and often critical relation to the state of the nation itself.

Similarly, Américo Paredes's novel *George Washington Gómez*, written between 1936 and 1940 but not published until 1990, concludes with the novel's main character returning to his hometown in the lower Rio Grande Valley in Texas before the United States enters World War II. Still known to his family as Guálinto Gómez, but now called George Gómez by everyone else, he claims to have returned to broker a land deal in Texas, but eventually reveals that he is "a first lieutenant in counter-intelligence ... My job is border security. That's why I must wear civilian clothes and keep my work a secret" (Paredes 299). While the Buffalo Soldiers National Museum celebrates military service as a path to integration and equality, Paredes's novel is much more cynical about what nationalism means for ethnic subjects. Rather than incorporating Mexican and Mexican-American subjects into the nation, George Gómez's national service entails abandoning his culture, signified most prominently in the novel by his remark that his children will not learn Spanish: "There's no reason for them to do so. They grow up far away from here" (Paredes 301).

While travel to the American West for the Buffalo Soldiers National Museum connotes newfound freedom and the rights of the citizen, being from the U.S.–Mexico borderlands in *George Washington Gómez* means that one must decide to be a member of the United States or not, and this decision means abandoning one's heritage or retaining it under an Anglo-dominated government. The military occupations that claimed the American West as U.S. territory are often represented as paving the way for a truer democracy, a more egalitarian society where individuals can realize their dreams. This idealistic national narrative is complicated by literature that documents what is lost during that process of nationalization. In *George Washington Gómez*, the title character has a recurring dream of an alternate history to Sam Houston's battle against Santa Anna for Texas, one that does not result in U.S. settlement of the Southwest, nor the retention of Santa Anna and the elite class of politicians that he represents: "Houston is easily captured. Santa Anna is joyous at what he thinks is his deliverance. But his joy does not last long. He is immediately hanged.... Texas and the Southwest will remain forever Mexican" (Paredes 281). This dream of a border never formed, a populist Mexico not established, and territory never acquired gestures to the power of alternative imaginaries in the American West, ways of thinking about geography, ethnicity, race, and culture that do not capitulate to the purportedly progressive vision of American settlement propagated by the ideology of Manifest Destiny.

## Uneven geographies

Along with homesteading, agriculture, and military service, the emergence and building of towns and cities in the American West is another major way that the promises and catastrophes of settlement are registered in literature. From mining, drilling, and ranching, to the construction of Western towns and, eventually, cities and suburbs, narratives about the West often detail the history of land development, and the tensions and inequalities that development often entails. Unlike the seamless, angelic progression across the West imagined in *American Progress*, the actual settlement of the West developed unevenly, among previous settlements and amid the boom-and-bust economies that led to both vibrant cities and ghost towns.

In D'Arcy McNickle's novel *The Surrounded* (1936), set in Montana, the divide between U.S. settlement and life on an Indian reservation is put in striking relief:

> The mission town of St. Xavier belonged to two ages. A brief sixty years separated its primitive from its modern, but the division was deeper than years.
>
> The opening up of the Indian reserve brought new townsmen and new houses. The newcomers, after one look at what was there before them – sway-backed cabins, rag-stuffed windows, refuse strewn about – moved on and erected their neat clapboard bungalows on the opposite side of Buffalo Creek. Over there they laid a few cement sidewalks, hid their outhouses in

woodsheds, planted round flower beds (which were soon neglected), and ran fences around their lots. That was the "Townsite," the up-to-date quarter.

> The old town, which was usually called Indiantown, was left to itself.... The center of life was the mission church.... Plain as it was, the hovels which were set against it gave it an air of grandeur. The newcomers thought Indiantown had been built without a plan, but they were wrong. There had been a plan, even if it didn't lend itself to street construction and regularity. Each cabin faced the church. Each door – there were no windows – gave a full view of God's tall house and the cropped poplar trees around it. The newcomers saw only the confusion. (McNickle 35–36)

While the post–Dawes Act settlement builds anew, "Indiantown" is structured around an older form of colonization than that initiated in the late nineteenth century. The contrast here between the new town and the old town registers, too, as the contrast between modern, economic development and older missionary outreach. In *The Surrounded*, both of these forms of colonization are displaced by the novel's main character, Archilde, who seems to reject both American models of success and the Catholicism his family has long practiced. Yet, in *The Surrounded*, Archilde struggles to find some way to live outside of those structures, only to be, ultimately, arrested at the novel's conclusion. As its title indicates, *The Surrounded* is about how Western development has continually sought to extinguished ways of life.[4] The survival of those ways of life would be further articulated in Native American literature in the later twentieth century. In works such as N. Scott Momaday's poetic memoir and history *The Way to Rainy Mountain* (1969) and Leslie Marmon Silko's novel *Ceremony* (1977), Native American identity is reconfigured from within the history of conquest in the American West.

In contemporary literature, the American West remains a site of fascination, and treatments of the West often continue to address the ramifications and meanings of settlement. Loosely based on William Shakespeare's tragedy *King Lear*, Jane Smiley's novel *A Thousand Acres* is set on an Iowa farm. The protagonist's father, a stoic, successful farmer, incorporates his farm and gives shares to his daughters. In the beginning of the novel, the implementation of tile drainage on the family farm creates a sense of man's command over nature:

> Most magically, tile produced prosperity – more bushels per acre of a better crop, year after year, wet or dry. I knew what the tile looked like (when I was very young, five- or twelve-inch culinders of real tile always lay here and there around the farm, for repairs or extensions of tile lines; as I got older, "tile" became long snakes of plastic tubing), but for years, I imagined a floor beneath the topsoil checkered aqua and yellow like the floor in the girls' bathroom at

the elementary school, a hard shiny floor you could not sink beneath, better than a trust fund, more reliable than crop insurance, a farmer's best patrimony. (Smiley 15)

This image of an artificial, prosperous surface underneath the farm takes on an ominous meaning later in the novel, when it is revealed that the father sexually abused his daughters. No longer registering as a sign of American prosperity and know-how, the farm instead seems to be a false front, a lie that masks a traumatic past. This idyllic turned traumatic past of American settlement is ingrained in the novel's narrator: "Lodged in my every cell, along with the DNA, are molecules of topsoil and atrazine and paraquat and anhydrous ammonia and diesel fuel and plant dust, and also molecules of memory" (Smiley 369). The persistence of the materials of the farm, and memories of life on the farm, make up the narrator of *A Thousand Acres*, and, by extension, any person who has been brought up in a nation that romanticizes the legacy of settlement, that mistakes the violence of land acquisition for the brilliance of individual initiative.

More recently, Justin St. Germain's memoir, *Son of a Gun*, details his mother's murder in a nearly vacant town outside of Tombstone, Arizona by her husband Ray, a former police officer in Tombstone. St. Germain finds in the iconic Western hero Wyatt Earp, whose famous shootout at the O.K. Corral remains central to the tourist industry in the otherwise rather desolate town, a long history to explain his mother's violent death:

We might as well blame Wyatt Earp. His legacy leads straight to Ray, right down to the mustache and the badge and the belief that a man solves problems with violence. If it weren't for Wyatt, grown men in Tombstone wouldn't still dress up like gunslingers, as if there weren't any other kinds of men in the frontier West. If it weren't for Wyatt, Tombstone might be known for its silver boom – it was once the largest city between Saint Louis and San Francisco – instead of a thirty-second gunfight that killed three men. If my mother made a wrong choice, it was moving to a town obsessed with Wyatt Earp, where a former deputy would kill her, and other men would say that she deserved it. (St. Germain 122)

The American West is still in the thrall of narratives of settlement – of heroic lawmen making frontier towns safe for businesses and families, of soldiers clearing purportedly savage indigenous peoples from land claimed by the United States, of immigrant families losing their ethnic heritages and becoming true Americans. These narratives of settlements' promises also entail violent loss – lynchings, shootouts, genocide, assimilation.

Looking through old family photographs from his childhood in Tombstone, Arizona, Justin St. Germain remarks, "I see guns everywhere"

(St. Germain 131). The legacy of violence, alternately heroized or forgotten in national narratives of settlement in the American West, cannot capture the reality of violence, although becoming aware of that violent history does possibly explain violence in the contemporary United States. Moreover, westward settlement is saturated with melancholy – it is a process that, in the twentieth century, is complete, yet still alive in our cultural imaginary. In the popular Western *Shane*, originally a 1949 novel by Jack Schaefer and adapted into a 1953 film by director George Stevens, the heroic gunfighter Shane rides off toward the mountains, after killing a group of ranchers and villainous gunfighters who have terrorized the new homesteaders in Wyoming. Wounded in the final showdown, Shane rides away on his horse, as a young homesteader's son, Joey, cries, "Shane, Come back!" (*Shane*). This final moment captures American culture's, and much of Western American literature's, relationship to westward settlement. An outgrowth of it, inextricably bound to its violent history, we are also drawn toward it as a kind of national, mythic origin, one that writers have increasingly presented as a myth, as something that obscures a more complicated set of promises and catastrophes.

## Notes

1 For an influential account of the "legacy of conquest" in the American West, see Limerick, *The Legacy of Conquest*.
2 For further accounts of women's writing about the West, see Halverson, *Playing House in the American West*; Kolodny, *The Land Before Her*; and Rosowski, *Birthing a Nation*.
3 For further reading on African Americans and Western American literature, see Johnson, *Black Masculinity and the Frontier Myth in American Literature*, and for further reading on Américo Paredes and Chicano literature, see Saldívar, *The Borderlands of Culture*.
4 For further reading on Native American literature and the West, see Piatote, *Domestic Subjects*.

## Works Cited

Anderson, Benedict. *Imagined Communities: Reflections on the Origin and Spread of Nationalism*. New York: Verso, 1991.
Baym, Nina. *Women Writers and the American West, 1830–1927*. Urbana: University of Illinois Press, 2011.
Buffalo Soldiers National Museum. Accessed Jan. 28, 2015. http://buffalosoldiermuseum.com/.
Cather, Willa. *My Ántonia*. New York: Vintage, 1994.
Ferber, Edna. *Cimarron*. New York: Vintage, 2014.
Halverson, Cathryn. *Playing House in the American West: Western Women's Life Narratives, 1839–1987*. Tuscaloosa: University of Alabama Press, 2013.

Johnson, Michael K. *Black Masculinity and the Frontier Myth in American Literature.* Norman: University of Oklahoma Press, 2002.

Kaplan, Amy. *The Anarchy of Empire in the Making of U.S. Culture.* Cambridge, MA: Harvard University Press, 2002.

Kolodny, Annette. *The Land Before Her: Fantasy and Experience of the American Frontiers, 1630–1860.* Chapel Hill: University of North Carolina Press, 1984.

Limerick, Patricia Nelson. *The Legacy of Conquest: The Unbroken Past of the American West.* New York: Norton, 1987.

McNickle, D'Arcy. *The Surrounded.* Albuquerque: University of New Mexico Press, 1978.

Paredes, Américo. *George Washington Gómez.* Houston, TX: Arte Público Press, 1990.

Piatote, Beth H. *Domestic Subjects: Gender, Citizenship, and Law in Native American Literature.* New Haven, CT: Yale University Press, 2013.

Riggs, Lynn. *Green Grow the Lilacs.* New York: Samuel French, 1931.

Rosowski, Susan J. *Birthing a Nation: Gender, Creativity, and the West in American Literature.* Lincoln: University of Nebraska Press, 1999.

Saldívar, Ramón. *The Borderlands of Culture: Américo Paredes and the Transnational Imaginary.* Durham, NC: Duke University Press, 2006.

*Shane.* Dir. George Stevens. Paramount, 2000. DVD.

Smiley, Jane. *A Thousand Acres.* New York: Anchor, 1992.

St. Germain, Justin. *Son of a Gun: A Memoir.* New York: Random House, 2013.

Turner, Frederick Jackson. "The Significance of the Frontier in American History." In Richard W. Etulain (ed.) *Does the Frontier Experience Make America Exceptional?* Boston, MA: Bedford/St. Martin's, 1999. 17–43.

Wilder, Laura Ingalls. *Little House in the Big Woods.* New York: HarperTrophy, 2004.

Will, Barbara. "The Nervous Origins of the American Western." *American Literature.* Vol. 70. No. 2 (June 1998): 293–316.

# 5

CATHRYN HALVERSON

# Gender and the literature of expansion

## Introduction

Among Mary Wilkins Freeman's many stories about women in rural New England, "A Poetess" specifically reports on the conditions of its own publication. Appearing in *Harper's Monthly Magazine* in 1890, the story narrates the sad fate of Betsey, the sentimental "poetess" whose local mode of literary production is shown to be superannuated. Betsey writes occasional verses on demand, and the tale opens with a bereaved mother commissioning an elegy for her son. So pleased is she with Betsey's poem, she has it printed on black-bordered paper to distribute to neighbors and friends. This wider circulation of her work, however, leads to Betsey's downfall. Upon reading it, the village's young new minister, she learns, declared she "had never wrote anything that could be called poetry" (202). The man speaks from a position of authority, as both a clergyman and a published magazine writer himself, and his criticism sends Betsey into a fatal decline. She exacts a promise from him on her deathbed to write a poem about her, making herself over from a producer of poetry into a subject of it.

Freeman (herself a hugely best-selling author) depicts two incompatible literary economies in dramatizing the evolution of authorship into a nationalized, male-dominated profession that embeds texts in market forces and institutional policies. Her fictional "Poetess" practices within an older system in which intimate textual exchanges strengthen personal bonds, and she literally dies at first exposure to its modern successor. However, for the real-life writers under consideration here, Elinore Pruitt Stewart and Hilda Rose, the meeting of these contrasting modes was not deadly but generative. As a consequence of inhabiting borderland frontier communities, Stewart and Rose also inhabited borderland literary space, producing texts that straddled the line between private and public textual production, and between gift and commodity. Their extended letters to distant middle-class friends – which for each originated in a need for a greater measure of women's culture and company than their adopted communities could support – resulted in *Atlantic Monthly* magazine serials and best-selling books, *Letters of a Woman Homesteader* (1914) and *The Stump Farm: A Chronicle of Pioneering* (1928).

Stewart and Rose had long addressed potent accounts of their farming experiences in Wyoming, Idaho, and Alberta to women far enough removed from such practice and places to take pleasure in reading about them. These distant interlocutors, in turn, served as mentor, muse, and agent. Over the years they coupled their replies with gifts of reading material, household objects, used clothes, and small sums, and they eventually initiated the publication of their work. The following explores this balancing act, whereby Stewart and Rose's records of western expansion connected them to easterners and urbanites. The farther they went, the closer they came.

We can speculate that their earliest training as writers took the form of letters to the family they left behind. Both embarked on homesteading after years of hard times. Born in 1876, Elinore Pruitt spent her childhood on Chickasaw Indian territory in what is now the state of Oklahoma. After a brief marriage and stint of homesteading in Kansas, she divorced and moved to Denver, where she worked in the home of the Massachusetts woman to whom she would later address her frontier letters. In 1909, she took a job as a ranch housekeeper for Clyde Stewart in southwestern Wyoming, only to marry him soon afterward and file on an adjoining claim of her own.

Hilda Gustafson also grew up poor, in a tenement neighborhood in Rockland, Illinois. Her parents had emigrated from Sweden in 1880 scant months before her birth, drawn by the city's burgeoning furniture industry. She worked as a kindergarten teacher and made plans for college but, suffering from tuberculosis, instead moved to Idaho with her family for her health. In 1911, she married Charles Rose, a Canadian twenty-eight years her senior (whom she always called Daddy). After fifteen years of farming in Idaho, the couple embarked on homesteading in Fort Vermilion, Alberta, the northernmost arable land in Canada and the world.

Despite the evident toll it exacted of exhaustion, sickness, and relentlessly precarious economies, Stewart and Rose were both staunch proponents of homesteading. They argued, moreover, that the system offered women special opportunities. Stewart asserted, "any woman who can stand her own company ... will have independence, plenty to eat all the time, and a home of her own in the end" (*Letters of a Woman Homesteader* 215), and she supported this claim by chronicling other women's achievements and her own. Rose presented her wilderness homestead as both a refuge from the horrors of modernity and the crucible of her strength,

strength that waxed as her husband's waned. Yet at the same time, their very need to write so volubly demonstrates a painful social lack. As Rose succinctly put it, "I have no woman to talk to, so I will write to ease my brain" (*The Stump Farm* 30).

The *Atlantic Monthly* made an apt venue for their texts. Since its inception it had been committed, like other quality magazines of the time, to regional writing. Harriet Beecher Stowe, one of the *Atlantic*'s founders, set it on a sure course with her 1858–1859 serialized novel, *The Minister's Wooing*. Other fiction writers, including Celia Thaxter, Rose Terry Cooke, and, most prolifically, Sarah Orne Jewett, joined Stowe in portraying rural New England. Contributions from the South included Rebecca Harding Davis's 1861 pioneering work of realism, *Life in an Iron Mills*; Mary Noailles Murfree's hugely popular stories about mountain life in Tennessee; and Charles Chesnutt's "conjure tales" of African American resistance. The *Atlantic*, moreover, had a special interest in the West. Bret Harte made literary history in 1871 with his $10,000 advance for a series of California stories. Western historians and naturalists, including John Muir and John Burroughs, made regular appearances, while Mary Hallock Foote's Idaho stories, Mary Austin's desert sketches, and Zitkala-Sa's memoirs of her Dakota childhood anticipated Stewart and Rose's life narratives.

In portraying frontier conditions and agrarian endeavors that recollected an earlier stage in the nation's history, *Letters of a Woman Homesteader* and *The Stump Farm* reassured American readers that "pioneer virtues are not deteriorating" (Eliot, vii, quoted in Rose), to quote from the foreword to the latter. The epistolary origins of these texts intensified their impact. As personal letters – vivid accounts of ongoing experience written by the participants themselves – they offered the semblance of unmediated contact between author and reader. They thereby satisfied what Nathaniel Lewis has shown to be the condition that publishers and readers sought first from literature of the West, authenticity.

Yet we can recognize their central subject as twofold, both life on western frontiers and the long-distance epistolary relationships that in consequence ensued. Ellery Sedgwick, the *Atlantic* editor whom Rose and Stewart shared, was both personally fascinated by such cross-class, cross-regional conversations and keenly aware of their market potential. This said, Stewart and Rose were not entirely community insiders, as their textual production itself confirms. The generative condition of so much Euro-American writing about the West was that sometimes uneasy, often exhilarating, subject position they held: at once insider and outsider. They were alert to the extraordinary nature of their lives in the West – which inspired them to record it – even as they were intent on preserving and developing social relationships elsewhere.

## Letters of a woman homesteader

Already versed in attempts to write travel essays and short fiction, Elinore Pruitt Stewart was flooded with new material on her move to Wyoming. The creative inspiration she found was given form and direction by her ongoing relationship with her former employer in Denver, Juliet Coney. Stewart responds in *Letters of a Woman Homesteader* not only to the people and places of frontier Wyoming, but also – quite literally – to Coney, a woman whose Eastern, high-culture affiliations were enduring enough that she continued to subscribe to the *Atlantic Monthly*, her hometown magazine.

Coney, often viewed as a wealthy standard-bearer of Victorian values – Stewart's genteel foil – has her own story of self-reliance and Western renewal. Raised on a farm just north of Boston, she married Edwin Sanborn Coney, a shoemaker, at the age of twenty-one. Edwin, a Civil War veteran, died of tuberculosis eight years later, and Juliet and her two daughters moved into the household of her grocer brother-in-law. For a time, she supported her family with work as a shoe stitcher for local factories. In the mid-1880s her daughter Florence moved to Denver to try ranching with her husband; after she, too, was widowed young, Coney joined her in Denver. Stewart entered the Coney household two decades later, to work as a nurse and maid.

*Letters of a Woman Homesteader* presents a frontier mix of peoples – French, Irish, English, Scottish, German, Mexican, Mormon – advancing toward community, with Stewart playing a key role. Much of the text consists of semi-fictional stories developed from local events, such as her rescue of Mormon women in distress or the family reunion she arranged for a mountain man far from his Tennessee home. Nevertheless, Sedgwick chose to publish the letters *as* letters rather than as a collection of stories, keeping Stewart's relationship with Coney on display. Although most exchanges of personal news were edited out, the salutations, valedictions, and, most important, self-reflexive commentary endemic to the genre were retained.

Stewart reveals considerable ambition for the letters she writes, her many apologies for their quality notwithstanding. The role that she asks Coney, her reader, to play is that of an urbanite psychically and even physically in dire need of what she can offer. In what reads as a near formulaic expression of the purported function of regional literature, she states, "I am so glad when I can bring a little of this big, clean, beautiful outdoors into your apartment for you to enjoy" (220); if only Coney and all other city dwellers could experience "this bracing mountain air ... the free, ready sympathy and hospitality of these frontier people" (221). In accord with Richard Brodhead's arguments in *Cultures of Letters*, that the literary "regional project" is linked to "the class project of vacationing" (145), Stewart conceived reading about her life as rejuvenating.

Stewart privately referred to Coney as "My Beloved," and her letters potently express her affection for her older friend. "I wish I could do nice things for you," she writes in response to a gift she received from her, "but all I can do is to love you" (142). Yet as this same statement suggests, the power imbalance between them was a source of unease. Stewart viewed Coney as both friend and judge. She looked to prove that she was no longer a servant (*her* servant), but rather an independent landowner and social equal, even as she admired Coney as a model of bourgeois comportment.

The distance between them is suggested by the crucial information Stewart long withheld: that she was no longer Clyde's housekeeper, but his wife. The "confession," to use her word, came a full year after the marriage. In an advance letter, she had warned Coney that she had something important to tell her, and she asked for a promise of forgiveness beforehand: "I know that is unfair, but it is the only way I can see out of a difficulty that my foolish reticence has led me into" (79). Coney did not reply. Instead, she only sent a card – three months later – that made no reference to Stewart's announcement. Impelled by the mute card, Stewart finally wrote, "I reckon I had better confess and get it done with. The thing I have done is to marry Mr. Stewart. It was such an inconsistent thing to do that I was ashamed to tell you" (79–80).

Stewart later explained of her methods, "She [Coney] was so very 'Bostony' that I used to try to shock her mildly and at the same time give her as nearly as I could a true picture of the West. She was so very conventional that some one who was not so had the best chance of being enteresting [*sic*] and entertaining" (George 38–39). Her paradoxical phrase expresses the gist of her challenge – one that other Western writers shared – "shocking mildly." Coney is so innocent as to be easily impressed, but a "true picture" of frontier life would upset her. Stewart describes a real crisis of representation:

> I was dreadfully afraid that my last letter was too much for you and now I feel plumb guilty. I really don't know how to write you, for I have to write so much to say so little, and now that my last letter made you sick I almost wish so many things didn't happen to me, for I always want to tell you. (45)

If the woman she sought to cheer was refined and fastidious, then how could she represent frontier conditions, which were otherwise? And if Coney modeled feminine decorum, then how could she send her stories starring the "Woman Homesteader" of Wyoming?

> From something you wrote I think I must have written boastingly to you at some time. I have certainly not intended to, and you must please forgive me and remember how ignorant I am and how hard it is for me to express myself properly.... If you only knew how far short I fall of my own hopes you would know I could *never* boast. (62–63)

This defense is followed by a closing she occasionally employs, "Your ex-washlady." The sign-off wryly reinforces her plea to "remember how ignorant I am"; it also emphasizes that their relationship has changed.

"If you only knew" is a phrase Stewart repeats, suggesting the gulf between Coney's experience and her own. For her part, Coney looked to align both their daily lives and their cultural orientation with a steady stream of modest gifts, all domestic in kind, of which *Letters of a Woman Homesteader* provides a catalog: books, magazines, cards, pictures, a tablecloth, a hassock, and a teapot. "I am sure this room must look familiar to you," Stewart comments in describing her home, "for there is so much in it that was once yours" (137).

Perhaps to assuage her discomfort about the one-way flow of gifts, Stewart emphasizes her own benevolence, her ability to give as well as receive charitably as she dispenses counsel and aid to her less privileged neighbors. A story about the Christmas celebration she arranged for two destitute families shows her literally passing on one of her presents: "Your largest bell, dear Mrs. Coney, dangled from the topmost branch" (208–209). Yet Stewart recognizes that she more than matches Coney's largesse with the letters she sends. Of a different order altogether than teapots, they require creativity, labor, and time – as she frequently points out.

Stewart's correspondence expanded hugely once she began publishing. The *Atlantic* highlights the development by capping the "Woman Homesteader" serial with Stewart's account of her fan mail, originally addressed to Sedgwick. "One dear old lady eighty-four years old wrote me that she had always wanted to live the life I am living, but could not, and that the Letters satisfied her every wish," she relays. "Then I had a letter from a little crippled boy whose mother also wrote, both saying how the Letters had cheered them" (113 [April 1914]: 552). Coney had helped Stewart imagine a readership at large, and she subsequently provided those same readers with a model for how to respond to her, for developing new social relations through writing. The *Atlantic* underscored the role it played in these emerging ties, reconstituting a "local" community that stretched across the continent. This community was composed of not only the professional and cultural elites commonly associated with the *Atlantic*'s readership, but also – as Stewart's letter reflects – the elderly, the sick, and the poor. She concludes, "The mother said she wanted to thank one who had brought so much of the clean, bright outdoors into her helpless little son's life. I wrote her it was you who ought to be thanked and not I." As embodied by Sedgwick, the professional male intermediary now appears as an agent in the affectionate exchange of texts – in high contrast to Freeman's "A Poetess," a story in which he terminates it.

Stewart supplied a sequel, *Letters on an Elk Hunt*, the following year. While these letters, too, are addressed to "Dear, dear Mrs. Coney," they were in fact sent directly to Sedgwick. Suggesting her discomfort with the contrivance, she opens one of them by stating, "It seems to be so odd to be writing you and getting no answers" (95). She then turned to writing fiction, including short stories and a novel, but made little headway in placing it. Her distrust of the mass-market magazines that might have welcomed her work checked the development of her professional career. The *Atlantic*, Stewart believed, should be her primary venue. As with her deference to Coney, her preference was rooted in both sentiment and class. Her affiliation with the magazine was launched by writing acts she conceived as donations of affection, and the community of *Atlantic* readers, accessed through Sedgwick, seemed to offer a way to continue in that vein even as she marketed her work.

Stewart enjoyed a measure of renewed success when she revived her epistolary efforts, routing through distant friends a provisional discursive mode exactly balanced between private and public expression. In introducing one dispatch, she explains:

> These letters are addressed to Mrs. Coney's sister. That was done to lend enterest [sic] if ever we should decide to send the letters to the publishers but that is a remote possibility so if my beloved friends can get any enjoyment out of them they shall as fast as I can find time and energy to get them in readable shape. It is little enough to do for you and all the rest who are so good to me. If you think they are worth while will you, after you have read them, send them on to Miss Ida Howorth, 17 Grove St. West Point Miss. That is, send the last two letters. She has had the first one, keep *that* until some time when you write me and tuck it in if you will. (George 69–70)

One of the letters to "Mrs. Coney's sister" did indeed get published in the 1923 *Atlantic*. "*Now* my Dear Miss Wood," Stewart gleefully reported, "See what you and my dear Mrs. Tidball have perpetrated upon the American Public" (George 77). A wide-cast women's community helped her produce, circulate, and publish her writing. She presents the set of letters as a gift to her friends even as she reminds them of the "time and energy" they consume and of her hopes for a sale.

Juliet Coney died in 1915, but Stewart wrote to her daughter Florence E. Allen until her own death in 1933. She annually marked Coney's birthday by sending Allen a special "memorial letter" (George 149) that included a freshly wrought Wyoming tale. Their relationship went deep; in the hard summer of 1927, Allen's loan helped save her farm. Here we see the full spectrum of Stewart's epistolary exchange, letters presented as actual gifts that were occasionally met with actual cash.

## The stump farm

In his 1946 memoir, *The Happy Profession*, Sedgwick recalled that while he "felt her friendship to be [near]," Elinore Rupert Stewart was "not the only heroine of my Northwest. There was Hilda Rose, whose arid farm was quite as stumpy as the claim staked by the Stewarts" (200). Like *Letters of a Woman Homesteader*, *The Stump Farm* is a collection of letters. Its history and composition, though, is more complex, in that Rose writes to an undisclosed number of unidentified women, some of them more patron than friend. Rather than the personal relationship on display in Stewart's text, *The Stump Farm* records a kind of joint sponsorship, the benevolent efforts of Rose's correspondents to allay her social and cultural impoverishment.

The origins of the book lie in Rose's endeavor to found a women's club in her remote mountain community in Idaho. Her "Civic Club" prospered, dedicated to self-improvement and uplift. In addition to tightening Rose's social bonds with working-class neighbors, the club created new bonds with distant middle-class associates by serving as a productive topic of conversation in the letters she sent them. Coupling club news with accounts of life on the farm, Rose produced an ongoing narrative of strife and striving that both made her new friends and induced charitable efforts on her behalf. Her correspondents collected secondhand clothes and reading material to send her (including the *Atlantic*). With farther-reaching impact, they also circulated her letters. We can see publication on the horizon in Rose's letter to one such early supporter: "In regard to my letters, you may do as you like. I didn't know they were interesting, but I suppose they are a contrast to the life of the city. The reading won't hurt me if you leave my name off" (Ellery Sedgwick Papers, Mrs. Austin, April 6, 1925).

Rose's letters eventually came to the attention of Florence Fisk White, a philanthropist in Southern California who hailed from one of the founding families of Helena, Montana. White recognized their literary quality and submitted a selection to the *Atlantic*, which published four installments in 1927. Perhaps through her club activities, Rose had also become acquainted with Dr. Mary F. Hobart in Boston (long a specialist in obstetrics at the New England Hospital for Women and Children), and the following year Hobart spearheaded the publication of *The Stump Farm*.

*Atlantic Monthly* income helped Rose survive her first long winter in Alberta, where she and Charles had moved in the summer of 1926 after a prolonged drought in Idaho. Publishing in the *Atlantic* also made for a substantial boost to her social capital in the form of important new correspondents. Rose counted as her favorites a group of "aged but brilliant old maids" (Ellery Sedgwick Papers, Jack Jensen, August 8, 1932). She grew closest to Margaret Emerson in New York City, a retired professor of English at Japan Women's University. Emerson coordinated aid for Rose in the 1930s (sending on heating oil, candles, and clothing), and some of Rose's letters to Emerson became *Atlantic* essays, too.

Educated by the like of Bret Harte, Mary Austin, and Elinore Pruitt Stewart, *Atlantic* readers were used to looking west. North, however, was a new direction. Rose guided them step by step to her new home:

> I see by one of your letters that you have no conception of how far north I am. Calgary is a large city crowded with cars. Farther north is Edmonton, also a big city. Next comes Peace River, a small town at the end of the railroad.... Then I went on a steamer that holds thirty carloads of freight in the bottom. We went north all the way until we came to the Great Slave Lake Region.... Get a map and find the Great Slave Lake. A little south of it – that's here.... Here is the primal wilderness. (*Atlantic* 140 [Sept. 1927]: 296–297)

*The Stump Farm* reads as a debate over whether the benefits of Rose's remote locations sufficiently compensate for their severity, a debate increasingly urgent once she emigrates. The experience of her son, Karl, helps her argue that they do. She believes that in Canada he can lead an authentic boy's life, learning to hunt, trap, and ride. "Boy will grow up, like Lincoln, in the wilderness" (92), she declares. "He needs to be in here" (163).

Evaluating her own experience is less straightforward. Whereas Stewart argues that women flourish on the frontier, Rose suggests they deteriorate. From Idaho, she writes, "You don't know how anxiously I look in the glass as the years go by and wonder if I'll ever get to look like the rest of the natives here. You have seen overworked farmers' wives, with weather-wrung and sorrow-beaten faces" (7). Conditions are still more extreme on the Peace River, home to a "lonesome sisterhood" that includes a woman whose mind had "shattered" (124) for lack of female company.

Rose's recompense is a more pronounced identity as author. In a private letter, she formulated her homesteading venture thus: "Daddy said he was going to take me so far from the world that it would never spoil me, so far from the world that it would never hurt me. So I can be myself without fear and have all the quiet needed to think in and write" (Ellery Sedgwick Papers, Jensen, n.d.). Here we see an endorsement of her isolation – it enabled her to write. Yet its extremity, she reveals, also compelled her to write: "I won't admit out loud that I'm lonesome, but it's a Robinson Crusoe existence. Like being alive yet buried. Books will save my reason, and letters" (150).

*The Stump Farm* is shaped by Rose's progress toward authorship. Early letters are studded with comments about her hopes to make money from writing, while later ones present their realization. Readers learn, for example, that her first *Atlantic* check reached her at her "blackest hour" (136), literally down and out with a back injury, and the book concludes with her jubilation over news of its coming publication. Sedgwick figures large in her musings: "At first I thought he was a young man, but now I believe he must be old, for age makes folks kindly and loving. And it's going to be a book. What color will the cover be? And some day I will hold it in my hand, and Daddy will be happy forever and ever" (175–176). While she had originally planned to support her family by trapping, her primary resource turns out to be not furs but all the "things to write about in a new country way out on the frontier" (78).

*The Stump Farm* was enthusiastically received as an inspiring testament of endurance and fortitude. "Are You Discouraged?" Charles B. Driscoll asked in the title of his widely syndicated review. "In case you ever feel that your affairs have come to about the worst possible pass, and you feel that a jump into the nearest and deepest river is about the next move, please do me a personal favor and read 'The Stump Farm.'" The book was circulated – just like the letters themselves – in the context of a supportive women's culture of exchange. The practice depressed sales, Rose complained, although as reparation "no one reading it forgets the name of the author and it is such a good lender that frequently people have to buy a new copy to replace the one worn out. This all is advertising of the best kind, also there is hardly a woman's club in the land that has not had it read aloud to them" (Ellery Sedgwick Papers, Jensen, n.d.).

Her sights set on professional authorship and her confidence high, after *The Stump Farm* Rose deliberately worked to produce poetry and stories that would sell. She also directed the literary efforts of her son, with plans to have him "start sending out little sketches of his life in here to the Boys' magazines" (Ellery Sedgwick Papers, Jensen, Dec. 9, 1934). Most important, she produced a full-length book manuscript, a memoir whose title announces its ambition: "The Land: An Epic of Today."

By one measure, her authorial career peaked just as it began. Rose never found a publisher for "The Land" (which, in arguing that the deck was stacked against small farmers, contested cherished scripts about Western opportunity), and she only placed a few more essays. Yet this does not mean that her writing no longer "paid." In 1928, with little effort on her part, a selection from her stream of letters had crystallized into a published book, *The Stump Farm*. Afterward, Rose's literary production dissolved back into correspondence – but now on a grander scale. Her epistolary project was her most fruitful literary labor, carefully managed for both the social relationships it supported and the forms of aid it evoked. "Tuck in an American dime now and then and I will talk with you," she informed one would-be correspondent (Ellery Sedgwick Papers, Jensen, June 6, 1932).

Over the years, the conditions of scarcity endemic to frontier life – of time, money, goods, and services – constricted Rose's ability to produce and market her writing. Yet the letters themselves, as the following demonstrates, allayed them:

> I was answering some fan mail, total strangers, I have a bunch every mail, and in two of them I said "I will close now for my fingers burn so bad with the mosquito bites and there is a lot of them hovering over my hands while I write." I always put my thoughts into words no matter how they sound and if it is true that is all I care about, I never think that my letter may shock. These did and both sent mosquito netting as a gift so the boys as well as daddy and I have nets over our beds. They sure surprised me but one might as well say that God looks after us and he does it in his own way. I shiver when I think what life would be this summer without them. (Ellery Sedgwick Papers, Jensen, n.d.)

Wilderness experiences like being swarmed by insects make it almost impossible for her to write. The narrative she manages to produce notwithstanding, though, is especially pungent, a "shocking" account to which readers respond with heaven-sent "surprises" that facilitate further efforts.

The evolution of Rose's readers into benefactors is on display in a later *Atlantic* publication, "Christmas at the Ranch" (1933). The essay, which despite its title spans a full year, begins, "There is not time enough to answer all the letters that come and all the questions people ask. I will try to answer them in this diary" (670). Rose plays fast and loose with genre. The carefully composed essay that she writes expressly for the *Atlantic* is ostensibly a diary, which itself is meant to substitute for personal letters. *The Stump Farm* had extended her epistolary range to the extent that she must publish once more to "answer all the letters" she owes. A near literal inventory of offerings that range in magnitude from flower seeds to "a new stove, a gift from an Atlantic reader, and it is a treasure" (676), "Christmas at the Ranch" demonstrates how her association with the magazine pervades her daily life.

By 1935, in the midst of the Depression and the aftermath of a flood, the Roses were destitute. Their plight led Sedgwick to engineer a "surprise party" (the term is Rose's), making a call to *Atlantic* readers to help the family take up a more viable homestead. An outpouring of support ensued, including $543.07 in cash, from both middle-class readers and the working poor. Rose itemized the purchases she made, among them "Radio license," "Washing machine," "Harness," "Seed Wheat," "Seed Oats," "Feed Oats," "Oil and Repairs," concluding with a postscript, "Besides cash everything that could be used arrived thru the winter – sacks of them every mail" (Ellery Sedgwick Papers, list, n.d.).

With the commencement of her *Atlantic* career, Rose felt like her life had been transformed. The rewards were at once social, financial, professional, and psychological. In a 1927 letter to Sedgwick, she wrote, "Instead of dreading the coming winter, I am looking forward to it. The work will let up and I can read all the books and magazines that have come and think about the friends out there in the busy world. They were there all the time, they just didn't know about me before. What a nice friendly world it is. How much I owe to you and the Atlantic. You took away all my loneliness, made me happy and gave me a winter grub-stake with that big check" (Ellery Sedgwick Papers, July 20, 1927).

## Conclusion

As narratives produced for Eastern markets and readerships, *Letters of a Woman Homesteader* and *The Stump Farm* reflect the salient condition of literature of the American West. Yet the multiple locations across their trajectories undo any simple binary of "Westerners" writing for "Easterners." Stewart was a self-identified Southerner from Oklahoma who reached Wyoming by way of Kansas and Colorado. Her relationship with a Western woman of another ilk brought her to the *Atlantic*, the "so very Bostony" Coney who in Denver found a new home. Rose, raised in an industrial Midwestern city by Swedish immigrants, also came west as an adult. Her narrative was routed to Boston by friends in California, among them a wealthy woman whose own mother was renowned for her vivid accounts of Montana pioneering.

Rose and Stewart's wider *Atlantic* readership was equally multifaceted. While concentrated in the urban Northeast and among the middle class, it also included working-class women and men in cities, towns, and farms across the nation. These readers found in their narratives not invigorating antidotes to modern life, but rather reflections of their own experience. Closing the circuit, Rose was joined in the flesh in Fort Vermilion by a family of seven who, as both *Atlantic* readers and aspiring homesteaders, took her book as a literal emigrants' guide. "The father lost his job and they read 'The Stump Farm' in the Atlantic and decided to pioneer in the Far North" ("Christmas," 675), she reports. Arriving at the onset of winter, they ended up sharing her cabin.

*Letters of a Woman Homesteader* and *The Stump Farm* demonstrate how regional and cultural distance, mediated through a national literary institution, could result in new forms of proximity. They thereby offer a more accommodating, real-life alternative to the severity of absolutely local production on display in Freeman's "A Poetess," in which a woman who writes a poem for a neighbor is undone when it reaches other eyes.

## Works Cited

Brodhead, Richard. *Cultures of Letters: Scenes of Reading and Writing in Nineteenth-Century America*. Chicago: University of Chicago Press, 1993.

"Colorado State Census, 1885." F. H. Allen.

Driscoll, Charles B. Review of *The Stump Farm*, by Hilda Rose. *New Castle News* (May 4, 1928): 4.

Ellery Sedgwick Papers. The Massachusetts Historical Society.

Freeman, Mary Wilkins. "A Poetess." *Harper's Monthly Magazine* 81 (July 1890): 197–204.

George, Susanne K. *The Adventures of the Woman Homesteader: The Life and Letters of Elinore Pruitt Stewart*. Lincoln: University of Nebraska Press, 1993.

Lewis, Nathaniel. *Unsettling the Literary West: Authenticity and Authorship*. Lincoln: University of Nebraska Press, 2003.

Rose, Hilda. "Christmas at the Ranch." *Atlantic Monthly* 152 (Dec. 1933): 670–677.

    *The Stump Farm: A Chronicle of Pioneering*. Foreword by Samuel Eliot. Boston, MA: Little, Brown & Co, 1928. First serialized in *Atlantic Monthly* 139 (Feb.–April 1927): 145–152, 334–342, 512–518; 140 (Sept 1927): 289–300.

Sedgwick, Ellery. *The Happy Profession*. Boston, MA: Little, Brown, & Co., 1946.

Stewart, Elinore Pruitt. *Letters of a Woman Homesteader*. Boston MA: Houghton Mifflin, 1914. First serialized in *Atlantic Monthly* 112 (Oct.–Dec. 1913): 433–443, 589–598, 820–829; 113 (Jan.–April 1914): 17–26, 170–177, 525–532. Reprint. 1988, with a foreword by Gretel Ehrlich.

    *Letters on an Elk Hunt*. Boston, MA: Houghton Mifflin, 1915. Reprint. Lincoln: University of Nebraska Press, 1979.

"United States Census, 1870." John H. Perkins, Massachusetts.

"United States Census, 1900." Chas O. Gustafson, Rockford Township Rockford City Ward 1, Winnebago, Illinois.

# 6

SUSAN KOLLIN

# The American West and the literature of environmental consciousness

In her recent memoir, Tlingit writer Ernestine Hayes recounts a story about the creation of Glacier Bay National Park in Southeast Alaska. Drawing on indigenous oral traditions from the region, she emphasizes the way glaciers have environmental agency and function as ecological actors in their own right. They decide when to retreat and advance, sometimes doing so in a "rush," and at other times as if they are "chasing things," pushing and pushing until they hit the "edge of land, some plants, some trees, a few caves ... a stretch of beach." After pushing as hard as they can, glaciers often give up and stop pushing. Then they rest while they plan their "capitulation" (36–37). Hayes focuses in particular on an oral narrative about a young girl from the powerful Chookeneidí clan who was placed in isolation behind a curtain when she reached puberty so she could learn to use her powers in a safe manner. For the Tlingit Indians of Southeast Alaska, a female's blood is her power. When a girl enters menarche, she must be separated from the community until she learns how to negotiate her new power and how to "control her glances and her words, for she is so powerful that one glance from her will turn a man to stone. One word from her will break a clan" (54).

One day the girl decided to call the nearby glacier from behind a curtain, just as one might call a dog. "That was not a good thing, to call a glacier like a dog. It was not a good thing to speak to the glacier at all," Hayes explains (55). A while later, the people noticed that the nearby glacier was advancing. The girl's mother explained to the community that her daughter had called the glacier and the people then knew they needed to move. "The people did not leave their homes without grief. They knew the land would grieve for them. They knew the land would miss them" (56). The people moved away, but waited until they could return home once "the ice moved back and decided to make room for them again." By that time, white people had moved in and taken their home, transforming it into a national park they named Glacier Bay. Afterward, the Tlingit were forbidden to return to the area, and now they are left "looking in the direction of that grassy place at the top of the bay, always waiting for the time when they can go home" (56).

In 1879, when John Muir traveled as one of the first cruise ship tourists through the Inside Passage of Southeast Alaska, the famed naturalist marveled at the "abundance of noble, newborn scenery" he encountered in the region. Accompanied by his friend, Presbyterian minister Samuel Hall Young, Muir expressed delight with the pleasures the coastal landscape offered, describing it as a "true fairyland" and noting that its beauty, "so charmingly brought to view," exceeded his ability to represent it. "Never before this had I been embosomed in scenery so hopelessly beyond description" (11–12). Muir's experiences in the region played a significant role in drawing attention to Southeast Alaska, as parts of his travel account would later be used in a brochure for the Northern Pacific Railroad in advertising the area as a new tourist destination (Kollin 28).

During their 1879 trip, Muir and Young also took an excursion through a region that would later become Glacier Bay, the area featured in Hayes's narrative. While indigenous oral traditions indicate that the Tlingit inhabited the region for thousands of years before contact with Europeans, and even though Muir and Young had indigenous guides accompany them, the two men nevertheless understood the space as *terra incognita*. The only map of the region that they knew about was drawn several decades earlier when George Vancouver sailed through the area, before receding glaciers had opened up additional passages to explore (Young 64). In his description of their travels, Young delighted in the fact that the space was undergoing such transformation, with new channels appearing and older areas closing. "Where Vancouver saw only a great crystal wall across the sea, we were to paddle for days up a long and sinuous fiord; and where he saw one glacier, we were to find a dozen" (65–66). The ever-changing landscape enabled the two men to imagine themselves as discoverers of new natures and new frontiers in an America that seemed to be fully explored; their travels thus allowed them to seize a new opportunity to leave their marks on the nation's maps (Kollin 30–31).

These accounts of the human place in nature, the divergent meanings assigned to glacial activity, and the complex understandings about land rights and cultural belonging in the region highlight the ways different and sometimes contested concerns shape the field of American environmental literature (Cruikshank 3). Rather than focusing on projects of discovery, naming, and mastery, for instance, Hayes's account of Tlingit oral narratives about Glacier Bay foregrounds beliefs about mutual interaction and dependency between humans and nonhuman nature. Meanwhile Muir's transcendentalist writings address the aesthetic, spiritual, and recreational-ist virtues of the natural landscape as well as the national meanings white Americans often associated with Western spaces (Buell 325). Ultimately Muir's understandings of nature would have important and lasting effects on generations of mainstream nature writers as well as environmental advo-cates across the region (Buell 137–138). A major figure in the history of the environmental movement, Muir advocated for the protection of Yosemite, fought for the creation of a national park system, and helped establish the Sierra Club. Rebecca Solnit notes that the famed naturalist had a specific vision of nonhuman nature, preferring his landscapes "wild, transcendent, unsocial, and unutilized – as far from the working world as he could get" (260). Indeed, Muir perceived Western nature through a lens shaped by spe-cific concerns, particularly by nineteenth-century white Protestant responses to industrialization, capitalist development, and national development.

Cultural geographer William Wyckoff recounts this well-known history, explaining that mainstream ideas of Western American landscapes have often worked hand in hand with larger national imperatives involving eco-nomic and political expansion. "The West became synonymous with the frontier and with unlimited individual opportunity, particularly for those who were white and male. The West also became the central political prize in the nation's nineteenth-century tale of Manifest Destiny, an imperial vision of continental conquest that marginalized Native peoples, people of color, and many immigrant groups," he notes. Alongside these visions were beliefs about the region as "a wild land of limitless natural resources, ripe for the taking by an entrepreneurial and acquisitive frontier population." Such views of the American West did not "appear overnight," but had to be developed, taught, and learned. "Politicians, travelers, writers and artists built a new visual lexicon of western landscape meanings, which changed from one generation to the next," such that contemporary understandings of what is valuable, aesthetically pleasing, or even "expendable" came out of these "earlier myths and cultural inventions" (Wyckoff 16).

This chapter assesses traditions of environmental literature about the American West and the role such writing played in shaping ecological con-sciousness about the region. While nineteenth-century European American nature writers such as Muir had a tremendous influence on how Western spaces were understood and later managed by the modern environmental movement, there is increasing recognition that mainstream nature advocates have overlooked many voices and concerns. A recent conference hosted in fall 2014 by UCLA's Institute of Environment and Sustainability took on the task of reevaluating Muir's legacy in the year marking the centennial of his death. At a time when globalization, the science of climate change, urbanization, and increased racial diversity in the American West have challenged the central concerns of the mainstream environmental movement, scholars are questioning the continued relevance of Muir's transcendentalist visions of nature, especially his message that Western wilderness is a "temple" that should be left undisturbed.

At the UCLA conference, a number of presenters noted that environmental concerns in the twenty-first century have largely moved beyond what Muir and his contemporaries were able to envision 100 years ago. Diverse populations in the American West have imagined their relationships with nature in different ways, often finding that the spaces of greatest significance are not necessarily located in Muir's sublime mountain peaks, but rather in their local parks, nearby mountains, and own backyards. Thus the natures that are most central to their lives often turn out to be familiar and nearby, rather than remote, faraway, or exotic. In the case of California in particular, large-scale organizations such as the Sierra Club and the Audubon Society have frequently struggled to connect with the state's communities of color who often do not place as much value in the organizations' central concerns and who rightfully critique the narrow racial perspectives through with environmental issues are typically framed (Sahagun; Taylor 4–5). In order to be relevant and successful in the twenty-first century, nature advocacy must take into consideration larger cultural frameworks and adopt more inclusive perspectives in defining its central philosophies and projects.

In an overview of ecological literary practices in the United States, Michael Ziser points to a growing shift toward expanding the scope of environmental study and notes how scholars are increasingly acknowledging nonhuman nature as agents and actors in history (13). Alongside this recognition of environmental agency is an understanding that humans are not discrete entities, but comingle and intersect with the natural world and in the process participate in a transformative interaction that shapes both parties. Ziser notes how the human subject in mainstream American nature writing has often been figured as isolated and alienated, marked by a "sense of being the helpless and solitary witness to a landscape of injury and loss [that] accounts for the predominant effect of twentieth-century environmental writing, a mournful desire for lost plentitude" (7). While such losses are no doubt real to nature advocates, he suggests that a "form of grievance that defines Nature as passive and victimized" continues the practice of separating humans from nature as autonomous entities rather than as "irredeemably implicated in nonhuman processes." His observations offer a shift toward thinking about humans as themselves wounded and compromised, as "split open to the more-than-human world" in profound ways (7). Ziser argues that mourning for a lost nature ultimately serves as a "defensive and recuperative gesture," a nostalgic response that places humans in a "comforting anthropocentric fiction" and that allows them to continue claiming a "central and dominant role in the cosmos" (8).

Ziser points to the ways nature advocates are increasingly acknowledging the interdependence between humans and nonhuman nature, turning to developments such as bioregionalism for a useful practice and philosophy. Emerging in the 1970s with the work of figures such as Allen van Newkirk, Peter Berg, and Gary Snyder, bioregionalism argues that mainstream U.S. culture suffers from a "loss of community, purpose, and sense of place" (Thayer 3). In outlining these problems, Robert L. Thayer suggests that the Cartesian dualism separating mind and body, the development of a global economy, the reliance on fossil fuels, the move away from organicism to mechanism, and the space and time compression that the digital revolution enabled are all factors shaping what he sees as a profound sense of homelessness (1–2). The "relocalization" movement central to bioregionalism provides solutions to these problems by offering a "means of living by deep understanding of, respect for, and, ultimately, care of a naturally bounded region or territory" (4). As Thayer explains, a bioregion may be understood as a "life-place," a region marked not by political but by natural boundaries. It is a space that has a distinct "geographic, climatic, hydrological, and ecological character" and is home to both human and nonhuman communities. Ultimately, he argues, the bioregion may prove the "most logical locus and scale for a sustainable, regenerative community to take root and to *take place*" (3).

Bioregionalism is often linked to the Deep Ecology movement, which argues for the inherent worth and intrinsic value of all living things. Influenced by thinkers such as John Muir, Henry David Thoreau, Mary Austin, Aldo Leopold, and Rachel Carson, Deep Ecology critiques the shallowness of mainstream environmentalism for its utilitarian ends and for what Arne Naess calls its "resource-oriented" and "growth tolerating" practices as well as a tendency to "subsume ecological policies under the narrow ends of human health and well-being" (48). In contrast, the Deep Ecology movement recognizes the complex web of interconnections between all living entities and the centrality of biodiversity, arguing that humans do not have a right to "reduce this richness and diversity except to satisfy vital needs" (Naess 50). Edward Abbey helped popularize the movement as the author of some of the best-known writings about the American West, including *Desert Solitaire* (1968) and *The Monkey Wrench Gang* (1975). Some environmentalists, however, criticize Abbey and other Deep Ecologists for a shallowness in their own thinking, including a deep-seated misanthropy and an unacknowledged racism often expressed in the movement's anti-immigration

stance, as well as various hyper-macho posturings that frequently appear in
the movement's acts of protest and visions of nature.

*The Monkey Wrench Gang*, advocated violence against industrial machinery and other forms of sabotage that could end up injuring human workers.
Later, in *Desert Solitaire*, Abbey acknowledged the difficulties of developing
a sense of place and forging new relationships with the natural world. He
once described the act of setting down roots in a region as akin to being stuck
with the "same old wife every night" (155). Writing about his move from
Boulder to Davis several years ago when he was offered a new university
position, Thayer echoes Abbey in depicting his initial resistance to settling
into a new space, noting that the natural features of the Colorado landscape
seemed to trump what his new home offered. He confessed that "if Boulder
was an affair with a flashy fashion model, the flat agricultural landscape
near Davis was a mail-order spouse whom I would grow to appreciate, then,
love, over a long time. Love at first sight, however, it was not" (xiii–xiv).

The gendered and sexualized discourses in some forms of Western environmental writing may be traced to the ways landscape narratives in general
have often inherited the erotic language found in American discourses of
conquest and discovery. Rebecca Solnit reminds us that much of this writing
has been shaped by white male fantasies of sexual possession that depict
nature as "virgin, untouched, undiscovered, unspoiled" (312). Some narratives by European American writers erase earlier place names in a "marriage" of sorts, whereby "the bride takes on the identity of her spouse."
Solnit notes that the land in these writings is figured as bride rather than
mother because mothers create their sons, thus preventing the authors from
imagining a space that "would yield to their will and bear their names, a
blank landscape waiting for them to begin writing a new history across her
rather than read what was already there" (313).

Throughout European American literary history, the West has especially
appeared as a blank space, as an empty land promising freedom from the
restrictions and confinements of the hyper-urban East. In his 1955 study of
the American Adam, for instance, R. W. B. Lewis described this movement
west as part of a national myth involving a "fresh initiative" and "divinely
granted second chance" for a new American self. The American Adam often
appears in mainstream U.S. literature as an "individual emancipated from
history, happily bereft of ancestry, untouched and undefiled ... an individual standing alone, self-reliant, and self-propelling" (5). Lewis's insights
were further extended and developed in 1960 by Leslie Fiedler in *Love and
Death in the American Novel*, in which he noticed a common obsession
with male mobility and self-creation in European American literature that
depicts heroes moving west in order to flee the domestic world of white

women and to escape their own adulthood (181, 259). Feminist literary critic Nina Baym later diagnosed the problem as a "melodrama of beset manhood," noting how the tradition tended to exclude female writers in studies of European American literature (130–132). More recently, Barbara Wills has called attention to this movement, noting how what she calls the "west cure" was developed as a solution to the nervous disorders seeming to plague elite white males in the eastern United States during the late nineteenth century. In contrast to the "rest cure" prescribed to their white female counterparts, which imposed immobility and bed rest as a remedy for their afflictions, elite white males were sent west to challenge themselves physically against the wild and rugged natures of the region (293).

A number of writers have countered these depictions of the American West as a place of rugged retreat and rejuvenation from a hyper-modernizing and diminished world. Wallace Stegner, for instance, addresses the environmental limitations of a life of constant mobility in *Big Rock Candy Mountain* (1943), while also showing the futility of retreat in his novel, *All the Little Live Things* (1967). Western narratives of environmental escape often suggest that it is preferable to move on to a new space of wildness than it is to deal with the places that have been diminished and destroyed. In recent works such as *Owning It All* (1987), *Hole in the Sky* (1993), and *Who Owns the West?* (1996), Montana writer William Kittredge notes how myths of the West as a place of escape ultimately do not provide sustainable ecological solutions. Likewise, California author T. C. Boyle offers a number of humorous takedowns of the retreat narrative in works such as *The Tortilla Curtain* (1996), which centers on the lives of a class-privileged white family who reside in a gated community in Southern California and their unacknowledged ties and debts to the Mexican workers whose undercompensated labor enables their privileged lifestyles. Boyle's novel *Drop City* (2004) also details problems faced by the early 1970s back-to-the-land movement as a countercultural group of dropouts tries to create a utopian community in California, but is thwarted when it fails to anticipate the problems of waste management and sustainable living. Things take a turn for the worse when the group is shut down by a public health inspector and flees to Alaska in hopes of finding a new Eden in the Last Frontier. In these novels as well as Boyle's many environmental short stories set in the region, dreams of escape ultimately appear as another form of male privilege while also proving to be thinly veiled expressions of white flight.

Based in the Pacific Northwest, Amanda Coplin's novel *The Orchardist* (2012) addresses limitations with the popular retreat story by replacing the typical Adam figure with an American Eve. The narrative is set in Washington State and spans several decades, beginning in the mid-nineteenth century and moving into the turn of the twentieth century. Coplin's story provides a different account for why the novel's white female characters, Jane and Della, might wish to flee community and history for a new life at a rural farm near Wenatchee and in doing so, addresses the gendered politics of mobility in popular Western retreat tales. After they manage to escape sexual captivity at the hands of a degenerate white settler, the young female characters do not find an Edenic space in the apple orchard where they eventually settle down. Instead, history comes back to haunt them as they are unable to forget their tormented memories of the past and cannot fully escape the reach of their captor. The novel deals with the disappearance and possible kidnapping of a female family member, the consequences of unwanted pregnancy, a devastating lack of social attachment, and an eventual suicide. For these American Eves, traumatic experiences of the past cannot be easily set aside with the move to a new environment, but serve as powerful forces that continue to exert control over the choices and decisions the characters make.

In a similar way, the late Colorado naturalist and environmental advocate Ann Zwinger also implicitly critiqued the gendered politics of mobility in her nonfiction writings about various trips through Colorado canyons, excursions along the Green River of Wyoming and Utah, and treks across desert landscapes and alpine tundra. Deep Ecologists often argue that environmental awareness is most successful when it is "implemented by persons who love what they are conserving, and who are convinced that what they love is intrinsically lovable" (Naess 49). As a nature writer, Zwinger aimed to educate others about sustainable environmental practices. In doing so, her work countered the exclusive American Adam nature discourse and contributed to the field of Western women's environmental writing by figures such as Terry Tempest Williams, Gretel Ehrlich, Barbara Kingsolver, Linda Hasselstrom, and Pam Houston, to name just a few authors who have devoted themselves to writing about various Western landscapes they have observed, described, and become deeply connected to over the years.

In her study *The Ecological Other*, Sarah Jaquette Ray extends discussions about problems of exclusion and inclusion in the literature of environmental consciousness, focusing in particular on issues of embodiment and national identity. In particular, Ray takes to task discourses of risk and the fetishization of the fit body in many of the most celebrated texts of nature writing. As Ray indicates, popular rhetoric of the virtuous and healthy body often contributes to larger biopolitical endeavors, particularly to a set of beliefs about the appropriate and representative American self. In the conservation movement, protecting nature frequently entailed protecting the larger "imagined body politic" (9). Such discourses often ended up policing immigrant bodies for being alleged threats to the nation; blaming urban bodies for disease, improper hygiene, or other ailments associated with urbanization itself; dispossessing indigenous Americans from their homelands; and overlooking disabled bodies that were excluded by design from the strenuous physical challenges entailed in the "wilderness model" (30). As Ray indicates, even attention to sustainable local and organic products in the contemporary environmental movement end up falling short if it focuses too narrowly on "enlightened consumption" and if it ignores diverse populations' "alienation" from the means of food production (3). Her observations thus offer a cautionary tale about how even well-meaning traditions of nature writing can obscure human connections and interrelationships with nonhuman nature, while also contributing to the further marginalization of certain bodies in the environment.

Rebecca Solnit likewise addresses problems with erasure and exclusion, turning specifically to issues of race and nature in regional environmental histories. In *Savage Dreams: A Journey into the Landscape Wars of the American West* (2000), she draws connections between Western environmental struggles over land and resources at the close of the twentieth century with the Indian wars of the nineteenth century. Solnit explains that events in the previous era continue to inform conflicts over Western nature in the present day, even as a gap exists "between our view of landscape" and our histories that are "full of lost stories, ravaged cultures, obliterated names" (222). Noting how projects of national security and environmental racism often go hand in hand, Solnit focuses on the toxic legacy of Nevada Test Site, which is situated on Western Shoshone lands, in order to examine the fate of tribal communities as well as other "downwinders" and "atomic veterans" who fight against nuclear testing in the region (xi). She also provides accounts of Yosemite, home of the Southern Miwoks and Yokuts, and now a celebrated national park as well as one of the most important spaces for landscape photography. The author notes the irony in which indigenous peoples are dispossessed from nature in order to create a national park that eventually undergoes such transformation that it becomes "suburb without walls rather than a wilderness with amenities," a hyper-developed space that distances rather than connects humans to the more-than-human world (229). In this way, Solnit's nature writing intersects with many Native American authors who also restore to memory histories of racial dispossession and ongoing struggles to reclaim Western homelands in their novels. Indigenous authors such as D'Arcy McNickle (Salish Kootenai), Leslie Marmon Silko (Laguna Pueblo), Linda Hogan (Chickasaw), and Louise Erdrich (Turtle Mountain Chippewa), to name just a few writers, present political sovereignty and cultural recovery as important concerns for environmentalist writing and politics in the West.

Emerging in the late 1980s, the environmental justice movement points to the centrality of issues such as race, class, labor, and public health as crucial concerns for ecological projects in the region. Influenced by the civil rights movement and problems stemming from environmental racism, Chicano novelist Rudolfo Anaya extends popular thinking about nature, employing the tradition of magic realism to depict more complex human relations with nonhuman nature in the Southwest borderlands. In works such as *Bless Me, Ultima* (1972), *Heart of Aztlán* (1976), and *Albuquerque* (1992), Anaya addresses issues of land rights and citizenship along with spiritual beliefs and racial conflict as central issues for a more inclusive ecological politics. Similar issues also inform the characters' lives in Ana Castillo's *So Far from God* (1993), which depicts labor, AIDS, and pollution in addressing how human bodies are always intermeshed with the more-than-human world in a way that highlights what Stacy Alaimo describes as an important but often overlooked "material transit between bodies and environments" (2). Likewise, Helena Viramonte's *Under the Feet of Jesus* (1994), which was inspired by the labor and environmental struggles of César Chávez, examines the lives of migrant Latino farm workers who work in California's beautiful but toxic and dangerous San Joaquin Valley.

The environmental justice movement calls attention to the natures and environments that are likely to garner the most consideration and the ways ecological concerns are often narrowly framed in the mainstream movement. Shifting the focus away from landscapes of leisure and recreationalist or aesthetic concerns, environmental justice advocates argue that the central cause of unsustainable environmental practices is a system built on the unequal distribution of wealth due to an ongoing history of racism and colonialism. "In this economic system, people of color are more likely to suffer environmental problems than white people are because the political and economic system is unequal, as a result of previous and present racist structures," Noël Sturgeon explains (9). Environmental justice advocates point to studies showing, for instance, that more toxic waste sites are located where communities of color live, poisoning from lead paint is more common among children of color, and the uranium mining with the most harmful environmental effects is carried out on Native American lands (Gamber 7–9; Sturgeon 8–10; Taylor 5).

Extending these environmental critiques, Mary Pat Brady recounts an oral history of Mexican American women and their insights about landscape, culture, and belonging. She refers to an interview with Patricia Preciado Martin in which Livia Leon Montiel describes her experiences growing up in a ranch family in Arizona, noting the changes in the land brought about by several decades of industrialization and deindustrialization. In particular,

Montiel addresses her family's experience of spatial loss with the development of new retirement communities and factories throughout the area. "Land is becoming extinct," she explains and then goes on to express her deep concerns that the area where she grew up will eventually be developed and lost forever (Brady 5; Martin 23). "Extinct" lands may be a surprising way to describe such transformations, but for Brady, the phrasing provides a useful explanation for what is at stake in the environmental justice movement, as land turns from "lived, embodied" place to an "abstract space of ícapitalism" (5). Brady notes how in Montiel's spatial descriptions, the land, "like the social and cultural, can disappear, go extinct, become only a memory" (6). Brady argues that Chicana literature frequently offers "alternative methods of conceptualizing space" by "seeing and feeling" the landscape as "performative and participatory." In *Extinct Lands, Temporal Geography*, she provides insights into how Chicana authors such as Gloria Anzaldúa, Sandra Cisneros, Cherríe Moraga, and other writers have reconfigured Western American landscapes and how they have "ungrounded its status as inert and transparent" (6).

Asian American authors in the West have also contributed to the development of environmental justice literature. In her novel *All Over Creation* (2003), Ruth Ozeki addresses food cultures and the transformation of nature in the region as a result of powerful agribusiness practices. The novel focuses on a group of environmental advocates aptly named "The Seeds of Resistance," who bring attention to the loss of biodiversity due to genetically modified crops introduced by multinational companies. Ozeki's narrative contributes to observations made by Michael Pollan and other activists who have popularized the food movement, drawing attention to problems in our modern industrial food practices. Shifting attention to issues of citizenship, inequality, and belonging, Julie Otsuka's *When the Emperor Was Divine* (2002) also addresses race and environmental justice by chronicling the experiences of a Japanese American family who are sent to internment camps following President Roosevelt's Executive Order 9066 in 1942. Otsuka's novel foregrounds how dehumanizing discourses often served as a means of justifying the dispossession, relocation, and internment of people of Japanese ancestry in the United States. In doing so, the novel shows how arguments based in nature carry authority by defining some populations as closer to nature or less civilized than other groups and thus deserving of unequal treatment. During World War II, a moral panic arose that framed the attack on Pearl Harbor as a barbarous and savage act. People of Japanese ancestry in turn were considered subhumans not worthy of their rights and were treated as animals, herded and held in the same spaces as cattle during internment. Sturgeon notes how such projects of naturalization try to justify inequality and social hierarchies through depictions of nature as "the legitimizing force, the source of truth and rational order" (11–12). She thus explains that it is important for environmental advocates themselves to remain vigilant about all arguments they make in the name of nature.

African American writers likewise address how arguments from nature have historically worked to situate black Americans as closer to nature and as less human while placing them outside certain natural landscapes as a threatening social force whose presence in the environment is suspect and must be policed. Noting the ways connections to the natural have often differed along "sharply divided racial lines," Paul Outka argues that scholars must attend to both the human and the "natural history of the ground we stand on when we speak." He suggests that in glancing down,

> there may be bones and ashes, breathing in, a sickly sweet smell; listening, the sound of dogs, looking out, strange fruit. When we see this, as well as the mountain, we may be seeing something that looks more like the American landscape in all its contradictory nature, rather than a mystical and romanticized construction writ sublimely large. (4)

Because the history and lingering effects of racialized slavery continue to shape African Americans' relationship to and understandings of nature, Kimberly Ruffin argues that black Americans "have not had much actual or conceptual refuge when it comes to environmental concerns in the United States" (4). In *Black on Earth: African American Ecoliterary Traditions*, Ruffin examines racial restrictions based on the intertwining politics of "ecological entitlement" for groups that are racialized positively while also examining what she calls "ecological deviance" for groups that are racialized negatively (124).

In a similar way, Kimberly K. Smith argues in *African American Environmental Thought* that black American writers often approach the environment with less sentimental perceptions of nature than European American populations. Understanding natural landscapes not as a "pristine and innocent wilderness but as a corrupted land in need of redemption," African American writers have frequently entered the conversation under different conditions (8). Smith contends that a central theme in African American environmental traditions is that the "denial of freedom to black Americans has distorted their relationship to the natural environment; indeed, it has scarred the land itself." She goes on to explain that for black writers "working in this tradition, America – not just the political community but the physical terrain – is a land cursed by injustice and the need of redemption" (8). African American writers in the West such as poet Wanda Coleman, science fiction novelist Octavia Butler, and *noir* author Attica Locke – to name just a few figures – are expanding the scope of environmental writing in the region by addressing issues of race and nature, divisions between urban and rural spaces, and relations between the human and the posthuman worlds.

Finally, the science of climate change, research on the Anthropocene, and studies of globalization are raising new concerns for environmental writing by challenging mainstream conceptualizations of the American West and of regions themselves as bounded spaces. In this context, Ursula Heise's call for a critically informed "eco-cosmopolitanism" may be a useful tool in confronting what Rob Nixon describes as "slow violence," the often invisible and gradual forms of environmental degradation that impact precarious populations in the Global South but that ultimately leave no place unaffected (Heise 8–9; Nixon 4). Likewise, Timothy Clark's analysis of "questions of scale" in a postnatural world where the border between "the natural" and "the artificial" has become increasingly porous may align with the work of critics calling for "resilience" as a way of making sense of new environmental challenges (Clark 130; LeMenager and Foote). In profound and as yet unimagined ways, these new concerns will likely direct and influence the themes, issues, and forms that emerge in the ongoing development of Western American environmental writing over the years to come.

## Works Cited

Abbey, Edward. *Desert Solitaire: A Season in the Wilderness.* 1968. New York: Touchstone, 1990. Print.

Alaimo, Stacy. *Bodily Natures: Science, Environment, and the Material Self.* Indianapolis: Indiana University Press, 2010. Print.

Baym, Nina. "Melodramas of Beset Manhood: How Theories of American Fiction Exclude Women Authors." *American Quarterly.* Vol. 33, no. 2 (1981): 123–139. Print.

Brady, Mary Pat. *Extinct Lands, Temporal Geographies: Chicana Literature and the Urgency of Space.* Durham, NC: Duke University Press, 2002. Print.

Buell, Lawrence. *The Environmental Imagination: Thoreau, Nature Writing, and the Formation of American Culture.* Cambridge, MA: Harvard University Press, 1995. Print.

Clark, Timothy. *The Cambridge Introduction to Literature and the Environment.* Cambridge: Cambridge University Press, 2011. Print.

Cruikshank, Julie. *Do Glaciers Listen?: Local Knowledge, Colonial Encounters, and Social Imagination.* Vancouver: University of British Columbia Press, 2005. Print.

Fiedler, Leslie. *Love and Death in the American Novel.* 1960. New York: Anchor, 1992. Print.

Gamber, John. *Positive Pollutions and Cultural Toxins: Waste and Contamination in US Ethnic Literature.* Lincoln: University of Nebraska Press, 2012. Print.

Hayes, Ernestine. *Blonde Indian: An Alaska Native Memoir*. Tucson: University of Arizona Press, 2006. Print.

Heise, Ursula. *Sense of Place and Sense of Planet: The Environmental Imagination of the Global*. Oxford: Oxford University Press, 2008. Print.

Kollin, Susan. *Nature's State: Imagining Alaska as the Last Frontier*. Chapel Hill: University of North Carolina Press, 2001. Print.

LeMenager, Stephanie and Stephanie Foote. "Editors' Column." *Resilience: A Journal of Environmental Humanities*. Vol. 1, no. 1 (January 2014): n. pag. Web. January 14, 2015.

Lewis, R. W. B. *The American Adam: Innocence, Tragedy, and Tradition in the Nineteenth Century*. Chicago: University of Chicago Press, 1955. Print.

Martin, Patricia Preciado. *Songs My Mother Sang to Me: An Oral History of Mexican American Women*. Tucson: University of Arizona Press, 1992. Print.

Muir, John. *Travels in Alaska*. 1912. San Francisco, CA: Sierra Club Books, 1988. Print.

Naess, Arne. "The Deep Ecological Movement: Some Philosophical Aspects." *Ecocriticism: The Essential Reader*. Ed. Ken Hiltner. New York: Routledge, 2015. 47–61. Print.

Nixon, Rob. *Slow Violence and the Environmentalism of the Poor*. Cambridge, MA: Harvard University Press, 2011. Print.

Outka, Paul. *Race and Nature from Transcendentalism to the Harlem Renaissance*. New York: Palgrave MacMillan, 2013. Print.

Ray, Sarah Jaquette. *The Ecological Other: Environmental Exclusion in American Culture*. Tucson: University of Arizona Press, 2013. Print.

Ruffin, Kimberly N. *Black on Earth: African American Ecoliterary Traditions*. Athens: University of Georgia Press, 2010. Print.

Sahagun, Louis. "John Muir's Legacy Questioned as Centennial of His Death Nears." *Los Angeles Times*, November 13, 2014. Web. January 15, 2015.

Smith, Kimberly K. *African American Environmental Thought*. Lawrence: University Press of Kansas, 2007. Print.

Solnit, Rebecca. *Savage Dreams: A Journey into the Landscape Wars of the American West*. Berkeley: University of California Press, 2000. Print.

Sturgeon, Noël. *Environmentalism in Popular Culture: Race, Gender, Sexuality, and the Politics of the Natural*. Tucson: University of Arizona Press, 2008. Print.

Taylor, Dorceta. *The Environment and the People in American Cities, 1600s–1900s: Disorder, Inequality, Social Change*. Durham, NC: Duke University Press, 2009. Print.

Thayer, Robert L. *LifePlace: Bioregional Thought and Practice*. Berkeley: University of California Press, 2003. Print.

Wills, Barbara. "The Nervous Origins of the American Western." *American Literature*. Vol. 70, no. 2 (June 1998): 293–316. Print.

Wyckoff, William. *How to Read the American West: A Field Guide*. Seattle: University of Washington Press, 2014. Print.

Young, Samuel Hall. *Alaska Days with John Muir*. 1915. Salt Lake City, UT: Peregrine Smith Books, 1990. Print.

Ziser, Michael. *Environmental Practice and Early American Literature*. Cambridge: Cambridge University Press, 2013. Print.

# 7

PIERRE LAGAYETTE

# California in late settlement

In the century that followed the Gold Rush, California experienced a series of major shifts that shaped it into a land of modernity, power, and success. The deepest and most inadvertent of these shifts was geological: tectonic plates that scarred the coastal West went for a violent change of topos in 1906 and left San Franciscans with no other choice than to turn piles of rubble into pillars for a restored prosperity. In the same period, California accomplished a large move from industrial mining to agriculture and horticulture, and attracted farmhands by the thousands, from all over the United States and neighboring countries. If gold had given wealth and power to Northern California, irrigated agriculture did the same for Southern California after 1880. The demographic and economic shift thus entailed was encouraged by the spreading of easy transportation as Central Pacific and Southern Pacific railroad lines crisscrossed California and put an end to the state's long-standing isolation. With railroads the wildest of capitalists bought for themselves a one-way ticket into California and enjoyed the bounties of monopoly. The land grants the "Big Four"[1] received from Congress turned them into the largest landowners of the state (with a cumulated property of more than 11.5 million acres), and made them the fiercest speculators whose rapaciousness Frank Norris exposed in his novel *The Octopus* (1901). Farmers violently protested as the ideal of the Homestead Act and the Jeffersonian dream of the yeoman farmer were buried for good. But the shift was permanent and the thirst for government land would never again be entirely quenched.

With the help of technology and industrialization another shift took place, from country to city. A massive migration, spurred by economic depression in the late nineteenth century, repeated droughts in the Great Plains, rising job opportunities in food-processing industries, and concentration in land ownership, brought a well-needed labor supply to California cities. In a span of twenty years (1900–1920) the population of the San Francisco Bay area doubled, while that of metropolitan Los Angeles increased fivefold.

73

By 1930 the City of Angels had shot up to fifth rank among American cities. Southern California, with its mild climate, beautiful landscapes, and romantic promises of happiness, revitalized the foundation story that located a terrestrial paradise in the vicinity. This represented another shift into the past, which perpetuated legends of Eden at the very moment when the "closing" of the frontier confronted Californians and Americans with the evidence of a heretofore unexpandable territory.

The shift from dream to reality was probably the most insidious, invisible, and yet essential that California had to endure in that period. The response that was required was neither demographic nor economic or even political: it had to be a cultural response left to the expert hands of artists and writers. For once Californians faced a challenge that only words, not material wealth, could cope with. In fact the shift here was rather a leap, and words were lacking. Ever since Bret Harte and Mark Twain had told their stories of miners and mining camps, hardly any major writer had come up to celebrate a "new" California, one that had become a mature society, with its beauties and tragedies, progress and evils. No one had taken the jump to bridge the old conventional vision of California-as-paradise and the emerging, darker view of post-frontier California as a closed space, irremediably bound by the natural barrier of the Pacific Ocean. At the turn of the twentieth century the state of California offered complexities that would not be easily erased, a mixture of openings and closures that somewhat kept the American Dream alive while, at the same time, pointing to its aporia.

## And the dream goes on

In spite of its remoteness, seismic risks, occasional economic hardships, and systemic aridity, California has exercised a permanent fascination on the minds of Americans and foreigners alike. In the years following the Civil War and the establishment of the transcontinental railroad, the state received exalted publicity from New York journalist Charles Nordhoff who, in his intriguing opus *California for Health, Wealth and Residence* (1873), claimed that Californians enjoyed "the finest climate, the most fertile soil, the loveliest skies, the mildest winters, the most healthful region, in the whole United States" (118). Nordhoff's euphoric praise balanced the views expressed by Major John Wesley Powell, whose *Report on the Lands of the Arid Region of the United States* (1878) voiced the strongest doubts about the inhabitability of the arid Western lands. Aridity was, indeed, a central issue in the development of the West, but Californians proved Powell wrong and found ways of "civilizing" the desert by turning it into a generous garden. The vision of California as cornucopia became an inexhaustible source of wonder and attraction.

This land was certainly bountiful and plenteous, but the waves of migrants who came to have their share of it soon raised the question of ownership. Statehood had hardly solved the problem: Californians of Mexican extraction had been despoiled of their properties. As for the original Indian occupants, they had been decimated by either disease or violence (from a total of about one hundred and fifty thousand at the time of the Gold Rush, there remained only twenty thousand by 1900), or they were simply displaced by multitudinous newcomers. The question of the survival of these "vanishing Indians" was taken up by reformers like Helen Hunt Jackson, who fought to bring to public light the sorry fate of this population. Her famous novel *Ramona* (1884) attempts to redress the wrongs done by Americans to both Indians and Mexicans. Beyond the romantic story of the tragic love between Ramona, the orphaned, mixed-blood, Scots-Indian girl, and Alessandro, the Indian sheepherder, it is the whole social fabric of late nineteenth-century California that is put to the test of prejudice, assimilation, and land greed. Each community present in Southern California, Mexican, Indian, and Euro-American, attempts to find its place in the social mosaic of the region, and racial stereotypes are hardly absent from the process. Ramona's foster mother, Señora Moreno, refuses to see the girl marry the Indian Alessandro even though she is half-native; American settlers drive off the young couple from the successive homesteads they tried to secure for themselves; as for Señora Moreno, she hates Americans for having left her "rancho" open to squatters and violating the terms of the Treaty of Guadalupe Hidalgo. For the first time American settlers are described as rapacious and malevolent, not rightful occupiers but illegitimate residents, and the U.S. government is seen as accessory to the institutional deprivation of the land titles held by the Mexican "Californios." "Tract after tract," writes Jackson, "her lands had been taken away from her; it looked for a time as if nothing would be left. Every one of the claims based on deeds of gift from Governor Pio Pico, her husband's most intimate friend, was disallowed.... No wonder she believed the Americans as thieves, and spoke of them always as hounds" (23).

Land spoliation, however, is not what will make Jackson's *Ramona* so immensely popular. The story's appeal is in its romanticizing of intercultural and interracial relations. For facts about the violation of Indian rights to their ancestral lands, one should turn to Jackson's documentary *A Century of Dishonor* published three years before *Ramona*. But the fictional tale of the orphan girl and Indian shepherd's stubborn quest for a place to live freely and happily revived the dream of an ideal, sun-drenched Arcadia. Southern California would again represent a land of second chances for the young couple as they scour the region for a place to settle and raise a family. Some thirty years later, Jack London would stage a similar pursuit of a suitable farmland, this time in Northern California, for newlyweds Billy Roberts and Saxon Brown in *The Valley of the Moon* (1913). Jackson's Ramona, in the words of historian Kevin Starr, "gave expression to a yearning that Southern California be a land of beauty and memory and sunny afternoons" (62).

For beauty, Mary Austin privileged the desert (which she experienced firsthand when she lived in Tejon Ranch near the Mojave Desert and later in Santa Fe) because it involved a distinct sense of place and could serve as the basis for the development of a regional culture. Nature, there, seemed untainted and customs carefully preserved. Austin spent most of her life trying to convey in words the spirit of California and should stand as the ur-author in any history of California literature. A native of Illinois, Austin came to California in 1888, at a time when the last frontier of settlement was disappearing. The uprooted Midwesterner was a wanderer at heart: after Tejon, she moved to Carmel and lived there a while among fellow artists, then traveled to Europe, stayed in New York for more than a decade, and finally settled in New Mexico where the desert called her. From her days at Rancho Tejon, she knew that the desert was the epitome of the West and deserved more than superficial investigation. She therefore probed the Western desert in a way that disregarded stereotypes (among them its supposed uninhabitable nature), transcended divisions (its native-sounding name, she decided, would be the "country of lost borders"), and rehabilitated Indian traditions. She joined her husband, Wallace Austin, in his fight against the attempt by Los Angeles to control the Owens Valley water supply, and she made a reputation for herself as a defender of nature in the West with one single book, *The Land of Little Rain* (1903). The success of this one book does some injustice to the thirty-five novels, stories, and essays she published in her lifetime; yet the impressions and experiences of California she wrote into this collection of sketches stand out as a true literary achievement. The book focuses on the arid and semiarid regions of Southern California, between the High Sierras south of Yosemite, the Ceriso, Death Valley, the Mojave Desert; and towns such as Jimville, Kearsarge, and Las Uvas. She writes, with quasi-ethnographic precision, of the region's climate, plants, and animals and of its peoples: the local Ute, Paiute, Mojave, and Shoshone Indians; Euro-American gold prospectors and borax miners; and descendants of Hispanic settlers. Unlike its reputation, in Austin's vision the desert becomes alive and nature hospitable for those who love solitude and purity. In this respect, *The Land of Little Rain* foreshadows Edward Abbey's *Desert Solitaire* and draws special attention to the centrality of water in the history of the American West. The little animals she describes in the story "Water Trails of the Ceriso" are quite capable, like the native Indians, to find concealed water in the most arid places; the subtext is that life in the desert depends on the adaptability of those who want to dwell there, not on the humanly engineered, forced transformation of the desert into a garden. The perfect coherence between desert and animal life is itself an indirect subversive exposure of man's inability to survive in nature without transforming it. More broadly, Austin addresses the question of a face-off between nature and culture. Her vision of the Western wilderness is only seemingly factual; she in truth is constantly reinterpreting the West, its symbols and history, in the light of the permanence of nature. To start with, the very title of the book is intriguing: it does not just indicate a geographical location; it becomes part of a renaming process that itself has social and cultural significance. Toponymy tells stories and makes history: in the Midwest, as Austin should have known, place names changed over time in the wake of the successive waves of migration and were closely linked to the history of settlement. Geography bears the marks of human occupation even when the word "desert" seems to refer to a land that cannot support human populations. Instead of this strongly connoted name Austin chooses the periphrastic (and more explanatory) "land of little rain." In so doing she symbolically turns her back to the whole frontier experience and, with this "new" name, seeks to inaugurate a fresh relation between Western man and his environment. Contrary to some of Steinbeck's titles, which are fundamentally inscribed in a biblical tradition,[2] Austin's "land of little rain" suggests that her inspiration comes rather from the ancestral Indian presence in California and native contact with nature. Steinbeck uses biblical metaphors to suggest that California offers an apotheosis to Western man's sweeping conquest of the world, with God's blessing. For Austin, traditions in the West are not inherited from the East. They are local, born of native and Mexican occupation. In the sketch "The Little Town of the Grapevines" ("El Pueblo de las Uvas") she describes an ideal village where inhabitants have learned to live harmoniously with their environment and found their true place in the scheme of nature. Grapes here are not connected with God's anger; on the contrary they express His benevolence and gentleness.

> Come away, you who are obsessed with your own importance in the scheme of things, and have got nothing you did not sweat for, come away by the brown valleys and full-bosomed hills to the even-breathing days, to the kindliness, earthiness, ease of El Pueblo de Las Uvas. (113)

This invitation to live a careless life in Southern California is predicated on the capacity of Californians to preserve memory while inventing a revised version of the American Dream. Reinterpretations assumed diverse, not to say antagonistic, shapes. John Muir, for example, was ecstatic when he first set his eyes on the "most delightsome" San Joaquin Valley. Robinson Jeffers, on the contrary, saw the wild Pacific Coast as "crying out for tragedy, like all beautiful places." For John Steinbeck the rural Salinas Valley was an epitome of how the noble saga of westering had ended in frustrating sociopolitical frictions. Clearly, by the first decades of the twentieth century, California had become a flawed paradise.

## Inventing the next California

The history of the American West is a story of rivers, mountains, and valleys, of water and stones. In this respect, the history of California is particularly emblematic: mountains and rivers yielded the region's earliest wealth in gold, but it was valleys that turned the state into an agricultural paradise. Rivers served to irrigate this blessed desert and to accommodate ever-increasing urban crowds. Geography and geology were central to the destiny of California and encouraged the regional culture. California writers loved valleys, not the biblical "valley of the shadow of death" inherited from the Puritan East, from which one is rescued by divine providence, but a valley of milk and honey and sunshine that announces a happy and fortunate future (Psalm 23:4). Mary Austin celebrated the Owens Valley and the neighboring Death Valley as places that made the "Frontier" obsolete, calling them a "Country of Lost Borders" where nature triumphs over legal or cultural divisions. Austin became embroiled in the famous Owens Valley water war, which began in the early 1900s, a project that sought to siphon the water of the Owens River to supply the quickly growing city of Los Angeles. She staunchly opposed the project, not to defy progress but to preserve the integrity of nature. The Owens Valley battle signaled a profound change: with the decline of mining, agricultural development became a favorable option and the Valley was uneasily caught between the old era and the new. Yet this fight between small valley ranchers and political heavyweights in the metropolis was too unequal and Austin was defeated. But her literary defense of rustic and pastoral life close to the soil informed all her "regionalist" writings, from *Isidro* (1905) to *The Ford* (1917), and, eventually, turned her into an early and original priestess of the environmentalist cult. Similarly, John Muir had fallen in love with the Hetch Hetchy Valley, a beautiful portion of the Yosemite National Park, which he described as "a grand landscape garden, one of Nature's rarest and most precious mountain temples" (*The Yosemite* 255). The valley was eventually dammed and flooded to secure a proper water supply for San Francisco and the Bay Area.

   Both Austin and Muir were confronted with a choice between preserving or transforming the California dream, between mourning a glorious, sacred past and promoting a shining, material future, between nostalgia and anticipation. As far as valleys were concerned, Owens and Hetch Hetchy pointed to the saga of Western settlement; San Joaquin and Imperial to the unstoppable advance of capitalism and commercialism. This new ambivalence of the American Dream spread to the remote corner of the Salinas Valley where the Tiflin ranch of Steinbeck's short story "The Red Pony" is located. The latter is part of the twelve-story collection Steinbeck published in 1938 titled *The Long Valley*. Besides being the author's birthplace, the Salinas area was reputed to have been far more than a simple backdrop to his narratives. Most of the tales in this opus were published in magazines before they were assembled at the instigation of Steinbeck's editor, Pascal Covici. The title, which is supposed to express the coherence of the volume, deserves closer attention. Reviewers and critics readily assumed that the "valley" referred to the Salinas, since Steinbeck admitted to having been durably inspired by the people, the geography, the culture, and some of the local events of this lush, fertile area. Actually the title brings no visible support to this interpretation: this "valley" is just "long," which gives us no clue to its identity nor any truth to the qualifier: the Salinas is definitely shorter than any of the great valleys in the state, San Joaquin, Sacramento, Imperial, Owens, and so forth. This valley is therefore devoid of geographical or topographical existence. On the other hand, most of California's valleys were named after individuals (discoverers, travelers, owners, etc.) or events. In other words the naming process inscribed them in history. Not here: this "Long Valley" has no historical existence either. It is placeless and timeless and represents an archetypal locus, detached from the contingencies of history and spatiality, where Steinbeck can freely play with symbols, myths, universal emotions, and even narrative techniques – which would justify the presence, in this collection, of the farcical, anachronistic tale of "St. Katy the Virgin." Finally, this all-purpose title may signify that the naming process in the West has come to an end and with it the whole process of continental conquest and appropriation of the land. The valley is a place closed off "from the sky and from all the rest of the world," that is from all spiritual and planetary coercions (3). Here, nature can be rearranged to suit the needs of obsessive gardeners like Elisa Allen ("The Chrysanthemums") or Mary Teller ("The White Quail"). Here, people are faced with their own frustrations and violence without the redeeming help of history, of great worldly, or national, or even Californian, schemes. Life in this valley is bared to essentials, made of trivial actions and thoughts and daily routines, which are so powerful that they anaesthetize the sense of past and future. Even the very process of memory seems to be coming to a halt. Take "The Red Pony" and the chapter concerning "The Leader of the People": the "westering" experience dear to Jody's grandfather is definitely over. The old man's nostalgia for a bygone era reinforces the "desolation of loss" that Steinbeck sought to illustrate in this collection of stories (*Steinbeck: A Life in Letters* 63). Grandfather's personal loss is obviously more spiritual than physical: it is the sudden closure of movement and advance that he mourns when he observes: "it wasn't getting here that mattered, it was movement and westering ... and the slow steps that made the movement piled up and piled up until the continent was crossed. Then we came down to the sea, and it was done" (303). This quest is precisely what makes California an icon of the continental conquest and a reason to perpetuate the American dream of grandeur. His daughter, Mrs. Tiflin, sees the latent urge to prolong the westering experience through Grandfather's reminiscences: "That was the big thing in my father's life. He led a wagon train clear across the plains to the coast ... and after he finished it, there wasn't anything more for him to do but think about it and talk about it. If there'd been any farther west to go, he'd have gone. He's told me so himself" (288). The impulse to pursue the quest in imagination and in words was kept alive by storytellers like Steinbeck, Jack London, and Nathanael West and became a sort of California trademark. Historian Gerald Haslam, paraphrasing Archibald MacLeish, identifies the place as "a region of the mind I call Fantasy California" (195). This land needed a redefinition to account for the spiritual quest that survived the tragic closure of the historical frontier. Such a continuum is perceptible in "The Red Pony" through intergenerational exchanges: Jody hears his grandfather's stories without ever resenting repetition. And the grandfather generously accepts to see his heroic defense against Indians minimized and downgraded to the ancillary level of mice hunting. But the new generation is ready to meet the challenge of movement, one they inherited from the pioneers in frontier days, or from displaced farmers at the time of the Dust Bowl.

Haslam talks of "a continuum of human experience" and quotes Ma Joad as saying: "... we're the people – we go on" (195; *The Grapes Of Wrath* 192). Going on, motion then is the key: even though Grandfather's grand journey across the continent has come to a halt, telling about it, turning experience into words extends the process of discovery and renewal. Ma Joad rightly prophecies: "A different time's comin'," which is another way of confirming the allure of California and its incarnation in second chances (192). *The Red Pony*, in a sense, paves the way for the migrants of *The Grapes of Wrath* by showing that despite the final barrier of the ocean, that ocean that stopped the "leader of the people" and his caravan for good, despite the incantatory tale-telling which ceaselessly tries to recapitulate the passing of an era, the impulse to move on endures and the desire for change never abates. Jody's childish war on mice translates the impermanence of settlement: those "overbearing and fat" mice that colonized the haystacks are doomed to be displaced and exterminated to clear the path for new crops and new farming activities. In this microcosmic California valley it is the whole saga of Western conquest and settlement that is being allegorically replayed.

## California, naturally

The stubborn need to progress westward is also what motivates the Oklahoma farmers whose adventurous voyage to mythic California is chronicled in *The Grapes of Wrath*. The Arcadian landscapes of the Salinas Valley are gone; here, dust and infertility dominate. The prerequisite of a benevolent nature, accessory to the human pursuit of success and happiness through the continent, is no longer valid. And the preeminence of a fictional narrative based on the author's control of his story and man's control of history is vanishing quickly in favor of a more balanced conception of man's relation to his natural environment. Humans must understand their place in nature and stop being deceived by the illusory promises and comforts of civilization. Nature may become at worst violent and lethal, at best indifferent to man's needs. Mary Austin had offered a benign view of the confrontation between humankind and nature, less romantic than Helen Hunt Jackson's yet redirecting attention to the nonhuman life in the desert. Nature was gradually becoming less of a setting and more of an actor in the destiny of Western settlers and in the stories told by Western writers. Robinson Jeffers was surely the most deeply impressed observer of man's insignificance in the natural world. Clearly the time had come for fiction writers to organize a comprehensive reevaluation of the old spiritual-mythic values and put the "modern" American to the test as they confront a potentially hostile or unmanageable Nature. On the other hand, the rise of industrialism and the gradual pauperization of whole strata of American society suggested that more people were being sacrificed on the altar of progress, irrevocably reduced to an animal state, and that, maybe, California was the only place left where a new social order more respectful of the individual and his environment would be reinvented. It would all start with a rehabilitation of the animal and physical worlds. Austin had shown how desert flora and fauna had developed what she called a "cheerful adaptation" to the peculiar ecosystem of the Mojave. Here were patterns of life that ignored the conventional vision of a man-centered universe: "There are hints to be had here," she notes, "of the way in which a land forces new habits on its

dwellers" (12). What Austin offered was a model of harmonious organization dependent on natural laws, not on social rules imposed by humans,
the implications being that man is no longer in control of nature (which
Austin refers to as "the land") but appears as just another species in the
animal world. Interestingly, the bestiary of California writers is quite extensive and animal imagery abounds. Random examples would include West's
"locust," Steinbeck's "red pony," Norris's "octopus," Jeffers's "roan stallion," or London's "wolf." Not to mention Grandfather's metaphor of the
"big crawling beast" in Steinbeck's "The Leader of the People," which dehu-
manizes the experience of westering at the very moment when the narrator
seeks to demonstrate the value of conquering the land. Settlement becomes
a mechanized operation, blind to anything else but its own purpose. Here is
one instance of Steinbeck's concessions to naturalist writing and thinking:

> It was a whole bunch of people made into a big crawling beast. And I was the
> head. It was westering and westering. Every man wanted something for him-
> self, but the big beast that was all of them wanted only westering. I was the
> leader but if I hadn't been there, someone else would have been the head....
> We carried life out here and set it down the way those ants carry eggs. (*The
> Long Valley* 302–303)

The glorious epic of Manifest Destiny is suddenly scaled down to the advance
of a creeping creature and the preprogrammed work of insects. Predatory
forces are evidently at play and challenge any human control of destiny.
A similar message can be read through *The Grapes of Wrath*. The narrative
is interspersed with moments of stasis when the author launches into detailed
descriptions of the natural environment as if to balance human actions with
the immanent power of natural laws. One instance is worthy of particular
attention: Steinbeck opens chapter 3 with the memorable scene of a small
land turtle confronted with the dangerous challenge of crossing a highway.
He goes into extreme detail to chronicle the event, which has led critics to
single out this passage as a fine example of Steinbeck's naturalism. At the
same time it appears legitimate to insist on the symbolic content of this short
episode: obviously Steinbeck's turtle signifies more than the ordinary "pet"
children are reputed to love,[3] more than an endangered specimen of a very
old zoological group (15). Steinbeck's minute description may seem to proceed from a scientific intent, as naturalistic writings commonly do. His interest, however, is elsewhere and bidirectional: for one, he introduces here an
incidental story in which the turtle's perilous journey toward the other side
of the road represents, in general, the crossing of the American continent
by courageous (although somewhat ill-equipped) settlers, and in particular
the Joads' equally audacious migration to California. The determination of

the socially oppressed Okies to reach their destination parallels the turtle's stubborn and instinctive resolve to climb the highway embankment, even though the space beyond that "hill" might prove hazardous or lethal. Yet the turtle's blindness to future trouble is not the product of social injustice, like the forced exile of Oklahoma farmers. It falls into place within the universal schemes nature devises for all living things – including mankind.

This is the second lesson of the fabulous adventures of the turtle: Nature is in command, not human beings. And there is no meanness in the turtle's ways, no desire to kill or to spare (like the two drivers on the highway) just a wonderful, objective need to obey forces that, naturally, guarantee survival and freedom. Turtles existed two and a half million years before man appeared and will probably outlast the human race by as much. Their survival might well depend on the toss of a coin: Steinbeck's turtle avoids being crushed by a malevolent roadhog only by a flip of fortune. Yet nothing can stop turtles, as a species, from riding out and enduring. These turtles are the perfect nomads (in the Deleuzian sense of the term), following a customary and predetermined direction (here the "southwest") (30).[4] They are not interested in roads; their life is tied to a territory that identifies them. Not so for the victims of the Dust Bowl: they are only migrants, moving from one place to another without certainty as to their final destinations. They are, so to speak "de-territorialized," caught in an historical process that functions like heredity: like the Mother Lode before, this "mother road" is the privileged agent of their destiny, that is, of their migration. The Joads' wanderings into and through the Golden State are a desperate attempt on their part to exchange vagrancy for ownership, and the socially degrading status of "migrants" (they are ruled by the government and stationed in canvas camps) for that of "nomads," people freely roaming within a familiar territory. They aptly illustrate Deleuze's remark on the contrast between nomads and migrants: "It is true that the nomads have no history; they only have a geography" (Deleuze and Guattari 384–395). The Oklahoma sharecroppers, ruled by the principles of migration, must each day repeat the well-known story of Western settlement told by trails, roads, or railroad lines, must reinvent a social order along the way, and must keep the dream alive of a bountiful California where they will secure a territory for themselves. Naturally; like the turtles.

## In my Eden is my beginning

The need for a place to improve one's life is the basis of all migrations to the Far West. But nowhere was the dream of an American Arcadia as permanent as in California, even after runaway urbanization and a large-scale agricultural boom in the early decades of the twentieth century had deeply affected the pastoral character of the Californian landscape. In the collective memory of Americans, California remained that legendary land Montalvo's medieval epic located "close to Paradise." Certainly Steinbeck described California as a flawed Eden: the deluge at the end of *The Grapes of Wrath* is no less damaging than the plague of dust the migrants fled from. But images of renewal and the promise of happiness supply an enduring sub-text to all California literature, even when the excesses of modern society induce the most radical protest and indictments on the part of regional authors. Decades before Steinbeck denounced the tragic fate of poor farm-ers and workmen, Jack London had challenged the social and economic model that bred urban poverty and decay, homelessness, street violence, and working-class despair. Nothing was more detrimental to the percep-tion of an edenic California than the sharp contrast between ostentatious wealth and the no less conspicuous drudgery laborers faced in the fields, the factories, or the sweatshops. Edwin Markham's famous poem "The Man with the Hoe" (1899) had decried the inhuman condition of small farm-ers and raised the question of whether California could still epitomize the American Dream. At the time, this daring remonstrance caused a cultural and political commotion on the West Coast. Markham had to insist that his scope extended far beyond California itself. He claimed to have recognized in Auguste Millet's eponymous painting the tragic fate of *all* laborers in *all* times at the hands of an oppressive society.

Years later, in some reflections on writing the poem, Markham observed: "The Hoeman is the symbol of betrayed humanity, the Toiler ground down through ages of oppression, through ages of social injustice. He is the man pushed away from the land by those who fail to use the land, till at last he has become a serf, with no mind in his muscle and no heart in his handiwork. He is the man pushed back and shrunken up by the special privileges conferred upon the Few" (1). Markham's iconoclastic views, his impulse "to write a poem that should cry the lost rights of the toiling multi-tude in the abyss of civilization" were attacked as un-American and undem-ocratic. Whoever dared go against the conventional wisdom of the beneficial effects of civilization, especially in California (the advanced outpost of pro-gress and success) ran the risk of being ostracized. Robinson Jeffers, in the 1940s, would suffer a similar bashing when he voiced his opposition to American involvement in World War II.

Oakland-born writer Jack London knew well those "slaves of the wheel of labor" Markham tried to rehabilitate. His writings reflect a lifelong concern with the real nature of the California dream and its adjustment to the evolutions of modern society. For the dream had a price: economic prosperity induced social agitation and even nature stirred a heated controversy between preservationists and conservationists over the persistence of the pastoral ideal in industrialized California. In other words, the crucial question had become whether California was still a kind of Garden of Eden, or rather a place to escape from – a question diversely answered by writers of future generations. On the surface, it seems that London chose the second option: his life was a succession of departures, flights, and travels. Yet departures involve returns and London kept returning to California. There he looked for his personal paradise, in the Sonoma Valley and his Glen Ellen ranch. He was not just a writer of "dog stories" or Alaskan adventures; rather he was the most successful California writer and the highest-paid American author at the time of his death. Many of his protagonists, like himself, looked for happiness and/or fortune in faraway lands; but they finally found the answer to their quest much closer to "home," in California. Such was particularly the case for Elam Harnish: the hero of *Burning Daylight* (one of London's most successful novels) comes back to California after having been for years a pioneer of the Yukon gold rush and having left "civilization" behind (5). *The Call of the Wild* and *White Fang* reawaken the old myth of the wilderness as an alternative to the complexities of modern life and, at the same time, present California as the ultimate place where a simple, pleasant existence can still be led. But no London novel succeeds like *The Valley of the Moon* in celebrating California as a last Eden. The adventures of the young couple Billy Roberts and Saxon Brown replicate in the form of a peripatetic voyage London's own pursuit of success and happiness. Gone is the attraction of the Arctic, where, as the Yukon stories testify, nature proved inhospitable and spoke only of man's insignificance. Gone is the alluring beauty of Polynesia, eulogized by Melville and Stevenson. London's *South Seas Tales* (1911) chronicles the wretched state of native society in those Pacific islands and shows how the latter have been contaminated by the evils of civilization. To dramatize his quest for paradise, in *The Valley of the Moon* London uses the well-known narrative device of peregrination, which allows the protagonists to explore, discover, and understand the realities of life while at the same time becoming aware of the historical depths of their quest. For Billy and Saxon's excursion into the California countryside is not merely geographical: theirs is the final version of the "westward movement" – not the vast migration of settlers Jody's grandfather rehashed ad libitum, but a sort of quintessential voyage into the most modern and advanced outpost of Western civilization. There is much of the *bildungsroman* in this novel, among the last London published in his lifetime. Billy and Saxon leave the violent, oppressive urban

environment of Oakland and start wandering through the region in search
of an ideal piece of land that they will own and cultivate, just like the
settlers of old. On the surface this errand into a not-so-wild West may
pass for another dystopian quest of the kind that had led Mary Austin to
Las Uvas (107). Not quite, though: London the socialist who exposed the
inhuman living conditions of "The People of the Abyss" in the East End
district of London similarly censured life in California's big cities, especially his native Oakland. What sends Bill and Saxon on the road is as
much the desire for Arcadia as a flight from the economic violence of hard
work, low wages, strikes, street riots, picket lines, scabs, Pinkertons, and
other offshoots of savage capitalism. *The Valley of the Moon*, however, is
in no visible way an anti-capitalist or pro-labor manifesto; it is a sweet,
anachronistic, and almost elegiac pursuit of that same ideal that had motivated previous generations to appropriate land in the West.

In a rather subtle way Billy and Saxon's determination to revive a bygone
past subverts the grand narrative of American history. Their move from city
to country (as opposed to the massive population shift from country to city
that fed the California urban sprawl) challenges the superiority of industrialized, urbanized America over the original pastoral scheme that brought
settlers across the continent to the Pacific. For the disturbing reality of a
changed world[5] they substitute a change of life of their own that revives the
old myths of free land and inexhaustible opportunities.

Along the way to their ever elusive destination the couple learn about
the changes California has gone through, learn from the cultural elite in
Carmel what modernity is all about, and learn from benevolent country-
men the basics of rational farming. Up in Sonoma, they fall upon their inevitable place, the famous "Valley of the Moon" Harnish ravingly watched
from his ranch house at the end of *Burning Daylight*.[6] The ecstasy of finding an idyllic land on which to build an entirely new life is a sign that,
against all odds, Billy the teamster and Saxon the laundry girl have proven
that California remains a land of second chances, that there is still room
for a piece of "the old pioneer-dream of land spaciousness" in this far
Western region (177). London presents the story's ending as the beginning
of a new life. One is tempted to see this apotheosis as another illustration
of the myth of American perpetual resilience, one that informs California
fiction to this day. On the other hand, the fact that Billy and Saxon end up
settling in the Valley of the Moon does not simply mean the fulfillment of
a dream, one that several people they met on the road deemed as impossible as reaching the celestial moon itself. It is also like going back home,[7] a
true return to origins, to pre-European occupation, since the name is the

English translation of the Native American toponym "Sonoma." And one is tempted to recall here T. S. Eliot's lines at the end of "Little Gidding":

> We shall not cease from exploration
> And the end of all our exploring
> Will be to arrive where we started
> And know the place for the first time. (222)

## Notes

1 The term refers to the four directors of the Central Pacific Corporation: Collis P. Huntington, Leland Stanford, Mark Hopkins, and Charles Crocker.

2 "East of Eden" refers to the "land of Nod" in Genesis 4:16, where Cain was exiled after having killed Abel. "The Grapes of Wrath" metaphorically refers to the remorseless sinners who will endure God's wrath, as described in Revelation 14.

3 In the next chapter, Tom Joad picks up a rambling turtle, just for fun: "Thought I'd take 'im to my little brother," he says, "Kids like turtles."

4 Steinbeck has Tom Joad and Casy, watching the turtle finally crawl away, comment: "Where the hell you s'pose he's goin'?" said Joad. "I seen turtles all my life. They're always goin' someplace. They always seem to want to get there."

5 "Times have changed," regrets Saxon, "They've changed even since I was a little girl. We crossed the plains and opened up this country, and now we're losing even the chance to work for a living in it." Jack London, *The Valley of the Moon*, 172.

6 "From where they sat they could look out over the world. Like the curve of a skirting blade, the Valley of the Moon stretched before them, dotted with farm-houses and varied by pasture-lands, hay-fields, and vineyards. Beyond rose the wall of the valley.... The air shimmered with heat, and altogether it was a lazy, basking day. Quail whistled to their young from the thicketed hillside behind the house. There was a gentle cooing of pigeons, and from the green depths of the big canyon arose the sobbing wood note of a mourning dove. Once, there was a warning chorus from the foraging hens and a wild rush for cover, as a hawk, high in the blue, cast its drifting shadow along the ground. Jack London, *The Works of Jack London*, vol. 3, *Burning Daylight*, 354.

7 On discovering the Sonoma Valley for the first time, Saxon exclaims: "Why, I feel just as if I was coming home." *The Valley of the Moon*, 172.

## Works Cited

Austin, Mary. *The Land of Little Rain*. Bedford, MA: Applewood Books, 2000.

Eliot, T. S. *Four Quartets*. London: Faber & Faber, 1963.

Deleuze, G and F. Guattari. *A Thousand Plateaux*. Minneapolis: University of Minnesota Press, 1987.

Haslam, Gerald. "Literary California: The Ultimate Frontier of the Western World," *California History*. Vol. 68, no. 4 (Winter 1989/1990).

Jackson, Helen Hunt. *Ramona*. Boston, M: Roberts Brothers Publishers, 1884.

London, Jack. *Burning Daylight*. London: W. Heinemann, 1911.

*The Works of Jack London*, vol. 3, *Burning Daylight*. New York: Review of Reviews, 1917.

*The Valley of the Moon*. Los Angeles: David Rejl, 1988.

Markham, Edwin. "How I Wrote The Man With the Hoe," *The Dearborn Independent*, Nov. 21, 1925.

Muir, John. *The Yosemite*. New York: Century Press, 1912.

Nordhoff, Charles. *California for Health, Wealth and Residence*. New York: Harper Brothers, 1873.

Starr, Kevin. *Inventing the Dream: California through the Progressive Era*. New York: Oxford University Press, 1985.

Steinbeck, John. *Steinbeck: A Life in Letters*. Elaine Steinbeck and Robert Wallsten (eds). New York: Viking Press, 1975.

*The Long Valley*. 1938. New York: Penguin Books, 1986.

*The Grapes of Wrath*. 1939. New York: Penguin Books, 2006.

# 8

GIOIA WOODS

# The West in modern verse

In "Letter to an Imaginary Friend," Thomas McGrath captures the West in modern verse: the West is "a real freedom: born/From the wild and open land our grandfathers heroically stole" (159). McGrath's ironic evocation suggests two central concerns operative in modern poetry from the region: the wild and open land, and its double ideological association with both freedom and colonialism. For many Western poets, the threat to Western environments stands metaphorically for an existential threat to human freedom. "There is our herd of cars stopped,/staring respectfully at the line of bison crossing," May Swenson's poem "Bison Crossing Near Mt. Rushmore" begins (146). Swenson conflates the closely observed bison with the "strong and somber remnant of western freedom," suggesting that we trade the benefits of close association with the natural world for a mechanistic simulation of organic wholeness, one that is robbed of agency. "And we keep to our line," the poem concludes, "staring, stirring, revving idling motors, moving/each behind the other, herdlike, where the highway leads" (147). Poet and publisher Lawrence Ferlinghetti, too, evoked the libertarian freedoms embodied by the American West. After World War II, it was a place of "born-again optimism" where a poet or artist could indulge "a vision of some wide open, more creative society" (*Howl on Trial* xi). In the 1950s, Ferlinghetti remembers, it was as if "the continent had tilted up, with the whole population sliding to the west ... [it] was still the last frontier in many ways, with its island mentality that could be defined as a pioneer attitude of being out there on your own, without reliance on government" (ibid. xi). In a curious way, it was the fashioning of a utopian landscape that united diverse poets. The American West itself was a utopian project: it offered the promise of social renewal and transformation. "There is no question but that San Francisco ... is radically different from what is going on elsewhere," poet Kenneth Rexroth observed in the late 1950s. "There are hand presses, poetry readings, young writers everywhere – but nowhere else is there a whole younger generation culture pattern characterized by total rejection of the official high-brow culture ... where magazines like the *Kenyon, Hudson* and *Partisan Review* are looked on as 'The Enemy' " (Rexroth, 507). Poets of the mid-century West used a whole host of modernist techniques to inform their poetry, including symbolism, realism, impressionism, expressionism, and, as modern verse turned to postmodern verse in the hands of the poets of the San Francisco Renaissance, a romantic surrealism.

There is the Western landscape itself, and then there are the ways humans make meaning about that landscape. Robinson Jeffers, perhaps the most influential modernist poet from the West, consistently situated humans as secondary to the powerful drama enacted by nature. We are, he believed, simply nature's interpreters, perhaps even nature's puppets. Jeffers, who lived most of his life on the rugged California coast near Carmel, found his images in his surroundings: hawks, mountain lions, rocks, trees, and ocean dominate his work. He frequently meditated on the austere beauty of the Western landscape and praised the fit and fierce animals that inhabit it. In a late poetic fragment, Jeffers acknowledged that "Mountain and ocean, rock, water and beasts and trees / Are the protagonists, the human people are only symbolic interpreters" (*Collected Poems 3* 484). The West, critic Robert Brophy explains, is not simply the setting for Jeffers' work; it is used "to explore the nature of being" and the nature of the relationship between humans and the cosmos ("Robinson Jeffers"). Brophy calls Jeffers the "metaphysician of the West" (ibid.). Like T. S. Eliot and other postwar modernists, Jeffers believed that Western civilization had played itself out. The extreme western coast where he lived came to represent for him civilization's geographical, intellectual, and spiritual end. Not surprisingly, the ideological violence wrought by Manifest Destiny and "progress" is a frequent theme in his work. In "The Purse-Seine," the narrator looks out over a city and compares the scene to a seine-net when "the crowded fish/ Know they are caught, and wildly beat from one wall/to the other of their closing destiny" (*Selected Poems* 61). Ultimately, it is the way humans have distanced themselves from nature that heralds their demise.

> Lately I was looking from a night mountain-top
> On a wide city, the colored splendor, galaxies of light:
>     how could I help but recall the seine-net
> Gathering the luminous fish? I cannot tell you how
>     beautiful the city appeared, and a little terrible.
> I thought, We have geared the machines and locked all together
>     into inter-dependence; we have built the great cities; now
> There is no escape. We have gathered vast populations incapable
>     of free survival, insulated

> From the strong earth, each person in himself helpless, on all
> dependent. (*Selected Poems*, 61–62)

Despite what some have called the extreme pessimism embodied in his philosophical "inhumanism," Jeffers was extremely popular with the reading public and with critics. Between 1924 and 1934 he published seven volumes of poetry, and in 1932 he became the first poet to appear on the cover of *Time*. During World War II, however, his belief in political isolationism caused his reputation to slide. In 1948, Random House published *The Double Axe and Other Poems* with an unusual disclaimer disagreeing with Jeffers' political views. In the postwar United States, his refusal to go along with national optimism earned him few friends. His attitude, however, is a crucial influence for other Western poets, who used the ideological freedom associated with Western landscapes as a way to develop a poetics of nonconformity. Jeffers made it possible for Western poets to condemn the machine-driven consumer culture that threatened Western environments and individuals. The West, after Jeffers, became a locus of rebellious poetic activity.

When *The Double Axe* was republished in 1977, poet William Everson wrote the introduction. In it he describes Jeffers as an incisive antiwar poet. Everson was deeply influenced by Jeffers, explaining "Jeffers showed me God. In Jeffers I found my voice" ("William [Oliver] Everson"). Everson himself was a pacifist who grew grapes in the San Joaquin Valley in the 1930s. Like Jeffers, he populated his poems with characters from the Western landscape. His first published collection of poems was a pamphlet called *These Are the Ravens* (1935). Throughout he evokes the power in nature, as in this excerpt from the poem "Muscat Pruning":

> All these dormant fields are held beneath the fog.
> The scraggy vines, the broken weeds, the cold moist ground
> Have known it now for days....
> There is a flicker swooping from the grove on scalloped wings,
> His harsh cry widening through the fog.
> After his call the silence holds the drip-sound of the trees,
> Muffling the hushed beat under the mist.
> Over the field the noise of other pruners
> Moves me to my work.
> I have a hundred vines to cut before dark.

When Kenneth Rexroth read the pamphlet, he favorably compared Everson to Jeffers, noting the prophetic language and "organic pulse" of Everson's lines (Davidson 48).

Everson became a conscientious objector during World War II and part of a unique arts community at Civilian Public Service Corps #56 in Waldport,

Oregon. Among the many cultural activities the camp's Fine Arts Group generated were several important publication venues for Western poets, including the Camp Waldport newsletter *The Tide* and the periodical *The Illiterati*. In his 1943 prospectus describing the mission of the Fine Arts Camp at Waldport, Everson wrote, "These are the years of destruction. We offer against them the creative," a mantra taken up in 1957 by Kenneth Rexroth: "Against the ruin of the world, there is only one defense – the creative act" ("Disengagement" 496).

Despite working long hours reforesting the area around Waldport, the Fine Arts Group founded and managed its own press, The Untide Press, which published works by Everson himself, fellow conscientious objector and poet Kenneth Patchen, and others. Not only did Everson become a master handset printer, he refined his poetic voice and went on to shape the San Francisco Renaissance and the Beat literary movement. In 1951, he joined the Dominican Order to become Brother Antoninus. He was sometimes referred to as the "Beat Friar."

Western poets Jeffers and Brother Antoninus were not alone in objecting to the legacy of Manifest Destiny. Much of the ideological protest centered around *Time/Life* publisher Henry Luce's famous 1941 advice to "accept wholeheartedly our duty and our opportunity as the most powerful nation in the world and in consequence to exert upon the world the full impact of our influence, for such purposes as we see fit and by such means as we see fit" (63). The postwar ideology of American exceptionalism increased pressure to conform to a society celebrating technological and economic progress. In response, media critic Marshall McLuhan described a media-induced social neurosis in 1949. He accused the *Time/Life* corporation of encouraging Americans to become "emotionally charged spectators" instead of engaged, informed citizens (15). In order to inoculate against the chauvinism of Luce's American Century, McLuhan prescribed the "untrancing of millions of individuals by millions of individual acts of will" (ibid. 15). In the American West, it was the "little magazine" that became the vanguard in the battle to "untrance" American readers.

In the 1940s, poet Kenneth Rexroth was involved in two important West Coast literary magazines, *Circle* and *Ark*. In addition to staking out a left anti-Stalinist position, part of the debate within Rexroth's sphere of influence centered on the appropriate poetic form populist literature should take. How should literature look if it is joined with revolutionary practice? Radical writers increasingly wished to appear anti-elitist, sympathetic to the working class, and supportive of literary experimentation. Rexroth himself resisted the New Critical ethos because it seemed to "neutralize much of the insurgent force behind the modernist enterprise, leaving behind a poetry of brilliant surfaces and technical virtuosity" (Davidson 34–35). What artwork could best contribute to social revolution? Contrary to some perspectives on the political influence of experimental modernism, perspectives that emphasize the potential elitism implicit in the use of obtuse form, Rexroth believed it was the work of surrealist and experimental writers, the work that consciously disrupted formal conventions, that could succeed in disrupting the dominant politics and cultural norms of mid-century America.

The Bay Area magazine *Circle* was at the avant-garde of these concerns: it championed free speech, resisted conformity, and helped develop an insurgent aesthetic, a new literary left. It was published beginning in 1944, in Berkeley, by George Leite, who was sometimes assisted by Bern Porter, an atomic bomb–era physicist turned experimental artist. Leite, like many of the writers he published in his magazine (including Kenneth Rexroth, Philip Lamantia, and William Everson), was a conscientious objector during World War II. Like his fellows, Leite was an anarcho-pacifist. He believed that any violence, especially that perpetrated by war, was a form of authoritarian control. The masses could not be subdued through force, state control, or propaganda; instead, if each individual was awakened, "untranced," people would enter freely into an enlightened social contract with one another. Unlike Old Left literature, notable for its propagandistic style, its realism, and its socialist conversion narratives, New Left literature tended to perform its cultural work by changing the reader's psyche through a combination of romantic mysticism and surrealism.

Perhaps its most important legacy was the way *Circle* advocated a repositioning of cultural centers from east to west; a "remapping" of literary and social space. Leite and Porter explain their position in this editorial statement from the inaugural volume of *Circle:*

> A circle can be measured beginning at any point: we decided to start our measure on the West Coast. There are many reasons for this choice: much excellent work is being done here without local representation.... We believe that to be of any value a work of art, whether poetry or prose, must be alive and virile; we are temperamentally unable to accept dullness. (Leite, 1)

The postwar left in California developed what historian Daniel Belgrad calls a "culture of spontaneity," a new humanism rooted in an alternate metaphysics (5). In bebop, gestural painting, modern dance, and, above all, Beat writing, spontaneity became a cultural style that resisted rationalism, mass cultural materialism (think *Time* magazine) and dullness, or conformity. Surrealism, especially, could awaken people to a world outside social constraint. It could untrance the spellbound masses. Within the surrealist framework, art did not change culture by producing propaganda in the service of the revolution; art changed culture by reawakening individual conscience. Writers whose work was published in *Circle* – including Rexroth, Lamantia, and Everson, along with Henry Miller, Kenneth Patchen, Anais Nin, e.e. cummings, and Robert Duncan – largely "forsook the topical nature of realist art in favor of the more 'abstract' project of transforming ... awareness" (ibid. 21).

In order to establish a new critical school of thought in the West, *Circle* editors Leite and Porter believed uncompromisingly in freedom of expression. Again, from their first issue:

> It is one of our major hopes in this world-wide struggle for freedom that there will be included a possible freedom of literary expression, which so far has existed in the Constitution alone. (Leite, 2)

Leite produced a total of ten issues of *Circle* until he went broke in 1948. Other little magazines continued with *Circle*'s example: the magazine *Berkeley* published by Bern Porter; *The Illiterati* published by the conscientious objector camp in Waldport, Oregon; *Ark*, published by Kenneth Rexroth's Anarchist Circle; and *City Lights*, published by Peter Martin.

From 1952 to 1955, *City Lights* published film and cultural criticism, poems, short fiction, and philosophical essays. The goal of heightening consciousness is made clear in poet Robert Duncan's "An Open Letter to CITY LIGHTS," published in the magazine's first issue in July 1952. The magazine's purpose, he wrote, should help citizens and artists understand "what we are" and "to make the city conscious of itself ... Now what I like about the idea of CITY LIGHTS at this point is that it invites us all to turn from the manufacture of culture ... back to the field of experience" (1). By choosing Duncan's open letter to introduce his first issue, Peter Martin endows the magazine with a widely recognized bohemian, antiauthoritarian tone. In 1944, Duncan had achieved notoriety for his essay "The Homosexual in Society," published in the magazine *politics*, in which he calls for a gay rights movement. Duncan's *City Lights* letter also established the existential nature of the magazine by insisting that the editorial focus remain "alive" with the experiences of the city, "experience" being the central touchstone of meaning-making of the avant-garde artistic left (ibid. 1). In its third issue, editor Herbert Kaufman recalls Duncan's introductory injunction in the essay "A Note on Reading Poems." To read a poem, Kaufman explains, is to enter an existential situation in which we "catch momentarily the essence of an experience" and "extend our accountability" (37). "What happens afterward," Kaufman concludes, "depends upon the success" of the poem (ibid. 38).

What Peter Martin and little magazine editors like him hoped would happen afterward was the "untrancing" of America. The little magazine supported experimental literature, nonconformist thought, and existential-ist values. The political, philosophical, and artistic ground these magazines laid shifted the nation's literary consciousness from east to west and made possible what Lawrence Ferlinghetti called "antiwar, anarchist ... antiau-thoritarian, civil libertarian attitudes, coupled with a new experimentation in the arts" (quoted in Schwartz 374). It was the cultural work of the little magazine that made the San Francisco Renaissance and Beat literature pos-sible; the little magazine helped shape the mid-century West into a literary utopia, fashioning itself to be what political scientist Lucy Sargisson calls a "critical" or "transgressive" utopia: a space with "subversive and trans-formative potential," a space with a dual function, one from which social critique can be mounted and alternative political spaces can be created (3).

In 1953, aspiring poet and painter Lawrence Ferlinghetti was coming home up Columbus Avenue in San Francisco's North Beach neighborhood when he met Peter Martin, a San Francisco State sociology instructor and publisher of the small film and literary magazine *City Lights*. Both men were political radicals: Martin, the son of an assassinated Italian anarchist, was determined to make books affordable for the underclass, and Ferlinghetti, a World War II veteran whose tour of duty took him to Nagasaki days after the bombing, was a radical pacifist. On that June morning in 1953, with a handshake and a $1,000 investment, Ferlinghetti and Martin became co-owners of a utopian ideal: a "left-leaning, anti-authoritarian bookshop and publishing house," the first in the nation to sell only paperback books (Emblidge 31).

Martin sold his share of the bookstore to Ferlinghetti and left San Francisco in 1955, and Ferlinghetti continued to fine-tune his vision of the bookshop. Like his own poetry, it was to become a space from which to crit-icize social norms and creatively construct alternative aesthetics. Informed by a tradition of political and literary bohemianism, San Francisco, by the mid-twentieth century, was the perfect setting in which to grow a utopian poetic and publishing movement.

Like the booksellers he so admired from his days in Paris studying at the Sorbonne on the GI Bill, Ferlinghetti soon began publishing books on the City Lights imprint. The press and the inaugural Pocket Poets Series became the central publishing venue for Beat poets like Allen Ginsberg, Gregory Corso, and Ferlinghetti himself. He also introduced readers to an inter-national avant-garde with translations of Russian, German, and Spanish poets. Beat and San Francisco Renaissance literature is often rightly criti-cized for marginalizing and objectifying women writers, but before 1960, Ferlinghetti's press had published Marie Ponsot, Denise Levertov, and Diane DiPrima. The iconic black-and-white cover design and pocket-sized format signaled a new direction in Western American poetry: it was avant-garde, it was international, and it challenged political and aesthetic restrictions. Best of all, the paperback books were affordable, putting poetry in the hands and pockets of the masses. "The aim," Ferlinghetti explained, "was to publish across the board, avoiding the provincial and the academic.... I had in mind rather an international, dissident, insurgent ferment" (Ferlinghetti, *City Lights Pocket Poets Anthology* i). Ferlinghetti's own collection of poetry, *Pictures of the Gone World*, inaugurated the series and firmly identified Ferlinghetti with the San Francisco Renaissance poets. What began as a series of meetings, readings, and poetic happenings in the 1950s in and around the city burgeoned into a poetic movement that was characterized by a revision of the romantic aesthetic. Poets like Kenneth Rexroth, William Everson, Allen Ginsberg, Jack Spicer, Gary Snyder, Helen Adam, Joanne Kyger, and Ferlinghetti himself evoked emotional, sensual, and "primitive" contact with nature and self, but updated it with neo-surrealism: "Dada would have loved a day like this/with its light-bulb sun/which shines so differently/for different people" (Ferlinghetti Pictures 23). A contemporary interest in existential philosophy, Buddhism, mysticism, and progressive politics surfaced among Renaissance poets: Gary Snyder's 1959 poem "Riprap" exhorts the reader to experience the poem like a Zen koan: "Lay down these words/before your mind like rocks" (Charters, 290). Many were influenced by Dylan Thomas' famed readings and by jazz; the Renaissance poets developed poems for performance and oral delivery. There was a heightened sense of populism, evidenced by Ferlinghetti's 1961 description of North Beach poetry as that which "should be called street poetry ... getting poetry back into the street where it once was, out of the classroom, out of the speech department, and – in fact – off the printed page" (Ferlinghetti, 124).

Each Renaissance poet developed a specific style, and Ferlinghetti's has been described as an American boulevardier, the biting, satirical "café poem" modeled after French populist poet Jacques Prévert. The twenty-seven poems collected in *Pictures of the Gone World* underscore Ferlinghetti's search for existential authenticity, his deep interest in art history, and the nature of representation. Often, the poems conflate personal observations with painterly ones: "Sarolla's women in their picture hats/stretched upon his canvas beaches/beguiled the Spanish/ Impressionists/And they were fraudulent/ pictures/of the world/the way the light played on them/creating illusions/of love? /I cannot help but think/that their 'reality'/was almost as real as/my memory of today" (Ferlinghetti, *Pictures of the Gone World* n.p.).

Ferlinghetti may not have received much attention for *Pictures of the Gone World*, but by 1957 his reputation as a publisher of avant-garde poetry was growing. Among the many poets with whom Ferlinghetti cultivated a relationship was Allen Ginsberg. The poet–publisher collaboration resulted in *Howl*, the fourth book in City Light's Pocket Poets Series. Ferlinghetti was charged with publishing and distributing obscene material and subsequently arrested by the San Francisco Police. The *Howl* trial made international headlines and Ferlinghetti, defended by the American Civil Liberties Union (ACLU), became known as a spokesperson for free speech. The final verdict, handed down in October 1957, judged Ferlinghetti not guilty, and his fame and the notoriety of City Lights Bookstore and press garnered worldwide attention.

After the *Howl* trial, Ferlinghetti continued his efforts at rendering poetry accessible, open, and, above all, oral. Along with poet Kenneth Rexroth and the Cellar Jazz Quintet of San Francisco, he performed and recorded the Long Play (LP) Poetry Reading at the Cellar. In 1958 New Directions published *A Coney Island of the Mind*, which included seven poems written expressly for jazz accompaniment, including the hauntingly rhythmic "I am Waiting." Here Ferlinghetti evokes American frontier ideology embodied in the American West: "I am waiting for someone/to really discover America/ and wail/and I am waiting/for the discovery/of a new symbolic western frontier/"). In this poem, Ferlinghetti mixes political observation with characteristic humor ("and I am waiting/for the American Eagle/to really spread its wings/and straighten up and fly right") with an ironic pastoral ("and I am waiting for the green mornings to come again/youth's dumb green fields come back again") and an environmental ethos (and I am waiting/for forests and animals/to reclaim the earth as theirs/ ... and I am awaiting/perpetually and forever/a renaissance of wonder" (49–50).

Ferlinghetti explained that these poems "should be considered as spontaneously spoken 'oral messages' rather than as poems written for the printed page" (Ferlinghetti, *Coney Island* 48). *A Coney Island of the Mind* became an instant best seller, and at more than one million copies sold, is one of the all-time best-selling volumes of poetry. By insisting on a wide-open poetry of engagement, Ferlinghetti succeeded in taking poetry out of the classroom and into the streets. As he wrote after being acquitted of obscenity charges in 1957, his mission as a poet and publisher was to challenge the "barren, polished poetry and well-mannered verse which had dominated many of the major poetry publications" (Ferlinghetti, 255). The press he founded in 1955 still thrives. The influence Ferlinghetti had on poetry in the American West cannot be overstated; as a poet he was a central figure in the San Francisco Renaissance; as a publisher, he promoted the new "wide-open poetry" to generations of readers.

Among these wide-open poets is Allen Ginsberg. In October 1955, Ginsberg first read his autobiographical poem *Howl* to an appreciative San Francisco audience. Ferlinghetti was there, and the next day sent him a telegram that read: "I greet you at the beginning of a great career. When do I get the manuscript?" Even though he thought of Ferlinghetti as that "square bookstore owner," the telegram was deeply symbolic for Ginsberg, who recognized the echo of another famous note. In 1855, Ralph Waldo Emerson had written Walt Whitman in praise of *Leaves of Grass*, in a note that read in part, "I greet you at the beginning of a great career" (Raskin 19). Ginsberg counted Whitman among his most powerful influences, evident in Ginsberg's search for the meaning of American democracy, his fully bodied poetic references, and his long, Whitmanesque lines cataloguing mundane observations. Although born in New Jersey and educated at Columbia, Ginsberg found his poetic home in San Francisco. When he arrived on the West Coast in 1954, he met Kenneth Rexroth, who urged him to drop formal poetic meter and write for himself. Like many poets before and after him, Ginsberg had found in the West a utopian ideal: a place from which to mount social criticism and to simultaneously reinvent self and society.

*Howl* is one of the most widely read poems of the second half of the twentieth century. In it, the narrator observes the collective madness of his peers whose voices were silenced by a society that pressed mechanization, conformity, and materialism. Part I famously begins: "I saw the best minds of my generation destroyed by madness, starving/hysterical naked,/ dragging themselves through the negro streets at dawn looking for an/angry fix, angelheaded hipsters burning for the ancient heavenly connection to the/starry dynamo in the machinery of night" (21). Like McLuhan before him, Ginsberg diagnosed a social illness and recommended treatment: an "untrancing" of individuals through individual acts of will. As Ginsberg explained in a letter to fellow poet Richard Eberhart in 1956,

> *Howl* is an "affirmation" of individual experiences of God, sex, drugs, absurdity ... an affirmative act of mercy and compassion, which are the basic emotions of the poem. The criticism of society is that 'Society' is merciless. The alternative is private, individual acts of mercy. The poem is one such

In Whitmanesque fashion, Ginsberg used long lines to, as he wrote, "free speech for emotional expression" (42). The logic among often surreal images is associative, and the rhythm moves between incantation ("The world is holy! The soul is holy! The skin is holy!") to freneticism ("Moloch! Moloch! Robot apartments! invisible suburbs! skeleton treasuries! /blind capitals! demonic industries! spectral nations! invincible/madhouses! granite cocks! monstrous bombs!") (27–28).

Ginsberg's *Howl and Other Poems* was published in November 1956 as number four in City Lights' Pocket Poets Series. It was seized by the San Francisco Collector of Customs in March 1957 on suspicion of obscenity.

In June 1957 City Lights clerk Shigeyoshi Murao was arrested for selling a copy to an undercover inspector. The jury trial began in August of that same year, and after two months of high-profile testimony, Judge Clayton Horn handed down the decision: "The freedoms of speech and press are inherent in a nation of free people," he wrote. "I do not believe that *Howl* is without redeeming social importance" (Horn 197). Although it contained "unorthodox ideas" and "coarse language," Judge Horn agreed that the poem was a clear "indictment of those elements in modern society destructive of the best qualities of human nature" (197). Ginsberg and Ferlinghetti made their mark; a new romantic poetry took hold in the American West, in which the development of individual consciousness became the antidote to the deadened, machine-driven world. Ginsberg's poetry, along with the poetry of Philip Lamantia, Michael McClure, Robert Duncan, and Gregory Corso, signaled a departure from the modern verse that dominated the New York publishing scene. There was plenty of criticism from the Eastern literary establishment. Ferlinghetti, however, continued to champion Bay Area poets: "well fuckem," he swears in a 1957 letter to Allen Ginsberg, "and fuck the partisan review ... we'll make it here in SF" (Morgan and Peters, 55).

By the early 1960s, the Bay Area literary scene had developed into a utopian space. Surreal, semi-confessional, and romantic poetic forms began to dominate. Poetry readings, small presses, and independent bookshops flourished. The "left coast" little magazine had seeded the ground for a bountiful bohemianism. The progressive cliques of writers, artists, and publishers, however, actively and sometimes hostilely excluded women. Male bonding was privileged in literary circles, and women were most often figured as sexual objects, as aesthetic inspiration, or as the reviled Other. In 1957, Denise Levertov attended a San Francisco reading during which Jack Spicer read a poem from his new series *Admonitions*. "The female genital organ is hideous," Spicer read, "We/don't want to be moved" (qtd. in Davidson, 172). Levertov responded with the poem "Hypocrite Women," which refers to Spicer as "a white sweating bull of a poet" who "told us/our cunts are ugly" (poetryfoundstion.org/levertov).

Women poets, of course, had long been subject to prevailing misogynist sentiment. For centuries, their capacity for poetic invention was thought to be inferior. Moreover, after World War II, women became associated with the Beat's protest against middle-class conformity and suburban life. Add to that the mythos of a West understood as a space for the exercise of male freedom and rebellion, and woman as the agent of domestication. Despite all this, there were a number of active women poets. It is just difficult to find their stories. Michael Davidson points to the privileged narrative of male poetic activity in the mid-century American West. When we hear women's voices, he explains, they are most often telling the stories of their male counterparts – Joanne Kyger's travels with Gary Snyder, or Carolyn Cassady's revelations about Neal Cassady, for example. But if we closely examine the fabric of Western poetic reinvention, many women emerge as crucial participants. Ruth Witt-Diamant is one of those women.

Witt-Diamant began her career as a professor of English at San Francisco State University in 1931 and began hosting lively poetry readings at her home on San Francisco's Willard Street. Her guests included Dylan Thomas, Marianne Moore, Robert Duncan, Langston Hughes, Allen Ginsberg, Anaïs Nin, and most often her friend Kenneth Rexroth. She established SFSU's Poetry Center in 1954, which quickly became the center of poetic activity in the region. Witt-Diamant herself became, according to Lewis Ellingham and Kevin Killian, "the most powerful figure in the postwar poetry world of San Francisco" (53). Although *she* was a highly visible figure during these years, women writing and publishing poetry between the war and the feminist revolution were rendered nearly invisible by the enabling fiction of female exclusion. There are, however, some notable exceptions, and if one retells the story, their dynamism and poetic influence are revealed.

Like most poets of the San Francisco Renaissance, many of the women poets were drawn from elsewhere by the city's poetry scene. Helen Adam came to the Bay Area via New York from her native Scotland. She met other local poets after attending Robert Duncan's poetry workshop in 1953, and soon became an active member of the Spicer-Duncan circle. Adam and Duncan developed a friendship and a regular correspondence. Duncan describes the profound influence her work had on him as "the wonder of the world of the poem itself, breaking the husk of my modernist pride and shame" (qtd. in Finch). Adam's work was informed by her extensive study in bardic tradition, lore, and language; her long poetic ballads are populated with werewolves, witches, and cautionary tales about the snares of love. She regularly read her work alongside Allen Ginsberg and Jack Spicer, but most of her poems remained out of print until 2007 when the National Poetry Foundation published *A Helen Adam Reader*. In it, editor and biographer Kristin Prevallet recovers Adam's extensive work and describes her influence not just on the San Francisco Renaissance and the Beats, but on the New York School and the Black Mountain Poets as well. Adam is among only four women (along with Denise Levertov) to be anthologized in Donald Allen's 1959 *The New American Poetry, 1945–1960*.

Like Adam, poet Joanne Kyger became part of the Spicer-Duncan circle in the late 1950s. Both were mystics, of a sort: Adam gave celebrated tarot card readings, while Kyger was a serious student of Zen Buddhism. In San Francisco she moved into the East West House where she lived with other students of Asian ideas and culture, including San Francisco Renaissance poet Philip Whalen. In 1958 Kyger gave a breakthrough reading to a mostly male audience at a Spicer-Duncan gathering. She read "The Maze," a poem in which the narrator's successful journey through a garden maze is held in relief against a woman, presumably Homer's Penelope, who is driven mad by the expectation of her long-suffering fidelity: "She tortures/the curtains of the window/shreds them/like some/insane insect/creates a/demented web/from the thin folds/her possessed fingers." In "The Maze," Kyger began a sustained exploration of Penelope. In other early poems, Kyger rejected the passive Penelope, and reimagined her instead as an active, creative, and erotic being surrounded by men – much like Kyger herself. Penelope became a powerful metaphor for female empowerment; she was "creating herself as a fold in her tapestry" (Kyger 31). Kyger traveled throughout Japan (with her then-husband Gary Snyder) and India (with Ginsberg and Peter Orlovsky) between 1960 and 1964; in 1965, her first collection *The Tapestry and the Web* was published. She went on to write more than twenty books, including the celebrated travel memoir *Strange Big Moon: Japan and India Journals, 1960–1964.*

Other women poets participated in the San Francisco Renaissance and Beat scene: Lenore Kandel, whose 1966 poem pamphlet *The Love Book* became infamous after being confiscated for obscenity, and Diane DiPrima, who coedited *The Floating Bear* newsletter in New York with LeRoi Jones (Amiri Baraka) before moving to San Francisco in 1969 to become a prolific Beat poet and memoirist. Part of the reason women poets were either invisible or exceptional before 1970 was the lack of publishing venues. In 1969, however, the first feminist press in the United States, Shameless Hussy Press, was founded in Berkeley.

Modern poetry in the American West considered the complex ways landscape stood in for human freedoms. Much of the poetry lamented the loss of freedom in the face of increasing mechanization. After World War II, the West became the site from which a new romantic poetry emerged that resisted conformity and mechanization, and invented a new utopia.

## Works Cited

Belgrad, Daniel. *Culture of Spontaneity: Improvisation and the Arts in Postwar America.* Chicago: University of Chicago Press, 1998.

Brophy, Robert. "Robinson Jeffers." *A Literary History of the American West.* Texas Christian University Press, 1987. 398–415. Rpt. in *Poetry Criticism.* Ed. Carol T. Gaffke and Margaret Haerens. Vol. 17. Detroit: Gale Research, 1997. *Literature Resource Center.* Web. Feb. 16, 2015.

GIOIA WOODS

Duncan, Robert. "An Open Letter to CITY LIGHTS." City Lights. July 1952.

Emblidge, David M. 2005. "City Lights Bookstore: A Finger in the Dike." *Publishing Research Quarterly*. Vol. 21, no. 4: 30–39.

Ferlinghetti, Lawrence. *Coney Island of the Mind*. New York: New Direction, 1958.
*Pictures of the Gone World*. San Francisco, CA: City Lights Books, 1955, 1995.

Davidson, Michael. *The San Francisco Renaissance: Poetics and Community at Mid-century*. New York: Cambridge University Press, 1989.

Ellingham, Lewis and Kevin Killian. *Poet be Like God: Jack Spicer and the San Francisco Renaissance*. Middletown, CT: Wesleyan University Press, 1998.

Finch, Annie. "Helen Adam and Jack Spicer: Birds of the Fifties." Harriet: A Poetry Blog. April 26, 2009. Accessed Feb. 2, 2015 (www.poetryfoundation.org/harriet/2009/04/helen-adam-and-jack-spicer-some-other-fifties/).

Jeffers, Robinson. *The Collected Poetry of Robinson Jeffers, Vol. 3, 1939–1962*. Ed. Tim Hunt. Redwood City, CA: Stanford University Press, 1991.
*Selected Poems*. New York: Vintage, 1965.

Kaufman, Herbert. "A Note on Reading Poems." *City Lights*. Spring 1953.

Kyger, Joanne. *The Tapestry and the Web*. San Francisco: Four Seasons Foundation, 1965.

Leite, George. 1944. Circle. Berkeley: s.n.

Luce, Henry R. 1941. "The American Century." *Life Magazine*. Vol. 10, no 7. February 17: 61–65.

McGrath, Thomas, "Letter to an Imaginary Friend." In Alison Deming (ed.) *Poetry of the American West: A Columbia Anthology*. New York: Columbia University Press, 1996. 155–160.

McLuhan, Marshall. 1949. "The Psychopathology of Time and Life." *Neurotica*. Vol. 5, Autumn: 5–16.

Morgan, Bill and Nancy J. Peters (eds.). *Howl on Trial: The Battle for Free Expression*. San Francisco: City Lights, 2006.

Powell, James A. "William (Oliver) Everson." In Ann Charters (ed.) *The Beats: Literary Bohemians in Postwar America*. Detroit: Gale Research, 1983. *Dictionary of Literary Biography* Vol. 16. Literature Resource Center. Web. Feb. 12, 2015.

Raskin, Jonah. *American Scream: Allen Ginsberg's Howl and the Making of the Beat Generation*. Berkeley: University of California Press, 2004.

Rexroth, Kenneth. "Disengagement: The Art of the Beat Generation." In Ann Charters (ed). *Beat Down to Your Soul*. New York: Penguin Books, 2001. 494–508.

Sargisson, Lucy. 2000. *Utopian Bodies and the Politics of Transgression*. New York: Routledge.

Schwartz, Walter. *New Directions in Poetry, 32*. New York: New Directions Publishing Corporation, 1976.

Swenson, May. "Bison Crossing Near Mt. Rushmore." In Alison Deming (ed.) *Poetry of the American West: A Columbia Anthology*. New York: Columbia University Press, 1996. 146–147.

# 9

LEE CLARK MITCHELL

# Noir fiction and the Western city

Nothing dictates that noir narratives require a Western setting even if they seem to occur more regularly in Los Angeles than other urban locales. Part of the West's attraction for noir was due to the influence of Dashiell Hammett, whose stories first appeared in the early 1920s in *Black Mask* magazine, the most successful of pulp monthlies. His Continental Op (like the author) worked as an investigator in San Francisco and shared a kinship with the dime novel heroes of decades before, the lone Western cowboys and solitary detectives in small towns who operated outside the law, paradoxically to ensure civic order. Hammett transformed that figure into an urban gumshoe working from a shabby office, cruising mean streets shadowed by crime, random violence, and the pressing failures of modern life. When Raymond Chandler inherited Hammett's mantle in the 1930s, he shifted the setting south to Los Angeles and played out the city's Manichean split between high style and low life, glitz and sleaze. Insubstantial housing matched the tinsel-town morals, enhanced by the allure of perfect weather and eye-catching scenery that made opportunity seem as easy as Hollywood promised on the big screen. Moreover, the confluence of Hispanic, Asian, black, and Anglo populations established a set of tensions as dramatic as in any American city.

Converting these possibilities into mass-fed dreams were the pulp magazines that emerged after World War I, published to satisfy a largely male, largely lower-class readership no longer engrossed by rural, gunslinger solutions to narrative crises (corruption, brutality) and newly enthralled by a "hard-boiled" vernacular: gritty, brusque prose conveying a freshly cynical view of emotions triggered by violent events. At *Black Mask*, energetic editor Joseph T. Shaw heavily promoted the style, declaring that "In the New Wild West you found private detectives going up against gangsters, gamblers, and crooked cops, all of it taking place in a sun-drenched, slightly surrealistic landscape where newly rich movie people mingled with newly rich criminals while old money millionaires and corrupt politicians looked on"

(Goulart, 96). As Ross Macdonald later observed, confirming the effect of the Western setting on Hammett: "From it emerged a new kind of detective hero, the classless, restless man of American democracy, who spoke the language of the street" (182). Hammett's anonymous hero, a lonely employee of the Continental Detective Agency, became transformed into Sam Spade, a figure even more independent, moody, and disconnected. As well, noir's seductive spider woman first emerges in Hammett's fiction, a self-sufficient moll living by her alluring inscrutability. The plot template of the genre is also Hammett's invention: having an initial crime resonate, proliferating in associations that entrap nearly everyone in a web of guilt. That proliferation may help explain the genre's apparent aimlessness, avoiding sequential narrative in favor of irrelevant events and red herrings. And that aimlessness is compounded by a generic language that scatters stylistic obstacles in the reader's path as a way to both enhance and delay the gratification of a mystery solved.

Hammett inspired countless imitators, not least out of admiration for his authentic details (garnered from his experience as a Pinkerton agent). Yet the taut resilience of his prose and the understated demeanor of his main character were what won a devoted readership. As Dorothy Parker effused about Spade, "after reading *The Maltese Falcon*, I went mooning about in a daze of love such as I had not known for any character in literature since I encountered Sir Launcelot when I hit the age of nine" (136). For the same reason, Gertrude Stein insisted on meeting Hammett when she toured America in the 1930s (O'Brien, 61). Beguiling readers, Hammett reshaped detective fiction, not least by taking the genre west to wild desert towns ("Corkscrew" 1925; "Nightmare Town" 1927). Even his first novel, *Red Harvest* (1929), plays to type in its "rotten town" scenario, of "Personville called Poisonville" near Butte, Montana: "an ugly city of forty thousand people, set in an ugly notch between two ugly mountains that had been all dirtied up by mining" (5). By the time of *The Maltese Falcon*, however, Sam Spade was firmly entrenched in San Francisco, with its international population and varied harbor locale that makes crime seem imminent everywhere, requiring a knowledge of actual streets and locales to fend off real from imagined threats. The novel takes us to the Geary Theater on Sutter Street, or Julius's Castle on Telegraph Hill, and "where Bush Street roofed Stockton before slipping downhill to Chinatown, Spade paid his fare and left the taxicab. San Francisco's night-fog, thin, clammy, and penetrant, blurred the street" (14). That urban precision seems odd as innovation, although Hammett clearly gives the reader an uneasy sense for the city itself, as if to authenticate experience in terms of geographical givens.

This is all part of a pattern Hammett perfects of details emerging over-abundantly as clues. The telltale traces that define the crime in "Bodies

Piled Up" (1923) are not themselves different from Poe's earlier sequences for
C. August Dupin or Conan Doyle's for Sherlock Holmes, as the Continental
Op cautions in language much like those detectives: "there must be – a trail
of some sort. And finding and following such trails is what a detective is
paid to do" (Nolan, *BM* 84). Yet where Hammett differs from his predecessors is in multiplying multiple false trails, relying on overly abundant
misconceived motives, combining willful confusion with artful dissembling
of all sorts. The point of *The Maltese Falcon* is precisely that the point keeps
shifting, as John Cawelti reminds us, "from the search for the client's sister,
to the investigation of his partner's death, to the hunt for the falcon until
finally it turns out that his real problem is not to find the killer but what
to do about a woman he has fallen in love with and who has turned out to
be a murderess" (146). The initiating crime does not in fact stay initiating
but moves us sideways into a different set of mysteries that in turn move us
obliquely once more. And that deliberate haphazardness to Hammett's fiction was only intensified by Chandler, making it difficult to know who killed
whom in *The Big Sleep*, and why. Or as David Lehman observes of the ran-
domness of murder in the novel, "the lack of a motive equal to the enormity
of the deed ... confirms a permanent rupture in the moral order" (129). Part
of the reason for this disconnectedness was simply functional: Chandler
wrote by pulling together separate stories for his novels (a habit initiated,
again, by Hammett). And this aspect of hard-boiled writing may, as Irvin
Faust remarks, be part of its sociocultural appeal: "Rather than plots in the
usual sense, these novels are composed of linked episodes – a sequence of
action-packed scenes, violence, drinking, and tough talk – that resonated
with everyday life in working-class communities. Reviewers' complaints
notwithstanding, these are not necessarily failed plots; they are plots that do
not respect the unities of bourgeois cultural organization and logic" (Smith,
83). Defying the dramatic principle of Chekhov's gun, this description aptly
defines the premise of the genre, given over to ample red herrings and otherwise flagrantly misleading, or at least distracting, elements.

As well, playing against type Hammett created a private eye who was
distinctly unromantic. His Continental Op, appearing in thirty-six stories,
becomes the model over the next half-century of someone about whom we
know very little – whose psychology is buried, whose past rarely emerges,
and who physically appears (in Hammett's version at least) nondescript, a
middle-aged "little fat guy" (Nolan, *BM* 96). Gertrude Stein wondered at
this erasure of character and physicality in a figure so otherwise distinctive:
"Why is it so important, so essentially 'modern,' to 'get rid of human nature,'
as the detective novel does?" (Lehman 14). Unlike nineteenth-century detectives with their hobbies and relationships, Hammett created a modern figure

who has endured in subsequent reincarnations with no other life outside detection, distinctive only in his hard-boiled voice and circumscribed indulgences (smoking, drinking, casual sex). In that sense, the private eye is merely a function of his employment, or as Hammett claimed: "I see him ... a little man going forward day after day through mud and blood and death and deceit – as callous and brutal and cynical as necessary – toward a dim goal, with nothing to push or pull him to it except he's been hired to reach it'" (*DH* ix). The figure of the Western gunman Shane stands behind that of Sam Spade: self-reliant, willing to stand outside the law, given to violence that matches the violence his world presents, but otherwise empty of interest.

Hammett's most distinctive contribution to the noir narrative was his verbal style itself, his Hemingwayesque understatement (although it's unclear who here influenced whom, or the extent to which both may have been swayed by a telegraphic journalistic mode). Instead of trying to match a vibrant plot with a similarly vivid style, Hammett regularly relied on prose that conveyed menace through terse broken English: "That was all. Three dead men, a broken gin bottle, blood" (Nolan, *BM* 81). As Peter Wolfe has claimed, Hammett "doesn't narrate. Instead, he makes things happen to people. Then he makes us wonder where the excitement came from and what it meant" (18). And Hammett's reluctance to describe his characters' thoughts compels us into becoming interpreters, as Dorothy Parker first observed: "He does his readers the infinite courtesy of allowing them to supply descriptions and analyses for themselves ... he sets down only what his characters say, and what they do'" (135). That reliance on laconic description is part of Hammett's (and the subsequent genre's) allure, with even his novels self-aware in their rejection of a sentimental tone. Consider Sam Spade's brush-off of Brigid O'Shaughnessy, "'You're good. You're very good. It's chiefly your eyes, I think, and that throb you get into your voice when you say things like 'Be generous, Mr. Spade'" (37). One might almost presume Spade here was indicting the melodramatic excesses of Hammett's own writerly peers. At other times an arch tone obtrudes, as when Spade returns to his apartment: "His rooms were not greatly upset, but showed unmistakable signs of having been searched" (56). But generally Hammett offers a series of direct statements notable for their restraint in describing what seem like bizarre events, as if willing a certain flat, emotionless expression in the face of the surreal. John Cawelti has nicely remarked of this in a gaudy simile: "like those paintings by Dali where flaming giraffes and melting watches are rendered with the most carefully drawn 'realistic' detail. This interweaving of flat realism and wild fantasy seems to grow out of Hammett's basic sense of life: the vision of an irrational cosmos, in which all the rules, all the seeming solidity of matter, routine, and custom can be overturned in a moment, pervades his work from beginning to end" (166). The breathless tone of events in his fiction is offset by his brusque expression, the "cold, slightly tired tone" (166) that is always calm, never unruffled, registering Spade's own noncommittal, detached perspective. It sometimes appears that rolling a cigarette, which he repeatedly does in *The Maltese Falcon*, takes on an importance equal to that of discovering a corpse; scrutiny seems given even more to the former, as if confirming the need for precise observation, freed from emotional involvement.

One question that arises with Hammett's fiction is why he then pays such close attention to physical description. Consider Elihu Willsson, the "czar of Poisonville" in *Red Harvest*: "The old man's head was small and almost per- fectly round under its close-cut crop of white hair. His ears were too small and plastered too flat to the sides of his head to spoil the spherical effect. His nose also was small, carrying down the curve of his bony forehead. Mouth and chin were straight lines chopping the sphere off" (14). And so on through neck and shoulders, arms, hands, and eyes, with detail that seems oddly excessive, giving no greater insight into the person behind the physical minutiae. Such descriptions abound, as they do in *The Maltese Falcon*, which opens: "Samuel Spade's jaw was long and bony, his chin a jutting v under the more flexible v of his mouth. His nostrils curved back to make another, smaller, v. His yellow-grey eyes were horizontal. The v *motif* was picked up again by thickish brows rising outward from twin creases above a hooked nose" (5). The parallelogram of Spade's face becomes a "motif" without a meaning, although later we are told: "The looseness of his lower lip and the droop of his upper eyelids combined with the v's in his face to make his grin lewd as a satyr's" (179). Still later, "Spade's smile made his v-shaped chin more salient" (194). And later again, as he ruminates: "The clefts at the root of his nose were deep and red. His lips protruded loosely, pouting. He drew them in to make a hard v and went to the telephone" (213).

This descriptive fascination, shifted from urban setting to physical bodies, seems likewise to serve little purpose other than its own elaboration, offer- ing a simple arabesque that deflects attention from immediate concern with the mystery. Moreover, this pattern continues throughout in the flamboyant descriptions of Joel Cairo and Brigid O'Shaughnessy in her Artoise gown, or even of Captain Jacobi, fatally wounded, finally presenting the titular falcon to Spade. Consider Spade's first meeting with the cunning Caspar Gutman: "The fat man was flabbily fat with bulbous pink cheeks and lips and chins and neck, with a great soft eff of a belly that was all his torso, and pendant cones for arms and legs. As he advanced to meet Spade all his bulbs rose and shook and fell separately with each step, in the manner of clus- tered soap-bubbles not yet released from the pipe" (107). The description graciously waylays the reader in a perfectly irrelevant series of elaborations that nonetheless beguile, in a pattern that the best of Hammett's successors would hone to verbal perfection. And such diversions extend to fulsome descriptions of items taken from Cairo's unconscious body, or the bureau drawer Spade secretly opens at Brigid's place, or her room as he searches. It is as if the meticulousness of simple portrayals not only diverted attention but offered a contrast to the imprecise, uncertain morality of the world Spade traverses. And in the detached style of narration that often shifts to the hero's perspective we are granted a clearer insight into how to respond, with restraint, emotional calm, even a certain flippant aplomb. Dialogue itself constitutes a form of moral attention, in the understated, unembellished quality of speech that becomes Hammett's signature. Given these various diversions from plot, it seems appropriate that even the coveted falcon seems irrelevant except as prod (in Alfred Hitchcock's term, a Maguffin, an object empty of significance that nonetheless drives the plot), establishing again a premise for noir. It is as if we were vouchsafed not meaning but merely the persistent desire for it, since the object everyone thirsts for is revealed as ultimately worthless: as Steven Marcus declares, "a mystified object, ... a *rara avis* indeed. As is the fiction in which it is created and contained, the novel by Hammett" (205–206). Still, our readerly appetite remains unabated, even knowing the hoax, as if obsession itself lay at the heart of the novel, inducing a need to know despite the fact that events occur with neither pattern nor discernable rationale.

A different version of noir, if also influential, is represented by James Cain's novels largely void of external description (either setting or personal), which focus instead on varieties of perverse psychological disturbance. Hammett had devised garden-variety crimes of greed, rage, lust, with only the narrowest moral boundary separating the investigator from those he stalks. Cain presents plots that instead heighten moral dilemmas in an automobile culture that everywhere seems an illusory liberation from civilized codes, as if being on the road in California could cancel out more stable moral understandings. In *Double Indemnity* (1936), a fast-talking insurance salesman establishes the sleazy premises of modern life, although Walter Neff's boss stands as a super-ego or agent of fate against whom his wily efforts at murder are unavailing. For Hammett, adultery had been a simple, almost mechanical proceeding, as Spade abruptly beds Brigid O'Shaughnessy after cuckolding his partner with nary an afterthought. For Neff, however, adulterous passion becomes an all-consuming, destructive compulsion, with the very unknowability of women making them ever more alluring.

In fact, Cain transformed the seductive female of Hammett's noir into a genuine femme fatale who ever after helps define the mode. Phyllis

Dietrichson emerges gradually as a monster, driven by murderous impulses that at first seem simply larcenous, then psychopathic when we learn she's killed repeatedly to cover earlier crimes. The odd "diabolism" of the plot that Ross Macdonald observed offers Phyllis as a figure caught between simple greed and murderous delight in killing for its own sake (Skenazy, 44). Compounding this is Neff's perverse desire to pull off the perfect crime. Similarly, in *The Postman Always Rings Twice* (1934), Frank Chambers is lured by Cora into a sadomasochistic affair that has them then plot the death of her husband – although the novel seems to take an eerie delight in all that goes awry (power outages, happenstance police appearances, injuries in a planned car crash, Cora's accidental death). And the absence of any genuine affection is signaled by the lovers' treacherous turning on one another at the merest provocation. Strikingly, both novels' distinctiveness lies in the first-person voice, confessing after the fact to failed crimes that reveal identities each has striven to hide. Or as Walter Neff memorably admits: "I had killed a man, for money and a woman. I didn't have the money and I didn't have the woman. The woman was a killer, out-and-out, and she had made a fool of me" (183). The passion of betrayal here is central to Cain's vision, in novels that each testify as confessionals beyond the grave revealing, in Paul Skenazy's words, "the paradox of confession as a literary form. The book reveals a character whose crime demands deception and secrecy. But in 'coming clean' … the character also creates himself" (50).

Inheriting the hard-boiled mode from Hammett and Cain, Chandler perfected it in his focus on character, style, and, especially, setting in ways his predecessors only hinted at. He seized on Los Angeles for its mix of tawdriness and edenic allure, the land of opportunity become the site of failure, of high-styled presumption colliding with low-life fraud. As William Nolan observes of "that unique landscape known as 'Chandler country,'" it extends "from seedy, paint-blistered beach bungalows to plush Bel Air apartments, from fog-draped piers to smoke-filled bars, from wide, sun-splashed boulevards to dank, narrow tenement hallways, from the broken-scrolled, decaying mansions on Bunker Hill to the foam-wet sands of Malibu" (230). Even more to the point, Chandler wove locale, weather, and mood together so that the twists of plot and the turns of psychology often seem driven as much meteorologically as psychologically. Granted, his early stories largely ignore the urban setting (as if he had not yet discovered this effect), but by the time of "Red Wind" (1938), he opens with "a desert wind blowing that night" (*S&EN* 368), a wind that continues to buffet emotions until the story's conclusion registers it finally dying down. A year later, *The Big Sleep* (1939) opens "with the sun not shining" (*S&EN* 589) and a view of "the old wooden derricks of the oilfield from which the Sternwoods had made their money" (602), linking the exploitation of land with the warped psychology of the Sternwood daughters. And a decade later, Philip Marlowe identifies Los Angeles as a "neon-lighted slum" (*LN&OW* 357), grown even more depressing:

> At La Brea I turned north and swung over to Highland, out over Cahuenga Pass and down on to Ventura Boulevard, past Studio City and Sherman Oaks and Encino.... Tired men in dusty coupes and sedans winced and tightened their grip on the wheel and ploughed on north and west towards home and dinner, an evening with the sports page, the blatting of the radio, the whining of their spoiled children and the gabble of their silly wives. I drove on past the gaudy neons and the false fronts behind them, the sleazy hamburger joints that look like palaces under the colors, the circular drive-ins as gay as circuses with the chipper hard-eyed carhops, the brilliant counters, and the sweaty greasy kitchens that would have poisoned a toad. (*LN&OW* 267)

It is as if Chandler had awoken to the broken promise of California, fed by the Hollywood dream machine, as two-dimensional as the landscape itself – or as Marlowe describes it, "California, the department-store state. The most of everything and the best of nothing" (*LN&OW* 268). Moreover, that duplicitous nature of setting finds a correlative in the verbal dissimulation of the novels' styles, not only their double entendres and bizarre similes but Marlowe's wisecracking patter, a wry cynicism more insistent than Sam Spade's. It is as if Chandler's developing eye for urban surroundings matched a more finely tuned ear for the poetic possibilities of hard-boiled expression itself, even when the laconic wit emerges from a deep dispiritedness about possibilities foreclosed. Hammett had earlier introduced this mode, but infrequently, as when Joel Cairo objects to Spade's "smooth explanation," only to have him respond: "What do you want me to do? Learn to stutter?" (*MF* 99). Chandler compounds that impulse through Marlowe's characteristic smart lip, responding to Carmen Sternwood's opening sally, "Tall, aren't you?" with "'I didn't mean to be.' ... I could see, even on that short acquaintance, that thinking was always going to be a bother to her" (5). But Chandler also treasured strange conceits of expression, compiling lists of bizarre similes he planned to invoke for Marlowe's disillusioned vision. In *The Big Sleep*, "The General spoke again, slowly, using his strength as carefully as an out-of-work show-girl uses her last good pair of stockings" (*S&EN* 593). Or "The gardens seemed deserted. The sunshine was as empty as a headwaiter's smile" (*S&EN* 753). Or famously, the hulking Moose Malloy appears in *Farewell, My Lovely*: "Even on Central Avenue, not the quietest dressed street in the world, he looked about as inconspicuous as a tarantula on a slice of angel food" (*S&EN* 767). If Chandler's outlandish conceits have long been admired, few have observed how fully this stylistic

tic playfully distracts the reader, pulling us out of the narrative flow into a verbal realm where developments occur more intriguingly than in banal plots of mayhem and murder. Words even seem to take on a life of their own, as when a character ends a phone conversation with "Abyssinia," stymying us until we recognize the colloquially cadenced "I'll be seeing you" (*S&EN* 496).

Chandler had a sensitive ear for expression, although having spent early years abroad, "I had to learn American just like a foreign language. To use it I had to study it and analyze it. As a result, when I use slang, colloquialisms, snide talk, or any kind of offbeat language, I do it deliberately. The literary use of slang is a study in itself" (*RCS* 80). Much of his deadpan humor involves slang and strained analogies that enjoyably divert our attention even as they disarm us. Regularly engaging the reader as Emerson notably did, Chandler relies on rhetorical rhythms that dispose us to him before we quite understand what is being said, simply by virtue of the meticulousness of prose that creates a calm descriptive surface, before exploding with similes that disrupt all we have seen. Consider how excess disrupts understatement in *The Big Sleep* in the initial description of General Sternwood's greenhouse, before quickly shifting registers: "The air was thick, wet, steamy and larded with the cloying smell of tropical orchids in bloom. The glass walls and roof were heavily misted.... The light had an unreal greenish color, like light filtered through an aquarium tank. The plants filled the place, a forest of them, with nasty meaty leaves and stalks like the newly washed fingers of dead men" (*S&EN* 592). That overheated, over-rhetorical realm occurs just after Marlowe chances upon Carmen Sternwood, as if to offer a physical setting for the psychological realm Marlowe encounters. Where Hammett seems suitably detached in terse descriptions, Chandler is once again fully invested, not only in setting but in inflections themselves.

The willingness to amble stylistically corresponds as well to Chandler's aimless plots, filled even more than Hammett's with diversionary ploys and narrative digressions. Marlowe authenticates this mode as he muses after somebody's death: "I went upstairs again and sat in my chair thinking about Harry Jones and his story. It seemed a little too pat. It had the austere simplicity of fiction rather than the tangled woof of fact" (*S&EN* 717). And that quality of "tangled woof" is something Chandler elaborates in his novels as another means of sustaining delight, keeping us alert. The secrets of the past regularly emerge in partial view, just as psychotic behavior reveals an obsessive line, although Chandler regularly ensures that the plot is reviewed, catching the reader up, explaining what has been obscured. In each of his novels, he re-describes what has occurred, attentive to the reader's confusion at plots that work by means of indirection and apparent aimlessness. Partly, that confusion owed to Chandler's habit of cannibalizing stories to compose his novels, but it is also meant to clarify the "lightning struck on every page," as Billy Wilder observed of his style (*World* 47).

By extending Hammett's palette, Chandler figured out other ways of delaying the plot, leading to Margaret Atwood's wry effusion: "An affair with Raymond Chandler, what a joy! Not because of the mangled bodies and the marinated cops and hints of eccentric sex, but because of his interest in furniture" (Smith 103). Where Hammett had passed his keen eye over hotel lobbies and city streets, Chandler scrutinized more carefully the clothing, interiors, and other apparently trivial metonymies that define social snobbery and class divides. Characteristically, he appears as interested in the random details of everyday life as in the secrets that form the mysteries Marlowe is hired to solve. Chandler himself explained his premise in recalling how editors edited his style, mistakenly pushing for plot because "their readers didn't appreciate this sort of thing, just held up the action. I set out to prove them wrong. My theory was that readers just *thought* they cared about nothing but the action; that really, although they didn't know it, they cared very little about the action.... The things they remembered, that haunted them, were not for example that a man got killed, but that in the moment of death he was trying to pick a paper clip off the polished surface of a desk, and it kept slipping away from him" (MacShane, 51). That premise of diversionary interest defines nearly all the most interesting aspects of Chandler's fiction, so that even a bet on a roulette table takes on a certain lingering charm: "The ball drifted along the groove, dipped past one of the bright metal diamonds, slid down the flank of the wheel and chattered along the tines beside the numbers. Movement went out of it suddenly, with a dry click. It fell next the double-zero, in red twenty-seven. The wheel was motionless" (*S&EN* 102). The focus on just such extraneous, engagingly rendered moments sustains our fascination in plot, as if the guided tour through the "half-savage country" of Southern California were an invitation (in Dennis Porter's words) "to stop and enjoy the strangeness, viciousness, and luxuriance of the region's flora and fauna" (63). Chandler understood, as others did not, that the mystery was less important than the mysteries of explanation themselves. In *Little Sister*, he even provided his own explanation, in a long description of Marlowe making coffee:

> I cut the flame and set the coffee maker on a straw mat on the table. Why do I go into such detail? Because the charged atmosphere made every little thing stand out as a performance, a movement distinct and vastly important. It was one of those hypersensitive moments when all your automatic movements, however long established, however habitual, become separate acts of will. You

are like a man learning to walk after polio. You take nothing for granted, absolutely nothing at all. (*LN&OW* 438)

The explanation offers a defense for all those moments of descriptive languor that are otherwise indulged. In this regard, Chandler transformed the figure of the private eye from Hammett's Continental Op as a short, fat, cynical figure who simply wants to expedite matters in achieving solutions to unavenged murder into Philip Marlowe, a more sympathetic if driven character but also more conventionally attractive: "Eyes brown. Height six feet, one half inch. Weight about one ninety. Name, Philip Marlowe. Occupation private detective. Well, well, nice to see you, Marlowe. That's all. Next man" (*LN&OW* 460). Marlowe establishes the template of other private eyes who drink to excess, share an eye for the ladies, and remain unmarried with no other interests than solving crime. He also has a certain savoir faire, a knowledge of culture and history, as well as an ear for correct language. As he observes when a client claims, "'I should not have called you, if it were not.' A Harvard boy. Nice use of the subjunctive mood" (*S&EN* 796). At other times, he refers to a repetitive character as "Hemingway," or names a dog Heathcliff. Even more characteristic than this knowing air is Marlowe's idealistic strain, or as someone says, "Phil Marlow … The shop-soiled Galahad" (*S&EN* 1136). Where Hammett's detectives are defined by a wryly cynical professionalism, Marlowe is anything but cool or detached, involving himself as much out of emotional sympathy as from a professional code. Chandler countered the hard-boiled, wisecracking public figure armored against urban disappointment with the solitary self-consciousness of a more generous, even sentimental, perspective on expectations unmet. Consider the death of Spade's partner, Miles Archer, in *The Maltese Falcon*, which bothers Spade very little, and compare the drawn-out poisoning of Harry Jones in *The Big Sleep*, which Marlowe overhears and immediately feels guilty about. Or compare Spade's firm condemnation of Brigid O'Shaughnessy at the novel's conclusion ("I won't play the sap for you," 221) with the more accommodating final response of Marlowe to Vivian Sternwood, encouraging her to get psychiatric help for her psychopathically murderous sister, Carmen. In short, Chandler has transformed the hard-boiled detective into a less hard-boiled (if also less two-dimensional), more conflicted figure capable of keeping the genre alive in different capacities.

The most influential writer to adopt the California setting of Hammett, Cain, and Chandler was Ross Macdonald, who transformed it (if counterintuitively) into a belated locale, haunted by the past. And instead of San Francisco or even the mean streets of L.A., he shifts to the upscale, beachside community of Santa Teresa (a fictional Santa Barbara), as if to showcase the stark divide between possibility and poverty, aspiration and sorry event. As *The Wycherly Woman* (1961) opens in describing this "promised land. Maybe it is for a few. But for every air-conditioned ranch-house with its swimming pool and private landing strip, there are dozens of tin-sided shacks and broken-down trailers where the lost tribes of the migrant workers live. And when you leave the irrigated areas you find yourself in gray desert where nobody lives at all. Only the oil derricks grow there, an abstract forest casting no shade. The steady pumps at their bases nod their heads like clockwork animals" (3). What Chandler introduced via desert wind and strained similes, Macdonald compounds in an even more forceful attention to the link between ecological damage and psychological trauma, in the process anticipating perspectives refined by Wallace Stegner and Edward Abbey into sustained critiques. *The Underground Man* (1971) centers on a wildfire linked to a murder in the present that was itself the result of a tangled series of homicides in the past. And the conflagration precipitated by the murdered son's dropped cigarillo serves as the present's revenge on the death of his father, a past unaccounted for. Regularly, Macdonald adds psychological depth to the motivation of those who employ his P.I., Lew Archer, although that motivation more often emerges through dialogue than description, as if Archer were a camera eye (or rather, ear) attuned to the rhythms of California speech in which disenchantment loomed larger than aspiration. Strangely, that discontent infects not only the urban environment, or characters themselves, but the very form of the detective novel as a belated fictional genre. Macdonald seems to express a nostalgia for the world Hammett and Chandler had treated with cynical eyes, and yet the very terms of that earlier mode are no longer feasible.

Sometimes, this occurs almost as a direct quotation of earlier moments, as when Archer initially enters a room: "The only strangeness was in the pattern of the cloth that covered the chesterfield and the armchair under the lamp: brilliant green tropical plants against a white desert sky, with single eyes staring between the fronds. The pattern changed as I looked at it. The eyes disappeared and reappeared again. I sat down on a batch of them" (63). This seems a clear invocation of the opening of *The Big Sleep*, while shifting the private eye's disorientation from hothouse orchids to tapestry, then compounding the surrealism with solitary eyes that bizarrely peer up, only then to be sat on. Macdonald not only repeatedly invokes Chandler's infatuation with furniture, but compounds it by lending objects a past that corresponds to the determining past of his characters. In another novel, Archer is invited to sit by his client, a woman with various dangerous secrets: "It was a small room, and it was as crowded with coffee- and end-tables, chairs and hassocks and bookcases, as a second-hand furniture store. The horizontal surfaces were littered with gewgaws, shells and framed photographs, vases and pincushions and doilies. If the lady had come down in the world, she'd brought a lot down with her. My sensation of stepping into the past was getting too strong for comfort. The half-armed chair closed on me like a hand" (174). And by the end, we are appropriately told that "The case ended where it began, among the furniture in Mrs. Lawrence's sitting room" (343), almost as if a commentary on Chandler's entire *mise en scene*.

Yet Macdonald is far more psychologically attuned than Chandler, with complicated plots that often turn on Archer's unearthing of family secrets, and of long-vanished criminals who have left emotional scars on his clients. Lost sons and wayward daughters populate the novels, even if by the end nearly everyone seems somehow related, with the present invariably revealed as a fated consequence of past events, often replicating them in the very shape of narrative plotting. One character agrees that "the facts are outrageous": "Are they not. The most outrageous of all is that you can't get away from the past. It's built into one's life. You can't wall it off or deny it or evade it or undo it. It's inescapably and inevitably there, like a deformed child in a secret room of one's house. How I've paid for my foolishness" (*Meet Me*, 180). And the efforts of Archer himself are unavailing, except insofar as he brings clarity to oedipal situations already foredoomed. Or as he once remarks, "I don't believe much in coincidences. If you trace them back far enough, they usually have a meaning" (444). Indeed, his best novel, *The Underground Man*, introduces a missing child as the rationale for Archer's efforts only as a Maguffin, appearing briefly at beginning and end but otherwise simply an engine to generate plot. Yet nearly everyone else in the novel matters just as little, since we never get to know their own mental processes. For a writer so given to irresistible psychological forces, it seems paradoxical that Macdonald succeeds best with the most fleeting of attempts at understanding, confirming how fully everyone has become an extension of everyone else. Still, despite the winning preposterousness of his plots, Macdonald induces belief through style itself, emptying out the personality of Lew Archer (who reveals little of himself) and allowing the reader only a view of events as he sees them, registering the anguish of those he meets.

That "chameleon aspect" of Archer (as Macdonald himself described it) allowed the Private Investigator (P.I.) "to move on various levels of society, ranging from the campus to the slums, and fade in and out of the woodwork on demand, ... and talk the language: a little Spanish in East Los Angeles, a little jive in Watts, a little Levi-Strauss in Westwood" (*SP* 19). Even so, characters cannot finally recreate themselves, for as Macdonald observes, "The Californian escapists of my books drag with them their whole pasts, rattling like chains among the castanets" (*SP* 61). One might even say that the resignation Lew Archer feels registers once again the belatedness of the detective novel itself, as if nothing can be done for him or for the world he hopes to save. Interestingly, however, he holds to a certain standard that Spade and Marlowe themselves articulated, if less wistfully, granting to traditional virtues an allure he hoped to pass on – for courage and loyalty, as he remarks on occasion. Even more than his predecessors, Archer feels committed to ethical values, as he explains: "There had to be a difference between me and the opposition, or I'd have to take the mirror out of my bathroom. It was the only mirror in the house, and I needed it for shaving" (127).

The shape of that wry observation, shifting from sober self-reflection to silly wisecrack, derives from Chandler. But Macdonald more dramatically reveals homage through his style itself, which improves on Chandler's fascination with similes by making them less simply gratuitous, more intimately linked to his novel's themes. Often these have to do with the Californian setting, already transfigured into a psychological force: "The edges of the sky had a yellowish tinge like cheap paper darkening in the sunlight" (*UM* 3). Or "The night died gradually, bleeding away in words" (*WSPA* 282). At other times, similes elicit the compelling hold of the past on the present, as when Archer sits in a bar that "had the air of having been there for a long time … The place had a cozy subterranean quality, like a time capsule buried deep beyond the reach of change and violence. The fairly white-coated waiters, old and young, had a quick slack economy of movement surviving from a dead regretted decade. The potato chips that came with my sizzling steak tasted exactly the same as the chips I ate out of greasy newspaper wrappings when I was in grade school in Oakland in 1920…. The rush and whirl of bar conversation sounded like history" (*MT* 325). For Archer, the literal becomes nearly always figurative, whether landscape is psychologized or conversation echoes some earlier history. As he says, "The past was unwinding and rewinding like yarn which the two of us held between us" (*UM* 231). Perfectly embodying this coalescence for Macdonald is *The Wycherly Woman*, about a daughter literally passing for her own mother because she mistakenly assumes she has killed her, although in fact we discover the murderer was an uncle who actually loved the mother. In Macdonald's universe, we become what we fear, for all our vain efforts to escape.

Clearly, the efforts of Hammett, Cain, Chandler, and Macdonald reveal the increasing reliance of noir fiction on distinctive urban settings. Starting with the heterogeneous populations of Southern California, with its often surreal blend of glamour and tawdriness, these writers defined the intersection of locale, psychology, character, and plot machinations that others would continue to explore in perhaps the most popular of readerly genres – popular, precisely because our urban experiences seem so untoward, unforgiving, unaccommodated. Detective novels ever since have played on the possibilities here transformed, and even when the urban settings of noir mysteries extend to Seattle or Boseman, San Antonio, Detroit, even west Miami Beach, they continue to offer fictional resolutions to our most pressing anxieties. It is the very detail of local settings, offered almost as travelogue, that allows readers to place their own uncertainties into an urban grid, with the private eye projected as once again a figure fighting for justice, however little he understands of that urban environment. As Raymond Chandler observed, "It is not a very fragrant world, but it is the world you live in, and certain writers with tough minds and a cool spirit of detachment can make very interesting and even amusing patterns out of it. It is not funny that a man should be killed, but it is sometimes funny that he should be killed for so little, and that his death should be the coin of what we call civilization" (*LN&OW* 991).

## Works Cited

Cain, James M. *The Postman Always Rings Twice, Double Indemnity, Mildred Pierce, and Selected Stories*. New York: Knopf, 2003.

Cawelti, John G. *Adventure, Mystery, and Romance: Formula Stories as Art and Popular Culture*. Chicago: University of Chicago Press, 1976.

Chandler, Raymond. *Later Novels and Other Writings*. New York: Library of America, 1995. Print.

   *Raymond Chandler Speaking*. Ed. Dorothy Gardiner and Katherine Sorley Walker. Berkeley: University of California Press, 1997. Print.

   *Stories and Early Novels*. New York: Library of America, 1995. Print.

Goulart, Ron. *The Dime Detectives*. New York: Mysterious Press, 1988. Print.

Hammett, Dashiell. *Dashiell Hammett: Complete Novels*. New York: The Library of America, 1999. Print.

   *Dashiell Hammett: Crime Stories and Other Writings*. New York: The Library of America, 2001. Print.

Lehman, David. *The Perfect Murder: A Study in Detection*. New York: Free Press, 1989. Print.

Macdonald, Ross. [Kenneth Millar]. *The Barbarous Coast* (1956). In *Archer in Hollywood*. New York: Alfred A. Knopf, 1967. 347–528. Print.

   *The Drowning Pool*. New York: Garland, 1976. Print.

   *Meet Me at the Morgue*. New York: Alfred A. Knopf, 1953. Print.

   *The Moving Target* (1949). New York: Vintage, 1999. Print.

   *Self-Portrait: Ceaselessly into the Past*. Santa Barbara, CA: Capra Press, 1981. Print.

   *The Underground Man*. New York: Alfred A. Knopf, 1971. Print.

   *The Way Some People Die* (1951). In *Archer in Hollywood*. New York: Alfred A. Knopf, 1967. 171–346. Print.

"The Writer as Detective Hero" (1973). In Robin W. Winks (ed.) *Detective Fiction: A Collection of Critical Essays*. Englewood Cliffs, NJ: Prentice-Hall, Inc., 1980. 179–187. Print.

*The Wycherly Woman* (1961). New York: Vintage Books, 1998.

MacShane, Frank. *The Life of Raymond Chandler*. New York: E. P. Dutton. 1976. Print.

Marcus, Steven. "Dashiell Hammett" (1974). In Glen W. Most and William W. Stowe (eds.) *The Poetics of Murder: Detective Fiction and Literary Theory*. New York: Harcourt Brace Jovanovich, 1983. 197–209.

Nolan, William F. *The "Black Mask" Boys: Masters in the Hard-Boiled School of Detective Fiction*. New York: William Morrow and Co., Inc., 1985. Print.

*Dashiell Hammett: A Casebook*. Santa Barbara, CA: McNally and Loftin, 1969. Print.

O'Brien, Geoffrey. *Hardboiled America: Lurid Paperbacks and the Masters of Noir* (1981). 2nd ed. New York: De Capo P, 1997. Print.

Parker, Dorothy. "Oh Look, A Good Book!" *Constant Reader*. New York: Viking, 1970. 134–136.

Porter, Dennis. *The Pursuit of Crime: Art and Ideology in Detective Fiction*. New Haven, CT: Yale University Press, 1981.

Skenazy, Paul. *James M. Cain*. New York: Continuum, 1989. Print.

Smith, Erin A. *Hard-Boiled: Working-Class Readers and Pulp Magazines*. Philadelphia. PA: Temple University Press, 2000. Print.

Wolfe, Peter. *Beams Falling: The Art of Dashiell Hammett*. Bowling Green, OH: Bowling Green University Popular Press, 1980. Print.

*The World of Raymond Chandler*. Ed. Miriam Gross. London: Weidenfeld and Nicolson, 1977. Print.

# 10

STACEY PEEBLES

# The Western and film

Will Munny enters the saloon and aims his rifle. First he shoots the saloon's owner. "You just shot an unarmed man," exclaims Little Bill Daggett, the town's sheriff and Munny's primary target. "Well, he should have armed himself," replies Munny, "if he's going to decorate his saloon with my friend." That friend is Ned Logan, whose corpse is on display outside the saloon's entrance. Munny confirms that he's a killer of men, but that he's also killed women, children, and "just about everything that walks or crawled at one time or another." And now he's here to kill Little Bill. When the shooting starts, Munny kills a number of Little Bill's men but then finds Bill himself wounded but still alive. Munny stands over him, preparing to shoot one more time. "I don't deserve this," protests Bill. "To die like this. I was building a house." "Deserve's got nothing to do with it," Munny growls, and a moment later, he fires his gun.

The film is *Unforgiven* (1992). On one level, Munny's response is a classic tough-guy comeback, the kind of appropriately biting response that we've come to expect from our masculine protagonists in the moments when life and death hang in the balance. Audiences loved it – as Munny and as the film's director, Clint Eastwood was bringing the full force of his stoic persona to bear, and Gene Hackman as Little Bill exerted a combination of charm and viciousness that always makes for a good villain. This, only their second scene together and the climax of the film, was a literally and figuratively dark encounter punctuated by a great line. Harold Schechter has written about hearing moviegoers in both Colorado and Paris whooping and applauding, enjoying what they saw as a "good old-fashioned shoot-'em-up."

It *is* a great line, and if all you're watching for is to see Eastwood come out on top physically and rhetorically, it serves that purpose. But in fact the line is a radical undoing of the primary purpose of the Western – not to mention a dramatic tradition going back to the ancient Greeks. From its inception in cinema and to a great degree in literature as well, the Western has been all about "deserve." Who deserves what on the frontier, in this liminal

Figure 10.1 Will Munny (Clint Eastwood) prepares to confront Little Bill (Gene Hackman) in *Unforgiven* (Warner Brothers, 1992).

space where justice is not yet fully administered by the law, and who, then, will do that administering? (The liminal space of the city in Greek tragedy, which, as J. P. Vernant argued, is where the values of heroic myth and of the modern polis come into conflict, also gives rise to questions about who deserves what and for what reasons.) If Will Munny is not killing the bad guy because he deserves it – as has happened in countless Westerns since *The Great Train Robbery* (1903) – then what exactly is going on here?

*Unforgiven* has drawn a good deal of scholarly attention, although many scholars note that the film may not be as revisionist as it's been celebrated to be, or the way I've just described it. Carl Plantinga notes that the violence in *Unforgiven* is indeed "[f]ar from regenerative" and that it progresses in a "steady downward spiral, [signaling] increasing loss and despair" (74), and also that the film "implies that the cycle of revenge and retribution is fueled by myth, exaggeration, masculine bravado, and willful misunderstanding" (74, 75). The final shootout, however, changes things, operating as a "compromise and throwback to the conventional Western myth," because although Munny clearly goes too far, "the film supplies Munny with a rationale and a motivation" (77, 78). In the end, Plantinga argues, "[t]he complexity of the [saloon] debacle ... stems from its combination of dramatic satisfaction with emotional and thematic ambiguity.... 'Deserve,' or justice, may have nothing to do with it, but audience desire certainly does" (79–80).

The film itself, then, may ultimately hew closer to the Western ideals that it initially seems to challenge. But even so, Munny's line is still a surprise

and a problem. The popularity and the satisfaction of the Western in literature, film, music, and visual art can be said to rely on many elements: the
aesthetic and thematic appeal of open landscape; the drama inherent in the
violent clash of cultures (whether Native American and white, outlaw and
sheriff, homesteader and cattle driver, to name just a few iterations); and the
historical/political resonance of the concerns of a nascent community in an
area previously unknown to the settlers. But especially in film, the Western
is built on its climactic moment: the violent rendering of justice. This is what
we want to *see* – a person or group of people getting what they deserve
even though they are beyond the reach of an established judicial system.
This is what we, the audience, deserve as well, to spin Plantinga's point a
different way.

And to satisfy that desire, we look to the Western hero, whose violent
righting of wrong has always been his most compelling and potentially
disturbing feature. Richard Slotkin has, of course, famously addressed just
this quality, as has Robert Warshow, who compared the Western hero to
the gangster. That other classic American cinematic figure is a mirror image
of the Westerner, he argued: twitchy and ambitious where the Westerner is
calm and unmotivated by financial or social success; a figure made by the
city instead of the frontier; and someone who shoots first and often rather
than only when necessary. But they both do shoot, and they are both violent
men. Nonetheless, because of these differences, the Westerner has "an image
of personal nobility that is still real for us" (707).

"What does the Westerner fight for?" Warshow asked. "We know he is
on the side of justice and order, and of course it can be said that he fights
for these things. But such broad aims never correspond exactly to his real
motives; they only offer him opportunity.... What he defends, at bottom, is
the purity of his own image – in fact his honor." And yet, noted Warshow,
the most interesting Westerns complicate that sense of honor or nobility.
"The truth is," he wrote, "that the Westerner comes into the field of serious
art only when his moral code, without ceasing to be compelling, is seen also
to be imperfect. The Westerner at his best exhibits a moral ambiguity which
darkens his image and saves him from absurdity; this ambiguity arises from
the fact that, whatever his justifications, he is a killer of men" (708).

The appeal of the Western hero, then, is akin to the appeal of a monarch –
an exceptional figure who acts as a font of order and justice, thus serving
as a model and a leader for those around him. After all, explains Socrates
in Plato's *Republic*, people "always tend to set up one man as their special
leader, nurturing him and making him great." The trouble comes, Socrates
notes, when good leadership degenerates into tyranny. And when does that
start to happen? It happens, Socrates says, "when the leader begins to act

out the tale that is told in connection with the temple of Lycaean Zeus in Arcadia" – "that the man who tastes of the single morsel of human inwards [innards] cut up with those of other sacrificial victims must necessarily become a wolf" (244). Lycaon, it is said, founded a sanctuary in Arcadia and offered a child as sacrifice; he was punished by being turned into a wolf, or *lykos* (469n26). Human blood, then, spilled in piety – or perhaps in honor – is what taints the good leader. The hero becomes the wolf, and that honor becomes complicated or lost entirely.

In the earliest Westerns, however, those complications were largely absent, and Westerns featured the spectacle of violence rather than its ambiguities or complexities. In Edwin S. Porter's one-reeler *The Great Train Robbery* (1903), the outlaws rob the train, ruthlessly killing a few innocent bystanders in the process, and are in turn gunned down by the pursuing heroes at the film's end. The eleven-minute film lacks the time – or, for that matter, the close-ups – that would allow either heroes or outlaws to deepen into more complex characters. It would be thirty-six years before the release of what I'll argue is the Western's "classic of classics," one praised for the elegant simplicity of its revenge plot as well as for the provocative complexity of its depiction – and interrogation – of societal, moral, gender, and even racial norms. That Western is *Stagecoach* (1939), a film that culminates and then recreates a fascination with the Western hero on screen and sets narrative patterns in place that later filmmakers might emulate or rebel against, but to which they would necessarily react.

When the Western on film was born with *The Great Train Robbery* in 1903, "Wild West" figures like Buffalo Bill were still alive but the frontier itself was, at least in the popular conception and that based on Frederick Jackson Turner's frontier thesis, entering the realm of storytelling. Convenient, then, that the movies came along just in time to pick up that mythologizing and run with it. Buffalo Bill himself turned to movie stardom in *The Adventures of Buffalo Bill* (1917), and Wyatt Earp appeared in *The Half-Breed* (1916). Actors like William S. Hart, Tom Mix, and Bronco Billy became the first big stars of the genre, and by the time James Cruze's big-budget epic *The Covered Wagon* came out in 1923, audiences knew to expect sweeping landscapes, dramatic conflict, and suspenseful set pieces. The film, set in 1848 and following a caravan of covered wagons heading from Kansas to Oregon, required (in the words of the film's program) "weeks of preparation, painstaking research, gigantic expenditure and a responsibility almost unequalled in the history of the films" (*"The Covered Wagon"*), and features a love triangle that is generally less interesting than the large-scale spectacle of buffalo hunts, river fordings, and prairie fires.

The success of Westerns like *The Covered Wagon* would pave the way for writers and directors interested in making characters and relationships as enthralling as their special effects. John Ford had his first big success the next year, in 1924, with *The Iron Horse*, a film about the construction of the Transcontinental Railroad that was shot on location. At twenty-nine, Ford had already directed more than fifty films, a number of them more forgettable Westerns. *The Iron Horse* is rightly remembered as a significant film, but Ford's first masterwork is *Stagecoach*, a film that marks the beginning of Hollywood iconicity for star John Wayne and serves as a milestone of cinema's deepening interest in the intersections of heroism, justice, violence, and what different people deserve in the vast space of the frontier. What makes *Stagecoach* compelling in this regard isn't, in fact, the hero's quest for revenge, which is so uncomplicated in its righteousness that it seems, in the words of one critic, to be the working of divine justice. But the network of personal histories, relationships, decisions, and consequences surrounding that hero's quest, and the ways that they are represented on film, are as subtle and thought provoking as any other example of the genre.

Certainly many other Westerns do, however, turn their spotlight on the complications of revenge or the violent rendering of justice. The most classic of these is *Shane* (1953), which builds up to the title character's inevitable confrontation with Ryker (Emile Meyer) and Ryker's hired gun, Jack Wilson (Jack Palance). Wilson fights for money, but Shane (Alan Ladd) fights on behalf of a town of homesteaders, threatened and intimidated by Ryker's desire to have free rein to run his cattle through the valley. On the surface it's as simple as it gets – the handsome, mysterious hero, clad in gold-colored buckskin and fighting for others who cannot defend themselves, faces off against the black-clad, serpentine villain Wilson. The bad guys don't even fight fair. Ryker pulls a hidden gun, and Ryker's brother draws on Shane as well from his hiding place in an upstairs balcony. Although the numbers are against him, we know who deserves to win.

And win he does, although not without sustaining an injury of uncertain severity. Shane mounts his horse and prepares to leave, explaining the decision to Joey, the young boy who idolizes him. "A man has to be what he is, Joey. Can't break the mold. I tried it and it didn't work for me … there's no living with a killing. There's no going back from one. Right or wrong, it's a brand. A brand sticks. There's no going back." It's an ostensible victory for the homesteaders, for the town, and for Shane the gunfighter, but for Shane the man it's a great and even tragic loss – confirmation that his essential nature is violent and unfit for society, or at least for the bucolic life of a farming community. "There's no living with a killing," he says, and as the last shot of the film reveals his darkened figure ascending into the uninhabited mountains, it's not clear if he's exiling himself to solitude or to death. The best thing he does is also the worst, and not even the desperate calls of Joey, the friendship and partnership of Joey's father, or the beauty and grace of Joey's mother ("Mother wants you! I know she does!" Joey cries out, unwittingly hitting the nail on the head) can bring him back.

Other Westerns offer variations on the theme. *The Ox-Bow Incident* (1943) shows what happens when those who are punished turn out not to have deserved it after all, and the devastating consequences of such a revelation. *The Searchers* (1956), which some have called John Ford and John Wayne's greatest partnership, features a hero whose notions of justice have twisted into racist hatred. And *The Man Who Shot Liberty Valance* (1962) focuses on a protagonist who, as it turns out, doesn't deserve the credit that he gets for killing the town baddie. (That credit goes, appropriately enough, to John Wayne's character, a man who doesn't entirely deserve the life he ended up with, either.) More contemporarily, 2007 saw three notable films engaging both the Western genre and the complicated intersections of violence and justice: the Coens brothers' *No Country for Old Men*, Paul Thomas Anderson's *There Will Be Blood*, and Andrew Dominik's *The Assassination of Jesse James by the Coward Robert Ford*. Each film challenges our expectations about why and how major characters live or die – and this is true even in the latter film, the climactic event of which comprises its very title.

*Stagecoach* initially seems like a comparatively shallow engagement with heroism and justice, but in fact its undercurrents run deep. The film follows a wildly disparate group of people traveling in cramped and dangerous circumstances to Lordsburg, New Mexico Territory, in 1880, and as such raises issues of class and morality almost immediately. Two of the characters, Doc Boone (Thomas Mitchell) and Dallas (Claire Trevor) have been kicked out of the town of Tonto in Arizona Territory by "the ladies of the Law and Order League" on the basis of their alcoholism and prostitution, respectively. They are defiant, but still they go, under the sharp, disapproving, and quite unbecoming gaze of said "ladies," one of whom is the wife of a prominent banker, Henry Gatewood (Berton Churchill). (Two lingering close-ups of the banker's dark, glowering face hint that he may not be quite the upstanding citizen that his status would suggest, and in fact he is attempting to steal $50,000 from his own bank.) They join a marshal, a stage driver, a married gentlewoman, a whiskey salesman, and an enigmatic Southern gambler for the journey to Lordsburg.

The final passenger shows up in one of cinema's great entrances. After the stage has left town and entered the desert, a man fires a shotgun into the air to get the driver's attention. It's John Wayne as the Ringo Kid, and the camera rushes up to meet him – temporarily losing focus in the process, as

Figure 10.2 The Ringo Kid makes his entrance in *Stagecoach*, and John Wayne becomes famous (United Artists, 1939).

if it can't wait another second to see the hero, either. The scene ushers in a new era for the Western hero, a character who had progressed from real-life figures like Wyatt Earp who were glimpsed briefly in film to silent-era romantic leads to the clean-cut, often snazzily dressed "singing cowboys" like Gene Autry and Roy Rogers. John Wayne is a new kind, and every succeeding Western actor would have his legacy to contend with one way or the other. Ringo, Wayne's character in *Stagecoach*, is an outlaw, broken out of the prison where he was sent on false charges and on his way to kill the Plummer brothers and avenge the murders of his father and brother. Marshal Curley Wilcox (George Bancroft) agrees with Buck, the stage driver (Andy Devine), that Ringo is "a fine boy," but nonetheless takes him into custody. As it turns out, however, the marshal wants to keep Ringo away from the Plummers not simply because Ringo should go back to prison or because he wants to prevent Ringo's illegal actions in seeking revenge, but rather because he fears for Ringo's life. In the eyes of the marshal, killing the Plummers wouldn't be wrong – but it would be dangerous, even lethal, and that the marshal can't abide.

*Stagecoach*, then, is very much a story of revenge, of a likeable, wrongly convicted outlaw on the road for justice. No one of high or low or even legal standing denies that the Plummers deserve to die, and the order of the cosmos itself seems to be against the brothers when Luke Plummer draws the "dead-man's hand" at cards before heading to the shootout or when a black cat crosses the brothers' path in the street. Barry Keith Grant writes that "Ringo's revenge quest is less a matter of personal than divine justice, a fated restoration of an overriding natural order.... In the end, *Stagecoach* asserts that there is no conflict between the moral individual and the demands of society, because moral authority will naturally subsume the legal" (16). Tom Schatz adds that because the film shows Ringo diving to the ground and firing his rifle, but then cuts back to his waiting friends rather than showing the gunfight or its results, it "removes Ringo's heroic act of vengeance to the realm of imagination and instantaneous legend, accentuated by the fact that the killings also serve to purify the town" (41).

If this is just a story about a good guy getting the bad guys in a way that is so uncomplicated as to be considered righteous, fated, and even divinely pure, then why has *Stagecoach* drawn such praise over the years? The film does have a number of impressive set pieces, including the climactic attack on the stage by Apaches near the film's end. And John Ford's use of deep focus and interior shots that rendered ceilings visible so impressed Orson Welles that, as the story goes, he watched the film some forty times and then employed those same techniques in *Citizen Kane* to famous effect (Cowie, 27). Significant though the aesthetics may be, however, scholars have found its plot and characters even more so. André Bazin wrote that it is "an ideal balance between social myth, historical reconstruction, psychological truth, and the traditional theme of the Western *mise-en-scène*" (149), and Slotkin said that the film shows how John Ford worked "with the elements of the 'B' formula, taking advantage of genre-based understandings – clichés of plot, setting, characterization, and motivation – to compose an exceptional work marked by moral complexity, formal elegance, narrative and verbal economy, and evocative imagery" (*Gunfighter Nation* 303).

This moral complexity, interestingly enough, isn't evident in the shootout or in Ringo's justification in pursuing it, but colors almost every other aspect of the film. *Stagecoach*'s best scene isn't a physically violent one, but rather a quiet masterpiece of the vectors of social and moral judgment. The group stops in Dry Fork and sits down to a brief lunch before it leaves for Apache Wells. Mrs. Mallory (Louise Platt), the upper-class, proper wife of a cavalry officer, is made visibly uncomfortable by the proximity of Dallas, the prostitute. The gambler Hatfield (John Carradine), in one of his many chivalric gestures toward Mrs. Mallory, offers her the excuse of moving to sit closer to the cool breeze from a window; the banker wordlessly follows them to the other end of the table, leaving Dallas and Ringo isolated. Ringo assumes

Figure 10.3 Ringo (John Wayne) and Dallas (Claire Trevor) take a liking to each other in Apache Wells (*Stagecoach*, United Artists, 1939).

the rejection is his fault: "Well, I guess you can't break out of prison and into society in the same week," he comments. He rises to leave, but Dallas grabs his arm. "Please. Please," she says, knowing the snub was actually aimed at her, and Ringo, innocent of the social norms at play and a bit confused, settles back down and engages Dallas in conversation. Dallas remarks on Ringo's fame as an outlaw, a status that Ringo explains by saying, "Well, I used to be a good cowhand, but things happen." "Yeah, that's it. Things happen," Dallas replies, just before Curley and Buck enter to round up the passengers for the next leg of the trip.

As Nick Browne has argued in an influential article, breaking down the scene's use of camera placement and editing reveals that it is largely structured around Mrs. Mallory's point of view – that is, the viewer is positioned to see things, quite literally, as she sees them. One might assume that this would lead the viewer to sympathize with Mrs. Mallory's position, but in fact, Browne argues, there is "a curious opposition between the empathetic response of a spectator toward Dallas and the underlying premises of the mechanism of the narrative which are so closely related, formally, to Lucy's [Mrs. Mallory's] presence, point of view, and interests" (125). We sympathize with Dallas and understand that this treatment is not, social norms to the contrary, what she really deserves, despite the ways that the scene is constructed cinematically. This "incongruity between feeling and formal structure" means that our position as spectators "is defined neither in terms of orientation within the constructed geography of the fiction nor in terms of social position of the viewing character" (125, 126–127). Instead, Browne writes, "our point of view on the sequence is tied more closely to our attitude of approval or disapproval and is very different from any literal viewing angle or character's point of view" (127). We know, in other words, who's right in this situation, regardless of what the social order or filmic structure may suggest. And it's the outlaw and the prostitute who are right, and continue to be as the film goes on.

Not only does the film make clear that Ringo and Dallas deserve better treatment from their companions, the characters themselves understand that they aren't to blame for their present circumstances – sometimes things just happen, as they say. Ringo lost his family because of the Plummer brothers, and Dallas, she reveals later, lost hers when she was a child in the massacre at Superstition Mountain. But "you gotta live, no matter what happens," she comments, and thus frames prostitution as her way of surviving. Ringo then proposes marriage and Dallas tearily demurs, assuming that he doesn't realize her profession. She seeks advice from Doc Boone, the other ostensibly lower-class character who proves to be a moral center of the film. The exiled drunkard not only manages to sober up and deliver the baby that no one knew Mrs. Mallory was pregnant with but also gives Dallas the validation she needs in order to assert her right to love and marry Ringo. "Who am I to tell you what's right or wrong, child?" Doc protests gently, but then adds, "All right, go ahead. Do it, if you can. Good luck." Doc questions his ability to judge her decision, but in his benediction proves that very ability to the viewer – and his opinion is the only one Dallas seeks out or seems to need.

After the couple arrives in Lordsburg, Ringo insists on walking Dallas home. "I gotta know where you live, don't I?" he says reasonably. Dallas leads him down an increasingly seedy street until she stops at a rough, dimly lit brothel. She assumes he'll leave her, but if he's surprised by the revelation, he doesn't show it at all. "I asked you to marry me, didn't I?" he says, again reasonably, and then tells her to wait while he goes to confront the Plummers. Dallas, the other passengers, and indeed the audience have been prepared to see Ringo reject Dallas when he realizes her prostitution, but that rejection never happens, nor even a note of surprise; it's entirely possible that he knew all along. When he tells Curley that Lordsburg "is no town for a girl like her," it sounds like the unintentional irony of a naïf, but Ringo, as it turns out, knows more than he lets on – he knows that Dallas deserves much more than what society or the "Law and Order League" would dictate. Not to mention cinema itself – the Hays Code, in effect beginning in 1930, strictly instructed filmmakers to be cautious in their depiction of "a woman selling her virtue." The words "prostitute" or "whore" are never uttered in the film, perhaps giving Ford plausible deniability for his portrayal of the unrepentant Dallas, who calls herself a survivor and is rewarded with validation, romance, and a ranch by the film's end.

Even *Stagecoach*'s treatment of Native Americans has been deemed by scholars to be more complicated than it initially appears. On the surface, they are a faceless horde threatening the white characters and supplying necessary tension for the trip to Lordsburg, which erupts during the climactic attack – this is a typical "cowboys and Indians" setup in which the latter deserve only to die. But J. P. Telotte writes that if John Ford's films "at various times seem callous or condescending in their ethnic portrayals, especially of Indians, then, they also and just as often seem to interrogate those identities in ways that are unusual for the American film industry and that reveal much about American culture and its traditions" (114). Telotte begins his discussion of this topic by describing a scene in *Stagecoach* when the timid whiskey salesman first lays eyes on Yakima, the Apache wife of Chris, who runs the station at Apache Wells. "A savage!" he gasps, and Chris smiles. "Sí, señor, she's a little bit savage, I think … she's one of Geronimo's people. I think, maybe not so bad to have an Apache wife, eh? Apaches don't bother me, I think." This scene, says Telotte, "illustrates how quickly and superficially determinations about other people are made here," especially Native Americans – and this echoes a scene that opens the film, when a soldier mistakes a Cheyenne cavalry scout for a renegade Apache (113). "They hate Apaches worse than we do," the soldier is assured. In a similar vein, Barry Keith Grant notes Dallas' statement about the scowling ladies of the Law and Order League that "there are worse things than Apaches" (15). It's not just cowboys and generic Indians who hate and are hated, and so the film's moral universe avoids an easy reduction into a Manichean system.

Telotte locates *Stagecoach*'s complexity in this regard most compellingly in a moment that passes between Hatfield and Mrs. Mallory during the Apache attack on the stagecoach. Ringo, Curley, and the others have run out of ammunition, and Apache victory looks imminent. Hatfield eyes his final remaining bullet, and then looks at Mrs. Mallory, who is turned away from him and fervently praying. We see Mrs. Mallory in close-up as the gun enters the frame and is aimed at her head, but then the hand holding it wavers and drops the weapon. Hatfield has himself been shot, just a moment before Mrs. Mallory hears the call of the bugle that heralds their rescue by the cavalry. Again on the surface, this seems like a xenophobic cliché, a heroic figure

Figure 10.4 Hatfield (John Carradine, offscreen) prepares to shoot Mrs. Mallory (Louise Platt) in order to save her from the attacking Apaches (*Stagecoach*, United Artists, 1939).

bravely preparing to kill a loved one in order to save her from sexual viola-tion and "unspeakably savage violence," indeed a "fate worse than death"; Telotte notes similar scenes in *The Birth of a Nation* (1915) and *Union Pacific*, released the same year as *Stagecoach* (115–116). But unlike those films, *Stagecoach* doesn't present Hatfield's actions as righteous or necessary:

> Here we find no unanimity, no agreement within this microcosm of west-ern culture on a better way out, no moral support or sanction for a death preferable to the suspected Indian fate. Ringo, for example, while offering similar attentions to Dallas, makes no effort to spare her a "fate worse than death," even though, as we later learn, he has retained three bullets to kill the Plummers. That response to transgression is Hatfield's alone, definitively placing him, like the banker Gatewood, outside the group, outside the society that has formed in the course of this stagecoach trip, and linking him, almost in spite of himself, to that broader cultural "imagination" that informs and makes possible what Doc initially termed the "disease" of "social prejudice." His effort at a "saving" murder … is simply another sort of prejudice. (126)

For reasons like these, argue Joseph McBride and Michael Wilmington, "*Stagecoach* leaves the question of American imperialism, the cavalry vs.

Figure 10.5 Marshal Curley Wilcox (George Bancroft) and Doc Boone (Thomas Mitchell)
send Ringo and Dallas away to Mexico, and celebrate their freedom from "the blessings of
civilization" (*Stagecoach*, United Artists, 1939).

the Indians, tantalizingly unresolved" (56). Thus the very premise that drives
the Western genre as a whole – that of Manifest Destiny, the imperative for
white Americans to live in this space – is called into question. This revision-
ism may be subtle, but it anticipates a number of later Westerns like *Little
Big Man* (1970), *Dances with Wolves* (1990), and *Dead Man* (1995).

In the end, the stage makes it to Lordsburg, and Ringo kills the Plummers.
When he returns from the shootout, the marshal makes as if he's going to
take Ringo back into custody; Dallas climbs in the wagon to ride with him,
and the marshal and Doc Boone suddenly rouse the horses to a gallop, sending Ringo and Dallas off together with a chorus of celebratory whooping
and shouting. "Well," says Doc – in a line that is rightly famous – "they're
saved from the blessings of civilization." Saved, then, from the "blessings"
of social norms, class structures, and systems of justice that so often fail to
account for what people really deserve. The Plummers deserved to die, and
Ringo and Dallas deserve to ride off to Ringo's ranch in Mexico, leaving
their traumatic and socially unacceptable – and, not incidentally, American –
pasts behind them.

It seems like a happy ending, and indeed it is happier for the characters we've been rooting for than many Westerns. Ringo is not leaving because he's been tainted by the violence of his killing – as do Shane, Ethan Edwards, and so many others – nor does Dallas have any reservations about accompanying him. But it's not a terribly rosy view of the American society that they ride away from. The momentary unity the group of stage passengers achieve when Mrs. Mallory's baby is born fragments again when they reach Lordsburg; although Dallas has proven herself brave and capable in her care for Mrs. Mallory and the child, she is once again reduced to an outcast by the ladies of Lordsburg. "I'll take the baby," one says curtly, leaving Dallas empty-handed.

Richard Slotkin found in *Stagecoach* a rendering of the ephemeral nature of American justice:

> Lordsburg justice is just good enough to punish Banker Gatewood, but it cannot provide the most positive sort of justice required by Ringo and Dallas.... The only justice they get is what they make for themselves, with the aid of a few friends: Ringo "rescues" Dallas by declaring his love for her in the midst of the red-light district, and kills the Plummers (with a little help from Doc Boone). Curly and Doc then render justice to Ringo and Dallas by allowing them to escape to Ringo's little ranch across the border in Mexico.... Democracy, equality, responsibility, and solidarity are achieved – are visible – only in transit, only in pursuit of the goal. When the goal is reached they dissolve, and society lapses into habitual injustice, inequality, alienation, and hierarchy. Our only hope is to project a further frontier, a mythic space outside American space and American history, for the original possibilities of our Frontier have been used up. (310–311)

Ringo, then, doesn't become the wolf – the blood he spills is spilled righteously, and he remains untainted by it. The wolf in *Stagecoach* is America itself, corrupted by the violence and social injustice of its own history. The only thing to do is to love someone regardless of her own history and ride out of the frame.

John Wayne is, of course, an icon of the Western, and *Stagecoach* makes him a star. But it's Clint Eastwood, from the 1960s until today, who has perhaps most been associated with Western justice and its stylish delivery. "Go ahead, make my day," he tells a robber in *Sudden Impact* (1983), playing a police inspector whose "unconventional methods" nonetheless "get results." Nothing would please him more, that catchphrase indicates, than delivering the kind of swift justice that San Francisco's lugubrious legal system so often obscures. Even in 2008's *Gran Torino*, in which Eastwood plays a Korean War veteran haunted by his killing of an enemy soldier attempting to surrender, his orchestrated suicide is in fact a deliberate and canny act of vengeance: he provokes the gang members who have harmed his friends into shooting and killing him in full view of a group of neighborhood witnesses, thus sending the wrongdoers to jail.

And so when Will Munny says that "deserve's got nothin' to do with it" before he shoots Little Bill, what does he mean? In the context of the Western genre and of Eastwood's career, it's a truly alien line. Munny may mean that because he is a killer of men (and women and children), Little Bill is simply the next to go. But he's also said that he will be killing Bill "for what you did to Ned," negating the possibility that it's simply an expression of his power or pleasure. The statement could be a denial of Little Bill's protest – "I was building a house," Bill says, as a way of countering the idea that he deserves to die. Perhaps Munny indicates with this line that he refuses to judge Bill's life in its entirety, productive constructions or other contributions, but will only respond to Ned's murder. (It should be noted here that the house is not very well constructed, although Bill himself takes great pride in it, much as he does his questionably violent attempts to ensure that the town he presides over is a safe and orderly one.)

When we watch a Western, how do we decide who deserves what? It often depends on the weight of our sympathies and antipathies, as encouraged by the acting, camera angles, editing, dialogue, and all the other elements of the film. By the end of *Stagecoach*, we know that the Plummers deserve to die, but we also know, in a subtler way, that Ringo and Dallas deserve to be together despite their pasts, and that they deserve more than what the fledgling communities of the West have to offer – more, in fact, than what America itself has to offer, and so they go to Mexico. Like Curley and Doc Boone, we're happy to see them escape the "blessings" of this particular civilization at film's end.

"They deserved that," we say – which is perhaps just another way of saying that we liked it, that we liked to see that. As a representation, it gives us – the audience, at a comfortable distance from the goings-on – satisfaction. In that sense, Will Munny, as a witness to his own actions, may simply be indicating that what he's doing is a necessary retributive response, but that he doesn't like it. Other characters in *Unforgiven*, like the dime novel author who spins tales of Western derring-do, may traffic in the aesthetic satisfactions of vengeance, but for Munny, any kind of killing – even that which is the most just – has lost its luster. Deserve, then, the pleasure of paying blood back with blood, has nothing to do with it. It's just killing. The wolf may carry out that killing, but the man recognizes his own corruption.

And do we, the audience? If we like this – and the Western's long-standing popularity, not to mention this particular film's, indicates that we do – then what, in turn, do we deserve? If it's a society that so often seeks righteousness in bloodshed but finds only chaos and suffering, then many would say that justice has indeed been served. Someone save us from the blessings of civilization.

## Works Cited

Bazin, Andre. "The Evolution of the Western." *What Is Cinema?* Vol. 2. Ed. and trans. Hugh Gray. Berkeley: University of California Press, 1971. 149–157. Print.

Browne, Nick. "The Spectator-in-the-Text: The Rhetoric of *Stagecoach*." In Leo Braudy and Marshall Cohen (eds.) *Film Theory and Criticism*. 6th ed. New York: Oxford University Press, 2004. 118–133. Print.

*The Covered Wagon*. Dir. James Cruze. Perf. Warren Kerrigan, Lois Wilson. Paramount Pictures, 1923. Film.

"*The Covered Wagon*." Film program. Paramount Pictures, 1923. The Silent Film Still Archive. Web. May 13, 2015.

Cowie, Peter. *The Cinema of Orson Welles*. New York: A. S. Barnes, 1965.

*Gran Torino*. Dir. Clint Eastwood. Perf. Clint Eastwood. Warner Brothers, 2008. Film.

Grant, Barry Keith. "Introduction: Spokes in the Wheels." In Barry Keith Grant (ed.) *John Ford's Stagecoach*. Cambridge: Cambridge University Press, 2003. 1–20. Print.

*The Great Train Robbery*. Dir. Edwin S. Porter. Perf. Alfred Abadie, Broncho Billy Anderson. Edison Manufacturing Company, 1903. Film.

*The Iron Horse*. Dir. John Ford. Perf. George O'Brien, Madge Bellamy. Fox Film Corporation, 1924. Film.

*The Man Who Shot Liberty Valance*. Dir. John Ford. Perf. John Wayne, James Stewart. Paramount Pictures, 1962. Film.

McBride, Joseph, and Michael Wilmington. *John Ford*. New York: Da Capo, 1975. Print.

*The Ox-Bow Incident*. Dir. William Wellman. Perf. Henry Fonda, Dana Andrews. 20th Century Fox, 1943. Film.

Plantinga, Carl. "Spectacles of Death: Clint Eastwood and Violence in *Unforgiven*." *Cinema Journal*. Vol. 37, no. 2 (1998): 65–83. Print.

Plato. *The Republic of Plato*. Ed. and trans. Allan Bloom. New York: Basic Books, 1968. Print.

Schatz, Tom. "*Stagecoach* and Hollywood's A-Western Renaissance." Grant 21–47. Print.

Schechter, Harold. "The Vigilante Soul Exposed." *The New York Times* March 31, 1993. Web. June 17, 2015.

*The Searchers*. Dir. John Ford. Perf. John Wayne, Natalie Wood. Warner Brothers, 1956. Film.

*Shane*. Dir. George Stevens. Perf. Alan Ladd, Jean Arthur. Paramount Pictures, 1953. Film.

Slotkin, Richard. *Gunfighter Nation: The Myth of the Frontier in Twentieth-Century America*. Norman: The University of Oklahoma Press, 1998. Print.

*Regeneration through Violence: The Mythology of the American Frontier, 1600–1860*. Middletown, CT: Wesleyan University Press, 1973. Print.

*Stagecoach*. Dir. John Ford. Perf. John Wayne, Claire Trevor. United Artists, 1939. Film.

*Sudden Impact*. Dir. Clint Eastwood. Perf. Clint Eastwood, Sondra Locke. Warner Brothers, 1983. Film.

Telotte, J. P. "'A Little Bit Savage': *Stagecoach* and Racial Representation." *Grant* 113–131. Print.

*Unforgiven*. Dir. Clint Eastwood. Perf. Clint Eastwood, Morgan Freeman. Warner Bros., 1992. Film.

Vernant, Jean-Pierre, and Pierre Vidal-Naquet. *Myth and Tragedy in Ancient Greece*. Trans. Janet Lloyd. Cambridge, MA: Zone Books, 1990. Print.

Warshow, Robert. "Movie Chronicle: The Westerner." Braudy and Cohen 703–716. Print.

# II

NICHOLAS MONK

# The Native American Renaissance

In her 1977 novel, *Ceremony*, Leslie Silko records, in the sacred lands of the Pueblo, the manifestation of the Western world's apocalyptic technology:

> Trinity site, where they exploded the first atomic bomb, was only three hundred miles to the southeast, at White Sands. And the top-secret laboratories where the bomb had been created were deep in the Jemez mountains, on land the Government took from Cochiti Pueblo: Los Alamos, only a hundred miles northeast of [Tayo] now, still surrounded by high electric fences and the ponderosa pine and tawny sandrock of the Jemez mountain canyon where the shrine of the twin mountain lions had always been. (246)

In Silko's vision hallowed sites have been usurped by the dark side of Western science: the novel records the terrible irony that resides in modernity's exploitation of these hitherto life-preserving landscapes to terrorize and destroy human beings, and lay waste whole environments on the other side of the Pacific Ocean. What could be more grotesque to Native Americans than the excavation of their sacred lands for such monstrous purposes? The yellow rocks of *Ceremony*'s Southwest have been transformed into weapons-grade uranium to provide the warheads for the bombs that would be unleashed on the cities of Hiroshima and Nagasaki: "a circle of death that devoured people in cities twelve thousand miles away, victims who had never seen the delicate colors of the rocks which boiled up their slaughter" (246).[1] The outrage implicit in such notions sat well in the constellation of ideas that emerged in the countercultural and revolutionary movements of the 1960s and 1970s. Environmentalists, for example, and the various peace movements that flourished in the moment read in Native American cultures models of organization and existence that were harmonious with the natural world, and offered a counter-narrative to the inevitability of economic growth and unregulated industrial expansion.[2] It became possible to understand Native American culture as exemplary of resistance to the notion – made manifest in the rampant exploitation of natural resources and the highly technologized prosecution of overseas wars – that human beings exist as separate from and outside the natural processes of the earth and the behavior of animals. A space was available in this time for such global concerns to be set alongside more local ones as Native American people, accustomed to "extinction, brutality, and racism," began to see conditions improve. People were "returning to their Indian culture for a sense of who they [were]." Something of this was "powerfully captured" in the work of writers like Silko and others belonging to what has come to be known as the Native American Renaissance.[3]

The beginnings of this renaissance, pinpointed in 1986 by Kenneth Lincoln in the publication of N. Scott Momaday's *House Made of Dawn* and manifested in higher education by the first ever Native American course taught in an American university (Professor Alan Velie at the University of Oklahoma in 1969), arrived at a moment of crisis in Western ontology.[4] Lincoln and others see *House Made of Dawn* as the work that opened the field and heralded this second renaissance in which American publishers began to welcome Native American writers to their lists, and it is certainly true that following Momaday's novel a whole range of work emerged that was diverse in form, content, and geographical location: the work of James Welch, for example, and his focus on the Blackfeet; Simon Ortiz with his novels of Keresan life; Chippewa Gerald Vizenor with his poetry, fiction, and criticism; and the poetry of Joy Harjo (Muscogee) from Oklahoma. *House Made of Dawn* was a notable attempt to juxtapose traditional Native American cultural practice with the elements of Western or Eurocentric modernity concerned with the desirability of progress, the Cartesian separation of mind from body and body from environment, and a globalizing cultural impulse, the economic manifestation of which were the twin phenomena of a burgeoning consumer capitalism and the growth of the military-industrial complex. The novel is, indeed, therefore, a landmark in the development of Native American fiction, but Leslie Silko's *Ceremony* is illustrative and exemplary of a new kind of literary response in Native American writers of the West. A response that, for the first time, and in ways that develop and refine Momaday's ideas, sets out a subtle agenda for resistance and change that is rooted firmly and wholly in the native cultural practices of the American West and, most importantly, in the land.

*Ceremony*, like *House Made of Dawn*, takes the return of a World War II veteran to his home in the Pueblos as a moment to explore the healing properties of native cultural practice in the face of psychological, physical, and emotional damage. In *Ceremony*, Tayo, Silko's protagonist, returns to the Laguna Pueblo suffering the trauma of his participation in the United

States' Pacific campaign. In this theatre Tayo, among a catalogue of other horrific experiences, sees his cousin killed and, along with his compatriots from the Pueblo, turns to alcohol and away from tradition in order to erase or diminish his trauma. Not only is this a response to the horrors of war, it is also Silko's reaction to the indisputable evidence that Native Americans such as Tayo have been subject to a monstrous confidence trick. Tayo and many like him have been persuaded to join forces with one version of modernity (represented by the U.S. government and its colonial and expansionist single-race empire), against another (Japan) that saw its own purity as paramount and sought, similarly, a greater empire through the deployment of industry and technology. That tragedy is, of course, that one version would destroy these young men as readily as the other. The progress of Tayo's understanding of these kinds of modernity is halting and piecemeal, and he struggles toward an understanding of their utterly debilitating effects via a series of engagements with tribal elders, "medicine men," and figures from the spirit world. Gradually Tayo becomes reacquainted with the traditional stories of his people, slowly reconstructs a spiritual relationship with the land, and begins to recover from the damage inflicted upon him in modernity's wars. In his hitherto losing battle with modernity, Tayo is redeemed from the point of destruction by the religious practices and rituals of his community. He returns to a spiritual relationship with a self that lies buried beneath his experiences of war, and in this way a symbiotic relationship grows between him, his land, and his community. Such is the case, too, for Abel in *House Made of Dawn*: although the realization of what will heal him arrives much later for him than for Tayo, with the death of the grandfather who raised him: "The old man had spoken six times in the dawn, and the voice of his memory was whole and clear and growing like the dawn" (172). That writing of this kind should emerge from the American West should be no surprise. The West is a region in which Native Americans have clung to established cultural practices and have achieved a measure of geographical and temporal continuity. The West has also been a notable location for the struggle between Western, or Eurocentric, capitalist modernity and its "other" over centuries – a process that began with the arrival of Spanish Catholic missionaries in the seventeenth century and that continues unabated in the exploitation of mineral, water, and other resources in the region and Native American resistance to the process. Indeed, the West is suffused with premodern culture and adorned with its ruins, even though the physical and temporal "reality" of its Native American communities exists on the sufferance of the U.S. government, the most powerful facilitator of capitalist modernity currently in existence. The modern and the "premodern" continue, thus, to confront each other on this ground in a variety of ways – indeed, the myths needed to sustain an ever-westward movement require such a confrontation: "even at the source of the American myth (of conquest) there lies the fatal opposition, the hostility between two worlds, two races, two realms of thought and feeling" (Slotkin, 17). I recognize, of course, that it would be reductive to suggest there is no overlap and influence in either direction, and there is, and has been, much miscegenation. The sheer number of representatives of the first nations groups – particularly in the Southwest – ensuring that Native American influence has not been swamped wholly. What is interesting, here, is that Silko, as a mixed-blood writer, is prepared to draw on the traditions of both the European and Native American elements in her heritage to generate a kind of literary activism that recognizes the reality of the spiritual, that questions the relationship of humanity to the landscape and the environment, examines war and conflict, and manifests a reverence for the ancient.⁵ Arnold Krupat quotes Hopi tribal council chairman Vernon Masayesva to this end: " 'Research needs to be based on the reality of our [Hopi] existence as we experience it, not just from the narrow and limited view American universities carried over from the German research tradition' " (*Turn to the Native* xix). Silko's fiction and the writing of other figures of the Native American Renaissance, such as Momaday, while clearly alive to the Eurocentric tradition Krupat mentions, and willing to deploy aspects of it, is profoundly suspicious of the notions that undergird it: progress, for example, instrumental reason, mechanization, and the grander claims of science.

At the same time Silko attempts to heal the "sickness" at the heart of her own community through a representation of a symbiotic relationship between humanity and the land. Frederick Turner writes of the dichotomy between the view of the "whites" of a hostile, dangerous environment, and the traditional indigenous attachment to a sacred earth. Beyond the trepidation created by the unknown, white settlers, possessing none of the belief systems that sustained the Native Americans in a seemingly hostile landscape, seemed to fear the "emptiness" of the environments of the West:

> [The Native American approach] amounted to a different kind of possession than the whites were prepared to understand as they looked about these spaces and found them empty of visible marks of tenancy.... To them the lands were satanic rather than sacred, and the traders and their employees could tolerate the wilderness only in the hope that eventually they could make enough money to leave it behind and return to civilization to live like humans. So they would grimly push out into the woods beyond the furthest reaches of civilization.... Here they would establish a post and make it known that they stood ready to supply the needs of the resident tribes in return for pelts taken in trapping and hunting.... Here again we encounter the clash between history and myth, with

the whites, driven to enormous technological ingenuity, producing a vast array of seductive items for the peoples of the globe whose spiritual contentments had kept their own technologies at comparatively simple levels.... We know now that there has been no people on earth capable of resisting this seduction, for none has been able to see the hidden and devious byways that lead inevitably from the consumption of new luxuries to the destruction of the myths that give life its meaning. (24)

Turner illuminates the manner in which whites, avowing Christianity rather than the sustaining myths of the indigenous peoples, countered their fear and filled the "emptiness" of what, to them, was a one-dimensional environment. Indeed, the potential of these attitudes to poison the continent were clear to Native American leaders, and were elucidated by Luther Standing Bear in *Land of the Spotted Eagle* as long ago as 1933: "'True, the white man brought great change. But the varied fruits of his civilization, though highly colored and inviting, are sickening and deadening. And if it be the part of civilization to maim, rob, and thwart, then what is progress?'" (quoted in Deloria, *God Is Red* 303).

Plainly, a version of spirituality that reconnects humanity with the land and the creatures that dwell on it is far more likely to preserve an environment that is at the point of becoming completely engulfed by modernity and capitalism, than one that advocates the earth as man's "dominion" – as both fundamentalist and, hitherto, institutionalized Christianity do. Gerald Vizenor amplifies the point in his history of the Chippewa:

"The single most important deterrent to excessive hunting ... was the fear of spiritual reprisal for indiscreet slaughter.... Nature, as conceived by traditional Ojibwa," Calvin Martin writes, "was a congeries of societies: every animal, fish, and plant species functioned in a society that was parallel in all respects to human families. There were 'keepers' of the game, or leaders of animal families." (21–22)

To Native Americans, the land and its creatures were sacred; to the European Christians who "discovered" and began to subjugate the Americas, they were not. As James Wilson notes in *The Earth Shall Weep*, the powerfully influential biblical story of the expulsion from Eden pits humanity against a hostile and torturing environment: "This primal catastrophe has left us profoundly dislocated: we are exiles in an alien wilderness which we must struggle to subdue. With every generation we move further and further from the gates of Eden, sustained only by dreams of somehow regaining our lost innocence or of creating a new heaven on earth" (5). Both acknowledge, though, that the cultural geography of the American West, and the relationship of its peoples to the landscape, have proved intensely resistant to the concerted onslaught of a version of Christianity heavily mediated by modernity and capitalism. As Vizenor remarks:

> Southwest Native Americans have retained "identity systems that have as an important element the symbol of roots in the land – supernaturally sanctioned, ancient roots, regarded as unchangeable," according to Southwesternist Edward Spicer. Such a perspective provides these groups with strong mythological sanctions for their residence, their right to live in the Southwest and their views of the land. The land is not something that can be controlled and changed; it is something of which all human beings are a part. (*The People Named Chippewa* 87)

*Ceremony* represents with great clarity the move that began in the late 1960s and early 1970s in the work of Native American artists to demonstrate levels of independence and separation from contemporary white (or Eurocentric) writers, while embracing some of the cultural forms in which the work of these white writers existed. The process is not, however, without its problems. As Louis Owens notes,

> [A] very real danger faced by the Native American, or any marginalized writer who would assume the role of scholar-critic-theorist, is that of consciously or unconsciously using Eurocentric theory merely as a way of legitimizing his or her voice – picking up the master's tools not to dismantle the master's house but simply to prove that we are tool-using creatures just like him and therefore worthy of intellectual recognition. (*Other Destinies* 53)

At the same time Native American practices, and the philosophies that underpin them, were appropriated consciously and unconsciously by the kinds of movements I describe in my first paragraph that sought to separate themselves from mainstream American culture. Vine Deloria Junior illustrates the point when he asserts that:

> [N]o real discussion was ever presented regarding American Indian knowledge of plant life, even though it is well known that Corn Dances are one of the chief religious ceremonies of the Southwestern Indians. In the schizophrenia that we know as America, Indians using songs and dances to improve crops is not significant, but a florist piping music into a greenhouse is astounding and illustrates a hidden principle of the universe. (*Red Earth* 44)

Deloria's argument, beyond the sly mockery of Western ignorance and arrogance, is that a glance at Native American practices and thinking might have led the West to the recognition of ecological and other crises earlier, and prevented Western thought in the years since Descartes honing a deadly policy of disconnection: Arne Naess's deep ecology (1972), for example, and the emergence in Western philosophy of the notion of Gaia arrived very late, and have been submerged beneath a welter of recent theories rooted in linguistic philosophy (at least in the academy) that have done little to counter – in terms of the lived reality of most people – the claim that there is a radical divide between interior and exterior, and between mind and "the rest." Writing of the Native American Renaissance, and that of Leslie Silko and N. Scott Momaday in particular, is not content to merely expose the manner in which Native American knowledge is ignored, trivialized, diminished, or stolen under capitalist modernity, but moves increasingly toward subtle manifestos and programs of political activism that reach far beyond simply demonstrating to the "master" that they are able to use the tools.

*Ceremony* is a novel that uses its postwar context to subvert myths of Western superiority, and it does this partly by examining the disjunctions of the kinds of rational Western philosophy that led, in Theodor Adorno's vision, from the arrow to the atom bomb (Horkheimer and Adorno, 222–223). The default position for many Native American cultures is to seek to connect layers of experience. The Navajo, for example, and the worlds in which they believe, are bound more closely together by the idea that these worlds exist on all temporal planes simultaneously. As James Wilson remarks: "The belief that we stand at the centre of a reality in which, in some way, past, present and future all converge, is common to many Native American cultures" (xix). From Wilson's perspective, the Native American cultures of the West, of which Silko is a part, have at their heart notions of multiplicity, yet such notions do not imply a separation from the worlds they describe. In Silko's version it is only human animals that resist unity with that which exists outside them in the natural world:

> Josiah said that only humans had to endure anything, because only humans resisted what they saw outside themselves. Animals did not resist. But they persisted, because they became part of the wind.... So they moved with the snow, became part of the snowstorm which drifted up against the trees and fences. And when they died, frozen solid against a fence, with the snow drifted around their heads? "Ah, Tayo," Josiah said, "the wind convinced them they were the ice." (27)

Again, these notions of multiplicity, simultaneity, and yet a paradoxical (to Western ears) move toward oneness tend to foster an automatic respect for, and easiness with, the environment that is often absent from Western perspectives. Tayo registers the experience of an existence in which rigid temporal and spatial demarcations are absent:

> He remembered the black of the sand paintings on the floor of the hogan; the hills and mountains were the mountains and hills they had painted in the sand.

He took a deep breath of cold mountain air: there were no boundaries; the world below and the sand paintings inside became the same that night. The mountains from all directions had been gathered there that night. (145)

In such ways Silko challenges white readers to rethink their own intellectual conditioning, and embrace as plausible ways of constructing an understanding of the world that seem counterintuitive to the dominant strands of Western thinking in the Western academy – notwithstanding the significant Emersonian tradition in the United States. Similarly, Momaday, in *House Made of Dawn*, makes a virtue of the Tanouan approach to the "conquerors" in which "[The Tanouan] have assumed the names and gestures of their enemies, but have held on to their own, secret souls; and in this there is a resistance and an overcoming, a long outwaiting" (52–53). This process of confrontation and juxtaposition is what lies at the heart of the Native American Renaissance of this period.

The keen awareness of the condition of the continent under the dominion of the white man that Silko shows in *Ceremony* contrasts vividly with the meretricious perceptions of the colonist. Vine Deloria quotes Walter M. Camp, for example, in a report to the Bureau of Indian Affairs (BIA) in 1920: "The savage is concerned only with the immediate necessities of life, while the civilized man looks beyond subsistence. In other words, the Indian is not a capitalist.... One might say he is lacking in industry, and that the dearth of capital is an effect and not the cause of his poverty" (*God Is Red* 331). The chilling dismissal of "subsistence" reveals a concomitant absence of a willingness to engage with the environment beyond the will to exploitation. Such exploitation as part of the "civilizing" processes of capitalism and cultural modernity has tended to lead to the destruction of those Native Americans seeking to maintain a "traditional" life. Walter Benjamin, in an oft-quoted passage, uses a Paul Klee painting to illustrate a similar but more general point concerning "progress":

A Klee painting named "Angelus Novus" shows an angel looking as though he is about to move away from something he is fixedly contemplating. His eyes are staring, his mouth is open, his wings are spread. This is how one pictures the angel of history. His face is turned toward the past. Where we perceive a chain of events, he sees one single catastrophe which keeps piling wreckage upon wreckage and hurls it in front of his feet. The angel would like to stay, awaken the dead, and make whole what has been smashed. But a storm is blowing from Paradise; it has got caught in his wings with such violence that the angel can no longer close them. This storm irresistibly propels him into the future to which his back is turned, while the pile of debris before him grows skyward. This storm is what we call progress. (*Illuminations* 261)

There are interesting comparisons to *Ceremony*: I think in particular of the initial stages of Tayo's visit to the "medicine-man," Betonie. Here, as Tayo is propelled blindly into the future (as though his back was turned to it), Betonie looks down from the foothills of the Ceremonial Grounds in Gallup (where he has placed his hogan) upon "tin cans and broken glass, blinding reflections off the mirrors and chrome of the wrecked cars in the dump below" (117). What Betonie sees is the detritus of modernity. The ever-mounting pile of refuse equates to the wreckage that lies before Klee's "new angel." Support for this claim appears later in Betonie and Tayo's first encounter as they watch the highway emerging from Gallup:

> [Tayo] looked at the old man.... He didn't seem to be listening. "There are no limits to this thing," Betonie said, "When it was set loose, it raged everywhere, from the mountains and the plains to the towns and cities; rivers and oceans never stopped it." The wind was blowing steadily and the old man's voice was almost lost in it. (132)

It may be that the "thing" to which Betonie refers is modernity, and it is fascinating (although probably coincidental) in the light of the quotation from Benjamin on Klee's painting that there should be a strong wind blowing at this moment.

What is plain, also, is that once modernity is unleashed it is extraordinarily difficult to resist its pernicious effects. Its progress seems irresistible and its appetite for new territory insatiable. The process in microcosm is detailed in *House Made of Dawn* when the assimilated Tosamah advocates a posture of gratitude and humility for returning Native American soldiers like Abel: "'They gave him every advantage. They gave him a pair of shoes and told him to go to school. They deloused him and gave him a lot of free haircuts and let him fight on their side. But was he grateful? Hell, no, man. He was too damn dumb to be civilized"' (131). In *Ceremony*, however, the crisis is scaled up:

> But there was something else now, as Betonie said: it was everything [the young Native Americans who had fought in the Second World War] had seen – the cities, the tall buildings, the noise and the lights, the power of their weapons and machines. They were never the same after that: they had seen what the white people had made from the stolen land. (169)

In Betonie's remarks resides the tragedy of the Native American experience at the hands of the colonial powers as the American Indian soldiers, already dispossessed and defeated by capitalist modernity, are confronted with its apotheosis in full panoply of steel, glass, shattering noise, and alien light. The moment of the Native American literary renaissance is captured in this moment of recognition, and it is no coincidence that this should occur in the Western United States as the region that has maintained enough of its indigenous population to support traditional perspectives and ways of life.

This recognition is also reflected more recently in the works of Louise Erdrich and Sherman Alexie. Very much associated with the "Second Wave" of the Native American Renaissance, which included Joy Harlo, Simon Ortiz, Paula Gunn Allen, and nila northSun, Erdrich is a registered member of the Turtle Mountain Band of Chippewas (also known as Ojibway). Her works include *Love Medicine* (1984), which won the National Book Critics Circle Award, *The Beet Queen* (1986), *Tracks* (1988), and *The Bingo Palace* (1994), among others. Her most notable novel is *Love Medicine*, and like many works emerging from the Native American Renaissance, the narrative blends the tradition of the Euro-American novel with the folktales, myths, and oral traditions of her Ojibway ancestors. Organized around a number of individual first-person narrations, the novel is centered around five chapters told from a third-person point of view. The story deals with an array of themes related to the move to reservation life: the clash with modernity, the effects of U.S. government policy on natives, the effects of new modes of imposed social organization on the family and the clan, and the clash of cultures that occurs as some natives assimilate to nonnative traditions. The transformation and diminution of spiritual life is also charted with tremendous pathos, and Erdrich provides another unique representation of Native American life in the twentieth century, clearly advancing the tradition that emerges with Silko and Momaday.

Not directly associated with the Native American Renaissance but certainly drawing on its innovations and impetus is the work of Sherman Alexie. Alexie traces his ancestry to a number of native tribes and grew up on the Spokane Indian Reservation. He is a writer of poetry, fiction, and screenplays, and some of his most notable works include *The Lone Ranger and Tonto Fistfight in Heaven* (1993), which is a book of short stories; *Reservations Blues* (1996); and the screenplay *Smoke Signals* (1998), based on the aforementioned short story collection. He is also known for children's stories and young adult fiction, having won the 2007 National Book Award for Young People's Literature for *The Absolutely True Diary of a Part-Time Indian*. His collection of poetry *War Dances* (2010) won the PEN/Faulkner Award for Fiction. Certainly not unlike Momaday, Silko, and Erdrich, but with his own more contemporary voice, Alexie works across genres to explore the traumas and complexities of reservation life. His works take that historically rooted experience and grapple with issues of cultural identity, recognizing that marked racial difference prohibits assimilation and necessitates the active preservation and reinvention of native cultural identity in the context of modernity. Vividly realistic in their portrayal of the violence, poverty, and degradation that often characterizes reservation life, his poems and short stories also point to that experience as a locus for cultural regeneration. With Alexie the motives and practices of what was originally called the Native American Renaissance continue in a fully active and vibrant tradition.

Silko's *Ceremony*, for me, however, is perhaps the most direct response to the confrontation of the indigenous with capitalist modernity, and it forms a significant part of what distinguishes the novel in its description and performance of activism from other work of the period. Not merely in the sense that the novel sets out the current position and is in many ways a manifesto for a reengagement of peoples of all colors with the natural environment, but in the sense that it is performative of the resistance it describes and it invites the reader to participate in something beyond a reading experience as consumption as typically understood in Western culture.

The mechanics of this process, in literary and philosophical terms, function in two separate but complementary ways. The concept of phenomenology is most helpful in understanding the first, and that of performativity the second. Phenomenology, as it is used here, was developed in the late nineteenth and early twentieth centuries to address the subject/object problem in which Western philosophy has become so frequently mired. The specific form relevant to Silko's work was developed in the West by Edmund Husserl and Martin Heidegger, and later used by literary critics – specifically Roman Ingarden in the 1930s, and "reader-response" theorists such as Hans Robert Jauss and Wolfgang Iser in the 1980s. This kind of work on phenomenology arose from a recognition that Western philosophy had not yet been able to close the gap, satisfactorily, between idealism (in a very reductive characterization, a school of thought that suggests there may not be a material world existing independently from thought), and empiricism (the view that what can be known is produced by that which acts externally upon mind or consciousness: there can be nothing innate.) What is interesting, however, in the light of my earlier remarks concerning the prevalence of a presumption of "connection" and "oneness" in Native American cultures, is that, as Robert Magliola argues: "Though opting for opposite horns of the subject–object dilemma, both idealist and empiricist agree there is no bridge between thought and world" (4). Phenomenology, however, has made attempts to build this bridge and in doing so has moved Western and Native American philosophies closer to one another. The work of Husserl shows how this might be the case:

Consciousness for Husserl ... is not a Cartesian knowing of knowledge but a real intercourse with the outside. Consciousness is an act wherein the subject intends (or directs himself towards the object), and the object is intended (or functions as a target for the intending act, though the object transcends this act). The subject intending and the object intended are reciprocally implicated (and, it should be added, the subject is real and the object is real, that is, truly emanating from the outside). (4)

Or framed in a way that might make sense to someone not familiar with the language of Western philosophy: "for the phenomenologist (to use one of Husserl's famous slogans), knowledge is the grasp of an object that is simultaneously gripping us" (17).

So, in phenomenology, the roles of both the perceiver and the perceived have a fundamental and important position in the creation of meaning while acknowledging that there is, indeed, a tangible world "out there" upon which consciousness acts and is acted upon. Crucially, in this regard, Silko and others of her generation have claimed of Native American societies that the subject–object divide has never been operative: "awareness never descended into Cartesian duality" (*Yellow Woman* 37).

As Silko suggests, the Western mind seems more inclined to focus on either subject or object, leading, inevitably, to either all-consuming individualism or crude materialism:

> They see no life
> When they look
> They see only objects. (*Ceremony* 135)

To extend these ideas to fiction, then, permits Silko to position herself as storyteller and her readers as audience in a traditional Native American sense that facilitates the co-creation of knowledge and understanding. These roles demand an integrated knowledge that depends not on the absolute authority of the author nor the whims of the reader, but on the participation of both in what phenomenology describes as "experiential unity." As Donald Fixico suggests, "The American Indian mind thinks inclusively. By seeing and believing that all things are related, this natural order is a sociocultural kinship. It is symbolic kinship based on an ethos of totality and inclusion" (48). Silko herself argues that: "The ancient Pueblo vision of the world was inclusive. The impulse was to leave nothing out. Pueblo oral tradition necessarily embraced all levels of human experience" (*Yellow Woman* 31). The Western insistence on the problem of a subject/object divide disappears – such a rupture is artificial even at the quotidian level. A position, therefore, in which there exist complex and tortuous divisions between storyteller and world, storyteller and audience, world and audience, and so on, is simply untenable:

> there are no inner or outer worlds, beginnings and endings, but a fluid circle of
> connections through which the several planes of being and doing, feeling and

thinking, seeing and dreaming, living and dying, are interrelated spokes on the single wheel of experience. (Niatum, 33)

In Silko's version of the function and action of the novel, as the Native American storyteller begins her story, the audience becomes, in that precise moment, part of a process that engages an entire listening/reading community – and by my use of the word "engaged" here, I do not mean merely that the author/storyteller commands the attention of the reader/listener, but, rather, that the reader/listener becomes a participant in a practice that redefines and reshapes the world in significant ways. Silko is not content to remain the mysterious, revered, quasi-shamanic author-figure, one that has been in gradual development as the dominant mode-of-being of the Western storyteller since the earliest manifestations of what Bakhtin has called "novelistic discourse." Indeed, drawing on the Native American practice of allowing the audience an important function in the telling of the story, Silko subverts the author function, inviting her audience to participate in the creation of meaning, thus offering them roles as co-activists.

The second element of Silko's novel that is a manifestation of a commitment to action and change is the notion of performativity: a performative linguistic act brings about that which it describes. The phrases, for example, "I award you this degree," spoken by a university official at graduation, or "I open this shopping mall," spoken by a celebrity, "are performative. Acts of this kind in speech or writing do, simply, what they say they do. They represent, in the moment, the action they describe. On a larger scale it seems to me that this is what Silko may be doing in *Ceremony*. The novel in its entirety, while it is faithful to Western and other conventions concerning description and narrative, from its opening word, "Ts'its'tsi'nako," to its closing word, "Sunrise," *performs* the ceremony of the title. In this moment literature is translated from a condition that could be characterized as passive (for the reader) and merely didactic (for the writer) to a condition approaching activism. Aristotle's division of poetry into mimesis (description) and diegesis (narrative) in *Poetics*, and in which the dominant reality is merely reproduced, is, it might be argued, able only to restate and emphasize the normative condition of the presiding cultural paradigm – in the case of post-Enlightenment fiction, an unfolding modernity (Genette 162–170). I want to argue that Silko's fiction, and that of Native American writers more generally, in adding the category of "performativity" to Aristotle's persistent formulation, resists the dominant paradigm in which Western culture is enmeshed and marks a renaissance for printed storytelling that has the potential to instigate meaningful change.

Silko is not alone in this: in *House Made of Dawn* Momaday recognizes that language brings "being" into the world: "She had learned that in words and in language, and there only, she could have whole and consummate being" (83). As Tosamah implies of the old Kiowa woman, words "do" things in the world: "[The words] were magic and invisible. They came from nothing into sound and meaning. They were beyond price; they could neither be bought nor sold. And she never threw words away" (85). Silko's method, however, is to fuse traditional Native American stories with her own activities as a writer. Her novel attempts to enact in the moment of writing the resistance it describes: "Ts'its'tsi'nako, Thought-woman,/is sitting in her room/and whatever she thinks about/appears" (1) therefore combines with: "I am telling you the story/she is thinking" (1). Both the Native American stories that Silko retells, and *Ceremony* itself, attempt to speak the thing into existence:

> Silko's *Ceremony*, like the mysterious witch's story which started the destruction in the first place, sets in motion the events that it describes, at least in the sense that Silko intends its characters and situations to be representative and its solutions to apply to the real world beyond its covers. (Hoilman 64)

Silko, thereby, travels beyond a merely mimetic rehearsal of literary tropes and techniques, and eschews a simple narrative framework in favor of a literary style that sets out to be politically active in a fashion that is far beyond a mere polemic or a straightforward call to arms. Silko seems to personify Edouard Glissant's dictum that "The artist's ambition would never be more than a project if it did not form part of the lived reality of the people" (235). Silko's novel is an extension of, and a participation in, the struggles of her people as *Ceremony* becomes ceremony: "Sunrise/accept this offering,/Sunrise" (262). If, says Silko, we can create or modify our own myth in opposition to their myth, it may be possible to de-nature the toxins of Eurocentric modernity. If we claim we created and invented the avatars of modernity we can, perhaps, uninvent and destroy them: "and I tell you, we can deal with white people, with their machines and their beliefs. We can because we invented white people; it was Indian witchery that made white people in the first place" (132). Let us contain them within our myth, *Ceremony* argues, as they have contained us within theirs: "Their evil is mighty/but it can't stand up to our stories" (2). Silko's is, therefore, a truly activist literary mode. The performative nature of the fiction, and the phenomenological condition of its form, guarantees as much. It represents an ability to encompass both Western and native ways of thinking in an intellectual rebirth that is rooted in indigenous culture and the relationship of that culture to the land. *Ceremony*, in ways that transcend any other work of the period, recognizes what has been lost in the process of colonization and seeks to suggest ways it might be replaced – not just for the benefit of the indigenous cultures of the American West, but for the entire population of the North American continent.

## Notes

1 The "living" land is sacred to many Native American groups: "the Blackfeet argued that the Forest Service's plans to allow Chevron and Petrofina to drill exploratory wells in a 100,000-acre roadless area of Montana south of Glacier National Park amounted to a violation of First Amendment religious rights. Traditionalists argued that it would 'cut out the heart' of their religion and that 'the land is our church.' " (Krech, 219) To "cut out the heart" of the land is both literal and metaphorical in this context. The importance of sacred sites to Native Americans should not be underestimated. As Deward Walker notes in "Sacred Geography in Northwestern North America":Ethnographic investigation of several hundred sacred sites suggests strongly that they are an essential feature of Native American ritual practice. Without access to them, practice would be infringed or prevented altogether in certain cases. Likewise all known groups possess a body of beliefs concerning appropriate times and rituals that must be performed at such sites.

2 See Edelman and Haugerud.

3 The quotations are from Richard B. Williams, president and CEO of the American Indian College Fund, in the foreword to *Indian Country Noir*, page ii. Of course, as Williams would be the first to acknowledge, Native Americans as a broad ethnic group remain socially deprived compared to other minorities, and prey to many of the social ills that accompany poverty.

4 Indeed, an earlier "renaissance" characterized by the work of John Joseph Matthews, Lynn Riggs, and D'Arcy McNickle in the late 1920s and early 1930s came about in a similar moment of calamity following the Wall Street Crash and marked the onset of the Great Depression.

5 Here, while acknowledging important objections from the likes of Jace Weaver and Elizabeth Cook-Lynn to "paracolonialism," and their support for "nationalist," "Nativist," and "anti-cosmopolitan" positions, I have no choice but to agree with Arnold Krupat: "Now, as Linda Alcoff notes of one Canadian case, 'white' critics are being asked by some Native people to 'move over,' to leave the field to those who are what they write about. I've already argued that, from an ethical and epistemological point of view, it makes no sense to exclude any would-be participant from the critical conversations that make up the contemporary interpretation of Native American literatures. Nor does it make sense politically to reject the aid of allies just because they are not 'us' " (*Turn to the Native* 89).

## Works Cited

Bakhtin, M. M. *The Dialogic Imagination*. Ed. Michael Holquist. Trans. Michael Holquist and Caryl Emerson. Slavic Series 1. Austin: University of Texas Press, 1981.

Benjamin, Walter. *Illuminations: Essays and Reflections*. New York: Schocken Books, 1969.

Cook-Lynn, Elizabeth. "Cosmopolitanism, Nationalism, the Third World, and Tribal Sovereignty." *Wicazo Sa Review*. Vol. 9, no. 2 (1993): 26–36.

Deloria, Jr., Vine. *God Is Red: A Native View of Religion*. 3rd ed. Golden, CO: Fulcrum Publishing, 2003.

  *Red Earth, White Lies: Native Americans and the Myth of Scientific Fact*. Golden, CO: Fulcrum Publishing, 1997.

Edelman, Marc, and Angelique Haugerud, eds. *The Anthropology of Development and Globalization: From Classical Political Economy to Contemporary Neoliberalism*. London: Wiley-Blackwell, 2004.

Genette, Gérard. "Boundaries of Narrative." *New Literary History*. Vol. 8 (1976): 1–13.

Glissant, Edouard. *Caribbean Discourse*. Trans. J. Michael Dash. Charlottesville: Ca raf-University Press of Virginia, 1989.

Heidegger, M. *Being and Time*. New York: State University of New York Press, 1962.

Hoilman, Dennis. R. "'A World Made of Stories': An Interpretation of Leslie Silko's Ceremony." *South Dakota Review*. Vol. 17, no. 4 (1979): 54–66.

Horkheimer, Max, and Theodor Adorno. *Dialectic of Enlightenment*. 1947. Trans. Edmund Jephcott. Ed. Gunzelin Schmid Noerr. Stanford, CA: Stanford University Press, 2002.

Husserl, Edmund. *Ideas: General Introduction to Pure Phenomenology*. London: Allen and Unwin, 1931.

Ingarden, Roman. *The Cognition of the Literary Work of Art*. Trans. by Ruth Ann Crowley and Kenneth R. Olson. Evanston, IL: Northwestern University Press, 1973.

Iser, Wolfgang. *Prospecting: From Reader Response to Literary Anthropology*. Baltimore, MD: Johns Hopkins University Press, 1989.

Jauss, Hans Robert. *Toward an Aesthetic of Reception*. Trans. by Timothy Bahti. Minneapolis: University of Minnesota Press, 1982.

Krech III, Shepard. *The Ecological Indian*. London: Norton, 1999.

Krupat, Arnold. *The Turn to the Native*. Lincoln: University of Nebraska Press, 1996.

Lincoln, Kenneth. *Native American Renaissance*. 2nd ed. Berkeley: University of California Press, 1992.

Magliola, Robert. R., *Phenomenology and Literature: An Introduction*. West Lafayette, IN: Purdue University Press, 1977.

Naess, Arne. *The Pluralist and Possibilist Aspect of the Scientific Enterprise*. London: Allen and Unwin, 1972.

Niatum. Duane. *Carriers of the Dream*. New York: Harper Collins, 1981.

Owens, Louis. *Other Destinies: Understanding the American Indian Novel*. Norman: University of Oklahoma Press, 1998.

Silko, Leslie Marmon. *Ceremony*. 1977. New York: Penguin, 1986.

  *Yellow Woman and a Beauty of Spirit*. New York: Touchstone-Simon & Schuster, 1996.

Slotkin, Richard. *Regeneration through Violence: The Myth of the American Frontier, 1600–1800*. Middletown, CT: Wesleyan University Press, 1973.

Turner, Frederick. *Beyond Geography: The Western Spirit against the Wilderness.* New York: Viking, 1980.

Visenor, Gerald. *The People Named Chippewa: Narrative Stories.* Minneapolis: University of Minnesota Press, 1984.

Walker, Deward, E., Jr. "Sacred Geography in Northwestern North America." January 19, 2015. www.indigenouspeople.net/sacred.htm. 1996.

Weaver, Jace. *That the People Might Live.* New York: Oxford University Press, 1997.

Wilson, James. *The Earth Shall Weep.* New York: Grove Press, 2000.

# 12

RAFAEL PÉREZ-TORRES

# Chicana/o literature in the West

The heart of Chicano literature lies in the Mexican Revolution, but its soul lies in the mists of the Mexica past. On one hand, Chicano/a literary texts focus on the material social conditions of Chicano life. Since the Mexican Revolution represents the birth of the modern Mexican nation, it has served as an iconic reference for social justice. While its eruption in the early decades of the twentieth century sparked an enormous migration to the United States, its role as a touchstone for equality and empowerment has profoundly shaped the content of Chicana/o literary expression. "Land and Liberty!" was after all a rallying cry of the Revolution. That cry for social representation resonates with much of modern Chicana/o literature.

In addition to its social dimension, the world of Chicano letters considers on the other hand the mythic, transhistorical dimensions of literary expression. The literature is drawn to broad questions of human consciousness, cross-cultural experience, and transnational states of being. This effort has underscored the importance of the psychic as well as sociopolitical terrain of the borderlands. To negotiate this treacherous contemporary cultural terrain, Chicana/o writers have deployed strategies of identification that call on premodern Mexica culture.

In the fourteenth century the Mexica formed a military alliance in the high plains of Central Mexico to create what we popularly call the Aztec Empire. Six centuries later, following the Mexican Revolution, the newly institutionalized Mexican government deployed Aztec imagery to celebrate (and simultaneously contain) Mexico's unique indigenous heritage.

Chicana/o artists, writers, and thinkers have freely drawn on and transformed the Mexican nationalist appropriation of Mexica iconography in order to confront and contest the difficult, violent, and genocidal legacies that constitute the modern moment. Through it all, Chicana/o literary culture has addressed processes of empowerment and cultural identity by calling on Aztec iconography in a strategy of ethnic affirmation and pride (Pérez-Torres 16). More importantly, the spiritual or religious aspects of this iconography highlight the transformative power of art to affect change on levels as intimate as the psychosexual and as encompassing as the economic and environmental.

The study of Chicana/o literature often clusters it in a series of socio-political eras: the great Mexican immigration of the 1920s and 1930s, the Mexican-American generation of the 1940s and 1950s, the civil rights movements of the 1960s and 1970s, the Third World feminist movements of the 1980s and 1990s, queers of color or jotería activism in the 1990s and 2000s, and the globalized call for immigrant and indigenous rights throughout much of these latter decades. Engagement with political discourse, commitment to social justice, and demands for collective agency form the activist scaffolding of Chicana/o literature in California.

At the same time, throughout its development, there has been a profound interest in the formal nature of aesthetic expression. The literature relies on a performative quality linked to the well-developed oral literacy characteristic of Mexican and Chicana/o cultures. The tension between the mythic and the historical, the aesthetic and the political has generated a rich and engrossing literary corpus delineating Chicana/o experiences in Western literature. Its literature is deeply imbedded in the neocolonial relationships between first Spain and then the United States and Mexico and their lasting effects on Mexico's long-suffering people both north and south of the border. The literature reveals how – for both individual and community – identities arise from a dynamic tension between displacement and attachment often impelled by tectonic historical shifts.

The novel *Pocho* by José Antonio Villareal (1959) provides an early example of a Chicana/o narrative following a character – a young man named Richard Rubio – torn by his family's displacement following the Mexican Revolution. Decades after its initial publication, the novel has come to exemplify for many critics the story of the so-called Mexican-American Generation (García). *Pocho* (originally published with the subtitle *A Novel about a Young Mexican American Coming of Age in California*) reflects an anxiety of identity. It traces the misadventures of Richard trying to measure up to the expectations of his revolutionary Mexican father while negotiating the impoverished landscape of his rural California farming community. The twin themes of cultural dislocation – "pocho" in Mexican Spanish refers disparagingly to deracinated Mexican-Americans – and labor exploitation haunt Richard's passage into adulthood.

While not successful when first published, the novel marks a significant and serious representation of a new identity: the Chicano (Ramón Saldívar, 70). The novel focuses on both the social conditions of the characters and the psychological impact of their multiple displacements. Desperate for a sense of belonging, Richard in the end decides to join the military in an attempt to assert some sense of national belonging. The decision to join the military, in the eyes of several of the book's critics, fulfills Richard's quest for assimilation and acceptance.

*Pocho* shares with other early Chicana/o literary texts a focus on the conflicts and complexities of self-formation in a multiethnic, multilingual, and primarily working-poor community. Hence these texts tend to emphasize an aesthetic realism that highlights the social and psychological dimensions of its Chicana/o characters. Realism remains a privileged aesthetic form due, in part, to an understanding that Chicana/o literature arises from a tradition of socially engaged art directly addressing the inequities of unjust social conditions.

John Rechy's best-selling 1963 novel *City of Night* has gained notoriety more as a gritty and salacious description of gay hustling in the urban demi-monde than as a direct mirror of Chicano social experience. Critics have argued that his 1991 novel *The Miraculous Day of Amalia Gómez* represents Rechy's most notable foray into writing ethnic literature. However, for more than fifty years his work has interrogated issues of marginalization – sexual, racial, ethnic, economic – drawn from Rechy's own experiences (Ortiz, 113). Rechy addresses how as a young, light-skinned, Mexican-American youth he had to balance an aggressive and rebellious sexual identity with the demands for social stability and incorporation. His texts at moments refer to the split identity he would experience when – in the home of a random sexual partner – he would spy his own books on the nightstand. The john had no idea that the author John Rechy and the cocky hustler in his bed were one and the same person.

The multiple dimensions inherent in identity and the graphic sexuality and assertive tone of rebellious confrontation have made Rechy a controversial figure in the corpus of Chicana/o literature. His status as a preeminent figure, however, can be little argued. Still, his work can evoke uneasiness (or enthusiasm!) in his readers because of its graphic and frank depiction of homosexual acts both casual and intense. Rechy's depictions of the socially outcast and his wildly vivid evocations of a multiethnic, multisexual Los Angeles in many ways prefigure themes that have come to predominate the study of Chicana/o literature.

While disparate in tone and interest from the books by Villareal and Rechy, the work of El Teatro Campesino – founded by Luis Valdez in 1965 to support the United Farm Workers (UFW) grape strike in Delano, California – similarly draws intense attention to conditions of injustice and exclusion. Rather than rely on a descriptive realism for its *actos* (short skits), however, the company drew on the traditions of the *commedia dell'arte* and its improvised, irreverent use of stock characters. The Teatro also called on the tradition of the *carpa* or traveling tent shows popular in Greater Mexico in the early twentieth century as well as the absurdist defamiliarization of Brechtian Epic Theater. The performances employ a repertoire of character types imbued with social stigma: the drunken father tormenting the passive and repressed mother; the delinquent son angry at the world paired with the shell-shocked veteran son angry at the world; the unwed pregnant daughter, and so on (Broyles-González, 140). While evoking stereotypical images of Mexican-American social pathology (particularly as regards gender roles), the types become tools by which social critique gets voiced (Heller, 769).

The work the Teatro produced in the fields, gymnasiums, auditoriums, and theaters – at first in Delano, then around California, later nationally and internationally – reflected a newly critical vision of U.S. society, inspired in no small part by the national and international social, political, and military struggles of the period. The function of Chicana/o literature began to change from mirroring unequal social conditions to hammering out new methodologies for liberation.

As part of the effort to remold the social landscape, activist academics at the University of California at Berkeley founded Quinto Sol Publications in 1965 in order to publish material relevant to a newly energized Chicana/o community. In 1967 they began publishing *El Grito: A Journal of Contemporary Mexican-American Thought* as a scholarly vehicle by which to counteract pathological representations of Chicanas/os prevalent in academic studies. Although geared toward a social science orientation, the journal always published short literary works and, in 1970, announced the first Premio Quinto Sol for the best literary writing by a person of Mexican descent residing in the United States. This begins a symbiotic relationship between Quinto Sol (and other publishing houses aimed at Chicano/Latino markets) and educational institutions that – because of aggressive and effective political activism – were beginning to offer Chicana/o studies courses (Cutler, 57). The prize money of $1,000 (while very welcome to hungry young writers) paled in comparison to the cultural capital that would eventually be accrued by the four books recognized by the Premio Quinto Sol.

The first recipient of the prize in 1971, Tomás Rivera, had only recently received his PhD in Spanish literature en route to a brief but stellar academic career that led to his being named chancellor at UC Riverside in 1979, a position he held until his death in 1984 (Calderón, 66). His short novel *...y no se lo tragó la tierra/...And the Earth Did Not Devour Him* enshrined – through a series of sometimes interrelated short chapters and vignettes – the migrant farm labor experience associated imaginatively and socially with César Chávez and UFW activism. Set in the late 1940s and early 1950s, Rivera's narrative traces among a disparate group of migrant farm laborers an arc from initial confusion and alienation to eventual self-awareness and community consciousness.

Influenced by Mexican author Juan Rulfo as well as Texan activist/academic Américo Paredes, Rivera's text generates a highly fragmented reading experience evocative of the dislocation and alienation the workers themselves experience daily. The theme of dislocation is embodied by the colloquial and formal registers of Mexican Spanish Rivera uses to compose the narrative: an English-language audience must rely on translation to make legible the book. More centrally, the hyper-fragmented narrative resonates with the broken conditions of a U.S. (post) modernity built upon the exploitation of dehumanized and denationalized labor.

Where Rivera's book opens to a discussion of social critique about workers' rights, the novel that won the Premio Quinto Sol the following year dealt with life in a remote rural town of New Mexico. Rudolfo Anaya's *Bless Me, Ultima* (1972) portrays the mystical power that a *curandera* has on the maturation of a young boy named Antonio Mares. The two other winners of the prize – Rolando Hinojosa for his portrayal of border life in Texas in *Estampas del Valle y Otras Obras (Sketches of the Valley and Other Works)* and Estela Portillo-Trambley for her collected stories *Rain of Scorpions and Other Writings* in 1974 – like Rivera focus on social conditions. Hinojosa's sketches focus on portraits of a shared border culture and struggles over land rights in the fictional south Texas town of Klail City. Portillo-Trambley's stories, for their part, explore the contentious position Mexican and Chicana women occupy caught between cultural expectations and a drive for new freedom and independence despite gendered restrictions. While not set in California nor written by authors originally from California, all four works awarded the Premio Quinto Sol served to solidify and shape the field of Chicana/o literature.

Along with this flourishing of art in fiction, poetry blossomed as an integral component of the Chicano movement. Alberto Baltazar Urista Herreria (better known by the *nom de plume* Alurista) has provided a brilliant body of poetry. His work, collected early on in *Nationchild Plumaroja* (1972) and *Timespace Huracan* (1976), draws together the experimentalism of Dadaist absurdism with the free-form improvisational style of bebop jazz, all the while calling up Aztec gods and warrior figures. As a young immigrant from Mexico in the 1960s, Alurista became deeply involved in student activism at San Diego State University. His poetry, experimental in form and written with an ear toward performance, represents some of the most aggressive and transformative work that, nevertheless, asserts the spiritual/mystical powers of language.

The poem that has drawn Alurista the most attention became a preamble for the "Plan Espiritual de Aztlán" adopted in 1969 by the First National Chicano Liberation Youth Conference, a statement advocating self-determination, mass mobilization, and social independence as the paths to justice and freedom. The plan, adapted by the conference attendees, articulated a separatist vision in which a new nation would be founded on the territory once known (according to legends shrouded in the shadow of recollected myth) as Aztlán.

The concept of Aztlán, the mythic homeland to the Mexica, came to embody a Chicano nationalist movement, one that underscores the transnational condition that makes up Chicana/o culture and experience. "We, the Chicano inhabitants and civilizers of the northern land of Aztlán, from whence came our forefathers," the preamble asserts, "reclaiming the land of their birth and consecrating the determination of our people of the sun, declare that the call of our blood is our power, our responsibility, and our inevitable destiny ("Plan" 402). The melding of social political activism with a mythical recollection of a utopian homeland and the near-biological imperative of race and liberation (the forefathers' "land of birth," the determination of the "people of the sun," the call of their blood as a "form of power") has generated a critique of Alurista's poetry as the expression of an essentialized and homogenized Chicano identity.

Yet, to view Alurista's opus as poetic dispatches from the frontlines of Chicano liberation is to misunderstand the breadth and diversity of his work. The territorial dream of an Aztlán as a site to be reclaimed does haunt some of the most ambitious aspirations for Chicano nationalism. Alurista has long asserted that Aztlán as an idea was meant to transcend borders and limitations in the quest for a transnational cultural and political freedom (Allen-Taylor; Bruce-Novoa, 276). His poetry offers a dynamic vision for Chicano subjectivity that lives culturally and literally across a hemispheric context, not only within the constraints of a nationalist model (López, 9).

It is indeed ironic, then, that Alurista's poetry is criticized as nationalistic. His poetry, rather, anticipates a turn toward a more global critical vision. In this respect, two books by Oscar Zeta Acosta reflect a fascination with Mexico and Central America as sites of authentic anticolonial struggle in juxtaposition to an anxiety about the historical significance of the Chicano movement's plans, proposals, protests, defeats, and triumphs.

*The Autobiography of a Brown Buffalo* (1972) and *The Revolt of the Cockroach People* (1973) portray the tumultuous decades of the 1950s and 1960s through the eyes of a young Chicano reporting on the mayhem and mischief that Acosta's alter ego in the books, Zeta Brown, generates as he seeks his place in the movement. The books are compelling not only because of the complicated and contradictory identities Zeta posits for himself, but also because of their focus on the historically and regionally specific quality of the movement, be its locale in the Central Valley of California where Acosta grew up or in the streets of Los Angeles where he became an activist lawyer. This regionalism stands in contrast to the global sensibility Zeta exhibited in his recognition of anticolonial struggle in the mountains of Guerrero in Mexico (López 8).

The books are marked by narrative excess: the tone soars from exuberance only to revel in acts of degradation; the very pages of *Revolt* are riddled with drawings of cockroaches crawling along the margins. So, too, the books reflect the personal excess of the narrator as he reels from one debauchery to another. Excess, to Zeta, is everything. The overt machismo, homophobia, and outright racism Acosta's alter ego spouts in the novels get undercut by the narrative voice that reveals the contradictions and degradations of Zeta Brown on his convoluted quest for decolonial liberation.

Several poets begin their writing career amid the aftershocks of the Chicano movement, developing themes and literary forms that resonate with the movement's activism but that sought new paths of understanding and expression. Generally imbued with a deep lyricism, the poetry of Gary Soto – especially in his first two published collections *The Tale of Sunlight* (1978) and *The Elements of San Joaquin* (1977) – evokes the beauty of the Central Valley landscape where he grew up. The poetic voice witnesses the landscape through a consciousness aware of the hours spent in backbreaking labor amid the limitless fields.

Having stumbled into college, Soto ended up studying with working-class poet (and later U.S. poet laureate) Philip Levine at California State University, Fresno. Soto developed a skill not just for the craft of poetry, but for conveying the brutishness and nobility of a life bound to labor (Lee, 188). His poems are often short, dramatic or lyrical pieces that convey the desolation of poverty, although often with a sense of humor and a profound sense of humanity underlying the desperation traced in his lines. A prolific writer, Soto has published numerous collections of poetry, literature for children and young adults, and personal recollections. Wary of being labeled exclusively a "Chicano poet," Soto has maintained a positon some distance from the poet as political activist.

More fully embracing the activist call of the movement, Juan Felipe Herrera began writing poetry in the 1970s and continues – in his role as the California poet laureate in 2012 and the U.S. poet laureate in 2015 – to contribute to Chicana/o letters with a sense of playfulness as well as seriousness of purpose when it comes to immigrant rights and social equity. Herrera's voluminous body of poems, while committed to addressing social issues, employs literary experimentation as part of the liberation practices his poetry champions. The tone of his always inventive poems can range from wryly observant to absurdly antic. In part, the purpose of all this play stems from Herrera's performance as poetic shaman and shape-shifting trickster. Poetry, for Herrera, bears witness to communal and individual responses, be they acquiescent or angry, to social injustice. More centrally, the poetry can serve as a salve that may ease into salvation. Participating in poetry serves as a secular communion, both invocation and evocation of community whose spiritual and social dimensions Herrera's poetry mirrors and provokes.

Although her list of publications does not reach the lengths of either Soto's or Herrera's, the figure of Lorna Dee Cervantes looms as large as any poet from California. Her work draws together the moral gravitas of the Chicano movement with a faith in the ancestral spiritual powers (she identifies as a member of the Chumash people). She evinces a dedication to her Chicana/o ancestors crossed with a strong feminist critique. Her collections of poetry, most notably *Emplumada* (1981) and *From the Cables of Genocide* (1991), reaffirm a commitment to spiritual awareness as a part of a psychic and emotional healing. Her work does not flinch, however, from evoking deeply personal and viscerally concrete poems chronicling sexual and racial abuse, social and cultural scars. Hauntingly beautiful in its descriptive power, Cervantes's poetry can be direct and confrontational as the title "Poem for the Young White Man Who Asked Me How I, an Intelligent, Well-Read Person, Could Believe in the War between Races" attests.

Cervantes's contributions do not stop with her invaluable poetic works. Her publishing house, Mango Press, founded in 1976, was among the principal outlets for several important Chicana/o poets. With the help of Gary Soto – who set up the Chicano Chapbook Series – Mango published or distributed poetry by Sandra Cisneros, Ana Castillo, Ray Gonzalez, Alberto Ríos, Victor Martinez, Luis Rodríguez, José Montoya, José Antonio Burciaga, and Luís Omar Salinas (Buckley, 23). All these poets, linked by their connections to California, share a sensibility about communal and individual human experience in relation to land and place. Labor and displacement are the means by which Chicana/o bodies interact with the places they and their loved ones occupy. The labor may be the domestic work of the household, the stoop labor of the field, the deafening shifts at the foundry, or the emotional labor required to maintain a family home. In every case, the sensibility of the poetic voice makes the reader aware of the costs engendered by one's occupation of land. Yet, simultaneously, these poets also point toward the possibility of change: each envisions a hope that may, in whatever attenuated way, affect the social conditions of the world beyond the poet's page.

Deeply committed to this vision of transformation, Gloria Anzaldúa takes up the call for decolonization, a journey toward self-identity both hard-fought and elusive, through the creative use of language. Anzaldúa's sense of self forms a privileged site of marginality. Bodies bounded by racial, sexual, or ethnic discourses take on the various categories of identification with which they have been constructed and engage in a critical, productive, but nevertheless jarring and deconstructive process of decentering. The mestiza/o body, as a racially and radically marked entity, moves through a critical borderland where different languages, cultures, economic stages of development, and technologized states of becoming all converge and clash.

The form and substance of her famous tome *Borderlands/La Frontera: The New Mestiza* (1987) proposes the twin journey for personal and social liberation. With its long history of philosophers, free thinkers, and new ageists (and the intellectual boiler room the History of Consciousness Department at UC Santa Cruz), California's intellectual cultures have clearly marked Anzaldúa's eclectic thinking and writing style. Her book mixes together various forms of literary and linguistic expression: essay, narrative prose, poetry (both lyric and dramatic), colloquial forms of Spanish and English, a smattering of *caló*, invocations of Mexica and Toltec mythology and religion. Because of its invocation (indeed, at times, intonation) of Mexica religious icons and imagery, Anzaldúa's work suggests a spiritual recentering of self and the social world becomes possible by accepting the transformational power of language.

The ability to speak critically in and about a specific place has influenced Chicana/o critical thought enormously. Through the arduous work of committed academicians, artists, and authors, Anzaldúa's writing has taken on international significance. Most centrally, her work provides a basis for the profoundly transformative Chicana critical theory developed by Norma Alarcón (founder and publisher of Third Woman Press), Chela Sandoval, Emma Pérez, and many other key thinkers, writers, and scholars.

While her work has profoundly influenced Chicana/o cultural critics and academics across generations, it has generated a great deal of controversy as well. Critics have attacked *Borderlands* for its invocation of ancient gods and goddesses and for its nostalgic reliance on mystical, mythological sources of power (Sáenz, 86). Other critics counter that her work, rather than escapist, is at heart a critique of the literal and spiritual displacement that results from the logic of late capitalism. The destructive economic and political disruptions inflicted by the needs of capitalism and nationalism lead to a painful but productively disruptive response in the mestiza body (Saldívar, 83).

Anzaldúa draws on mythic indigenous imagery to envision or embody the necessary psychic journey through the "Shadow Beast," the archetypal rebellious being, en route to an awakening in the new consciousness of the Coatlicue state. Coatlicue in Mexica mythology is a mother figure at once creating life and voraciously consuming the living. The Coatlicue state thus represents a transformative but highly disruptive spiritual and psychic state that is at once a death and rebirth. This leads the "new mestiza" to undergo a profound transformation of identity through a break or rupture that, for Anzaldúa, represents a new creative power. Thus Anzaldúa famously appropriates the ancient imagery of Mexica religious iconography to signal and symbolize processes of personal and artistic creative rupture. This rupture, while potentially psychological and spiritual, ultimately represents a new form of knowledge, a mestiza political hermeneutics (Saldívar-Hull, 66–67).

Anzaldúa, as do many Chicana/o writers and artists, uses Aztec iconography because it helps focus attention on the many ruptures and violations comprising the collective experiences of Mexicans in the United States. For Anzaldúa, the central spiritual significance of the iconography cannot be denied, yet Aztec imagery serves as part of a critical cultural repertoire evoking the long colonial history of the Mexican people and their descendants. The appropriation of ancient indigenous imagery mirrors the valorization of Aztec culture found in Mexican and Chicano nationalist discourse, yet one that wrests control from a discourse that often relies on the disparagement and disempowerment of female figures. Anzaldúa – along with other Chicana feminist writers, artists, and activists – embraces powerful female icons associated with Aztec culture and revisits, rewrites, or rejects figures associated with betrayal, treason, and capitulation (Chabram-Dernersesian, 84–85). Nationalist scripts, whether Mexican or Chicano, have served to silence women's voices in the formation of empowered Mexican and Chicana subjectivities. Anzaldúa's evocation of Aztec goddesses responds to the gender constraints enacted by male-centered visions of Chicano identity.

While her book has been extraordinarily influential, Anzaldúa's editorial work has also proven of lasting worth. Along with Cherríe Moraga, she coedited the transformative and groundbreaking collection *This Bridge Called My Back: Writings by Radical Women of Color* (1981) while the two were attending writers' workshops in the Bay Area. The book, having gone through multiple editions since its original publication, draws together personal essays, testimonials, interviews, and poetry responding to the complex social and political forces that influence and affect U.S. third world women (a term Chela Sandoval expanded on in her equally groundbreaking essay, "U.S. Third World Feminism," from whence arises her notion of oppositional consciousness as a methodology of the oppressed). The collection brought women of color together as a collective to talk about shared forms of oppression and explore the possibility of coalitional activism. By recognizing race, gender, class, sexuality, national affiliation, linguistic fluency, and so forth as components of subjectivity, it becomes possible to bridge differences strategically for specific political or community ends. Turning away from essentialized notions of identity, the contributors to *Bridge* reflect on the numerous confluences that have gone into the formation of identities that can – through commitment to the principles of social justice – transform the social landscape for women of color in the United States and, consequently, for the whole population.

Such aspirational hopes are evident in the work of playwright, poet essayist, and Anzaldúa's co-conspirator Cherríe Moraga. Her writing addresses the significance of multiple forces at work in formulating a socially conscious subjectivity. Serving as an artist in residence at Stanford University, Moraga is widely regarded for her theatrical work that ranges in topic from realistic portrayals of labor activism to the deployment of mythic icons from a variety of ancient civilizations. Her published plays include *Heroes and Saints and Other Plays* (1994), *Watsonville/Circle in the Dirt* (2002), and *The Hungry Woman* (2001). In Moraga's work, the appropriation of Aztec imagery and the reclamation of female power resonates with the strategies Anzaldúa employed. These myths sustain their potency as a potentially transformative force, but they also generate allegorical figures within the logic of the theatrical experience where ancient Greek and Aztec gods embody the social, sexual, cultural, and political conflicts of the contemporary world.

Attuned to the literary implications of mythic figures in his own fictional work, Arturo Islas gained fame as both an exceptional educator at Stanford University, where he held a professorship, and as an author of some renown with the publication of his novel *The Rain God* (1984) and its sequel *Migrant Souls* (1990). His novels recount the semi-autobiographical tales of the Angel family from south Texas. Drawing on realist and modernist literary techniques, they forge a complex portrait of a family in conflict as it negotiates numerous borders: national, economic, social, linguistic, religious, and sexual, among others. The melding of the past into the present is a hallmark of the narrative, just as the characters transition from one state of consciousness or existence into another, most poignantly evoked by the closing scene at the Angel family matriarch's deathbed surrounded by the wayward, confused, and alienated members of the conflicted family making – out of the U.S./Mexico borderlands – a sense of place and home.

A brilliant essayist, Richard Rodriguez traces in his writing the difficulties he has had in finding a sense of either home or place. He has generated a great deal of controversy – for his stance against bilingual education in the classroom and multiculturalism as a value – and garnered admiration for the stylish and sophisticated tone of his essays. They have been collected in books – beginning infamously in 1982 with his contribution to the culture wars, *Hunger of Memory: The Education of Richard Rodriguez* – that address the complex feelings and experiences the author endured as a scholarship student at Stanford University. He senses he is disparaged yet oddly privileged within U.S. society because of his ethnicity and strikingly racialized features. Consequently, he struggles with feelings of unworthiness and alienation due to his cultural and racial position, a sensibility compounded by the ideologically overwhelming promise of American exceptionalism and inclusion that seems to not take Rodriguez's own individualism into account. (Interestingly, another Stanford scholarship boy, Arturo Islas, presented a university lecture in 1985 that scathingly critiqued Rodriguez's denial of "a private self" [Islas, 223]). Out of his personal anxiety, Rodriguez has launched – deploying impeccable prose and stylistic flair – an attack against what he views as simplistic, overly rigid, orthodox, even puritanical attitudes toward the politics of diversity in U.S. society.

In many ways standing as a contrasting intellectual figure to Richard Rodriguez, Louis J. Rodríguez has long championed diversity as a necessary corrective to social inequality. Before becoming a poet and politician, Rodríguez as a young man fell in with the Los Angeles gang life but – in part thanks to a community arts center in his barrio and his work with the L.A. Latino Writers Workshops – he became a writer and editor of the literary arts magazine *ChismeArte* (literally meaning gossip and art as well as a pun on the act of gossiping as a communal form of communication). Arts and writing, a means of expressing his creativity, offered Rodríguez an avenue of escape from the violence of the barrio. In 2001 Rodriguez founded Tía Chucha's Press, which has published poets Patricia Smith, Terrance Hayes, and Elizabeth Alexander. Rodríguez's efforts have grown into the community cultural arts learning center Tía Chucha's Centro Cultural. In 2014 he was named the poet laureate of Los Angeles (Olivas).

Literarily most acclaimed for his 1993 memoir *Always Running: La Vida Loca, Gang Days in L.A.*, Rodríguez portrays his years living the gang life, employing realist narrative techniques in order to convey the need for spiritual and social revival and renewal. His memoir asserts that the social conditions leading to gang violence are linked to the economic and social injustices that marginal communities face daily without recourse to protection or defense.

A fellow Angelino, Helena María Viramontes first gained attention for her collection of short stories *The Moths and Other Stories* (1985) that deals with primarily Latina characters whose stories center on the transgression of borders, whether national, economic, or cultural. Given the literal or implicit sense of movement inherent in the lives of the characters, the notion of a monolithic or traditionally constructed family gets undone. Viramontes's stories consider the formation of family in new configurations: often oriented in an international context, the family becomes organized around a political commitment rather than blood ties. Her narratives align a Chicana feminist sensibility with the conditions of various political (usually Central American, usually women) exiles. Her novels *Under the Feet of Jesus* (1994) and *Their Dogs Came With Them* (2007) also trace the lives of women characters whose lives are delimited by the laborious conditions in the migrant farm fields and lives of displacement due to urban development.

The themes of displacement and an awareness of social responsibility as a mark of the moral life again manifest themselves as central concerns. Although his literary output was limited before succumbing to complications of AIDS in 1996, Gil Cuadros composed a number of extraordinary stories and poems. They call up the issue of displacement and social injustice, and cast these concerns in the context of the AIDS crisis in the Chicano community. In his collection of stories and poems *City of God* (1994), Cuadros portrays a hard-edged urban landscape in which queer Latino characters struggle to find acceptance and community, seeking to affirm the fulfillment of social justice for all Chicanas and Chicanos no matter their sexual orientation.

Other texts worthy of mention that attend to the moral dimensions of ethnic identity are Ernesto Galarza's compelling autobiography *Barrio Boy* (1971), Ron Arias's magical realist novel *The Road to Tamazunchale* (1975), and in the mid-1980s to the 1990s José Antonio Burciaga's poems and essays, Alfred Arteaga's poetry and Mary Helen Ponce's prose pieces. Other authors who have contributed to the opus of Chicana/o literature in California include, beginning in the 1980s, poet and performance artist Marisela Norte; journalist, essayist, musician, and activist Rubén Martínez; and playwright, director, and performer Luis Alfaro. These last three artists have been part of the downtown Los Angeles cultural life and all continue to contribute in multiple ways to the development of Chicana/o literary arts. Among newer authors – engaging Chicana/o literary traditions while moving in innovative and completely original directions – are fictionalist Manuel Muñoz, writing movingly and profoundly about life in California's San Joaquin Valley, novelists Alex Espinoza and Felicia Luna Lemus magically reimagining the cultural and historical landscape of Los Angeles, and brilliant novelist and Los Angeles native Dagoberto Gilb.

"One cannot be pessimistic about the West. This is the native home of hope," Wallace Stegner famously observed. He continued, "When it fully learns that cooperation, not rugged individualism, is the quality that most characterizes and preserves it, then it will have achieved itself and outlived its origins. Then it has a chance to create a society to match its scenery" (Stegner, 38). Certainly less concerned with scenery than with the hard realities of living on and by the land, Chicana/o writers in California have long sought to point out the necessity of collective cooperation, social renewal, and a call to justice and inclusion. This call recognizes the important social struggles that sought to correct the destructive legacies of a complex and extensive colonial history. In this regard, the poet Alurista may have more in common with Wallace Stegner than might instinctively seem evident: a shared sense of optimism and a faith in the possibility of renewal.

Alurista notes: "Some people say my poetry is protest poetry." Rather than fully embrace this position of oppositionality, he rejects the view that his work provides only negative critique: "No. It's also about reconstructing. To reconstruct ourselves, because being colonized people, the self that we possess, the view that we have, is colored by the colonization that we have suffered, by the schooling that we have been subjected to. We have to expel the Yankees from our heart" (Bruce-Novoa, 276). The processes of internal colonization form the ideological battleground upon which Chicana/o literature has sought to array its repertoire of illusion and illustration. It represents worlds of experience invisible to the U.S. national imaginary. It considers how identity gets shaped at the crossroads of various social, economic, linguistic, racial, and cultural forces. Ultimately, it evokes for its readership worlds of knowledge devalued by colonization, avenues for exploration that suggest transformative paths of awareness. Chicana/o literature looks to the future. It does so with one key distinction: in order to understand its future, it recalls the past and finds connection with communities of the exploited, discriminated, and outcast. The rooted quality of the literature grounds the range of hope and optimism for which the West is renowned. Hope, transformative and empowering, is in Chicana/o literature anchored to the violent colonial history that has inescapably forged the political, social, and cultural state of the West.

# Works Cited

Acosta, Oscar. "Zeta." *The Autobiography of a Brown Buffalo.* San Francisco, CA: Straight Arrow Books, 1972. Print.

*The Revolt of the Cockroach People.* San Francisco, CA: Straight Arrow Books, 1973. Print.

Allen-Taylor, Douglas. "Wizard of Aztlán." *Metro: Silicon Valley's Weekly Newspaper.* August 5–11, 1991. San Jose, CA: Metro Publishing Inc. Web. Accessed June 17, 2015.

Alurista. *Nationchild Plumaroja, 1969–1972.* San Diego, CA: Centro Cultural de la Raza, 1972. Print.

*Timespace Huracan: Poems, 1972–1975.* Albuquerque, NM: Pajarito Publications, 1976. Print.

Anaya, Rudolfo. *Bless Me, Ultima.* Berkeley, CA: Quinto Sol Publications, 1972. Print.

Anzaldúa, Gloria. *Borderlands/La Frontera: The New Mestiza.* San Francisco, CA: Spinsters/Aunt Lute Books, 1987. Print.

ed. *Making Face, Making Soul/Haciendo Caras: Creative and Critical Perspectives by Feminists of Color.* San Francisco, CA: Aunt Lute Press, 1990. Print.

Broyles-González, Yolanda. *El Teatro Campesino: Theater in the Chicano Movement.* Austin: University of Texas Press, 1994. Print.

Bruce-Novoa, Juan. *Chicano Authors: Inquiry by Interview.* Austin: University of Texas Press, 1980. Print.

Buckley, Christopher. "Chicano/Latina Poets: A Special APR Supplement." *The American Poetry Review.* Vol. 40, no. 5 (2011): 23–30. Web. Accessed June 20, 2015.

Calderón, Hector. *Narratives of Greater Mexico: Essays on Chicano Literary History, Genre, and Borders.* Austin: University of Texas Press, 2005.

Cervantes, Lorna Dee. *Emplumada.* Pittsburgh, PA: University of Pittsburgh Press, 1981. Print.

*From the Cables of Genocide: Poems on Love and Hunger.* Houston, TX: Arte Público Press, 1991. Print.

Chabram-Dernersesian, Angie. "I Throw Punches for My Race, but I Don't Want to Be a Man: Writing Us – Chica-nos (Girl, Us)/ Chicanas – into the Movement Script." In Lawrence Grossberg, Cary Nelson, and Paula Treichler (eds.) *Cultural Studies.* New York: Routledge, 1992. 81–95. Print.

Cuadros, Gil. *City of God.* San Francisco, CA: City Lights Books, 1994. Print.

Cutler, John Alba. *Ends of Assimilation: The Formation of Chicano Literature.* Oxford: University of Oxford Press, 2015. Print.

García, Mario T. *Mexican Americans: Leadership, Ideology, and Identity, 1930–1960.* New Haven, CT: Yale University Press, 1991. Print.

Heller, Meredith. "Gender-Bending in El Teatro Campesino (1968–1980): A *Mestiza* Epistemology of Performance." *Gender & History.* Vol. 24, no. 3 (2012): 766–781. Print.

Hinojosa, Rolando. *Estamas del valle y otras obras/Sketches of the Valley and Other Works.* Berkeley, CA: Quinto Sol Publications, 1973. Print.

Huerta, Jorge A. "Introduction." In Jorge Huerta (ed.) *Necessary Theatre: Six Plays about the Chicano Experience.* Houston, TX: Arte Público Press, 1989. Print.

Islas, Arturo. *Migrant Souls*. New York: William Morrow, 1990. Print.
  *The Rain God*. Palo Alto, CA: Alexandrine Press, 1984. Print.
  "Richard Rodriguez: Autobiography as Self-Denial." In Frederick Luis Aldama
    (ed.) *Arturo Islas: The Uncollected Work*. Houston, TX: Arte Público Press,
    2003. 220–228. Print.
Lee, Don. "About Gary Soto." *Ploughshares*. Vol. 21, no. 1 (1995): 188. Print.
López, Marissa. *Chicano Nations: The Hemispheric Origins of Mexican American
    Literature*. New York: New York University Press, 2011.
Moraga, Cherríe. *Heroes and Saints and Other Plays*. Albuquerque, NM: West End
    Press, 1994. Print
  *The Hungry Woman*. Albuquerque, NM: West End Press, 2001. Print.
  *Watsonville/Circle in the Dirt*. Albuquerque, NM: West End Press, 2002. Print.
Moraga, Cherríe, and Gloria Anzaldúa, eds. *This Bridge Called My Back: Writing
    by Radical Women of Color*. 2nd edition. New York: Kitchen Table Press, 1983.
    Print.
Olivas, Daniel. "Daniel Olivas Interviews Luis J. Rodriguez." *Los Angeles Review of
    Books*. March 19, 2014. Web. Accessed February 20, 2015.
Ortiz, Ricardo L. "Sexuality Degree Zero: Pleasure and Power in the Novels of John
    Rechy, Arturo Islas and Michael Nava." *Journal of Homosexuality*. Vol. 26, nos.
    2–3 (1993): 111–126.
Pérez-Torres, Rafael. *Mestizaje: Critical Uses of Race in Chicano Culture*. Minneapolis:
    University of Minnesota Press, 2005.
"Plan Espiritual de Aztlán." In Luís Valdez and Stan Steiner (eds.) *Aztlan: An
    Anthology of Mexican American Literature*. New York: Knopf, 402–406. Print.
Portillo-Trambley, Estela. *Rain of Scorpions and Other Writing*. Berkeley, CA:
    Tonatiuh International, 1975. Print.
Rechy, John. *City of Night*. New York: Grove Press, 1963. Print.
  *The Miraculous Day of Amalia Gómez*. New York: Arcade Publications, 1991. Print.
Rivera, Tomás. *...y no se lo tragó la tierra/...And the Earth Did Not Part*. Herminio
    Rios, trans. Berkeley: Quinto Sol Publications, 1971. Print.
Rodríguez, Luis J. *Always Running: La Vida Loca, Gang Days in L.A.* Willamtic,
    CT: Curbstone Press, 1993. Print.
  *It Calls You Back: An Odyssey through Love, Addiction, Revolutions, and
    Healing*. New York: Touchstone Press, 2012. Print.
Rodriguez, Richard. *Brown: The Last Discovery of America*. New York: Viking,
    2002.
  *Darling: A Spiritual Autobiography*. New York: Viking, 2013.
  *Days of Obligation: An Argument with My Mexican Father*. New York: Viking,
    1992. Print.
  *Hunger of Memory: The Education of Richard Rodriguez*. New York: Bantam
    Books, 1983. Print.
Sáenz, Benjamin Alire. "In the Borderlands of Chicano Identity, There Are Only
    Fragments." In Scott Michaelsen and David E. Johnson (eds.) *Border Theory:
    The Limits of Cultural Politics*. Minneapolis: University of Minnesota Press,
    1997. 68–96. Print.
Saldívar, José David. *The Dialectics of Our America: Genealogy, Cultural Critique,
    and Literary History*. Durham, NC: Duke University Press, 1991. Print.

Saldívar, Ramón. *Chicano Narrative: The Dialectics of Difference*. Madison: University of Wisconsin Press, 1990. Print.

Saldívar-Hull, Sonia. *Feminism on the Border: Chicana Gender Politics and Literature*. Berkeley, CA: University of California Press, 2000.

Sandoval, Chela. "U.S. Third World Feminism: The Theory and Method of Oppositional Consciousness in the Postmodern World." *Genders*. Vol. 10 (1991): 1–24. Print.

Soto, Gary. *The Elements of San Joaquin* Pittsburgh, PA: University of Pittsburgh Press, 1977. Print.

*The Tale of Sunlight*. Pittsburgh, PA: University of Pittsburgh Press, 1978. Print.

Stegner, Wallace. *The Sound of Water Mountain*. New York: Penguin Books, 1997.

Valdez, Luis. *The Shrunken Head of Pancho Villa*. [publisher not identified], 1967. Print.

Villareal, José Antonio. *Pocho*. New York: Doubleday & Co., 1959. Print.

Viramontes, Helena María. *The Moths and Other Stories*. Houston, TX: Arte Público Press, 1985. Print.

*Their Dogs Came With Them*. New York: Atria Books, 2007. Print.

*Under the Feet of Jesus*. New York: Plume, 1996. Print.

# 13

LINDA RADER OVERMAN

# Mestiza consciousness of La Frontera/ Borderlands in Sandra Cisneros and Helena María Viramontes

Gloria Anzaldúa, Chicana poet, essayist, fiction writer, and feminist critic, defines the "place of contact between the dominant culture and non-dominant cultures" (Wheatwind) as the "borderlands," the place from whence a consciousness of difference derives. Looking at Chicana culture "with all our differences amongst us as well as looking at the clash of dom-inant culture and Mexican culture, with the use of the border as a met-aphor," (Wheatwind) she expounds on this metaphor in her seminal text *Borderlands/La Frontera*, which explores the complexities of the Chicana identity and what she theorizes as *la consciencia de la mestiza*.

A Chicana-*tejana* growing up in the Lower Rio Grande Valley of south Texas and a lesbian, Anzaldúa is of working-class origins. Embracing a hybrid identity, she asserts she is not claimed by any one specific category of sexuality, race, culture, class, or gender, but proclaims:

> I am a border woman. I grew up between two cultures, the Mexican (with a heavy Indian influence) and the Anglo (as a member of a colonized people in our own territory). I have been straddling that *tejas*-Mexican border, and oth-ers, all my life. (v)

By exploring a consciousness of the Borderlands, Anzaldúa argues that the Chicana identity is hybrid rather than fragmented. *Las Chicanas* are a border people confronting the challenges of living between the United States of America and the United States of Mexico. In confronting their challenges, these women are shaped by a mestiza consciousness that "assumes a pro-phetic voice to create – by mythic, spiritual, mystic, intuitive and imagi-native means – a new vision of different kinds of borderlands, sexual or cultural, religious or racial, psychological or creative" (Ramírez, 185–186). *La mestiza*'s domain contains "various kinds of borders simultaneously"; tolerating contradictions, *la mestiza* operates "in a pluralistic mode" as the "supreme crosser of cultures" (Anzaldúa, 79, 84).

Anzaldúa speaks of this struggle in "keeping one's shifting and multiple identity and integrity" (58) intact by generating the condition of the uncomfortable familiar, that is, "no not comfortable but home." In acknowledging mestiza consciousness and the multiplicity it engenders, Anzaldúa creates "a third space, the in-between, border, or interstice that allows contradictions to co-exist" (Yarbro-Bejarano, 11). Anzaldúa proclaims in *Borderlands/La Frontera* as well that "the culture and the Church insist that women are subservient to males. If a woman rebels she is a *mujer mala*" (Anzaldúa, 17).

Sandra Cisneros and Helena María Viramontes inhabit this space through their literary allegiance to Chicana women of color. Each constructs women who grasp their hybridity, and through the act of writing, give themselves the ability to ultimately transcend repressive lives and embrace being *mujeres malas*.

Echoing Anzaldúa, Cisneros feels trapped by constricted patriarchal paradigms: "I guess as Mexican daughters we're not supposed to have our own house. We have our father's house and then he hands us over to our husband's" (Aranda, 73). Challenging this cultural paradigm, Cisneros examines the *mujer mala* through her character Esperanza Cordero in the story "The House on Mango Street," from the eponymous novel.

A preadolescent Esperanza's desire for "a real house" expresses, by metaphoric extension, her need to break free of the Chicano cultural prototype about which Anzaldúa writes. Dreaming of her own home that is not dilapidated, shabby, and shameful, Esperanza wants another house/identity to be hers. Esperanza wants not just "a room of her own," but a house of her own, signaling her ascent into middle-class achievement, and the house her mama "dreamed up in the stories she told us before we went to bed" (Cisneros, 4):

> The house on Mango Street is ours, and we don't have to pay rent to anybody, or share the yard with the people downstairs, or be careful not to make too much noise, and there isn't a landlord banging on the ceiling with a broom. But even so, it's not the house we'd thought we'd get. (3–4)

Esperanza discovers that a dwelling is a reflection of who one is; and in the eyes of the dominant culture, she ascertains just who she is perceived to be:

> You live *there*?
> *There*. I had to look to where she [a nun from my school] pointed – the third floor, the paint peeling, wooden bars Papa had nailed on the windows so we wouldn't fall out. You live *there*? The way she said it made me feel like nothing. (4–5)

Esperanza's realization of her *otherness* is glaringly brought to light in this passage. By answering truthfully (as most children do) and pointing to her tattered and rundown living space, Esperanza is observed to be just as shabby as the apartment above a laundromat. Hence she proclaims: "I knew then I had to have a house. A real house. One I could point to. But this isn't it. The house on Mango Street isn't it. For the time being, Mama says. Temporary, says Papa. But I know how those things go" (5). Esperanza soon discovers that she does not simply want to deny an identity associated with poverty, but rather desires to create an independent identity. Rather than embracing a white, middle-class norm, Esperanza adopts the identity of a borderlands writer, who chooses to become a self-autonomous person. Anzaldúa expounds:

> For a woman of my culture [and Esperanza's] there used to be only three directions she could turn: to the Church as a nun, to the streets as a prostitute, or to the home as a mother. Today some of us have a fourth choice: entering the world by way of education and career and becoming self-autonomous persons. (17)

Esperanza refuses to affiliate herself with any of these "three directions." And in order to reach an empowered identity, she must understand her relationship to the past. As Maria Elena de Valdés emphasizes, Esperanza's "sense of alienation is compounded because she is ethnically Mexican, although culturally Mexican American; she is a young girl surrounded by examples of abused, defeated, worn-out women" (57).

Esperanza's great-grandmother, and her namesake, is just such a person. Esperanza identifies with her great-grandmother's rebellious spirit; however, she prefers not to inherit her future. Esperanza, hope in English, explains that in Spanish "it means sadness, it means waiting":

> My great-grandmother. I would've liked to have known her, a wild horse of a woman, so wild she wouldn't marry. Until my great-grandfather threw a sack over her head and carried her off.... She looked out the window her whole life, the way so many women sit their sadness on an elbow.... I have inherited her name, but I don't want to inherit her place by the window. ("My Name," 10–11)

Although Esperanza focuses on the oppression internalized in her culture, Anzaldúa points to the historical roots of that oppression, tracing her own great-grandmother's suffering from similar repression: losing her cattle and all of her land, Anzaldúa's grandmother loses her identity. Her story, however, begins when a gringo swindled her land away following "the Treaty of Guadalupe-Hidalgo on February 2, 1848" (Anzaldúa 7), creating the border fence that "divides the Mexican people," leaving "100,000 Mexican citizens on this side, annexed by conquest along with the land."

Anzaldúa describes, in her usual code-switching manner, the repression that happened after:

> Mexican-American resisters robbed a train in ... Texas ... in 1915, Anglo vigi-
> lante groups began lynching Chicanos. Texas Rangers would take them into
> the brush and shoot them. One hundred Chicanos were killed in a matter of
> months ..."
>
> "Drought hit South Texas," my mother tells me. "*La tierra se puso bien seca
> y los animales comenzaron a morrirse de se'. Mi papá se murió de un* heart
> attack *dejando a mamá* pregnant *y con ocho huercos*, with eight kids and
> one on the way. *Yo fuí la mayor, tenía diez años.* The next year the drought
> continued *y el ganado* got hoof and mouth. *Se calleron* in droves *en las pastas
> y el* brushland, *pansas blancas* ballooning to the skies. *El siguiente año* still
> no rain.... A smart *gabacho* lawyer took the land away *mamá* hadn't paid
> taxes. *No hablaba inglés*, she didn't know how to ask for time to raise the
> money.... Mama Locha had asked that we bury her there beside her hus-
> band. *El cemeterio estaba cercado.* But there was a fence around the cemetery,
> chained and padlocked by the ranch owners of the surrounding land.... [A]
> sign read: "Keep out. Trespassers will be shot." (8)

Fictively and historically, we see cogent examples by Cisneros and Anzaldúa of the oppression of La Chicana/Mexicana by, not only the dominant culture, *Anglos* who murdered and pillaged, but worse – by Mexicanos/Chicanos who oppress the women of their own race. Nevertheless, Esperanza will not *wait by the window and wonder how it could have been.* Esperanza's connection to "a wild horse of a woman" gains ground as Esperanza "comes to an understanding of herself, her world, and her culture" (González-Berry and Rebolledo, 114). The ties to her great-grandmother are bonds to that part of herself that "no one sees" and to her namesake who was prevented from obtaining her own vision.

Esperanza, however, looking at her own small society, sees the portraits of many entrapped women. For instance, Rafaela is one woman who seems to be a representation of ideal beauty, exactly what a woman would want to be. But what does it get her: a jealous husband who traps her by the window. This happened to Esperanza's great-grandmother in the past, but it is also happening in the present. In fact the very women who seem to be the luckiest – the most beautiful – can also be the ones who are most entrapped. Hence, in "Rafaela Who Drinks Coconut & Papaya Juice on Tuesdays," Rafaela is ultimately trapped, although she yearns to live *la-mala-vida-de-una-mala-mujer*:

> [O]n Tuesdays Rafaela's husband comes home late because that's the night
> he plays dominoes. And then Rafaela, who is still young but getting old from

leaning out of the window so much, gets locked indoors because her husband is afraid Rafaela will run away.... Rafaela leans out the window and leans on her elbow and dreams.... On the corner there is music from the bar, and Rafaela wishes she could go there and dance before she gets old. (79)

The truth is Rafaela will get old and will not in fact "go there and dance." She won't live the life of *la mala mujer* since the rebel in her is not strong enough. Anzaldúa would argue that instead of being the "perfect" woman, one should take on another role, that of the Shadow-Beast:

It is a part of me that refuses to take orders from outside authorities.... It is part of me that hates constraints of any kind, even those self-imposed. At least the hint of limitations on my time and space by others, it kicks out with both feet. Bolts. (Anzaldúa, 16)

Yet some of these Chicanas will never empower the Shadow-Beast in themselves to bolt far enough or at all. Only Alicia, like Esperanza, in "Alicia Who Sees Mice," is driven by her Shadow-Beast to leave a miserable life of internal oppression imposed by a tortilla-eating father and culture. Alicia's father continually insists:

Close your eyes.... And anyway, a woman's place is sleeping so she can wake up early.... Alicia, whose mama died, is sorry there is no one older to rise and make the lunchbox tortillas. Alicia ... is young and smart and studies for the first time at the university. Two trains and a bus, because she doesn't want to spend her whole life in a factory or behind the rolling pin. Is a good girl, my friend, studies all night and sees the mice, the ones her father says do not exist. (31–32)

Alicia, through the avenue of education, escapes on "two trains and a bus." Anzaldúa too chose a similar path to Alicia's and Esperanza's:

I was the first in six generations to leave the Valley, the only one in my family to ever leave home. But I didn't leave all the parts of me: I kept the ground of my own being. On it I walked away, taking with me the land, the Valley, Texas. *Gané mi camino y me largué. Muy andariega mi hija.* Because I left of my own accord *me dicen, "¿Cómo te gusta la mala vida?"* (Anzaldúa, 15–16)

In Esperanza's tales we see a "girl who didn't want to belong" (Cisneros, 109), but likes "to tell stories," and we see that she will eventually find a form of liberation by being a "budding writer of poems" (González-Berry, 117): "one day ... I will pack my bags of books and paper. One day I will say goodbye to Mango. I am too strong ... to keep me here forever" (Cisneros, 110).

Anzaldúa, Esperanza, and Alicia all inhabit a borderland arena, an "in-between," from which they write and remember. Sometimes, memory/

re-memory enables our "ability to retrieve and organize images and events from the personal past" (Hampl, 313). It is then that we can "carry our wounds" forward and "learn not only to tell stories but to listen to what our stories tell us." Through re-memory Esperanza and Alicia will affirm what they were, what they were not, and what they have become.

In *The House on Mango Street*, Cisneros primarily focuses on one woman; in *Woman Hollering Creek*, a collection of short stories, she focuses on many women. Although some are defeated, some resist by embracing the ultimate *mujer mala* – La Llorona – "the weeping woman" (Madison, 12). According to the standard myth, La Llorona was a woman "who, upon discovering her husband's infidelity, murdered their children and was condemned to an eternity of sorrow and weeping. According to legend, she continues to wander through the night crying out for her children." La Llorona, however, comes in many versions. The image that is most significant for Cisneros is the woman who by choice or circumstance fails to conform to obligatory feminine roles.

Anzaldúa interpolates her version of such roles with pronouncements of resistance:

> My Chicana identity is grounded in the Indian woman's history of resistance. The Aztec female rites of mourning were rites of defiance protesting the cultural changes which disrupted the equality and balance between female and male, and protesting their demotion to a lesser status, their denigration. Like *la Lorona*, the Indian woman's only means of protest was wailing. (21)

Cisneros, in *Woman Hollering Creek*, gives us women who attempt to free themselves from a paradigmatic world of constricted roles in which the *ideal* woman represents admirable suffering and absolute love. If she does not choose the role of the nun or the mother, a woman risks stigmatization as a *mujer mala*, or if she does not marry she is made to feel like a total failure. Yet Cisneros acknowledges the woman who challenges these paradigms pays a cost.

In her title story, "Woman Hollering Creek," Cisneros first creates a character who wants to live under the guise of wife/mother, but finding herself in an abusive relationship she must choose some mode of resistance. Ultimately, she finds this choice no less dangerous than the first and she ends up escaping back to the man who said, "I am your father, I will never abandon you" (Cisneros, 43).

And so Cleófilas Enriqueta de León Hernández, the young Mexican bride whose father gave Juan Pedro Martínez Sánchez permission to marry, originally comes north of the border to live with her new husband, an icehouse worker. This journey from North to South is a common one. Cleófilas and Juan must drive:

> over several miles of dirt road and several miles of paved, over one border and beyond to a town *en el otro lado* – on the other side … their new home in Seguín [Texas].… Poor thing. And without even a mama to advise her on things like her wedding night. Well, may God help her. What with a father with a head like a burro, and those six clumsy brothers. (43–45)

Cleófilas foresees her life like the many *telenovelas* she watches. What she's "been waiting for … has been anticipating since she was old enough to lean against the window displays of gauze and butterflies and lace, is passion" (44). However, she couldn't help wondering "why the name Woman Hollering" (46) of the creek behind her not-exactly-new-house fascinated her so:

> La Gritona. Such a funny name for such a lovely *arroyo*.… Though no one could say whether the woman had hollered from anger or pain. The natives only knew the *arroyo* one crossed on the way to San Antonio, and then once again on the way back, was called Woman Hollering, a name no one from these parts questioned, little less understood. (46–47)

Cleófilas's dreams lay in the display window she enjoys looking at with its gauze, butterflies, and lace. Perhaps she should have looked beyond it, rather than focus merely on the frills that first catch the eye and hide the defects. Hence, Cleófilas justifies her choice, of what Anzaldúa calls "to the home as a mother" (17), for "the man I have waited my whole life for" (Cisneros, 49). Cleófilas, however, begins to question herself:

> She has to remind herself why she loves him.… Or wonder a little when he kicks the refrigerator and says he hates this shitty house and is going out where he won't be bothered with the baby's howling and her suspicious questions, and her requests to fix this and this and this because if she had any brains in her head she'd realize he's been up before the rooster earning his living to pay for … the roof over her head … why can't you just leave me in peace, woman. (49)

Here the frills in the display window fail to hide the cruelty of a *telenovela* gone wrong, and ugliness erupts, actuality intervenes. Reality in *la frontera* betrays Cleófilas and her dreams. Now in her *telenovelas*, "the episodes [get] sadder and sadder. And there [are] no commercials in between for comic relief. And no happy ending in sight" (53) with her man in Texas. Cleófilas decides going back home to Mexico and facing the looks "with one baby on her hip and one in the oven" (50) is better than remaining in the borderland – a "town of gossips."

Cleófilas is trapped not only by her husband's machismo, but by five hundred years of *history/His-tory* that has imposed silence and social ostracism on her story/*Her-story*, making her and others like her indiscernible, silent, and unseen. It is this legacy that Cisneros gives her women to fight against and against which Anzaldúa protests:

> The dark-skinned woman has been silenced, gagged, caged, bound into servitude with marriage, bludgeoned for [five hundred] years, sterilized and castrated in the twentieth century. For [five hundred] years she has been a slave, a force of cheap labor, colonized by the Spaniard, the Anglo, by her own people.... For [five hundred] years she was invisible, she was not heard ... she concealed her fire; and she kept stoking the inner flame. (22–23)

The flame that burns is that of the ultimate *mujer mala*, who cultivates that inner fire, who drowns her own children rather than submit them or herself to further subjugation. *La mujer mala* calls to Cleófilas, albeit there is one place she could go, not to the houses on either side of her two neighbors, but to the creek "now in the springtime, because of the rains, a good-size alive thing, a thing with a voice all its own, all day and all night calling in its high, silver voice. Is it La Llorona, the weeping woman? La Llorona, who drowned her own children?" (Cisneros, 51). Accordingly, Cisneros revises the myth about a woman who kills her children into one that points the way for resistance for Cleófilas. In fact, she soon meets her own *llorona* figure, Felice, a social worker at the women's shelter, who belongs to herself alone. She brings joy and laughter to Cleófilas, who is astonished by her liberated state, her freedom with language, and the fact that she actually drives a pickup truck:

> when they drove across the *arroyo*, the driver opened her mouth and let out a yell as loud as any mariachi. Which startled not only Cleófilas, but Juan Pedrito as well.
>
> *Pues*, look how cute. I scared you two, right? Sorry. Should've warned you. Every time I cross that bridge I do that.... Woman Hollering. *Pues*, I holler.... Did you ever notice, Felice continued, how nothing around here is named after a woman? ... She was laughing. (55)

Felice has arrived at that place, "the epitome of happiness" (Fiore, 70), where by choice she is independent, and instead of hollering from anger or pain she can laugh, scoff even, at one of the Chicano patriarchal bastions: the-definition-of-a-good-girl is a virgin. Instead, Felice aligns the word *arroyo* (which in Spanish means brook or stream, and in the context of street means gutter) with anything but a virgin. Felice subverts the idea of "feminine sorrow" by being the embodiment of happiness as her name suggests:

That's why I like the name *arroyo*. Makes you want to holler like Tarzan, right? ...

I used to have a Pontiac Sunbird. But those cars are for *viejas*. Pussy cars. Now this here is a *real* car. (Cisneros, 55)

In driving a car that is typically designed for a man, Felice challenges the stereotype of the dependent woman. These new partners/sisters holla/laugh while crossing the arroyo, which commands that the women holler. Cleófilas still cannot believe a woman like this exists:

What kind of talk was that coming from a woman? Cleófilas thought. But then again, Felice was like no woman she'd ever met. Can you imagine, when we crossed the *arroyo* she just started yelling like a crazy.... Then Felice began laughing again, but it wasn't Felice laughing. It was gurgling out of her own throat, a long ribbon of laughter, like water. (55–56)

Stepping away from her victimization and silence, Cleófilas makes a small stride toward freedom in her encounter with Felice. Felice inhabits all aspects of the borderland identity. Thus, Anzaldúa might just characterize Felice as "a new *mestiza* ... [con] *una consciencia de mujer* [mala] ... a consciousness of the Borderlands" (Anzaldúa, 77).

Like Sandra Cisneros, Helena María Viramontes explores the repression of women and the means by which they resist oppression. In *The Moths and Other Stories*, Viramontes exemplifies the struggle these women must undergo simply to survive one day "of a life ruled by unfairness" (Badeaux, 4). Viramontes creates women resistance fighters who in their own way take on the role of Anzaldúa's Shadow-Beast:

Some of [them] conform to the values of the culture, push the unacceptable parts into the shadows. Which leaves only one fear – that [they] will be found out and that the Shadow-Beast will break out of its cage ... Yet still others ... take it another step: [they] try to waken the Shadow-Beast inside. (Anzaldúa, 20)

However, to wake the Shadow-Beast can be dangerous as the role of resistance often comes with a measure of sacrifice.

The young fourteen-year-old narrator of "The Moths" does not fit in at home among her perfect sisters who crochet and embroider, nor does she feel at home in church, where "the coolness of the ... frozen statues with blank eyes" (Viramontes, 25) reminds her that she "was alone" (25) and why she "had never returned" (25). Although her father demands that she must go, she wants to escape from church; however, when she rebels, she causes dissension in the family. Her father insists she attend church: "he would grab my arm and dig his nails into me to make sure I understood the importance of catechism" (25). When he sees he has no effect on her, he directs his anger at her mother, causing her sister to turn upon her: "Can't you see what it's doing to Amá, you idiot?" (25). In the end the idiot ultimately relents.

Her grandmother, though, accepts her, even her shadows. Abuelita has seen the girl through all the "rages" (23) of her early childhood, scarlet fever, whippings, and puberty. Only at Abuelita's does her *nieta* learn the power of folk medicine as she plants Abuelita's "wild lilies or jasmine or heliotrope or cilantro or hierbabuena in red Hills Brothers coffee cans" (24). Only while Abuelita watches does she feel "safe and guarded and not alone." Abuelita constructs a place her *nieta* feels she has potential to be healed and be a healer – a *curandera*.

As a young *curandera* she comes to learn the comfort of place, and the power of life and death. Abuelita offers her *nieta* an awareness of difference, creating within her a borderland space, a mestiza consciousness allowing her to confront life's own shadows – her grandmother's death. As a result the young narrator cradles Abuelita's wasted body in a ceremonial bath of baptism and cleansing of the dead. Now as a young priestess, she submerses Abuelita into the water, and the "tub overflowed and poured onto the tile of the floor":

> Then the moths came. Small, gray ones that came from her soul and out through her mouth fluttering to light, circling the single dull light bulb of the bathroom. Dying is lonely and I wanted to go where the moths were.... I wanted to rest my head on her chest with her stroking my hair, telling me about the moths that lay within the soul and slowly eat the spirit up. (28)

It is at this point that the young girl transforms into a Shadow-Beast of rebellion who finds a borderland arena of healing. Unlike her sisters, she cannot conform to society's norms, but she can become a *curandera* and a priestess. Her anger at her mother melts away:

> The bathroom filled with moths, and for the first time in a long time I cried, rocking us, crying for her, for me, for Amá, the sobs emerging from the depths of anguish, the misery of feeling half born, sobbing until finally the sobs ripped into circles and circles of sadness and relief.

As Virginia Adán-Lifante writes:

> *A pesar de que rodear la luz es un comportamiento normal de las polillas, en el cuento refuerza la idea de regeneración como búsqueda de nuevos valores, ya que aquí la luz tiene la misma función que el fuego purificador.* (369)

> [In spite of the fact that circling the light is a normal behavior for moths, in the short story it reinforces the idea of regeneration as a search for new values since here the light has the same function as the purifying fire.]

Through this purification process, the child becomes the woman *curandera*, the rebel becomes the priestess. Therefore as *curandera*-priestess she now has the ability to "[picture] herself ... located at this moment of life and death" (Stockton, 214) transitioning magically between one world and another. Ultimately, with her grandmother's help, her Shadow-Beast finds an alternate space – the space of healing. Yet Viramontes's women do not always find an alternate space, sometimes only a space of resistance.

Viramontes critiques the restrictive culture that imposes such rigid gender roles upon its women that they are forced to take excessive actions in order to individuate their Shadow-Beasts, to challenge society's dismissive words: "Tu eres mujer" (Viramontes, 32). Anzaldúa reminds us:

> "You're nothing but a woman" means you are defective.... The modern meaning of the word "machismo" ... is actually an Anglo invention. For men like my father, being "macho" meant being strong enough to protect and support my mother and us, yet being able to show love. Today's macho has doubts ... [h]is "machismo" is an adaptation to oppression and poverty and low self-esteem ... loss of a sense of dignity and respect in the macho breeds a false machismo which leads him to put down women and even to brutalize them. (83)

Women respond to this false machismo with "defiant resignation" (Viramontes, 56), as Viramontes's last story presents a woman who takes a gun, the phallic symbol of a man, and finds herself going against a woman.

Ironically, in "Neighbors," a Chicana in the act of resistance kills, not an angry husband or a threatening male, but another woman. Aura Rodriguez is so isolated from her community over the "past seventy-three years" (102) that the first thing we learn is that she "always stayed within her perimeters, both personal and otherwise, and expected the same of her neighbors." Suffering from the pain of her aged body and its aching joints, she's terrorized by the Bixby Boys, a local gang, who play loud music and throw "beer cans in her yard" (108). After calling the police, who respond with excessive force, Aura realizes her vengefulness toward them is a mistake. Toastie, a boy she has watched grow up, runs from the police toward her:

> it was not until he lunged for the door that she was able to see the desperation and confusion, the fear in his eyes, and he screamed at the top of his lungs while pounding on her door ... he screamed to her, "Pleeeeeeeease." (109)

Soon his supplications turn into threats of "We'll get you," by his other friends.

In the meantime Aura's elderly and lonely neighbor, Don Fierro, who lives in the small house behind her, has a visitor one day: "a massive woman with a vacuous hole ... a distinct scent accompanying her. She was barefooted and her feet, which are cracked, dirty and encrusted with dry blood, were impossible to imagine once babysmall and soft" (102). Fierro and his visitor bond in such a way that Aura becomes curious enough to "peer into their bedroom window" (110) and listen along with them to their music playing on the record player. A healing presence, the woman with the caked-hairsprayed-on-wig dances and feeds Don Fierro's mouth as well as his soul. He could only pronounce that everything she cooked was "all so good [as] he reached over the table to touch her hand" (116). But for Aura things take on a darker turn.

Threats turn to reality as the Bixby Boys desecrate Aura's garden and home, and Aura refuses to sit passively: "she refused to be their sacrificial lamb" (112). She readies herself for the next wave of "we'll get you" (109) with an old gun, clumsy and cold, but lethal just the same. Finally Don Fierro dies, but not before enjoying the happiness from this warm mass of sleeping woman, in effect a *curandera*, who comforted him and stayed with him until the end, when "in short fits of spasms, his life snapped" (117). What she does not know is what is waiting for her on the other side of the front house door; she has run for help to the Shadow-Beast of the darker side ready to shoot at anyone or any snakes, "rattlers," who might strike out at her (in the guise of the Bixby Boys). Aura is ready with her gun "held high with both hands, squeezing, tightly squeezing it as she aimed at the door" (118) where the barefooted woman stood panting.

In their article "With a Pistol in *Her* Hand: Rearticulating the Corrido Narrative in Helena María Viramontes's 'Neighbors,' " JoAnn Pavletich and Margot Gayle Backus argue that Aura becomes a "male corrido hero":

> she confronts an ambiguously culturally situated adversary who stands outside her ... literal and conceptual field of vision. Poised in ambiguous self-defense of her ambiguous right, Aura Rodrigues takes up an ancient pistol she finds in her basement and assumes, while she simultaneously transforms, the conventional stance of the male corrido hero, with *his* pistol in *her* hand. (128)

To take a pistol in hand indeed is an act of resistance, but ultimately she kills another woman rather than undergo a transformation. Aura deteriorates into a disconnected self, fragmented by isolation, distrust, envy, and revenge. The Chicana she murders has committed no crime other than to embrace the light-bearing-side of her Shadow-Beast as a healer/*curandera*. The deadly cost of Aura's "ambiguous right" imperils both herself and her sister within the culture and within her community. She gains nothing and is not transformed into anything other than a murderess, appropriating her own "false machismo." The woman, whose name we are never told, could have been Aura's *curandera* as well. "*His* pistol in *her* hand" (128) does not empower Aura, but creates a broken Shadow-Beast sitting in a cell and never rising to an awareness of herself nor of *la consciencia de la mestiza*.

*Las Chicanas*, in the fictional works of Cisneros and Viramontes, have been shaped by Anzaldúa's *consciousness*/theory of the Borderlands. This theory enables these characters to inhabit an alternate "third space" (Yarbro-Bejarano, 11), thereby creating a mestiza consciousness, which drives them to resist multiple forms of oppression: internal and external. However, they come to the realization that by taking on the form of the resistance fighter – whether in the figure of *la mujer mala, la llorona*, or the Shadow-Beast – such resistance does not come without great price, to the one and to the many.

## Works Cited

Adán-Lifante, Virginia. "Relaciones intergeneracionales en la cuentística femenina chicana." In Renate von Bardeleben (ed.) *Gender, Self, and Society*. Frankfurt: Peter Lang, 1990. 247–255.

Anzaldúa, Gloria. *Borderlands/La Frontera*. San Francisco, CA: Aunt Lute, 1987.

Aranda, Pilar E. Rodriguez. "On the Solitary of Being Mexican, Female, Wicked and Thirty-Three: An Interview with Writer Sandra Cisneros." *The Americas Review*. Vol. 18, no. 1 (Spring 1990): 64–80. Print.

Badeaux, Alyce Claire. "Las Lloronas Ya No Lloran (The Weeping Women Cry No More): A Discussion and Analysis of the Work of Chicana Author Helena María Viramontes." Thesis. University of Southern Mississippi, 1993.

Cisneros, Sandra. *The House on Mango Street*. New York: Vintage, 1984. Print.
    *Woman Hollering Creek*. New York: Vintage, 1991. Print.

de Valdés, Maria Elena. "In Search of Identity in Cisneros's *The House on Mango Street*." *Canadian Review of American Studies*. Vol. 23, no. 1 (1992): 55–72. Academic Search Premier. Web. May 9, 2015.

Fiore, Teresa. "Crossing and Recrossing 'Woman Hollering Creek.'" *Prospero*. Vol. 1 (1994): 61–75. Print.

González-Berry, Erlinda, and Tey Diana Rebolledo. "Growing Up Chicano: Tomás Rivera and Sandra Cisneros." *Revista Chicano-Riqueña*. Vol. 13, nos. 3–4 (1985): 109–119. Rpt. in *Contemporary Literary Criticism*. Ed. Lawrence J. Trudeau. Vol. 352. Detroit: Gale, 2014. *Literature Resource Center*. Web. Apr. 9. 2015.

Hampl, Patricia, "Memory and Imagination." In Robert Root and Michael Steinberg (eds.) *The Fourth Genre*. New York: Pearson, 2005. 306–315. Print.

Madison, D. Soyini (ed.) *The Woman that I Am: The Literature and Culture of Contemporary Women of Color*. New York: St. Martin's, 1994. Print.

Pavletich, JoAnn, and Margot Gayle Backus. "With a Pistol in Her Hand: Rearticulating Corrido Narrative in Helena María Viramontes' 'Neighbors.'" *Cultural Critique*. Vol. 27 (Spring 1994): 127–152. Print.

Ramírez, Arthur. Rev. of *Borderlands/La Frontera: The New Mestiza* by Helena María Viramontes. *The Americas Review*. Vol. 17, nos. 3–4 (1989): 185–186. Print.

Stockton, Sharon. "Rereading the Maternal Body: Viramontes' The Moths and the Construction of the New Chicana." *The Americas Review*. Vol. 22, nos. 1–2 (Spring–Summer 1994): 212–229.

Viramontes, Helena Maria. *The Moths and Other Stories*. Houston: Arte Publico Press, 1985.

Wheatwind, Mare-Elise "Gloria Anzaldúa Interview." *NuCity* [Albuquerque, NM]. 11–17 Apr. 1994. n. pag.

Yarbro-Bejarano, Yvonne. "Gloria Anzaldúa's Borderlands/La Frontera: Cultural Studies, 'Difference,' and the Non-Unitary Subject." *Cultural Critique*. Vol. 28, no. 28 (1994): 5–28. *JSTOR*. Web. Apr. 9, 2015.

## 14

MARGUERITE NGUYEN

# The West and the Asian American experience

Scholars have shown the somewhat dichotomous manner in which Asian Americans have figured in portrayals of the "American West," both written *out of* them as perpetual foreigners and written *into* them as exceptional American subjects. Asian American literary production can be said to grapple with the narrative tensions inhering in these representational modes. This chapter prioritizes Asian American literature and literary criticism and focuses on what I posit are four prominent tropes and forms – the linguistic fragment, the letter, the iconic/un-iconic image, and the mixed genre – to unpack how Asian American literary Wests confront prevailing notions of the U.S. West.[1]

### Linguistic fragments

Dorothy Fujita-Rony writes that in the early days of her teaching, she often went West – resorted to "standard ways [of analyzing] Asian Americans" that typically start with the Chinese Americans in Gold Rush California, proceed to Asian exclusion laws, move to the World Wars and the issues of citizenship that they raise, and conclude with Southeast Asian refugee arrival in the United States. Fujita-Rony notes that by taking the West as a bounded space and positing a succession of Asian American migration, this model reproduces American exceptional ideologies that equate the passing of time with a gradual integration of Asian Americans into U.S. cultural, social, and political life (Fujita-Rony, 563–564).

Such hegemonic thinking has turned some Asian American writers toward the fragment to open alternative paths of representation. Maxine Hong Kingston's *The Woman Warrior*, for instance, thematizes the linguistic fragment to question prevailing paradigms of California's geography and significance in American culture and history. Kingston's coming-of-age is largely scripted through the many ghost stories that family members tell, and a word that recurs throughout her childhood is *kuei*. In one tale the repetition of "Sit Dom Kuei" causes young Kingston to belabor the phrase's meaning: "I kept looking in dictionaries under those syllables. 'Kuei' means 'ghost,' but I don't find any other words that make sense.... How do they translate?" (88). Her piecemeal grasp of Chinese creates an insistent desire to find correct and complete English translations so that she can appropriate Chinese terms into daily life – something important for not only Maxine but also her Chinese American classmates whose "voices were too soft or nonexistent" (167). By the end of the text she is an active participant in "talk story," an interactive, open-ended form that joins historical events and narrative imagination. *The Woman Warrior* dialecticizes translatables and what Emily Apter calls "untranslatables" of Asian American literature – not just from word to word or phrase to phrase, but also of intergenerational memory and history.

The flow of linguistic fragments within California geography in Kingston's *The Woman Warrior* recalls the Chinese-language poetry that detained immigrants carved into the barracks walls at Angel Island. About one hundred and seventy five thousand Chinese and sixty thousand Japanese were processed at Angel Island during Asian exclusion, housed in barracks separated by gender (Lai, Lim, and Yung, 8, 15). Lamenting the facility's conditions, "coaching" future detainees, and contrasting expansive Angel Island views with realities of imprisonment, these early twentieth-century poems posit the West as transpacific – a movement of peoples, objects, and texts across the ocean.

Poetic fragments become grounds for dialogue and intertextuality, as they are extended, repurposed, and revised by detainee-poets. Poems 47–49 cluster around the Island's disciplinary regime: "I am distressed that we Chinese are detained / in this wooden building" (Lai, Lim, and Yung, 47); "I thoroughly hate the barbarians because they do not respect justice" (48); "I cannot bear to describe the harsh treatment by the doctors" (49). By contrast, poems 59–60 relate self-perseverance: "not to worry too much. / They mistreat us but we need not grieve" (59); "you must cast your idle worries to the flowing stream" (60). Subsequent poems 61–62 then overturn the theme of affective labor: "My heart trembles at being deported back to China" (61); "In the wooden jail, I was imprisoned for days. / Now I am to be deported back" (62). Situated within yet excluded from U.S. national boundaries, the poems – once referred to as a "bunch of graffiti" (Lee and Yung, 302) – write back to processes of detention and immigration, restyling the edifice of the incarceration facility itself.

Asian American linguistic fragments relate not only issues of immigration but also concerns with U.S. imperialism, colonialism, and militarization. Craig Santos Perez's experimental chapbook series, *from unincorporated territory*, scrutinizes Guam as an American "unincorporated territory" – a term used in the 1950 Organic Act of Guam to secure territorial control of the major Pacific harbor and land mass without the word *colony*. Santos Perez's interest in fragments manifests in his own poetic extractions, a process he calls "trans-book threading" that shows how his "poems change and continue across books" ("The Page Transformed"). Excerpts from *"ginen all with ocean views" from unincorporated territory [saina]* remix fragments from travel magazines and news sites, resulting in semantic reappropriations that cast a critical gaze on the tourist industry's fetishistic one:

'we have shampooed the
beaches' 'laid
on a nice sunset'          'reserved one of our
last hunter-
gatherer tribes' 'all
mirrors end in golf's | exclusive | domain' 'curio
city' 'speak English!' | 'to cope with | / wreckage formations'

Santos Perez's "threading" critiques the tourist industry's dissemination of alluring snippets of Guam's history, culture, and topography, de-sanitizing America's heavily edited paradigms of the Pacific. Indeed, as he points out, "On some maps, Guam doesn't exist; I point to an empty space in the Pacific and say, ... 'I'm from this unnamed place'" ("Preface" 7). Linguistic fragmentation and its sense of incompletion in Santos Perez's poems convey what Cynthia Tolentino calls an "archipelagic" perspective – "the partial perspectives and politics of location of islands" that shape Santos Perez's poetry and the potentially decolonizing politics of "incorporation."

In a similar spirit, Barbara Jane Reyes' *Poeta en San Francisco* juxtaposes English, Spanish, Tagalog, and Baybayin script to confront the cognitive dissonances of colonial history in the Bay Area and beyond. Indeed, Tagalog was Spain's first big translation project and a major act of scale-jumping, attempting to consolidate the archipelago's thousands of islands within one language. Referencing El Camino Real, "Orient" queries the old Spanish highway's role in organizing West Coast history: "we find ourselves retracing the steps of gold / hungry arrogant Spaniards. Walking on knees / behind their ghosts, could we ever know how much blood has seeped into the soil – " (19). Conjuring a religious procession, but kneeling to inspect the violence on the ground rather than revere those whose steps "we" are "retracing," "Orient" portrays potentially interminable processes of assessing colonial bloodshed. Colonial and neocolonial violence in *Poeta en San Francisco* thus endure in the speaker's personal experience:

en esta ciudad, where homeless 'nam vets
wave old glory and pots for spare change;

she grows weary of the daily routine:

fuckinjapgobacktochina!
allthemfuckingooknamessoundthesame!

and especially:
iwasstationedatsubicbay.

…

Maganda ka mahal kita magkano ka² (21)

Connecting gendered and sexualized discourse at home to U.S. colonialism and neocolonialism in Vietnam, Japan, and the Philippines, these linguistically hybrid lines also dialogue explicitly with William Carlos Williams's "To Elsie" – specifically, the line "The pure products of America go crazy" (Ponce 211–212). Engaging that poem's question of what is "American," Reyes enlists poetic fragments to evince the mixed soils and sounds of American poetry.

Linguistic mixing compels a turn to humor in David Henry Hwang's play *Chinglish* (or *Chíng-lish*). The play's premise of American Daniel Cavanaugh's business ambitions with China – as "the Chinese have maintained consistent growth over decades, at levels the West can only dream about" (9) – stages the semantic misunderstandings that occur as China and the United States rival for global dominance. On a mundane level, since transliteration can be done in various ways the result is often a nonsensical phrase. Thus "Dry Goods Pricing Department" becomes translated to "Fuck the Certain Price of Goods" (8). But there is no romanticized transcendence of or fundamental difference posited between "East" and "West." Instead, *Chinglish* shows that variations in interpretation are not simply a matter of misunderstanding or mistranslation but are intertwined with hierarchies of knowledge and uneven flows of capital. *Chinglish*'s reception implicates theatre production itself in marketing and shaping epistemology. The play did well on the West Coast and in Chicago but did not last long on Broadway partly because, according to the *New York Times*, "non-English dialogue is very rare on Broadway" (Healy).

Rachel Lee argues that "the sentiment that Asian American literary studies consists of fragmented, separate 'threads' still reverberates in the early years of the twenty-first century," and that it is necessary to relate these threads to specific contexts of time and space (*Exquisite Corpse* 9). By circulating linguistic fragments to weave the paradigmatic West with Asian American Wests, the works discussed elucidate histories of and responses to U.S. immigration, colonialism, and imperialism, demonstrating linguistic and sonic fragments' potential to critique interlinked Euro-American empires.

## Letters

William Decker notes that letters in American literature have importantly connected individuals across the United States' vast space (10). Following Decker, if the West is the country's premier frontier space, letters play an important part in illuminating its dynamics. However, Asian American writers clarify this characterization because they show how epistles relate and separate Asian American subjects to and from each other and the American body politic.

In Carlos Bulosan's *America Is in the Heart*, letters record the effects of the American war in the Philippines and on the plights of itinerant Filipinos in America. Letters are often the bearers of bad news across this expanse. They relate Carlos's brother Amado's time in prison and his father's devastating death: "he had been dead for five days when his neighbors found him.... He died alone in the place where he had been born" (*America* 164). In "Be American," Bulosan complicates ideas about authorship in light of Filipinos' status as U.S. nationals but noncitizens: "When I received a box of grapes from a friend, I knew he was working in the grape fields in either Fresno or Delano, ... There were no letters, no post cards – ... But these surprising boxes, crates, and barrels that arrived periodically were the best letters in the world" (1124). Filipino workers forge fraternal intersubjectivity – a shared frame of experience and consciousness – by sending and receiving packages. Yet they lack a return address – a sense and structure of "home." As Martin Joseph Ponce points out, "letters represent epistolary *acts*" that "draw connections and deliver critiques across the sites of ... social dispersal" (23). Epistles in Bulosan's works evidence the intergenerational effects of U.S. imperialism and the peripatetic journeys of Filipino migrant laborers.

Although Bulosan critiques "white chauvinism," Rachel Lee shows that *America Is in the Heart* privileges relationships of "brotherhood" and contains a "regulation of sexuality" at its core (*Americas* 18). Jessica Hagedorn's works offer a queer, feminist counterpoint to Bulosan's, evident in her different use of epistolary modes. In the first chapter of *Dogeaters*, Rio Gonzaga looks back to a 1956 Manila through the cultural heterogeneity of her youth, from her fascination with the "perfect picture-book American tableau" of Hollywood films (3) to a Filipino radio show called *Love Letters* (14). This transpacific scale of cultural influence echoes her family's mixed racial and national background, whose colonial and neocolonial contexts the younger Rio does not yet grasp.

By the end of *Dogeaters*, the pleasures of childhood give way to mixed opportunities under the Marcos regime's martial law. The final chapter,

"Kundiman," takes the form of a lyrical prayer – a variation on the letter and act of address – but combines the sacred with the profane: "*Our Mother, who art in heaven... Hallowed be thy name, thy kingdom never came. You who have been defiled, belittled, and diminished*" (250). By substituting the Virgin Mary for "Our Father" as the final addressee of the novel, *Dogeaters* upends the woman's conventional status as a passive object of affection and idealized symbol of the nation, in effect queering the Lord's Prayer (Ponce, 144). That the grievances are made in Catholic prayer and Filipino song thrusts the kundiman's message into eternity, inviting responses yet to come.

John Okada's posthumously published *No-No Boy* offers another way to think about Asian American letters in the context of Japanese American internment. One striking image in the novel are the bundles of letters that Mr. Yamada hides from his wife because he knows her fervent Japanese nationalism will deny Japan's defeat: "I read these letters and drink and cry and drink some more because my own people are suffering so much and there is nothing I can do.... Your mama is sick, Ichiro. She says these letters are not from Japan" (37). Mikhail Bakhtin notes that epistles' processes of sending, receiving, and responding render the epistolary form dialogic (205). Yet the conversation extended to Mrs. Yamada is here foreclosed. Moreover, letters in *No-No Boy* point to those beyond the text, including government notices posted along the West Coast instructing Japanese Americans to report for internment and the "loyalty" forms Japanese American internees were asked to sign. These examples show how forms of address, deployed as instruments of the state, have the power to define and redefine Japanese American subjects. Indeed, as Ichiro notes in an unvocalized address to his mother (and, obliquely, the U.S. nation-state), "it is not enough to be American only in the eyes of the law ... I am not your son and I am not Japanese and I am not American" (16). His thoughts outline a geopolitics of address and identity as shifts in world power render certain grievances censored in the public sphere.

Ruth Ozeki's *A Tale for the Time Being* enlists multiple epistles to frame a young girl's diary within varied historical contexts. Ruth, a writer in British Columbia, discovers a diary that has washed ashore in a Hello Kitty lunchbox wrapped in barnacle-coated plastic bags. Incorporating English, Japanese, kanji, and emoticons, Nao Yasutani's entries about her life as an inquisitive teenager invite Ruth into a shared experience of time: "My name is Nao, and I am a time being. Do you know what a time being is? ... A time being is someone who lives in time, and that means you, and me, and every one of us who is, or was, or ever will be" (*A Tale for the Time Being* 3).

Yoking together past, present, and future, the novel includes a subplot centered on Jiko, Nao's great-grandmother, and Haruki, Jiko's son who dies as a kamikaze pilot in World War II. Ozeki forges an intergenerational, transpacific frame by embedding within Nao's diary Haruki's two diaries – one in Japanese and one "secret French diary" detailing his transition from a nineteen-year-old philosophy student to a "sky soldier" enduring sado-masochistic abuse from a superior. In turn, these epistolary layers frame and are framed by Ruth's reading context, which is largely shaped by images of whirlpools, debris, and contaminated seawater from the 2011 tsunami and Fukushima meltdown. The Asian American West here is thus an ecological one where "memories, leaking out" (248) connect the Pacific as much as the leaks of radioactive water that cross the ocean. Moreover, by implicating strangers, epistles in A Tale for the Time Being push the form into specula-tive possibilities for Asian America. As Haruki notes in his last letter to his mother, there are no definitive "last words" – only "other words and other worlds" (258).

In the provocative debate about the role of letters in Edgar Allan Poe's "The Purloined Letter," Jacques Lacan noted that all letters are "dead letters" – that the contents of a letter never reach the recipient the way we intend (72) – while Slavoj Žižek paraphrased Barbara Johnson's variation on Lacan as such – "A letter always arrives at its destination since its desti-nation is wherever it arrives" (12). Attention to Asian American letters clari-fies the geopolitical conditions within which one can write and if, when, and how writings reach their audiences – illuminating what Johnson describes as "economies of justice" and "effects of power" that characterize Asian American literary Wests (458).

## Iconic/un-iconic images

Pacific Islander literature has long wrestled with a cultural iconography that depicts the region as a paradise ripe for enjoyment, exploitation, and com-modification. In turn, much Pacific Islander literature attempts to undo these forms of shorthand and grapples with what J. Kēhaulani Kauanui describes as "discourses and relations of domination" that posit Pacific Islands as landlocked and dependent (9).

Epeli Hau'ofa writes of his challenging experience as a professor trying to overturn students' belief that the Pacific Islands are "too small, too poor, and too isolated to develop any meaningful degree of autonomy." Hau'ofa calls for a shift in perspective: "There is a gulf of difference between view-ing the Pacific as 'islands in a far sea' and as 'a sea of islands'" (89–91). The prepositional change in Hau'ofa's statement creates a significant deictic shift; the Pacific is not simply located in, but is an active part of, an expansive and dynamic space in which land and sea are connected through indigenous interaction.

Similarly, Haunani-Kay Trask's poetry undoes iconographies of Hawai'i while grappling with their ongoing force. In "Hawai'i," Trask evokes a sensual experience of Hawai'i through familiar tropes – "The smell of the sea," "the puckered sand," being "mesmerized by the sun" (170) – but joins them with images of tourism – a hula dancer "smiling stiffly / into the haze of white faces; / a spiteful whiteness" (171). Indicting Japanese development, the poem references a proposed project that required "two thousand bodies / exhumed for Japanese / money, developers' dreams, / and the archaeology / of *haole* knowledge" (173). Images of razed indigenous edifices indicate overlapping American and Asian imperialisms, which attempt to reconstitute indigenous ecology, economy, and knowledge. Troubling notions of Hawai'i as a mythic space of "racial harmony" and "egalitarian pluralism" (Kauanui, 21), Trask's poetry highlights the commercial motor of such pastoralized ideals and shows how poetic geographies can organize and disorganize knowledge.³

Hsuan Hsu writes that local or regional space in American culture "often serves as a focus of nostalgia and a privileged site of geographical feeling" ("Literature and Regional Production" 36). Oliver de la Paz's "In Defense of Small Towns" wrestles with these iconographies of the U.S. small town, depicting a man who shifts between loving and hating the time he spent as a youth in rural Oregon. Here there was "no room // for novelty or change" (1), yet he acquired an appreciation for "stillness" and the textures of nature's transitions (2). The poem's couplets suggest balance and consistency, yet the speaker is unsettled by his ability to remember selectively:

> If I've learned anything, it's that I could be anywhere,
> staring at a hunk of asphalt or listening to the clap of billiard balls
>
> against each other in a bar and hear my name. Indifference now?
> Some. I shook loose, but that isn't the whole story. The fact is
>
> I'm still in love. And when I wake up, I watch my son yawn,
> and my mind turns his upswept hair into cornstalks (1–2)

The town's lack of change and novelty reflects a conservative aversion to difference yet generates expansive possibilities that its "smallness" would seem to foreclose. That the rural Pacific Northwest, implicitly set against the city, is both limiting and generative exposes description as effects of active memory-making and not simply details of passive perception. De la Paz's poem compels critical focus on the small towns that constitute Asian

American literary Wests and the politics of nostalgia that place and displace individuals within them.

Dao Strom's *Grass Roof, Tin Roof* reconsiders the symbolism of California mining towns by depicting a Vietnamese refugee family's resettlement in the Sierra Nevada foothills. Tran, a Vietnamese refugee, migrates to the United States after the Vietnam War and marries Hus, a Danish immigrant. Hus's enduring belief in the American frontier leads him to build a family home by the Coloma Valley near the American River, on "a piece of land in those once fabled hills of gold" (48); the novel places Vietnamese refugees within the ideology of the American West as a space for what Richard Slotkin calls "spiritual and secular regeneration" (33). Yet Tran and Hus's children expose that symbolic structure as in crisis after the Vietnam War. Beth views the house as a cold place with "poor water pressure, thin walls, no heat, and no windows on the entire south-facing side" (182). As a mixed-race figure caught in the throes of postwar national shame and America's desire to forget "Vietnam," she points to strained efforts to "connect [her] fate to the fate of current events" (185). *Grass Roof, Tin Roof* portrays an American frontier myth undergoing revision in changing geopolitical conditions, as the Coloma Valley signifies the alienation and violence of westward expansion rather than opportunity and rootedness in the nation.

One of the most iconic images of the American West is Chinatown. Asian American depictions of Chinatown yield surplus contexts that exceed the spatial and racial boundaries that American popular culture has imposed on the term. Staged in terms of a family's move away from San Francisco Chinatown into a white suburb, Gene Luen Yang's graphic novel *American Born Chinese* delineates the problems of multicultural ideology after Asian exclusion. The narrative shows that as Asian Americans disperse outside ethnic enclaves, "un-iconic" figures like the young Jin Wang are caught in more indirect and subtle forms of racism.

Jin's first day in a new school is framed as the failure of liberal multicultural education when the teacher "welcomes" him in good faith but mistakes him for a Chinese national rather than an American citizen (31). The most disturbing figure in the text, Chin-Kee, appears with "slant-eyes, short stature, sallow skin, predictably Chinese clothing, claw-like fingertips, and long menacing queue" to, as Min Hyoung Song points out, link nineteenth-century stereotypes of the Chinese coolie with more recent stereotypes of Asian American model minorities; Chin-Kee is also a star student who answers questions more readily than his white classmates (Song, 80). Yet Yang enlists graphic narratives' frames and gutters to deconstruct Chin-Kee's ideological layers, bordering Chin-Kee's appearances with capitalized, bold-font laugh lines that recall the filming of a sitcom. Inviting and interrupting familiarity with Chin-Kee's character, the narrative points to iconography-making as process and shows how iconographies work in flexible, ideologically varied ways; stereotypes of Asian Americans do not necessarily become obsolete but rather attach to the stereotyped in refashioned forms.

If Asian American graphic narratives have become a provocative way to disturb iconographies, GB Tran's *Vietnamerica: A Family's Journey* achieves this through a transnational, intergenerational autobiographical rendering of his family history. The text's prominent use of flashbacks outlines Tran's attempt to access less-studied pasts, opening up Vietnam War narratives to the complicated affiliations that multiple imperialisms and wars in Southeast Asia have produced. Temporality is thus non-teleological, evincing what Tran describes as "comic's ability to suspend stories in time" ("A Thousand Pictures"). As Harriet Earle shows, "*ligne claire*" becomes one way Tran stylistically creates disorienting temporal jumps. Associated with the iconic comics style of Hergé, the Belgian cartoonist and author of *Les Aventures de Tintin*, *ligne claire* enlists "'smooth, continuous linework, simplified contours and bright, solid colours'" (C. Hatfield as quoted in Earle, 1–2). *Tintin* is itself a theme in *Vietnamerica*, cherished by Tran's father, Tri Nghi, a painter of romanticized and impressionistic Vietnamese landscapes. The juxtaposition of Tran's *ligne claire* with Tran's rendering of Tri Nghi's technique connects Vietnamese, European, American, and Vietnamese American art styles. Thus in *Vietnamerica*, the West is a Euro-American epistemology and aesthetic in need of decentering. As Tri Nghi tells Tran: "You can't look at our family in a vacuum and apply your myopic contemporary Western filter to them" (11).

Erwin Panofsky defines iconology as the attempt to comprehend the symbolic meanings of icons, while W. J. T. Mitchell clarifies iconology as also entailing scrutiny "of the image as such" (2). By interrogating the iconographies that have defined circumpacific spaces in ways that serve U.S. hegemony, these texts advance critical understandings of the Asian American "un-iconic" in portrayals of the American West.

## Mixed genres

Ruth Ozeki remarks in her "Foreword" to the 2014 edition of John Okada's *No-No Boy* that there is a new area of inquiry afoot called "agnotology" – "the study of ignorance, how it is produced and maintained, what is lost and forgotten, and most importantly, why." As the production of ignorance partly relies on standard epistemologies and watershed moments or motifs, many Asian American writers have turned to the messier nature of knowledge production, often resulting in mixed genres.

Theresa Hak Kyung Cha's *Dictée* is perhaps the most prominent example of a mixed-genre Asian American text, enlisting photographs, calligraphy, prose, poetry, epistles, drama, French Catholic prayer, and archival documents as well as English, French, Korean, Greek, Latin, and Chinese. Thus one important theme in *Dictée* is translation. On the first page Cha includes what appears to be a translation exercise from French into English, but when we find that the French words "virgule" ("comma") and "les guillemets" ("French quotation marks") have been translated as words rather than incorporated as punctuation marks, the translation practice is exposed as a dictation exercise that involves bodily and psychic labor (1). Illustrating what Lisa Lowe describes as the text's "aesthetic of infidelity" – in which there is no one-to-one match between word and referent (130) – this moment stages a Korean girl's experience in a French Catholic school to draw attention to the somatic experiences of the colonial and postcolonial woman's body. As such *Dictée* links to other texts of feminist historical recovery, including Nora Okja Keller's *Comfort Woman*. While taking a seemingly conventional novelistic form, *Comfort Woman* draws from interviews, testimonies, and archival documents to elaborate the force of specifically feminine relationships that queer the heteronormativity of wartime "recreation camps." Both Cha and Keller use plural genres in different ways to foreground women's bodies and narratives variously exchanged, used, and edited out of cultural and historiographic works.

Karen Tei Yamashita's *I-Hotel: a Novel* is a mixed-genre text that was, to some extent, imagined into being, starting out as "an article about a book I'd never written" (609). Ten years and at least 150 interviews later, *I-Hotel*'s ten novellas, illustrations by Leland Wong and Sina Grace, pseudo-screenplays, documentary structures, dossiers, oral narratives, and other forms organize 1968–1977 Asian American history and activism around the I-Hotel in San Francisco's Manilatown/Chinatown. Therein, the strength of the Yellow Power movement is as salient as its uncertainties. In "What Is to Be Done?" the title's hearkening of class struggle plays out as a series of study questions about intersectionality that a group of young activists explores in Berkeley. Questions such as "*When did we become Asian American?*" recur throughout the novel, pointing to the problem of organizing along a united front, particularly in relation to other racial groups, and echoing enduring questions in Asian American cultural criticism (321). As a structure that has been moved, demolished, and rebuilt, the I-Hotel becomes an apt architecture through which to relate processes of archiving and narrating Asian American history, culture, and politics, as the tenuousness of built ethnic environments – and of literary categories – compels documentation, but in a way that does not reproduce hegemonic consolidations.

The recent publication of Hmong American anthologies has questioned foundational assumptions in literary inquiry. The largest populations of Hmong Americans live in California, followed by Minnesota and Wisconsin, with a large concentration along the agricultural strips of California's Central Valley. Anthologies such as *Bamboo among the Oaks* (2002) and *How Do I Begin?* (2011) have transformed Asian American literary history, made possible by Hmong American cultural organizations founded in St. Paul, Minnesota, and Fresno, California, respectively. These patterns of Hmong diaspora delineate an American West that is transpacific and linked to the American interior.

The artworks of artist Seexeng Lee in *How Do I Begin?* depict Hmong women in a range of contexts. "Mother's Love" places a Hmong woman draped in Hmong-patterned textiles at the center of a scene of mother–child bonding, while "Hmong Woman Playing a Hmong Flute" sets the eponymous image against geometric patterns one might find on Hmong cloth. "Hmong Woman Sewing a Paj Ntaub [Hmong embroidery]" illustrates a woman intently embroidering a large swath of fabric, whose swirling, undulating patterns and folds evoke the other two pieces (93–94). Together, the three works form a triptych thematizing Hmong women and embroidery. Ma Vang argues that Hmong have been largely defined through a perceived lack of written language, and their supposed illiteracy has translated to a lack of full subjecthood and citizenship ("The Refugee Soldier" 700). Lee's works link to other examples of Hmong story cloth to show that *paj ntaub* constitutes a "mode of telling and mode of reading" and, moreover, figure it through feminine action. Thus it is more the case that prevailing literary paradigms are not equipped to recognize Hmong narrative practices than that Hmong have lacked writing.

Dana Williams and Marissa Lopez note that "the ethnic archive" presents a chance for scholars to "invoke a multiethnic cacophony of voices that require reconsiderations of established knowledge and knowledge production alike" (358). The Asian American texts discussed in this chapter engage this issue through narratives that challenge, reinscribe, and remain ambiguous about prevailing notions of language, letters, iconography, and genre in American literature. As a geographic space and conceptual idea through which the United States has established racial and sexual borders while emerging as a world power, the American West, reconceived as an Asian American literary West, is mainland, transpacific, transnational, and interior. It stages the potential unraveling of normative geographies, myths, archives, and temporalities of the American West – even raising questions about what constitutes writing itself.

## Notes

1   Hsuan Hsu's model of "chronotopes of the Asian American West" and James Lee's comparative analysis of Asian American and Latina/o literature in Los Angeles have offered insightful models for thinking about works related to the topic of this chapter. See Hsu, "Chronotopes of the Asian American West," and J. K.-J. Lee. Some of the omissions in this chapter are addressed in their pieces, for instance South Asian American literature.
2   "You're beautiful, I love you, how much are you?"
3   There is still a marginalization of Pacific Islands studies within Asian American studies, thus it is necessary to bear in mind the distinct material conditions, critical methods, and decolonizing frameworks that characterize Pacific Islander studies even as we link it to Asian American studies. See Kauanui and Diaz.

## Works Cited

Apter, Emily. "Untranslatables: A World System." *New Literary History: A Journal of Theory and Interpretation.* Vol. 39, no. 3 (2008): 581–598. Print.

Bakhtin, M. M. *Problems of Dostoevsky's Poetics.* Trans. Emerson, Caryl. Theory and History of Literature. Minneapolis: University of Minnesota Press, 1984. Print.

Bulosan, Carlos. *America Is in the Heart: A Personal History.* Classics of Asian American Literature. 2014 edition. ed. Seattle: University of Washington Press, 2014. Print.

"Be American." In Nina Baym (ed.) *The Norton Anthology of American Literature.* Shorter Seventh ed. Vol. 2. New York: W. W. Norton & Co., 1995. 1122–1127. Print.

Cha, Theresa Hak Kyung. *Dictee.* 1st Calif. pbk. ed. Berkeley: University of California Press, 2001. Print.

De la Paz, Oliver. "In Defense of Small Towns." *Requiem for the Orchard.* 1st ed. Akron, Ohio: University of Akron Press, 2010. 1–2. Print.

Decker, William Merrill. *Epistolary Practices: Letter Writing in America before Telecommunications.* Chapel Hill: University of North Carolina Press, 1998. Print.

Diaz, Vicente M. "'To "P" or Not to "P"?': Marking the Territory between Pacific Islander and Asian American Studies." *Journal of Asian American Studies.* Vol. 7, no. 3 (2005): 183–208. Print.

Earle, Harriet E. H. "Traumatic Analepsis and Ligne Claire in Gb Tran's Vietnamerica." *The Comics Grid: Journal of Comics Scholarship.* Vol. 4, no. 1 (2014): 1–4. Print.

Fujita-Rony, Dorothy. "Water and Land: Asian Americans and the U.S. West." *Pacific Historical Review.* Vol. 76, no. 4 (2007): 563–574. Print.

Hagedorn, Jessica Tarahata. *Dogeaters.* 1st ed. New York: Pantheon Books, 1990. Print.

Hau'ofa, Epeli. "Our Sea of Islands." In Rob Wilson and Arif Dirlik (eds.) *Asia/Pacific as Space of Cultural Production*. Durham, NC: Duke University Press, 1995. 86–98. Print.

Healy, Patrick. "Do You Know What I Mean? Probably Not." *New York Times*, October 20, 2011. Print.

Hmong American Writers' Circle (ed.) *How Do I Begin?: A Hmong American Literary Anthology*. Berkeley, CA: Heyday, 2011. Print.

Hsu, Hsuan L. "Chronotopes of the Asian American West." In Nicolas S. Witschi (ed.) *A Companion to the Literature and Culture of the American West*. Wiley-Blackwell, 2011. 145–160. Print.

"Literature and Regional Production." *American Literary History*. Vol. 17, no. 1 (2005): 36–69. Print.

Hwang, David Henry. *Chinglish*. New York: Dramatists Play Service Inc., 2012. Print.

Johnson, Barbara. "The Frame of Reference: Poe, Lacan, Derrida." *Yale French Studies*. Vol. 55.55, no. 56 (1977): 457–505. Print.

Kauanui, J. Kēhaulani. *Hawaiian Blood: Colonialism and the Politics of Sovereignty and Indigeneity*. Narrating Native Histories. Durham, NC: Duke University Press, 2008. Print.

Keller, Nora Okja. *Comfort Woman*. New York: Viking, 1997. Print.

Kingston, Maxine Hong. *The Woman Warrior: Memoirs of a Girlhood among Ghosts*. Vintage International ed. New York: Vintage International, 1989. Print.

Lacan, Jacques. "Seminar on 'the Purloined Letter.'" *Yale French Studies* (1972): 38. Print.

Lai, H. Mark, Genny Lim, and Judy Yung. *Island: Poetry and History of Chinese Immigrants on Angel Island 1910–1940*. Seattle: University of Washington Press, 1991. Print.

Lee, Erika, and Judy Yung. *Angel Island: Immigrant Gateway to America*. Oxford; New York: Oxford University Press, 2010. Print.

Lee, James Kyung-Jin. "Pacific Rim City: Asian-American and Latino Literature." In Kevin R. McNamara (ed.) *The Cambridge Companion to the Literature of Los Angeles*. Cambridge; New York: Cambridge University Press, 2010. 87–100. Print.

Lee, Rachel C. *The Americas of Asian American Literature: Gendered Fictions of Nation and Transnation*. Princeton, NJ: Princeton University Press, 1999. Print.

*The Exquisite Corpse of Asian America: Biopolitics, Biosociality, and Posthuman Ecologies*. Sexual Cultures. New York: New York University Press, 2014. Print.

Lee, Seexeng. Ed. *Circle, Hmong American Writers'*. Berkeley, CA: Heyday, 2011. Print.

Lowe, Lisa. *Immigrant Acts: On Asian American Cultural Politics*. Durham, NC: Duke University Press, 1996. Print.

Mitchell, W. J. T. *Iconology: Image, Text, Ideology*. Chicago: University of Chicago Press, 1986. Print.

Moua, Mai Neng. *Bamboo among the Oaks: Contemporary Writing by Hmong Americans*. St. Paul: Minnesota Historical Society Press, 2002. Print.

Okada, John. *No-No Boy*. Seattle: University of Washington Press, 1981. Print.

Ozeki, Ruth L. *A Tale for the Time Being*. New York: Viking, 2013. Print.

"Foreword." *No-No Boy*. Seattle: University of Washington Press, 2014. Print.

Panofsky, Erwin. *Studies in Iconology; Humanistic Themes in the Art of the Renaissance*. The Mary Flexner Lectures on the Humanities. New York: Oxford University Press, 1939. Print.

Ponce, Martin Joseph. *Beyond the Nation: Diasporic Filipino Literature and Queer Reading*. Sexual Cultures. New York: New York University Press, 2012. Print.

Reyes, Barbara Jane. *Poeta en San Francisco*. Honolulu, HI: TinFish Press, 2005. Print.

Santos Perez, Craig. *From Unincorporated Territory [Hacha]*. Kane'ohe, HI: TinFish Press, 2008. Print.

Interview by Iris. "The Page Transformed: A Conversation with Craig Santos Perez." *Lantern Review Blog*. March 12, 2010.

"Preface." *From Unincorporated Territory [Hacha]*. Kane'ohe, HI: TinFish Press, 2008. Print.

Slotkin, Richard. *Gunfighter Nation: The Myth of the Frontier in Twentieth-Century America*. Oklahoma paperbacks ed. Norman: University of Oklahoma Press, 1998. Print.

Song, Min Hyoung. "'How Good It Is to Be a Monkey': Comics, Racial Formation, and *American Born Chinese*." *Mosaic*. Vol. 43, no. 1 (2010): 73. Print.

Strom, Dao. *Grass Roof, Tin Roof*. Boston, MA: Houghton Mifflin Co., 2003. Print.

Tolentino, Cynthia. "Equatorial Archipelagos." In Rachel C. Lee (ed.) *The Routledge Companion to Asian American and Pacific Islander Literature*. London; New York: Routledge/Taylor & Francis Group, 2014. 268–78. Print.

Tran, GB. Interview by Tran, Ky-Phong. "A Thousand Pictures Tells a (Epic) Story: Interviewing Gb Tran." *diaCRITICS*. DVAN. March 17, 2011 2011.

*Vietnamerica: A Family's Journey*. New York: Villard Books, 2010. Print.

Trask, Haunani-Kay. "Hawai'i." In Rob Wilson and Arif Dirlik (eds.) *Asia/Pacific as Space of Cultural Production*. Durham, ND: Duke University Press, 1995. 170–174. Print.

Vang, Ma. "The Refugee Soldier: A Critique of Recognition and Citizenship in the Hmong Veterans' Naturalization Act of 1997." *positions: east asia cultures critique*. Vol. 20, no. 3 (2012): 685–712. Print.

Williams, Dana A., and Marissa K. Lopez. "More Than a Fever: Toward a Theory of the Ethnic Archive." *PMLA*. Vol. 127, no. 2 (2012): 357–359. Print.

Yamashita, Karen Tei. *I Hotel: [a Novel]*. 1st ed. Minneapolis: Coffee House Press, 2010. Print.

Yang, Gene Luen, and Lark Pien. *American Born Chinese*. New York: First Second, 2006. Print.

Žižek, Slavoj. *Enjoy Your Symptom!: Jacques Lacan in Hollywood and Out*. Routledge Classics. Routledge Classics ed. New York: Routledge, 2008. Print.

# 15

ERIC GARDNER

# African American literature
# and the early West

John Mifflin Brown's January 19, 1861 letter to the African Methodist
Episcopal (AME) *Christian Recorder* praised new editor Elisha Weaver
and emphasized Weaver's youth in Indiana, positing the American West as
a source of power for emergent black print culture. "It takes our Western
boys to lead off," Brown wrote; "I thank you for proving that we can do
something." While Brown's praise inaccurately narrows the gender of black
Western participants in print culture, his emphasis on black Westerners
"doing something" in print speaks volumes about African American literature in and of the early West. It flies in the face of the sense – still often predominant – that there was no black literary engagement with the early West,
and it usefully locates much of the African American textual engagement
with the West in periodicals. Working with a wide geographical sense of the
West (Indiana to California), Brown reminded readers of important recent
history, from the founding of an AME magazine (the *Repository of Religion
and Literature*) in Indianapolis in 1858 to the launch of a short-lived but
important black newspaper in San Francisco, *The Mirror of the Times*, in
1856. Brown also suggested a capacious definition of "doing something,"
recognizing "literature" as not just fiction, poetry, and drama but also public letters, essays, sketches, travelogues, journalism writ broadly, and a host
of other genres.[1]

This chapter builds from the work of recent literary historians to more
fully sketch out the nexus of African American literature and the early West.
It explores an eclectic sampling of texts from the later nineteenth century
and the early twentieth century to begin to suggest the diversity of black literature in the West and argues for strong connections between this literature
and the black press. While it focuses on questions of witnessing and testifying
about the black West through print, it recognizes the impossibility of marking any single representative "black West," and it mixes discussion of texts
that are essentially unknown with consideration of works that are becoming better known. Given the dearth of scholarship on the earliest African

American literary West, it begins with more extended treatments of two mid-nineteenth-century sets of texts – William Newby's mid-1850s letters from San Francisco to *Frederick Douglass's Paper* and Annie E. Vincent's early 1860s work for the San Francisco–based *Pacific Appeal*. These discussions lead to shorter biblio-historical comments on a much broader range of texts, grouped to hint at the contours of literature tied to the black West published between the 1850s and the 1920s. The chapter concludes with a brief analysis of Delilah Beasley's 1919 history *Negro Trail Blazers of California*, a text that emphasizes a witnessing that is encyclopedic in scope and execution, and more extended consideration of Emma and Lloyd Ray's 1926 Seattle-centered autobiography *Twice Sold, Twice Ransomed*, a text that implicitly challenges approaches like Beasley's.

The dozen-plus letters that William Newby (1828–March 24, 1859) published under the playful penname "Nubia" in *Frederick Douglass's Paper* between September 1854 and early 1856 are arguably among the most important early texts by a black Western writer. Newby's letters came in the midst of broad Eastern interest in California, a push by Douglass to gain a California audience, and black Californians' growing recognition that they needed a voice in American print culture. Trained as a barber and daguerreotypist, Newby was the son of an enslaved father and free mother. After her husband's death, Newby's mother moved her family from Virginia to Philadelphia, exposing the young Newby to early African American print. Still, frustrated by racism in the East, he joined a small but growing community of free African Americans in San Francisco and became a leader in the efforts of the 1850s tied to the all-Black San Francisco Athenaeum and California's version of the "colored convention" movement so critical to black activism in the East.[2]

Much of the conventions' efforts and Newby's sociopolitical events focused on the fact that African Americans could not testify in legal proceedings involving white people. The importance of black participation in a public written record was emphasized every time African Americans were misrepresented by whites; texts like Newby's are thus instances of black writing functioning as much to "un-tell" (to use John Ernest's term) stories of blackness as to tell them (86).[3] Correspondence like Newby's also helped black Californians participate in broader national conversations and was an essential reminder to far-flung family and friends that African Americans in the West existed, persevered, sometimes even flourished.

Like many nineteenth-century correspondents, Newby used providing news as a warrant for writing but quickly expanded beyond basic reporting. He represented San Francisco not simply as a destination but as a portal, a conduit to the wider West – the gold fields, Northern California, the Pacific

Northwest, even the broader Pacific – and he repeatedly marked these sites as locations for (potential) black elevation. He began this narrative in his very first letter to *Douglass's Paper*: "You can form no idea of the progress made by the colored people in this city within the short space of two years." He described San Francisco's black churches, cultural and benevolent societies, and West Indian emancipation celebrations. This progress was in the face of "many deprivations," and Newby felt obligated to testify about such: "we have no oath against any white man or Chinaman. We are debarred from the polls." Later letters further detailed the trials African Americans faced in the West and thus broadened the chronicling of national discrimination in *Douglass's Paper*. Newby's April 6, 1855 letter, for example, critiqued the furor over African American minister John Jamison Moore's invitation to attend a San Francisco teachers' convention: "A man may be shot down in the street without causing a remark," Newby wrote, "but the circumstances of a colored man voting in a convention of whites causes the public mind to heave and surge like an angry sea." Newby's letters thus brought readers into textual proximity with both the hopes and the trials of the black West.

That work, though, sometimes exhibited Newby's own doubts and struggles with the racism at the core of American society and American print. Many moments show an ambivalent dance with Manifest Destiny, immigration, internalized racism, and racial difference. Newby's critique of American expansionism is perhaps most pronounced in his March 16, 1855 letter to *Douglass's Paper*, where he shifted into the voice of a travel writer, observing white America's multifaceted dominance in the third person. Spanish Californians, he wrote, "are being rapidly dispossessed of their immense property by the shrewd Americans … They complain that the Yankees have changed everything, even the climate." Newby then argued that "the Yankees" were especially effective in dividing those they wanted to rule: "The Americans here, as everywhere, have succeeded in imbuing" Spanish Californians "with the proper amount of prejudice against colored people[,] for it seems to be the settled policy of the people in this country, in their intercourse with foreigners, to fill them with their beastly and disgusting prejudices." For all this outrage, though, Newby fell into dominant American views on the growing population of Asian immigrants. His very first letter to *Douglass's Paper*, for example, noted that the immigrants "exhibit a most grotesque appearance. Their 'unmentionables' are either exceedingly roomy or very close fitting.… Their habits are filthy, and their features totally devoid of expression." This construction of Chinese Americans as Others marks Newby's participation in what Helen Jun's "Black Orientalism" describes as "the discursive production" by black Americans "of an utterly foreign, premodern, alien Oriental in opposition to a rational, modern, Western subject," which created chances for African Americans to "perform heteronormativity" to allow stronger positions in debates over black citizenship (1049, 1054). Newby's print testimony of and from the black West thus demonstrated how fraught that location could be – and even illustrated how key emergent Western genres (like the letter to the East and the travelogue) were already imprinted with racial hierarchies and conflicts.

Understanding the complex politics of representation in Newby's letters aids us in thinking about the text that many histories of the (literary) black West mark as a key first, the 1856 *Life and Adventures of James Beckwourth*. Published less than a year after Newby's letters, this (auto)biography – written "as told to" the white Thomas Bonner – tells of the exploits of a trader and explorer in and beyond the Sierra Nevada range. *Life and Adventures*, however, never mentions Beckwourth's racial heritage, and that de-racing is paired with representations of Beckwourth as a "solitary frontiersman." Read against the emphasis on black communities in Newby's letters, *Life and Adventures* looks even more like a proto-dime novel, predicting, for example, the thematics of nation and exclusion in the 1907 *Life and Adventures of Nat Love*, the most important early black "cowboy" narrative. Newby's linkage of black manhood and the development of black collective efforts was simply much easier for white culture to "forget."

The promise Newby and colleagues like J. H. Townsend saw for and in black communities of the West soon led to a local black newspaper, the *Mirror of the Times*, designed to share the voices of the black West. Scholars of the American West and of African American literature generally have often failed to acknowledge that, while the *Mirror* failed in 1858, this work eventually meant that San Francisco would support two long-lived black periodicals (the *Pacific Appeal* and the *Elevator*) simultaneously – a feat few cities in the East achieved. Brown was right; black Westerners could indeed "lead off." Still, while longtime *Elevator* columnist Jennie Carter has received some scholarly attention and *Elevator* editor (and writer) Philip Bell less, Anne E. Vincent (ca. January 1847–January 18, 1873) – usually "A. E. V." to her readers – represents a wider range of black Western writers who are often still unknown to or ignored by scholars and who found public voice through California's black press (Carter 2007, Gardner 2012).[4]

The earliest publication by Vincent found to date appeared in yet another black California periodical, the short-lived religious paper *The Lunar Visitor*. Her half-column essay on "The Destiny of Man" in the February 1862 issue was signed "Miss A. E. Vincent" and echoed the airy philosophical generality of her title. As work from a young woman writer, Vincent's essay embodied what *Visitor* editor John Jamison Moore wanted young women in the black West to be: accomplished, intelligent, and publicly engaged but always "proper." However, the dozen-plus letters she later wrote for the *Pacific Appeal* show a much more individualized voice, one that applied such general principles to her specific Western life.

That transformation was rooted firmly in Vincent's biography, which we are just beginning to recover. Much of her short adult life was devoted to teaching, and she was a force in the Sacramento AME Sabbath School program for several years, although she also lived in San Francisco, Petaluma, and Virginia City, Nevada. Her June 7, 1862 letter to the *Pacific Appeal* thus began by marking her own reading and the *Appeal*'s place within the larger print culture of the United States: "you stated that you had not room for all of your communications in the last week's paper, and it made me think that ... the day is fast approaching when the *Appeal* ... shall not only ring and resound throughout the State of California, but throughout the Eastern and Western States." That ringing was essential "so that our people may know that we are not yet dead, but alive and awake to the sense of our incumbent duty, and live in hopes of the long-wished-for day when our people will be recognized as a nation." Vincent wrote that "Knowing the oppression which we have been laboring under for so many years past – knowing the obstacles ... that our ancestors have borne ... let the *Appeal* increase ... tenfold in circulation." Like Newby, Vincent was testifying to the hopes and trials of African Americans attempting to build new and free lives in the West.

Vincent's letters moved toward a stronger "I" and a greater emphasis on her educational work in Sacramento. Her massive August 29, 1863 column, for example, gives a detailed account of a "Sabbath School Presentation," transcribes speeches, describes recitations, and meticulously lists the participating children's names. As in Newby's letters, Vincent's initial warrant was to provide news, but she soon went beyond basic reporting to, for example, suggest that "all the Sabbath schools in the State" annually "unite in heart and hand, in a general assembly." This "Sabbath School Convention" – and note the echo of the California conventions – also moved her to remember "some of the good times ... when I was a scholar of the boarding Sabbath school in the old Connecticut State, where we would have from five to six hundred scholars, teachers and friends congregate." Those memories of the East still touched her as she wrote from the West and pushed her to argue that other students, including young women like herself, would grow from this kind of communal and community work, especially when shaped by a setting "where nature had been unrefined."

Vincent's work demonstrates the growing ability of the black press in the West to provide space for a wide range of black voices, both mature and maturing, both men and (albeit in more circumscribed ways) women. She shared the columns of the *Appeal* and the *Elevator* with both pseudonymous women like "Violet," who sparred with Philip Bell, and the poet "Cassandra," as well as women like Mrs. J. E. Dove, who wrote letters lamenting California abolitionist Thomas Starr King's death, and, much later, Jennie Carter. Like Vincent's letters, the work of many of these black women was deeply marked by a sense of class and faith-centered propriety and the expectations of the papers' male editors. But while they often struggled to move beyond the generic sentiments and didactic tone that flooded the periodical press of the time, they *did* write and thus testified to what they witnessed in the early American West.

I treat California's black press in some depth here because it remains a generally unacknowledged birthplace for much black literature of and from the West and because it soon attracted contributors from not just California but also a range of surrounding states and territories. James Monroe Whitfield, whose 1853 *America* has recently been recognized as crucial to understanding nineteenth-century American poetry, for example, concluded his career with commemorative poetry shared first in public recitations in California and then in the *Elevator* (Levine and Wilson 2011).[5] James Madison Bell was, in essence, the *Appeal*'s house poet before leaving California in 1867 for his native Ohio, where he had a long poetic career culminating in his 1901 *Poetical Works*. Thomas Detter, whose 1871 collection *Nellie Brown* is generally recognized as containing the first piece of extended fiction from the black West (the title novelette), cut his teeth writing for the *Appeal* and especially the *Elevator*; his long letters detailed experiences in California, Idaho, and Nevada and moved freely between personal narratives, travelogues, and belletristic essays.[6] James Williams, whose slave narrative *The Life and Adventures of James Williams, a Fugitive Slave* was published in San Francisco in 1873 and is beginning to garner serious critical attention as a Western variation of the genre, also had deep ties with the black press in the West, including significant conflicts with *Appeal* editor Peter Anderson.[7] Years before his murder in 1900 in the midst of the fight for the vote in Kentucky, Robert Charles O'Hara Benjamin worked with both the *Los Angeles Observer* and the *San Francisco Sentinel*. He eventually experimented with an amazing range of genres – publishing his *Life of Toussaint L'Ouverture, Warrior and Statesman* in Los Angles in 1888; a pamphlet on "the Negro Problem" (that began as a lecture to Portland, Oregon's African Methodist Episcopal Zion church) in San Francisco in 1891; and an early contribution to conduct books for black youth, *Don't: A Book for Girls*, also in San Francisco in 1891.[8] And Mifflin Wistar Gibbs, whose black press efforts in the West dated back to the *Mirror of the Times*, ventured into autobiography with *Shadow and Light* (1902), part of which chronicled his time in California and British Columbia. Complete with a preface from Booker T. Washington, Gibbs' work placed economic power as a prime driver of success in the West and beyond. *Shadow and Light* was republished by the University of Nebraska Press in 1995. Washington's influence was notable in some sectors of the West. Note, for example, Josie Briggs Hall's *Hall's Moral and Mental Capsule for the Economic and Domestic Life of the Negro*, which was published in Dallas in 1905.

In short, many of the books of the African American West that we have begun to recover have roots in and connections to the massively understudied field of black periodicals. That set of venues offered the best and sometimes the only sites for publication by and about African Americans in the West. While California's black press – including exciting later examples like the *California Eagle* – was the most developed and perhaps produced the richest flowering of early black texts, future recovery efforts will need to consider other locations. Gayle Berardi and Thomas Segady have found more than forty black newspapers founded in the West between 1880 and 1914, including a notable understudied cluster in Kansas (resulting in part from the Exodusters) and titles from the 1890s as diverse as the Oklahoma-based *Langston City Herald* and the *Salt Lake City Plain Dealer*. These periodicals suggest not just a number of budding black editors and writers but also a black readership hungry for print. Determining who they were, what they read, how they saw literature, and what other modes they used to circulate texts will also be a critical next step in understanding African American literature in the West.

The later nineteenth century and early twentieth century also saw a broader range of African American authors separate from the West's growing black press at work in both fact and fiction. James Young's novel *Helen Duval: A French Romance*, published in San Francisco in 1891 with a frontispiece picture of the author, suggested again that African Americans in the West were thinking globally. (One thinks, too, of Peter Cole's *Elevator* columns sent from the small black expatriate community in Japan.[9]) Zachary Withers's *Poems of Slavery*, published in San Francisco in 1905 (by the Pacific Coast Appeal Publishing Company, invoking but unrelated to the earlier *Appeal*), attempted to use the West as a space for remembering slavery. In different ways, Pauline Hopkins's 1902 novel *Winona, a Tale of Negro Life in the South and Southwest*, which was serialized in the Boston-based *Colored American Magazine*, attempted to use the West (and specifically Kansas) as a landscape for considering proslavery violence as an ancestor of lynching and abolitionist protection of the West as a national call to action.[10] While Hopkins had little experience with the West of her fiction, the other turn-of-the-century black novel of the West that has generated much recent notice, Sutton Griggs's amazing 1899 *Imperium in Imperio*, reenvisions Griggs's own home state of Texas. Griggs's imagined Texas was the location for a wide-reaching secret black organization (notably tied to black higher education) that considers revolutionary violence, large-scale black migration to Texas, black nationalism, and even separation from the United States. Griggs's Texas is not only both South and West, but is hemispheric in its reach, as, in John Gruesser's words, it "profoundly engages with the Spanish-Cuban-American and the Philippine-American Wars and their domestic implications" as it explores potential responses to the murder of a black postmaster (62). Maud Cuney-Hare's 1913 biography of her father, *Norris Wright Cuney: A Tribune of the Black People*, envisions a very different Texas, in which a handful of black and white politicians attempted to salvage the possibility of cross-racial political progress post-Reconstruction. Published in New York City by the offices of W.E.B. Du Bois's *Crisis*, it was advertised as a story of "a red-blooded man who was one of the great leaders of Negro Americans" and mourned both the death of the Republican Party of Lincoln and the Nadir's destruction of black political power. For a sample of this ad, see the inside front cover of the March 1915 issue of *The Crisis*.[11]

The sense of a Western black hero so critical, albeit in very different ways, to Griggs's and Cuney-Hare's work (and often gendered male) is worth some special study. Mentioned earlier, Nat Love's autobiography, published in Los Angeles in 1907, has perhaps received the most critical attention of any early black Western text, in part because it addresses Langston Hughes's still-famous call to historians of black experiences "Don't leave out the cowboys," and in part because it places Love as the archetypal lone wolf having amazing adventures before riding off into the sunset (Katz, xi).[12] The book's full title alone hints at this: *The Life and Adventures of Nat Love, Better Known in the Cattle Country as "Deadwood Dick," by Himself; a True History of Slavery Days, Life on the Great Cattle Ranges and on the Plains of the "Wild and Woolly" West, Based on Facts, and Personal Experiences of the Author*. While the crucial difference – "Slavery Days" – is marked, Love's text, for example, tends to treat American Indians in ways that echo Newby's representations of Asian immigrants – as savage Others that allow a (lone) African American to side with white people. As radical as Love's presence in the West might be, his book repeatedly marks him as unique. Oscar Micheaux's early books brought a different set of experiences – those of a black South Dakota homesteader – to these questions. His autobiographical novels *The Conquest* (1913) and *The Homesteader* (1917) – the latter of which served as the basis for Micheaux's lost silent film of the same title released in 1919 – in the words of Michael K. Johnson "feature less gunslinging and more farming" (6).[13] Nonetheless, they explore the solitary black male hero in the West in dialogue with both the potential for black community and the potential for (then-controversial) interracial love. These texts not only testified to black presences in the West; they argued that African Americans could participate in the growing mythos of the West and are thus crucial ancestors of the textual and filmic traditions of the black Western studied richly in Johnson's *Hoo-doo Cowboys and Bronze Buckaroos: Conceptions of the African American West.*[14]

The flowering of textual representations of and from the black West in the early twentieth century unfortunately coincided with a time when the last original pioneers of the African American West were passing away. Ohio-born Delilah Leontium Beasley (September 9, 1871–August 18, 1934), a nurse and sometime journalist who wrote for the black *Oakland Sunshine* and the white *Oakland Tribune*, became fascinated with this almost-lost history when she moved to the Berkeley area in 1910 and, after much research, decided to write a series of lectures that she hoped to give across the state. However, the project continued to grow – turning first into material on slavery in California published in Carter G. Woodson's *Journal of Negro History* in January 1918 and then into the 1919 *Negro Trail Blazers of California*, which ran over three hundred pages of close-set type and tiny margins attempting to salvage all of the testimony she could.

The book's division into a "historical section," a "biographical section" devoted to early California African Americans, and a section on "The Present Day Negro in California," as well as its range of chapter headings – from "Slavery in California" to "Doctors and Dentists" – marks the volume's encyclopedic approach, as do its diverse lists and seventy-plus illustrations.[15] This structure also emphasizes the book's cross-disciplinary approach, argues for a chronologic trajectory of progress, and, in Nina Baym's words, sees "black achievement in California and recognition of black citizenship in the West" as "the aims and ends of Manifest Destiny" (74). Beasley's witnessing was thus in some ways what Newby hoped for, with all of the joys and concerns embodied in those hopes. Her narrative of progress also reached across gender (although pieces of it were clearly gendered). One of the book's key later chapters focuses on "Distinguished Women"; like the other portions of the book, it weaves together narrative, personal reflection, citation of external sources (often periodicals), and material collected in individual interviews to mark efforts and accomplishments. Perhaps of equal interest is the "Literary Department" chapter, which argues that "the greatest literary work done by the Negro is through his weekly papers," and is thus organized around sketches of various black periodicals and, again in a nod toward "progress," black writers for white newspapers (251). Beasley, like John Mifflin Brown, emphasizes repeatedly that black periodical writing was multi-generic; indeed, the chapter itself contains biographical sketches, historical narrative, excerpts of letters and press accounts, literary criticism, pieces of speeches and essays, and the full text of twenty poems. Her bio-critical considerations of Eloise Bibb Thompson and William Edgar Easton are also among the earliest extant.[16]

Although sometimes layered in cumbersome prose and an arcane voice reminiscent of some late nineteenth-century local histories, Beasley's testimony was saving – and making available through print – much of what white culture in the West had ignored, dismissed, and sometimes even destroyed. Nonetheless, Beasley's narratives of progress were not borne out by the events that followed the release of *Negro Trail Blazers*. Although more recent historians have seen its value, Woodson's *Journal of Negro History* panned the book for its compendium style – saying "there is something about almost everything" – and dismissed it as a "hodge-podge" (129). And although the book in part led to a larger relationship with the *Oakland Tribune*, for which Beasley wrote regularly in the mid-1920s, the costs tied to the book's publication and promotion nearly bankrupted her.

Among the ironies of the *Journal of Negro History*'s attacks on *Negro Trail Blazers* is the simple fact that Beasley's book did *not* begin to address "everything" about the black West. To hint at landscapes much broader than Beasley's gloriana and to expand consideration of black Western literature's witnessing, this chapter thus closes with *Twice Sold, Twice Ransomed*. Often bylined to both Lloyd P. Ray and Emma J. Smith Ray, the book was copyrighted and essentially authored by Emma Ray (January 7, 1859–November 25, 1930). Released in late 1926 by the Chicago-based Free Methodist Publishing House, the book has elements of both spiritual autobiography and missionary tale: it tells the Rays' life stories and features their decades of evangelical work, especially among people Ray referred to, in language common to missionary tales, as "the most illiterate and degraded class of humanity" (159). But *Twice Sold* is much more – a postbellum slave narrative, a temperance story, a study of urban poverty and an argument for reform, and a book about African American evangelists (rather than white missionaries) and about Seattle (rather than Mozambique or South Africa, the locations featured in other Free Methodist missionary books that year).

That mingling of genres witnesses versions of the West rarely captured; it is prominent from the very first page of *Twice Sold*'s narrative proper: "I was born twice, bought twice, sold twice, and set free twice. Born of woman, born of God; sold in slavery, sold to the devil; freed by Lincoln, set free by

God" (15). For all of the promise of a detailed treatment of Emma Ray's life in slavery, though, the book covers those experiences in only seven pages; Lloyd's time in slavery takes only a few sentences. What the first chapters of *Twice Sold* emphasize instead are legacies of slavery in Missouri, Texas, and Kansas: Emma's Missouri family was poverty-stricken and often hungry; her mother, who "had been worked hard as a slave," died when Emma was only nine; her father had to "hire out" the children – although he kept most of the family together (24). Recovery from such legacies is paired with both the Rays' moves further West and their growing evangelical activism. Still, that pairing and the parallelism of the narrative's first sentence are much more fraught than the rhythmic, preacherly language suggests – in part because, by the 1920s, the romanticizing of the "old South" (and concurrent attempts to shame formerly enslaved people) were multilayered and multi-generational, and in part because *Twice Sold*'s West is deeply frightening.[17]

In what Nina Baym calls an "indirect" history of Seattle – with some emphasis on the years surrounding Seattle's great fire of 1889 and the Alaskan gold rush – the Rays often depict a West of urban nightmare, at times of almost apocalyptic struggle (52). This representation of the West, tightly linked to the language of slavery and yet curiously distanced from it, both complicates their remembrance of chattel slavery and opens up spaces for African American engagement with the West. The first sentence's quick analogy between slavery and bondage to sin, for example – with freedom depicted in the second as holiness rather than a culmination of massive sociopolitical struggle – threatens, at its worst, to equate being enslaved with lacking willpower and faith, especially as the book often specifies such "sin" as substance abuse and addiction. Simultaneously, this very de-racing gave the Rays some power to work and, ironically, to more clearly mark race.

Consider the chapter "The Addict," whose title figure is a young white woman living in a burned-out building who "when it was dark ... would make her way out on the streets and alleys to beg money to buy some more of the drug that enslaved her" (163). At the request of the woman's parents, Emma Ray brings her tracts and, in a fascinatingly domestic gesture, flowers after finding her in a "filthy" room passed out on "an old, half-burned mattress"; the woman was "*something* ... dead to the world" (162–163; emphasis mine). A page later, the woman *is* dead – as taking cocaine "like snuff" eats "a hole up into her head" (164). Loaded with the language of blame, this section nonetheless, echoing abolitionist literature, shows how "enslavement" turns people into suffering "things."

Nonetheless, the narrative's regular labeling of individuals' color reminds readers of just how *many* of the people the Rays aided (how many prostitutes, how many addicts, how many criminals) were white. In an astounding reversal to abolitionist and missionary tales, *Twice Sold* regularly depicts whites in "bondage" and places the black Rays as the missionaries. The book does this work even as it reminds readers that the Rays were once enslaved as chattel – as when, for example, the Rays talk about how central song is to their evangelism and Ray directly asserts, "We always sang some of our own songs. They seemed to grip the hearts of the hearers more ... and blessed our own souls also. We were not ashamed of them; they were given to our forefathers under the pressure of slavery. We had sung them all when we were young, and ... we did not forget them" (73–74).[18]

In fact, in a crucial continuance of the messy equation between chattel slavery and slavery to sin, the Rays regularly remind readers of black presences in the West and submit that the lessons of emancipation are crucial to broader progress. Ray, for example, describes a 1914 Seattle temperance parade, which leads her to remark, "I had witnessed such a sight once before when but a child, and that was when the Negro race celebrated" emancipation; "I felt just such a thrill ... as I did when in the parade. Every one that could walk marched.... Mothers with ... babies in their arms, some of the returned soldiers from the war, and old ex-slave men" (243). Ray then places the whites in the temperance parade as former "slaves" – saying, "This same joy of freedom was in the hearts of some of the men in the prohibition parade. Had not they, too, been slaves, and had not the Lord delivered them?" (243) Here as elsewhere, she calls attention to how the Rays marched alongside both white reformers and whites "converted" from addiction. The book's discussion of cross-racial evangelical work and the Rays' bonds with white evangelicals suggest that the frightening landscape that is the Rays' Seattle – and the Rays' West – also opens broader egalitarian possibilities.[19]

As Michael K. Johnson has argued in *Hoo-doo Cowboys and Bronze Buckaroos*, "from the earliest incursions into the Americas by Spanish explorers to the California Gold Rush and to the Oklahoma land rush, African Americans have been present at every frontier and have been active participants in transforming those frontier settlements into thriving communities" (4). Building from the work of historians like Quintard Taylor and Shirley Ann Wilson Moore as well as the germinal bibliographic efforts of scholars like James Abajian and deep archival work, a generation of literary critics like Johnson is recognizing not only the significant presences of African Americans in the West but also their fascinating print traces – traces that testify to literary aspiration and praxis. In this vein, this chapter, to use Abajian's words about his *Blacks and Their Contributions to the American West: A Bibliography and Union List of Library Holdings through 1970*, "is not a definitive bibliography" of summary but "a foundation on which future reference works can be built" (vi). Scores of African Americans in the early West proved that they could "do something" in and with print; it is our task to recover and understand their efforts.

## Notes

1 See chapter 2 of my *Unexpected Places: Relocating Nineteenth-Century African American Literature* (2009).

2 On Newby, see my *Unexpected Places*, 105–107.

3 The published proceedings of the California conventions are another example of early black print in this vein.

4 On Carter, see my *Jennie Carter: A Black Journalist of the Early West* (2007). On Bell, see my "Early African American Print Culture and the American West" in Jordan Stein and Lara Langer Cohen's *Early African American Print Culture* (2012). See also chapter 3 of my *Unexpected Places*.

5 *America* was republished along with most of Whitfield's California poems in Robert S. Levine and Ivy G. Wilson's edition of *The Works of James Monroe Whitfield* (2011).

6 Detter's book was republished in 1996 by the University of Nebraska Press.

7 Williams's narrative was republished under the title *Fugitive Slave in the Gold Rush* in 2002 by the University of Nebraska Press. While slave narratives tended to focus on and be published in the East, there was a thin strand linked to the West, beginning at least as early as the 1849 *Narrative of the Life and Adventures of Henry Bibb*, which includes scenes in Texas, Arkansas, and a nebulous "Indian Territory." Henry Clay Bruce's *The New Man* (1895; republished by the University of Nebraska Press in 1996) is perhaps the best known of these; it offers a narrative of slavery and freedom that touched both Missouri and Kansas. Select texts published in St. Louis and Chicago can be included in this strand, as can Eliza Suggs's *Shadow and Sunshine* (published in Omaha in 1906), J. Vance Lewis's *Out of the Ditch: A True Story of an Ex-Slave* (published in Houston in 1910), and Daniel Arthur Rudd and Theodore Bond's *From Slavery to Wealth: The Life of Scott Bond* (published in Madison, Arkansas, in 1917). All are available online through the "North American Slave Narratives" project at http://docsouth.unc.edu/neh/.

8 Benjamin's *Life of Toussaint* is of especial note when placed in dialogue with his youth in St. Kitts, reminding readers of how geographically diverse the roots and concerns of black Westerners were.

9 On Cole, see my *Unexpected Places*, 92–105.

10 Among the growing body of scholarship on *Winona*, chapter 3 of Jill Bergman, *The Motherless Child in the Novels of Pauline Hopkins* (2012) is useful as is the crucial biographical work in Lois Brown, *Pauline Hopkins: Black Daughter of the Revolution* (2008).

11 For a sample of this ad, see the inside front cover of the March 1915 issue of *The Crisis*. While Cuney-Hare's book is thoroughly Du Bois-ian, another Texas woman writer leaned more toward ideas Marcus Garvey would espouse; see the 1916 novel *Five Generations Hence* in Karen Kossie-Chernyshev's *Recovering Five Generations Hence: The Life and Writings of Lillian Jones Horace* (2013).

12  Hughes's quote comes from William Loren Katz's conversations as he was writing his landmark history *The Black West*. Love's narrative was republished by the University of Nebraska Press in 1995 and is treated usefully in chapter 3 of Michael K. Johnson, *Black Masculinity and the Frontier Myth in American Literature* (2002), which places it in dialogue with Hopkins's *Winona*.

13  On Micheaux, in addition to Johnson's *Hoo-Doo Cowboys*, see chapter 2 of Johnson's *Black Masculinity* and chapter 2 of Blake Allmendinger's *Inventing the African American West* (2005).

14  Although not published until 1963 (under the title *Negro Frontiersman: The Western Memoirs of Henry O. Flipper*) Henry Ossian Flipper's 1916 manuscript functions in dialogue with such texts, too. This autobiography of a black West Pointer was written as part of Flipper's lifelong attempts to clear his name; he had been dishonorably discharged after being falsely accused of embezzlement and was finally pardoned posthumously in 1999.

15  The fullest biographical treatment of Beasley, although often deeply negative, is in Rodger Streitmatter, *Raising Her Voice: African American Women Journalists Who Changed History* (1994).

16  Bibb Thompson moved to California in 1911 with her journalist husband, Noah Davis Thompson, and began expanding beyond poetry and journalism to write plays and short fiction. Easton moved to Los Angeles from Texas in 1901, less than a decade after authoring his important early play *Dessalines, a Dramatic Tale: A Single Chapter from Hayti's History*.

17  The American West was deeply involved in the revisionist history of the "old South"; one thinks not only of the California ties of D. W. Griffiths's 1915 *Birth of a Nation* but also the ways early twentieth-century historians of the West generally removed African Americans and traces of slavery from view. A full study of black Western responses to *Birth of a Nation* – including work by both Beasley and Bibb-Thompson – remains needed.

18  *Twice Sold* includes lyrics in a chapter titled "Favorite Songs."

19  That said, Ray notes that the black population in Seattle remained quite small: "There were but a few of our own people in Seattle when we came, and at times I got very lonely" (43).

## Works Cited

Abajian, James. *Blacks and Their Contributions to the American West: A Bibliography and Union List of Library Holdings through 1970*. Boston, MA: G. K. Hall, 1974.

Baym, Nina. *Women Writers of the American West, 1833–1927*. Urbana: University of Illinois Press, 2011.

Beasley, Delilah L. *The Negro Trail Blazers of California*. Los Angeles, CA: np. 1919.

Berardi, Gayle, and Thomas Segady. "The Development of African-American Newspapers in the American West: A Sociohistorical Perspective." *Journal of Negro History*. Vol. 75, no. 3–4 (Summer–Autumn 1990): 96–111.

Ernest, John. *Liberation Historiography: African American Writers and the Challenge of History, 1794–1861*. Chapel Hill: University of North Carolina Press, 2004.

Gruesser, John. "Empires at Home and Abroad in Sutton E. Griggs's *Imperium in Imperio*." In Tess Chakkalakal and Kenneth W. Warren (eds.) *Jim Crow, Literature, and the Legacy of Sutton E. Griggs*. Athens: University of Georgia Press, 2013. 49–68.

Johnson, Michael K. *Hoo-doo Cowboys and Bronze Buckaroos: Conceptions of the African American West*. Jackson: University Press of Mississippi, 2014.

Jun, Helen. "Black Orientalism: Nineteenth-Century Narratives of Race and US Citizenship." *American Quarterly*. Vol. 58, no. 4 (December 2006): 1047–1066.

Katz, William Loren. "Introduction" to *The Black West: A Documentary and Pictorial History of the African American Role in the Westward Expansion of the United States*. Rev. Ed. New York: Harlem Moon/Broadway, 2005.

Ray, Emma J. *Twice Sold, Twice Ransomed: Autobiography of Mr. and Mrs. L. P. Ray*. Chicago, IL: Free Methodist Publishing House, 1926.

Review of *The Negro Trail Blazers of California* in *Journal of Negro History*. Vol. 5, no. 1 (January 1920): 128–129.

# 16

ROBERT THACKER

# Wallace Stegner and the literature of historical memory

Throughout his unequaled career as writer of the West, Wallace Stegner often dismissed its most pervasive myth, the Western. He wrote of people "so eager to adopt and wrap themselves up in the myth," people both in the West and those looking west from the East and elsewhere, people who made far more of the cowboy – a "very mean, dirty, low-paid job," he once called it – than was warranted (Simons, "The West of Wallace Stegner" 30, 31). This dismissal was pervasive throughout his work. For good reason: just a few years after Stegner was born in 1909 on his grandfather's farm in Iowa, in 1912, Willa Cather wrote a friend describing her first trip to the Southwest earlier that year and named the two men most responsible for the myth, describing the people she saw out West then as "so outrageously over-nourished and self-satisfied and so busy living up to Owen Wister and Remington" (Cather to Guiney). These two men, both visitors from the East, really began the Western myth Stegner so scorns: Frederic Remington first visited Montana in 1881, just five years after the death knell of the Plains Native way of life had been sounded by the June 1876 battle the Natives had ironically won there on the Greasy Grass/Little Big Horn River. Owen Wister followed during the same decade for his health. By the turn of the century Remington and others had established the imagery of romantic nostalgia – Natives, cavalry, cowboys confronting one another in the West amid high plains, mountain, and desert landscapes – through the outpouring of illustrations he produced to slake the appetite of Gilded Age America gone mad with such visions of its West. And with Wister's *The Virginian* (1902) the cowboy Western myth became powerfully articulate. Writing of them both together in a foreword to a set of letters between Wister and Remington, Stegner once asserted: "Remington – active, restless, aggressive, ironic, as romantic as Wister but in less literary ways – was primarily an eye, a quick, accurate, unsentimental eye, a hand that could record swiftly what the eye saw." For his part Wister similarly "set out ... to preserve and record the facts of range life," Stegner continues, "but he wanted to do it in fiction, which outlives fact" (vii, viii).

Yet while Remington produced mythic images during the 1880s and '90s, and branched into sculpture with his ubiquitous *The Bronco Buster* (1895), by 1900 he had begun to show himself largely done with mythic Western illustration. Instead, from then and through the rest of his career, one cut short in late 1909, Remington's prime interest was not the mythic West he had illustrated and become synonymous with. Rather, his later paintings – powerful in their use of color, often twilight or nocturnal scenes – picture another place: the American West as living space (see Anderson). But if Remington was the first major artist of the West to turn from its myth, he was followed along this path by Cather, who, with the novels she published during the 1910s – *O Pioneers!* (1913), *The Song of the Lark* (1915), and especially *My Ántonia* (1918) – wrote what Janis P. Stout has called "a different West" (20). That is, a place where people are not cowboys but individuals, members of families, inhabitants. Again, the American West as living space. As such, both Remington and Cather should be seen as predecessors to Stegner, who, for his part, wrote of the West in just this way and much more comprehensively through his massed fiction, history, biography, short stories, and essays. Throughout the latter half of the twentieth century he was the West's most prominent voice. More than they, or anyone else, he articulated the difficulties of what he called "living dry" – living in the arid West. His biography of the career of John Wesley Powell, *Beyond the Hundredth Meridian* (1954), has been seen by many as the most important book on the West published during the twentieth century.

When he died in 1909, Remington had been struggling with the colors of the West, with getting them just right, accurate and luminous. In 1913 in *O Pioneers!* Cather wrote that on the prairie-plains "the great fact was the land itself" – and that phrase, "the great fact," was one she would repeat at key moments in other novels (21). In 1962, Stegner named one of his masterpieces, *Wolf Willow*, after a smell, an odor recalled from his boyhood spent on the prairie-plains of southern Saskatchewan, a smell that confirmed to him as a middle-aged man revisiting the town of his youth that the "sensuous little savage that [he] was then is still intact inside [him]." There he defines his personal connection to it: "The tantalizing and ambiguous and wholly native smell is no more that shrub we called wolf willow, now blooming with small yellow flowers. It is wolf willow, and not the town or anyone in it, that bring me home" (18–19). Later, concluding this opening chapter, Stegner proclaims of this smell and its associations with this town in memory that "If I am native to anything, I am native to this" (21). That smell, and the aridity of the West, were to him two of its "great facts" (see West 61–71).

That opening chapter is followed by one called "History Is a Pontoon Bridge." There Stegner sounds a theme that anchors *Wolf Willow* but much more than that exemplifies the whole of its author's accomplishment. Remembering himself still as the "sensuous little savage" he once was, Stegner writes, "I still sometimes dream, occasionally in the most intense and brilliant shades of green, of a jungly dead bend of the Whitemud below Martin's dam. Every time I have that dream I am haunted, on awaking, by a sense of meanings just withheld, and by a profound sense of nostalgic melancholy" (21–22). This river valley is sanctuary from exposure on the prairie, Stegner explains, and remembering it as he revisits the place for his book, he asserts that "I may not know who I am, but I know where I am from," writing further that "however anachronistic I may be, I am a product of the American earth, and nothing quite so much as in the contrast between what I knew through the pores and what I was officially taught" (23).

Stegner wrote these words when he was about fifty, when his memories of Eastend, Saskatchewan and of his family's homestead south of there on the Canada–U.S. border were his alone – his older brother, Cecil, his mother, and his father all long dead. And he wrote them into an unusual book: *Wolf Willow* is a mélange, as its subtitle makes clear, "a History, a Story, and a Memory of the Last Plains Frontier." Referring to the history he wrote there, Stegner often called himself "the Herodotus of the Cypress Hills"; he was "unearthing and imagining and writing the history he hadn't known," John Daniel has maintained, and while Stegner himself saw the autobiography and fiction in the book as "adjuncts" to the history there, Daniel sees *Wolf Willow* "as shaped and powered by the needs of memory seeking its wholeness" (36). (Stegner once remarked in an interview, after mentioning the "great gush" of awful writing the Grand Canyon inspired, that "I think prairie dwellers with nothing so spectacular to see begin to see what really matters.") Drawing further on an essay in which Stegner asserted that the Sierra Nevada, especially Yosemite, had taught Ansel Adams how to see, Daniel suggests that "the Northern Plains taught Wallace Stegner how to see and made him the writer he was" (Stegner and Adams 38). *Wolf Willow* demonstrates this unequivocally through autobiography, history, and fiction – its "Genesis" is seen to be among Stegner's best fictions – and Daniel concludes his essay with a comprehensive assessment of Stegner that is a coda here: "The wholest writers are those with a complex sense of responsibility to nature, history, community, culture – to values that transcend their private epiphanies and memories, to whatever it is that holds them in its sights and demands the most of them. Wallace Stegner was that kind of writer" (39).

In *Wolf Willow* too Stegner recalls, in "History Is a Pontoon Bridge," his younger self: "Once, in self-pitying frame of mind, I was comparing my background with that of an English novelist friend." The other had been "brought up in London, taken from the age of four onward to the Tate and the National Gallery" and had every cultural advantage while Stegner "had grown up in this dung-heeled sagebrush town on the disappearing edge of nowhere" and "was nearly twelve before [he] saw either a bathtub or a water-closet." Hearing this, the Englishman looked at Stegner and "said dryly, 'Perhaps you got something else in place of all that.'" Tellingly, Stegner continues here to liken himself to Cather, "that bright girl from Nebraska," who "tried, and her education encouraged her, to be a good European." While he saw the parallel in their circumstances, Stegner concludes that Cather "ended by being neither quite a good American nor quite a true European nor quite a whole artist" (24–25). Recent Cather scholarship – most appearing after Stegner's death in April 1993 – has disproved this evaluation, but the connection Stegner made here is salient: like Cather, he first headed east only to return west; like her too, but writing well beyond fiction alone, he offers a West that is at once felt, historically detailed, well-informed, and understood. The American West as living space.

Wallace Stegner really began as a writer of fiction. After publishing his PhD thesis, his first novel, *Remembering Laughter* (1937), won a publisher's prize and so earned him both attention and cash, then sorely needed by Stegner and his wife, Mary, as they began their long life together. It was followed by three more – *The Potter's House* (1938), *On a Darkling Plain* (1940), and *Fire and Ice* (1941) – before Stegner produced his first significant extended fiction, *The Big Rock Candy Mountain* (1943), a novel that drew on his family's peripatetic history moving about the West when he was a boy. After failing as a homesteader in Saskatchewan, George Stegner took his family to Montana and to Washington before eventually settling in Salt Lake City, where they moved about frequently – twelve houses in four years at one point, Stegner has his autobiographical character Bruce Mason recall – in order to avoid the police. Stegner's father was a bootlegger and ran a "Blind Pig," a place where illegal liquor was available. Bo Mason shares George Stegner's dreamer's attraction to, and movement toward, the next thing, the scheme that will pay off handsomely and provide the largesse of the Big Rock Candy Mountain of the hobo's song. Yet, while fiction was Stegner's primary focus during the early stages of his career, after *The Preacher and the Slave* (1950; later retitled *Joe Hill*), Stegner abandoned the form of the novel for more than a decade. (And after some success with the form of the short story, he did the same thing there, permanently.)

The year before *The Big Rock Candy Mountain* appeared Stegner published *Mormon Country* (1942), a collection of essays on Mormon culture and sociology. Teaching then at Harvard and missing the West generally and Utah in particular – he told Richard Etulain, who has published an excellent book of interviews with Stegner – that his motive for writing it was "sheer nostalgia": "I wanted to get back west in flesh or in spirit, and the book gave me an excuse to come in both" (Stegner and Etulain, 116). Less than *Mormon Country* itself – most critics rightly see Stegner's *The Gathering of Zion* (1964), his history of the Mormon Trail, as the better book on the Latter-Day Saints – the earlier book nevertheless shows where Stegner was going, both as a writer and in relation to the West: toward its history, toward its facts, toward its realities. Jackson J. Benson, who published the first major Stegner biography and has paid especial attention to him as a writer of fiction, has described the output of years as "a very uneven career in writing fiction," seeing it as "a slow evolution toward the creation of a fictive personality with a voice that is at the heart of his success in the last, great period when he won both the National Book Award and the Pulitzer" (Finding, 205). When Stegner spoke to Etulain about *Mormon Country* he maintained that it was "simply reporting not only what I knew about Mormon history, which at that point wasn't a great deal, but also what I knew about Mormon sociology, about what living in Utah was like." By the time he wrote *The Gathering of Zion* in the 1960s he had read a lot more history, both Mormon and more broadly.

Just as Stegner concludes the initial memoir portion of *Wolf Willow*, he writes of "the dump ground" in Eastend as the repository of all the history anyone living there then knew, writing, "It is all *we* had for the civilization we grew up in. Nevertheless there was more, much more. If anyone had known that past, and told us about it, he might have told us something like this": and he then shifts to the book's second section, "Preparation for a Civilization," with its extended history of the region (36). By the time he wrote this "perfectly personal book" in the early 1960s he had been writing history for some time, but even so the point stands: Stegner was, as Benson has written, "a writer who was also a historian, someone who became a historian because he felt so ignorant of his own past" ("Writing as the Expression of Belief" 25).

In 1945, along with the editors of *Look*, Stegner published *One Nation*, a caustic analysis of separation and mistrust based on race in all of the United States. In its first chapter, "The Unaccepted," Stegner writes that "There is a wall down the middle of America, a wall of suspicion, distrust, snobbery, hatred and guilt. On one side is the majority of our people – white, Protestant, and gentile – with social, economic, and religious patterns of behavior derived from Anglo-Saxon and North European ancestors. On the other side are people who because of color, religion, or cultural background are not allowed to become full citizens of the United States" (3). Writing about *One Nation* in an appreciation of Stegner after his death, Patricia Nelson Limerick asserted that "with its full ethnic inclusiveness and demand for justice, with its careful attention to the western half of the United States in the picture of national race relations," the book "was evidence enough that Stegner had the jump on the New Western History" (113). In a similar vein, Arthur Schlesinger Jr. – a friend from Stegner's Harvard years – maintained that "His ambition was to make sense of an ordinary American life, to delineate the historical continuities between past and present and thereby to transform the chaos into human order" (20). *One Nation* was a remarkable early attempt at this – there would be many others as Stegner lent his efforts more and more to the conservationist cause in the 1950s and '60s and later.

After publishing *The Preacher and the Slave*, his novel set mostly in Salt Lake City focused on Joe Hill and the circumstances of his actions, trial, and execution there, to almost no critical notice in 1950, Stegner turned to the writing of biography and history with *Beyond the Hundredth Meridian: John Wesley Powell and the Second Opening of the West* (1954). The Hill novel required considerable biography from Stegner, although the evidence surrounding him was both limited and contradictory. That experience let him to conclude that he was "on the wrong track" for, as Curt Meine has argued, "he seems to have recalculated his bearings on the middle ground between history and literature" (127). Having been well aware of Powell through his doctoral dissertation on Clarence Dutton during the 1930s, Stegner saw him as central to any real understanding of the trans-Mississippi West. Meine has foregrounded Stegner's work in biography as critical to his vision of the West, noting that he, in effect, wrote three biographies: Powell's, Bernard DeVoto's – *The Uneasy Chair: A Biography of Bernard De Voto* (1974) – and, throughout the whole of his work, most especially through his fiction, his own. As such, the two biographies he actually did write are critical to Stegner's sense of the relation between the present and the past in the West. Stegner confirms this himself when he begins his author's note in *The Uneasy Chair* with the commonalities he shared with his subject: "We were both boys in Utah, though at different times and in different towns. We were both Westerners by birth and upbringing, novelists by intention, teachers by necessity, and historians by the sheer compulsion of the region that shaped us" (*The Uneasy Chair: A Biography of Bernard De Voto* ix).

That last phrasing captures the allure Powell offered and Stegner grasped. An autodidact, wounded Civil War officer and veteran – he lost his right arm at Shiloh under General Grant – explorer ("the Front Range of the Rockies in 1867–1868 and then his glorious and harrowing expedition down the Colorado in 1869," Walter Nugent has written), and then longtime

Washington bureaucrat, Powell was perfect for Stegner. His experience and career embodied the whole process of coming to know the substance, the salient qualities, of the American West during the latter half of the nineteenth century – that is, just as throngs of Easterners and immigrants, the question of slavery settled, were hell-bent on moving into and settling the trans-Mississippi West. Nugent writes that in chapter 3 of Stegner's *Beyond the Hundredth Meridian* – the biography, really, of Powell within the context of his career – "Powell regains center-stage ... developing and presenting his famous 1878 *Report on the Lands of the Arid Region of the United States*, containing his audacious proposals to junk the homestead system and replace it with a combination of four-section rangeland tracts and, in the few places where water existed, small irrigated farms." A professional historian, Nugent assesses Stegner's book as "a fine history not only because it is source-based and Stegner knew the turf," but also because it "is a great *story*, as exploration stories almost always are. The space in question, the plateau province, is almost unsurpassed in grandeur." "It was, and is, the 'deep West,' the 'unambiguous West' " (102–103, 104).

This work confirmed Stegner's thinking on the aridity of the region and, once his story took Powell to his career in Washington, allows him to compellingly construct his subject as – literally – a solitary voice in what amounts to a wilderness. As Stegner said to Etulain thirty years after he had done his work on Powell, "I would say that there's a very definite constraint upon Western growth, and Powell knew why. Aridity is something that you simply cannot fake out. You can only make maximum use of the water you've got. Beyond that, there isn't any, unless you resort to what the boosters call augmentation. That means bring it in from the Columbia, the Yukon, or somewhere else" (Stegner and Etulain, 181). By the early 1980s, Stegner certainly knew what he was talking about. The year after the Powell biography appeared Stegner edited and published *This Is Dinosaur: Echo Park Country and Its Magic Rivers* (1955), a well-illustrated collection by several hands that Alfred A. Knopf rushed through the press so as to send a copy to every member of Congress. There Stegner writes in his foreword that as "this book goes to press, Dinosaur National Monument is the storm center of a controversy, fought over by those who would preserve its beauty and its National Park integrity and those who would convert the Green and Yampa canyons into a storage vessel for impounding water and creating hydroelectric power" (*This Is Dinosaur* v). As Knopf's action suggests, the book was an exercise in environmental lobbying, one that succeeded in this case, although ultimately it failed in the Glen Canyon Dam, which created the ironically named – as Stegner well knew – "Lake Powell."

*This Is Dinosaur* also marked the beginning of Stegner's association with the conservationist movement, an association that took various forms. Born of, and borne by, *Beyond the Hundredth Meridian* – a book that has often been seen as required reading for any incoming secretary of the interior, and by some who served in that office – it saw Stegner spending a short time in Washington during the Kennedy administration as a special assistant to the then secretary, Stewart L. Udall. Just before that and most famously, Stegner wrote his "Coda: Wilderness Letter" (1960). This letter – a real letter – is Stegner's single most famous piece of writing, republished continually. There he "speaks for the wilderness idea as something that has helped form our character and that has certainly shaped our history as a people," and continues to assert that we "need wilderness preserved – as much of it as is still left, and as many kinds – because it was the challenge against which our character as a people was formed." "For it can be a means of reassuring ourselves of our sanity as creatures, a part of the geography of hope" (*The Sound of Mountain Water* 146, 147, 153). This last phrase has become synonymous both with Stegner and with the environmental movement – an idea that burns bright yet, however challenging the goal of the wilderness idea remains. Stegner kept to his conservationist commitments, both national and local, and regularly turned his typewriter to this cause throughout the rest of his life. He did so, doubtless, for many reasons, but his one overarching "great fact" was always the aridity – and so the vulnerability – of the American West: as wilderness, as landscape, as living space.

After Powell, when Stegner turned to biography again his subject was his friend De Voto (1897–1955) – a man he had met in in 1937 and came to know when they were together summers at Bread Loaf. After teaching at Northwestern and Harvard (1922–1936), De Voto left the academy to edit *The Saturday Review of Literature* briefly and then wrote "The Easy Chair" column in *Harper's* (1935–1955), became the literary editor of the Mark Twain Estate, and most significantly wrote a trilogy of synthetic popular histories that told the story of the American West and of its expansion (*The Year of Decision: 1846* [1943], *Across the Wide Missouri* [1947], and *The Course of Empire* [1952]). Writing in his column, Meine asserts, De Voto "took up the cudgels in the western land grab battles of the late 1940s" while "Stegner was writing himself more deeply into the canyonlands with Powell. If Stegner was the one person who could do justice to Powell, De Voto was the one person who could provide a fully appreciative introduction to *Beyond the Hundredth Meridian*, which he did. And in the years to come, Stegner would assume a role – conservation's literary standard bearer – that De Voto had practically invented" (131). With De Voto as his biographical subject in *The Uneasy Chair*, Stegner was writing a different type of biography from his book on Powell: he was writing from life and, more than that, and, as Meine maintains, "Stegner was as much participant and observer in the life he wrote" (132).

In 1945 Stegner left Harvard to create and lead the creative writing program at Stanford University, a program famous for the writers – mostly called Stegner Fellows while they were there – it produced, Edward Abbey, Wendell Berry, Ken Kesey, Larry McMurtry among the most notable, but many others too. Building a home in the Los Altos hills south of Palo Alto, a rural area when he and Mary settled there but ultimately a place from which to watch urban encroachment, Stegner established himself permanently there as a notable member of his communities, as a writer, and as a teacher. When, after the turbulent 1960s Stegner decided that he had had enough at Stanford and retired in 1971 to write full time, he almost simultaneously published *Angle of Repose*, his best-known novel and winner of the Pulitzer Prize.

After his decade-long hiatus from the novel during the 1950s following *The Preacher and the Slave /Joe Hill*, Stegner had returned to the form with *A Shooting Star* (1961) and *All the Little Live Things* (1967). He also continued to write the historical West with *The Gathering of Zion: The Story of the Mormon Trail* in 1964 and, in 1969, when he gathered his Western essays together in *The Sound of Mountain Water*. After his retirement, the De Voto biography and the publication of a collection of De Voto's letters would be Stegner's first major projects, and he followed them with another novel, *The Spectator Bird* (1976), which won the National Book Award. This says nothing of numerous speeches, essays, introductions, and other occasional pieces.

Stegner's best biographer, Philip L. Fradkin, offers the most detailed and cogent account of the making of *Angle of Repose*, the book he rightly sees as the fictional equivalent to the nonfictional *Beyond the Hundredth Meridian* within the writer's *oeuvre*. There, he writes, "Stegner took the basic outline of the lives of Arthur and Mary Hallock Foote and bent it to his fictional needs." Doing so, Stegner created a firestorm, for the "characters and plot that drew on the stories of others in *Angle of Repose* brought allegations of slander and plagiarism," and, as Fradkin continues, "Stegner was vulnerable to such accusations. He found his material in life, and then used his imaginative powers to shape the accounts into the fictions that fit his needs" (226, 228). "'I begin with the real world, obviously. I hope I don't end there,' he said." In an unpublished draft of a reply to a query about the writing of the novel Fradkin quotes, Stegner wrote:

> For years I have wondered why no western writer has been able to make a
> continuity between the past and the present, why so many are sunk in the

mythic twilight of horse opera, why the various Wests seem to have produced no culture or literature comparable to those of New England, the South, and the Midwest, why no westerner had managed to do for his territory what Faulkner did for Yoknapatawpha County. Well, here was my chance to give it a try. (229)[1]

Stegner certainly did this, and, without any question and with the controversies regarding his use of the Arthur and Mary Hallock Foote papers to one side, he succeeded admirably. And, as Jackson J. Benson has written, he succeeded to a degree not before seen in his fiction. The great strength of *Angle of Repose* is in the telling: maimed and wheelchair-bound historian Lyman Ward narrates his investigations of his grandparents' – Susan and Oliver Ward – marriage, reading through and reproducing the letters they left. As Melody Graulich, by far among the most perceptive critics to analyze the novel, has argued, in reading *Angle of Repose*, Stegner "attempts to capture readers in the web of our enduring literary heritage, to turn us into literary historians." Reading it, we "have to look over Lyman's shoulder to do it" ("Book Learning," 233, 247, 246), and "Stegner lets us read many of Susan's letters on our own, read Susan's story from the inside." "Lyman's judgments are shaped by his reading and by his cultural inheritances. His presence turns *Angle of Repose* into a story about interpretation, how the myths of our literary tradition affect our readings" ("Ruminations," 44).

In the essay by Arthur Schlesinger Jr., which began as an address to the American Academy of Arts and Letters on November 4, 1993 as tribute to his friend after his death in April of that year, Schlesinger wrote, as I have noted, that Stegner's "ambition was to make sense of an ordinary American life, to delineate the historic continuities between past and present and thereby to help transform natural chaos into human order." He then continues to assert that Stegner "succeeded triumphantly in his books, with their unforced penetration and power. And he succeeded triumphantly in his own life." Knowing the West and its history as well as he did, respecting those who deserved respect and excoriating those who did not – those he consistently called "the boosters" – Stegner had what Charles Wilkinson has called "the rigor of civility" (20). Ever writing the literature of historical memory, Stegner felt, described, and analyzed such stupidities wherever he found them as he ranged about the West. And he did so with commitment, with precision, and with artistry. Wallace Stegner wrote the West as his West, a place felt, lived in, and understood: the American West as his living space. As he once said, and as can be seen everywhere throughout his work: "I seem to have been born with an overweening sense of place, an almost pathological sensitivity to the colors, smells, light, and land and lifeforms of the segments of the earth on which I've lived" (*A Sense of Place*).[2]

## Notes

1 "'I begin with the real world ... '": Fradkin is quoting a letter Stegner wrote to Jame Hepworth July 2, 1985. See Fradkin, 347, n. 2.
2 The quotation from Stegner is from his audiocassette, *A Sense of Place.*

## Works Cited

Anderson, Nancy K. *Frederic Remington: The Color of Night.* Washington, DC: National Gallery of Art.

Benson, Jackson J. "Finding a Voice of His Own: The Story of Wallace Stegner's Fiction." In Charles E. Rankin (ed.) *Wallace Stegner: Man and Writer.* Albuquerque: University of New Mexico Press, 1996.

*Wallace Stegner: His Life and Work.* New York: Viking, 1996.

"Writing as the Expression of Belief." Ed. Curt Meine, Forward by Paul W. Johnson. *Wallace Stegner and the Continental Vision: Essays on Literature, History, and Landscape.* Washington DC: Island Press, 1997.

Cather, Willa (from 225). *O Pioneers!* (1913). Eds. Charles W. Mignon, Susan J. Rosowski, and David Stouck, the Willa Cather Scholarly Edition. Lincoln: University of Nebraska Press, 1992.

Daniel, John. "Wallace Stegner's Hunger for Wholeness." In Curt Meine (ed.) *Wallace Stegner and the Continental Vision: Essays on Literature, History, and Landscape.* Foreword Paul W. Johnson. Washington, DC: Island Press, 1997.

Flores, Dan. "Bioregionalist of the High and Dry: Stegner and Western Environmentalism." In Charles E. Rankin (ed.) *Wallace Stegner and the Continental Vision: Essays on Literature, History, and Landscape.* Albuquerque: University of New Mexico Press, 1996.

Fradkin, Philip L. *Wallace Stegner and the American West.* New York: Knopf, 2008.

Graulich, Melody. "Book Learning: *Angle of Repose* as Literary History." *Wallace Stegner: Man and Writer.* Albuquerque: University of New Mexico Press, 1996.

"Ruminations on Stegner's Protective Impulse and the Art of Storytelling." In Curt Meine (ed.) *Wallace Stegner and the Continental Vision: Essays on Literature, History, and Landscape.* Forward Paul W. Johnson. Washington DC: Island Press, 1997.

Hepworth, James R. "The Art of Fiction CXVIII." Interview with Wallace Stegner. *Paris Review* 115 (Summer 1990).

Limerick, Patricia Nelson. "Precedents to Wisdom." In Charles E. Rankin (ed.) *Wallace Stegner: Man and Writer.* Albuquerque: University of New Mexico Press, 1996.

Meine, Curt. "Wallace Stegner: Geobiographer." In Curt Meine (ed.) *Wallace Stegner and the Continental Vision: Essays on Literature, History, and Landscape.* Forward Paul W. Johnson. Washington, DC: Island Press, 1997.

Nugent, Walter. "Wallace Stegner, John Wesley Powell, and the Shrinking West." In Curt Meine (ed.) *Wallace Stegner and the Continental Vision: Essays on Literature, History, and Landscape.* Forward Paul W. Johnson. Washington, DC: Island Press, 1997.

Schlesinger, Arthur, Jr. "No Agenda but the Truth." *The Geography of Hope: A Tribute to Wallace Stegner.* San Francisco, CA: Sierra Club, 1996.

Simons, Paula. "The West of Wallace Stegner." Published excerpts from a broadcast interview made July 1992 with Stegner. *Brick* 46 (Summer 1993).

Stegner, Wallace. *A Sense of Place.* Louisville, CO: Audio Press, 1989.

*The American West as Living Space.* Ann Arbor: University of Michigan Press, 1987.

"Ansel Adams and the Search for Perfection." *One Way to Spell Man: Essays with a Western Bias.* New York: Doubleday, 1982.

"Coda: Wilderness Letter" (1961). rpt. in *The Sound of Mountain Water: The Changing American West.* New York: Penguin, 1997.

"'I Dreamed I Saw Joe Hill Last Night.'" *Pacific Spectator* 1 (Spring 1947): 184–187.

Foreword. *My Dear Wister: The Frederic Remington–Owen Wister Letters.* Ed Ben Merchant Vorpahl. Palo Alto, CA: American West, 1972.

"Foreword." *This Is Dinosaur: Echo Park Country and its Magic Rivers.* Ed. Wallace Stegner. New York: Knopf, 1955.

"Joe Hill: The Wobblies' Troubadour." *New Republic* 118 (January 5, 1948): 20–24.

"Living Dry" (1987). *Where the Bluebird Sings to the Watermelon Springs: Living and Writing in the West.* Afterword T. H. Watkins, 1992; rpt. New York: Modern Library, 2002.

*The Uneasy Chair: A Biography of Bernard De Voto.* Garden City, NY: Doubleday, 1974.

"Wallace and the Editors of *Look.*" *One Nation.* Boston, MA: Houghton Mifflin, 1945.

*Wolf Willow: A History, a Story, and a Memory of the Last Plains Frontier.* 1962; rpt. New York: Penguin, 1990.

Stegner, Wallace, and Richard W. Etulain, *Conversations with Wallace Stegner on Western History and Literature.* Revised ed. Salt Lake City: University of Utah Press, 1983.

Stout, Janis P. *Picturing a Different West: Vision, Illustration, and the Tradition of Cather and Austin.* Lubbock: Texas Tech University Press, 2007.

Tatum, Stephen. *In the Remington Moment.* Lincoln: University of Nebraska Press, 2010.

Topping, Gary. "Wallace Stegner and the Mormons." *South Dakota Review* 23 (Winter 1985): 25–41.

"Wallace Stegner the Historian." In Charles E. Rankin (ed.) *Wallace Stegner: Man and Writer.* Albuquerque: University of New Mexico Press, 1996.

West, Elliott. "Stegner, Storytelling, and Western Identity." In Charles E. Rankin (ed.) *Wallace Stegner: Man and Writer.* Albuquerque: University of New Mexico Press, 1996.

Wilkinson, Charles. "Wallace Stegner and the Rigor of Civility." In Chris Turner (ed.) *The Geography of Hope.* New York: Random House, 1996.

# 17

STEVEN FRYE

# Cormac McCarthy:
# narratives and borders

Cormac McCarthy is one of the most radically innovative authors of our time, in many ways extending the modernist pattern of experimentation to its logical conclusion. But like T. S. Eliot, he claims with forthright honesty that a thoughtful use of influence is central to any genuine transformation of literary tradition. Essential to this aesthetic is a respect, even reverence, for the primacy of story, the revolutionary power of language, and the active participation of the audience as witness. Through a creative alchemy unprecedented today, McCarthy's works claim tradition, language, and narrative as a mode of literary empowerment. All these elements are integrated in the singular consciousness of the artist and reader, which in its beauty and embodied reality stands against the cosmological void McCarthy so frequently explores. In his Western works, the evocation of the border serves a multiple purpose. First and most clearly, they are an exploration of America's frontier past, but also and most presciently they constitute a borderland between the material and the transcendent, the subjective and the objective in human perception, the perceivable and the mysterious, the known reality of "the world" and the ghost reality of "the world in its making."

In considering McCarthy's use of influence as well as the intertextual patterns in his work, it has now become standard to refer to the 1992 interview with Richard B. Woodward in the *New York Times Magazine*, titled "McCarthy's Venomous Fiction." In his encapsulation of a conversation with McCarthy, Woodward quotes him saying: "The ugly fact is that books are made out of other books. The novel depends for its life on the novels that have been written." McCarthy cites a few writers, particularly Melville and Dostoevsky. Without question *Blood Meridian* depends for its life on *Moby-Dick*, and many of McCarthy's other novels, specifically his play *The Sunset Limited*, are innovative recreations of *The Brothers Karamazov*. But there are a host of allusions throughout his novels and plays – large leitmotifs, overarching structural metaphors, and individual references – that enrich his works, forming an important part of what makes them beautiful, McCarthy's own singular creative genius what makes them sublime. Homer, Dante, the Bible, the Gnostic gospels, the works of Milton and Shakespeare are only a few of the many, and they are so numerous that even if readers miss some they will comprehend others. T. S. Eliot based his creative life on the idea that the great poet is endowed with "historical sense" and writes with the spirit of the past in his "bones," thus creating literary art that is simultaneously traditional and innovative. McCarthy's aesthetic seems to comport well with this idea. But McCarthy seems to be about something else, something more mystically generative, less firmly classicist, embracing rather than rejecting romantic concepts of sublimity, and depending on the mind of the reader to participate in the act of creation. He is by no means a relativist, nor do his works lend themselves to acts of wholesale reconceptualization on the part of the audience. They are too pressing, too informed, too full of substance and moral urgency to fall prey to reader response. But there is one word that is perhaps unavoidable when considering the relationship of author and reader as they come together in McCarthy's canon. That word is *empathy*. It may seem strange to suggest that intimate identification is a primary purpose in novels that court situations so foreign, so alien to our daily experience, often so horrific and violent. But to echo *Child of God*, each of his characters appears to us as "children of God," much like ourselves. From John Wesley Rattner in *The Orchard Keeper*, to Lester Ballard, to Culla Holme in *Outer Dark*, onward to the unnamed kid in *Blood Meridian*, and to the sympathetic heroes of the Border Trilogy, we are meant to identify in intimate ways with the characters and their struggles, striving to understand them even as we strive to understand ourselves.

McCarthy's last novel, *The Road*, achieves a certain character inertia early in the narrative with the father's thoughts. As he ponders a wasted and threatening world, "He knew only that the child was his warrant. He said, if he is not the word of God God never spoke" (5). Later in the novel, after the man has used one of his bullets to kill a cannibal, the father admonishes the boy like all of us might in a moment of threat: "My job is to take care of you. I was appointed to do that by God. I will kill anyone who touches you. Do you understand?" (77). In situations such as these, which occur in McCarthy's novels from the beginning, we are drawn to empathy, a deep, even intimate sense of identification, and we are confronted with the singular fact that grounds the study of phenomenology, that human consciousness is perhaps the most unique, beautiful, compelling, and mysterious thing the universe has created.[1] For all of his philosophical portentousness and the apparent objectivity of his narration, McCarthy is first and primarily an artist of the personal; his novels are an externalization of consciousness, his characters deeply human. Insofar as he shares this with the greatest works of literature, with Shakespeare, Milton, Melville, and Dostoevsky, his works are not derivative but participatory, not only in the realm of objective experience, but in the subjective realm of the human mind itself. In McCarthy's view, consciousness, in Whitmanesque terms, casts silken threads of acute awareness outward into the air, inviting this interconnection of minds, and it does this by asserting the primacy of narrative, the human story perpetually told.

In the first novel of the Border Trilogy, *All the Pretty Horses*, this emphasis on the relationship of personal consciousness to narrative appears most fully in the dream motif. In the broadest possible sense, John Grady Cole is a dreamer, an idealist, and he is willing to risk all to realize a dream that possesses inescapably mystical characteristics.[2] Early in the novel, the dream is conscious, as he rides out into the country and projects himself into a past that is simultaneously real and imagined:

> At the hour he'd always choose when the shadows were long and the ancient road was shaped before him in the rose and canted light like a dream of the past where the painted ponies and the riders of that lost nation came down out of the north with their faces chalked and their long hair plaited and each armed for war which was their life and the women and children and women with children at their breasts all of them pledged in blood and redeemable in blood only. (5)

Standing alone and pondering the act of crossing the physical border between the United States and Mexico, John Grady projects himself across an interior borderland, between the conscious and the unconscious, past and present, in a waking dream across centuries in a singular act of identification with an ancient enemy, recognizing even in their warlike brutality a fundamental humanity and connection to the narrative that even unrecorded becomes absolute in its relation to his own story.[3] In this act of idealistic projection, his life and his hopes for a future on the land become inextricably connected to the Comanche. John Grady responds to a narrative that he has been told or has read, but that same universal story has become a part of the woven substance of his consciousness both in waking and in sleeping. His is ultimately a search for purpose and a form of meaning he cannot fully articulate or make concrete to others except through the hopes he articulates for a life across the Mexican border, where he will live "like the old time Waddies." His narrative as it appears in his dreamlike projection is by no means void of reality, particularly the reality of violence, and his final conversation with the Texas judge who has exonerated him is quite telling. The judge has characterized the story John Grady has told in court as extraordinary and heroic, and for many reasons John Grady rejects being characterized as special. In part, this is because of the guilt he feels for killing the young man in prison. But it is primarily because the judge has separated John Grady from the narrative that he has worked so hard to imbed himself within. To be special is in some sense to occupy his own realm, to stand apart. But John Grady Cole has sought throughout the novel to participate in a historically constituted universal story that he perpetuates intentionally and unintentionally in projected memory and dreams. John Grady does achieve, from the point of view of the reader, a kind of mythic status, but it is a recognizable myth. This appears most fully when John Grady is in jail, as he dreams of horses and his inextricable connection to them:

> That night he dreamt of horses in a field on the high plain ... and in the dream he was among the horses running and in the dream he himself could run with the horses and they coursed the young mares and fillies over the plain where their rich bay and their rich chestnut colors shone in the sun. (161)

In an unconscious state he achieves a state of total identification with the horses, animals that to him have a unique connection to a mystical order he can only obliquely comprehend. What distinguishes John Grady Cole, then, is his internal drive and external commitment to a mythic story, a frequently articulated story about man and horse in an unsettled West in which he can both bind himself to the landscape and its living occupants and participate in an experience that is storied in nature. Through dreams imagined and unimagined, through consciousness itself, John Grady seeks and in many ways finds himself, at least for a time.

This emphasis on the dream as universal narrative achieves perhaps its fullest expression at the conclusion of the last novel in the Border Trilogy. John Grady Cole has died in a knife fight with the pimp Eduardo, in pursuit of the same ideal that gave him identity and purpose in *All the Pretty Horses*. Many years have passed, and his friend Billy Parham in old age listens to and as such participates in the dream of a mysterious stranger. The stranger tells the story of his dream, and a dream within a dream, and a reluctant and even skeptical Billy listens, acting in a sense as witness, questioning the dream's validity as he encourages the stranger to continue. The stranger perceives a deep and vaguely consequential portent in the dream, even as Billy struggles to diminish its meaning. In this context the stranger makes a claim for the universality of story, saying that "it is the narrative that is the life of the dream while the events themselves are often interchangeable" (283). The stranger throughout his telling attempts to challenge the line that separates dream from waking, just as he tries to blur the distinction between life and afterlife.[4] When Billy asks him where we go when we die, the stranger says

"I don't know.... Where are we now?" (268). The stranger's purpose is not to challenge the nature of lived experience but to bind it to the concept of narrative. He argues:

> The world of our fathers resides within us. Ten thousand generations and more. A form without a history has no power to perpetuate itself. What has no past can have no future. At the core of our life is the history of which it is composed and in that core are no idioms but only the act of knowing and it is this we share in dreams and out. Before the first man spoke and after the last is silenced forever. (281)

Here the concept of borders is most fully and conceptually articulated. Borders are exterior and interior, conscious and unconscious, and each is bound together by history which is itself constituted as narrative. That universal story achieves its meaning through the perpetual act of knowing, and knowledge can only be constituted and understood through tales, stories, and dreams, all of which have a narrative form. The emphasis on the concept of sharing is central here, because this is where the empathy resides. Billy originally notices the stranger from across the highway and ponders the possibility that he is the angel of death. At seventy-eight, death appears perhaps as more friend than enemy, and Billy is willing to share both food and conversation with the man. As the dream narrative is told, the stranger reaches out to Billy, trying with a genuine confidence to cause Billy to understand that the dream, the dream within the dream, and the narrative they constitute are in effect Billy's own. While Billy resists, he cannot help but listen and in a certain way without his fully knowing it Billy's identity is absorbed and merged with that of the stranger and also that of the dreamer. All act as witness, all participate in the unity of the one universal narrative that is the human experience, and all simultaneously constitute and eradicate the borders that identify the self and its relation to the other.

We experience this idea throughout McCarthy's novels, in their dialectical structure, in the intricate blend of narration, description, dialogue, and extended monologue. But the idea that as humans we live within narrative, circumscribed and empowered by language, bound together by the act of telling and the role of the witness, is most clearly thematized in *The Crossing*.[5] Ostensibly an adventure story with a picaresque structure, this second novel in the Border Trilogy proves to be, in a different way than *The Road*, McCarthy's confession, revealing directly for the first time perhaps what motivated his many sacrifices as an author. To live is to speak; to find meaning is both to hear and speak again. In three crossings over both geographical and spiritual borders, the main character Billy Parham comes of age through a series of confrontations with incarnate evil and a set of encounters with people who have been tempered by experience. They stand ready to tell him their stories, and from them he gains a provisional wisdom as he comes to apprehend, at least vaguely, that he is a player in a universal drama, a single story written by a silent author, who pens the trajectory of single lives with sublime vision and insight beyond human comprehension. In his border experiences, Billy listens to the priest at Huisiachepec and his tale of the pensioner, to the blind revolutionary and his wife, and to the *gitano*, the gypsy in charge of the wrecked airplane. All of them present stories that emerge as re-inscriptions of a single narrative of human fate and destiny. They contain and order all in a sweeping story that lends form and purpose to what remains the mystery of human experience and the mystery of the suffering that at times brings us to our knees.[6] This idea is most directly told by the priest. McCarthy writes:

> What does Caborca know of Huisiachepec, Huisiachepec of Caborca? They are different worlds, you must agree. Yet even so there is but one world and everything that is imaginable is necessary to it. For this world also which seems to us a thing of stone and flower and blood is not a thing at all but is a tale. And all in it is a tale and each tale the sum of all lesser tales and yet these are also the selfsame tale and contain as well all else within them. So everything is necessary. Every least thing. This is the hard lesson. Nothing can be dispensed with. Nothing despised. Because the seams are hid from us you see. The joinery. The way in which the world is made. We have no way to know what could be taken away. What omitted. We have no way to tell what might stand and what might fall. And those seams that are hid from us are the course of the tale itself and the tale has no abode or place of being except in the telling only and there it lives and makes its home and therefore we can never be done with the telling. Of the telling there is no end. And whether in Caborca or in Huisiachepec or in whatever other place by whatever other name or by no name at all I say again all tales are one. Rightly heard all tales are one. (143)

Central to the priest's synthesis of his own story is a series of relationships: between the experience and the teller, the teller and his own conscious awareness and response, the tale and the witness, the witness and Billy the silent interlocutor. Binding them all is the shared moment of hearing and the empathy that emerges as the tale is recognized and relived, both in the moment of telling and in perpetual memory. Human experience in its richest and most meaningful form takes place in the realm of the phenomenological, through hearing and apprehending, again in Whitmanesque terms, through "peering, absorbing, translating." The tragic even horrific travails of the priest, the revolutionary, and the *gitano* find no genuine compensation in the telling, but their stories rearticulated are nevertheless received, taken into the singular consciousness of the witness, and retold, ultimately in the novel itself. We are given clearly to understand that truth value in *The Crossing* has nothing to do with the fictiveness of the story. For McCarthy, the border that divides fiction and nonfiction is an illusion. The epistemological relevance of the novel form does not derive from fictional events that carry a thematic import. It derives from the universal, even transcendent legitimacy of the fiction itself, which is grounded not in a single set of historical events but in the universal story that binds human bodies and human minds to the world in all its mystery. McCarthy makes more than a romantic gesture here, and the linkage of *The Crossing* to Hegelian dialectics is reasonably well established.[7] In a move reminiscent of Emerson, Thoreau, and Whitman, he seeks to bind all into the irreducibly complex but orderly weave of the world. In this tapestry we see the role of influence and the manner in which his literary forebears empower his works. McCarthy writes:

> Who can dream of God ... seated solely in the light of his own presence. Weaving the world.... A God with a fathomless capacity to bend all to an inscrutable purpose. Not chaos lay outside of that matrix. And somewhere in that tapestry that was the world in its making and in its unmaking was a thread that was he and he awoke weeping. (149)

The world in its making, the thread that was he, the tapestry and the matrix, all integrated physically in an inconceivable process that is nevertheless purposeful. This image of the weaver-god is drawn directly from "The Bower of the Arsacides" chapter in *Moby-Dick*. In that book, Melville's world is made metonymic in the vast, immemorial, unremembering sea, where move "endless processions of the whale" and one "grand-hooded phantom ... like a snow-hill in the air." Lurking there also is the world in its making, where like McCarthy's world, "are all the horrors of the half known life." Melville writes:

> The weaver-god, he weaves; and by that weaving is he deafened, that he hears no mortal voice; and by that humming, we, too, who look on the loom are deafened; and only when we escape it shall we hear the thousand voices that speak through it. (480)

In Melville's concept, God himself is deafened by the action of his own creative process. McCarthy imbues *The Crossing* with the same foreboding and a deeper recognition of the reality of violence. But he takes power from the original reference and reorganizes its meaning, rearticulating it in such a way that the weaver-god cannot help but hear, being himself synonymous with the tale, its telling, and its perpetuation by the witness.

In a more subtle but nevertheless substantial way, the creative relationship of story to human identity precedes the Border Trilogy, notably in

McCarthy's masterpiece *Blood Meridian; or, the Evening Redness in the West*. This novel entered the scene with little fanfare, with scant attention from critics and a limited readership. In many ways this was odd, given that McCarthy had so recently won the coveted MacArthur Fellowship. But the staggering portrayal of violence and the portentous philosophy of destruction Judge Holden expressed certainly consign the novel to a specialized readership, despite the fact that it is now recognized as one of the cornerstones of world literary art in the late twentieth century. *Blood Meridian* is a frontier narrative, a metaphysical and epistemological romance, a "book" that transcends genre. But it is essentially a dark picaresque that in its chapter captioning evokes the explorer narratives of the late nineteenth century. It tells the story of an unnamed "kid" who journeys west and becomes involved first with an ill-fated army troop and then with the infamous gang of scalp hunters led by John Joel Glanton. The story takes its basis from an actual history written by Samuel Chamberlain, *Recollections of a Rogue*, which is the only source in which the horrific and ultimately compelling Judge Holden can be found. Again the chapter captioning immediately calls attention to the events as narrative, even as we come to know that they are founded in an actual history.[8] The fact that events and people are drawn from a written recollection suggests that the circumstances recounted are simultaneously real, recollected, and in the end storied, forming inevitably the narrative weave of the world. McCarthy is supremely conscious of the interrelationship of truth and the web of telling that forms the epistemological logic of this and other novels, beginning with a poetic, lyrical, almost fable-like tone and style:

> See the child. He is pale and thin, he wears a thin and ragged linin shirt. He stokes the scullery fire. Outside lie dark turned fields with rags of snow and darker woods beyond that harbor yet a few last wolves. His folk are known for hewers of wood and drawers of water but in truth his father was a schoolmaster. He lies in drink, he quotes from poets whose names are now lost. The boy crouches by the fire and watches him.
> ... All history present in that visage, the child the father of the man. (3)

Foregrounded in the direct address to the reader is the act of telling and the invitation to witness: "See the child" draws the reader into the narrative and in no way sacrifices the distanced, storied, and folkloric quality of a series of events that are rooted in only a half-known history. The borderland here embodies what Mary Louise Pratt refers to as a "contact zone," a porous boundary, in this case an embodied space that eradicates the distinction between fiction and history, that blends and makes inextricable the relationship of truth and the narratives that give it structure.[9]

Drawn into this one narrative, the reader is yet again enfolded into a version of the one tale, but the content of *Blood Meridian* reminds us that the one story does not involve a simple through-line but a tapestry, and here the threads are rough woven and dark, connoting that part of the weave involves violence, indiscriminate bloodletting, and a bleak justification for degradation in the extreme.

The reader as witness becomes involved then in more than the story being told, but in the complex of influences and direct allusions that give it texture and bind it to the very tradition that makes it most innovative. "The child the father of the man" is taken from William Wordsworth's "My Heart Leaps Up When I Behold," and the novel is imbued with the Jacobean language and cadences of the King James Bible, with Dante, Shakespeare, and the dialectical interchanges echoing Melville and Dostoevsky. Among many more developed allusions, the judge and the miter scene is drawn from Milton's *Paradise Lost*, and Judge Holden, seven feet tall, bald, cold-white, and ubiquitous, is a clear reconfiguration of the great white whale, the "grand hooded phantom" of *Moby-Dick*. In her talk in the Yale Lecture Series, Amy Hungerford sees the judge as an allusion to Captain Ahab. Hungerford is excellent with a host of references and is certainly correct in emphasizing the importance of Melville's masterpiece, but the judge is re-conceptualized from, not Ahab, but the white whale itself. Ahab is too monomaniacal, too human, too obsessed, and in the end it is the very transformation of Ahab into a Satanic figure that divorces him from the judge as reference. To call the judge "evil" is a massive oversimplification. Like the white whale, he suggests a universal force of destruction that no mythic concept of evil can contain. It is right to say that the judge may be what is behind the pasteboard mask, the mystery of the human plight that Ahab hopes to strike through in killing Moby-Dick. Destruction, malevolence, and brutality define him, but so do they provide the dark texture that adds a portentous meaning to the one tale rightfully told. In a powerful moment in the novel when the judge addresses the band, he demonstrates the innate process whereby even scientific facts become threads in the elaborate tapestry:

> In the afternoon he sat in the compound breaking ore samples with a hammer, a feldspar rich in red oxide of copper and native nuggets in whose organic lobations he purported to read news of the earth's origins, holding an extemporary lecture in geology to a small gathering who nodded and spat. A few would quote him scripture to confound his ordering up of eons out of the ancient chaos and other apostate supposings. The judge smiled.

> Books lie, he said
> God don't lie.

No, said the judge. He does not. And these are his words.
He held up a chunk of rock.
He speaks in stones and trees, the bones of things. (116)

The judge continues later, speaking to them "in the old epic mode," and it becomes clear that nothing lies external to language. Not that in the Derridian sense words are arbitrary signifiers, but, as Emerson argues, the earth itself is logos, language itself an emanation of an absolute reality, however mysterious and frightening. In a novel that presents itself as a picaresque fable and a history together, for the judge and his witnesses, all books are lies unless they speak the universal tale of wandering and woe, of destruction and violent regeneration.

In *The Road*, McCarthy continues and heightens this theme, although he softens it significantly. Ironically, he does so with a peculiar aesthetic sleight of hand. The idea of the world as tale is retained, but *The Road* is terse and seemingly unadorned, sparse and tactile, as if the world has been stripped of illusions and reduced to its darkest essentials. But even the minimalist language is drawn from tradition, and while displaying his own voice, McCarthy echoes the style of Ernest Hemingway, even using playful allusions to Hemingway's short stories "Indian Camp" and "Cat in the Rain." But the novel (pun very much intended) is a road narrative, containing many of the same features as any adventure tale: a journey, a spiritual quest, a post-apocalyptic, character-driven story full of conflict and striving. McCarthy conceptualized *The Road* in this manner from the beginning. In the McCarthy papers and manuscripts held in the Wittliff Collections at Texas State University, San Marcos, we have discovered that the working title of the novel was "The Grail," and in excised passages the boy is much more clearly a messianic figure. Thus, *The Road* is built out of some of the oldest of stories, the Christian Gospels and the Arthurian legends. But the story elements are not merely structural features employed formally to construct an externalized tale. In *The Road*, they are linked to the deepest recesses of human consciousness, to dreams. McCarthy writes:

> In his dream she was sick and he cared for her. The dream bore the look of sacrifice but he thought differently. He did not take care of her and she died alone somewhere in the dark and there is no other dream nor other waking world and there is no other tale to tell. (32)

In dreaming of his departed wife the past becomes present and inescapable. Dream, thought, and memory are all one, forming the substance even of the waking world, and taking shape through narrative, again in the one tale first fully conceived in *The Crossing*. Dreams themselves, although an aspect of human consciousness, are never removed from the oldest and most resilient form of narrative construction – sacrifice – which in the course of history is central to ritual, romance, theatre, and the binding tapestry of story structures that seem for McCarthy to form the essence of human perception. "The dream bore the look of sacrifice but he thought differently." As the man is forced for one torturous moment to think outside the dream, he is confronted with darkness, the inexpressible loneliness of a Godless death, and a cosmological void bereft of meaning. *The Road* is at times a composite of frightening internal monologues that frequently contradict one another, standing in tense dialectical relation, and this one expresses the horror of the world outside the dream and external to the one tale rightfully told. The novel refers to these dreams repeatedly, sometimes in a positive and sometimes in a negative sense. At one point, the man even ponders the idea that dreams of death suggest the presence of the survival impulse. At other times, however, dreams perform a more generative function, as the man ponders their contours:

> And dreams so rich in color. How else would death call you? Waking in the cold dawn it all turned to ash instantly. Like certain ancient frescoes entombed for centuries suddenly exposed to the day. (21)

As we consider the figurative meaning of the universe as cosmological void (although it later takes on the more rich association with the typological wilderness of the Bible), the only defense from oblivion is dreams rich in color that must be protected like ancient works of art that are the visual embodiment of narratives, myths, and ancient histories. The one tale to tell then emerges from the deepest recesses of consciousness, and the basic phenomenological fact is that the mind, the dream, the story, the ritual, the "frescoes entombed" are the bound substance of human experience and of the highly determined matter of which we are comprised, as they spin through space-time, bending, to echo *The Stonemason*, the very warp of the world.

In the end, *The Road* may be the re-inscription of many works within the Western literary tradition, but in many ways it is most obviously a synthesis of the Bible. It may not be an overstatement to say that if *The Road* were the only book found after the great cataclysm it might be the new Genesis or the first gospel. It places two people into a typological wilderness under the most trying of circumstances, confronts them with the grandest question, that of the existence, purpose, and nature of the divine. Job-like it confronts the question of suffering and redemption, and similar to the Gospel of John it seeks to define the interrelationship of physical matter and spiritual reality. As a novel containing an Existential Christian subtext, the boy cannot pray to God but only to the father who has loved him, and the believing woman responds with understanding:

> The woman said that was all right. She said that the breath of God was his breath yet though it pass from man to man through all of time. (286)

With a revealing and perhaps coincidental similarity in Ingmar Bergman's *Through a Glass Darkly*, God quite simply is love, and to pray is to pray to the father who, perhaps unknown to himself, was the divine fully realized for the boy. Thus the sacred nature of this text, drawn with explicit references to other religious works, is inextricably bound to tradition, narrative, story, and the one tale carried forward.

Thus the role of influence has a distinctive meaning in McCarthy's works. It can reasonably be said that any allusion in any work of literature, whether a sweeping structural metaphor or a brief line reference, empowers by bringing the whole of the previous work into the body of the new. All of the themes, meanings, subtle associations, the totality of the reader's memory of the original novel, poem, or play, imbue the new work with intensity and significance through the memory of the reader. In constituting his own aesthetic and implementing it throughout his work, McCarthy is acutely aware of this mode of literary empowerment, but unlike other writers, the body of his novels suggests that writing and art are more essential than we might have supposed, that the grand and ordered architecture of the world itself can never be made separate from its expression in narrative. Stories told and retold, the world in its making, the threads that are each of us, are made real through the act of expression and witness, and from this living dream we must all wake weeping, but the grief that inspires those tears is tempered with the deepest empathy, a half-known apprehension of our connection to each other, in a borderland so to speak, that like threads in a weave binds the ordered and harmonious tapestry of the universe.

## Notes

1 For a detailed discussion of the theological implications of character interaction in *The Road*, see Allen Josephs.
2 Edwin T. Arnold discusses in detail the role of dreams in the Border Trilogy. See also Rick Wallach.
3 See Douglas Canfield, and Nick Monk's "*All the Pretty Horses*, the Border, and Ethnic Encounter."
4 Note also Kim McMurtry and Linda Woodson.
5 See Dianne Luce's "The Road as Matrix," the first essay to explore the role of narrative and witness in *The Crossing*. Note also my own essay dealing with romantic naturalism in *The Crossing* as well as my reading of the novel in *Understanding*

*Cormac McCarthy.* For additional treatments of romantic naturalism and naturalism, see Giles and Link.
6  For a discussion of theodicy in *The Crossing*, note James Keegan. See also Timothy Parrish.
7  Note again Dianne Luce in "The Road as Matrix."
8  For a detailed exploration of sources, see John Sepich.
9  See also Nick Monk's "'An Impulse to Action and Undefined Want.'"

## Works Cited

Arnold, Edwin T. "'Go to Sleep': Dreams and Visions in *The Border Trilogy*." In Edwin T. Arnold and Dianne C. Luce (eds.) *A Cormac McCarthy Companion: The Border Trilogy*. Jackson: University of Mississippi Press, 2001. 37–72.
Canfield, Douglas J. "Crossing from the Wasteland to the Exotic in McCarthy's The Border Trilogy." In Edwin T. Arnold and Dianne C. Luce (eds.) *A Cormac McCarthy Companion: The Border Trilogy*. Jackson: University of Mississippi Press, 2001. 256–269.
Frye, Steven. "Cormac McCarthy's 'world in its making': Romantic Naturalism in *The Crossing*." *Studies in American Naturalism* 2 (Summer 2007): 46–65.
Giles, James R. *Outer Dark* and Romantic Naturalism." In Steven Frye (ed.) *The Cambridge Companion to Cormac McCarthy*. Cambridge: Cambridge University Press, 2013. 95–106.
Josephs, Allen. "The Quest for God in *The Road*." In Steven Frye (ed.) *The Cambridge Companion to Cormac McCarthy*. Cambridge: Cambridge University Press, 2013. 133–148.
Keegan, James. "'Save Yourself' The Boundaries of Theodicy and the Signs of The Crossing." *Cormac McCarthy Journal* 1 (Spring 2001): 44–61.
Link, Eric Carl. "McCarthy and Literary Naturalism." In Steven Frye (ed.) *The Cambridge Companion to Cormac McCarthy*. Cambridge: Cambridge University Press, 2013. 149–161.
*Understanding Cormac McCarthy*. Columbia: University of South Carolina Press, 2009.
Luce, Dianne C. "The Road as Matrix: The World as Tale in *The Crossing*. *Perspectives on Cormac McCarthy*. Rev. ed. Jackson: University of Mississippi Press, 1999. 195–219.
McMurtry, Kim. "'Some Improvident God.' Metaphysical Explorations in McCarthy's Border Trilogy." In Wade Hall and Rick Wallach (eds.) *Sacred Violence: Cormac McCarthy's Western Novels*. Vol. 2. El Paso: Texas Western Press, 1995. 143–157.
Monk, Nick. "*All the Pretty Horses*, the Border, and Ethnic Encounter." In Steven Frye (ed.) *The Cambridge Companion to Cormac McCarthy*. Cambridge: Cambridge University Press, 2013. 121–132.
"'An Impulse to Action and Undefined Want': Modernity, Flight, and Crisis in the Border Trilogy and *Blood Meridian*." In Wade Hall and Rick Wallach (eds.) *Sacred Violence: Cormac McCarthy's Western Novels*. Vol. 2. El Paso: Texas Western Press, 1995. 83–103.
Parrish, Timothy. "History and the Problem of Evil in McCarthy's Western Novels." In Steven Frye (ed.) *The Cambridge Companion to Cormac McCarthy*. Cambridge: Cambridge University Press, 2013. 67–78.

Sepich, John. *Notes on Blood Meridian*. Austin: University of Texas Press, 1993.

Wallach, Rick. "Theatre, Ritual, and Dream in the Border Trilogy." In Wade Hall and Rick Wallach (eds.) *Sacred Violence: Cormac McCarthy's Western Novels*. Vol. 2. El Paso: Texas Western Press, 1995, 159–177.

Woodson, Linda. "McCarthy's Heroes and the Will to Truth." In Steven Frye (ed.) *The Cambridge Companion to Cormac McCarthy*. Cambridge: Cambridge University Press, 2013, 15–26.

# FURTHER READING

## Critical studies and essay collections

Abbott, Carl. *"It's Your Misfortune Not My Own": A New History of the American West*. Norman: University of Oklahoma Press, 1993.

Ainswoth, Len, and Kenneth W. Davis, eds. *The Catch-Pen: A Selection of Essays from the First Two Years of the National Cowboy Symposium and Celebration*. Lubbock, TX: The Ranching Heritage Center, 1991.

Allmendinger, Blake. *The Cowboy: Representations of Labor in an American Work Culture*. New York: Oxford University Press, 1992.

Athearn, Robert G. *The Mythic West in Twentieth-Century America*. Lawrence: University Press of Kansas, 1886.

Baym, Nina. *Women Writers in the American West, 1833–1927*. Urbana: University of Illinois Press, 2011.

Bennion, Sherilyn Cox. *Equal to the Occasion: Women's Editors of the Nineteenth-Century West*. Reno: University of Nevada Press, 1990.

Billington, Ray Allen. *Land of Savagery, Land of Promise: The European Image of the American Frontier in the Nineteenth Century*. New York: Norton, 1981.

Bredahl, A. Carl, Jr. *New Ground: Western American Narrative and the Literary Canon*. Chapel Hill: University of North Carolina Press, 1989.

Calder, Jenni. *There Must Be a Lone Ranger: The Myth and Reality of the American Wild West*. 1974. Rpt. London: Abacus, 1976.

Calvin, Ross. *Sky Determines: An Interpretation of the Southwest*. 1934. Rpt. Albuquerque: University of New Mexico Press, 1975.

Campbell, Neil. *The Rhizomatic West: Representing the American West in a Transnational, Global, Media Age*. Lincoln, NE: Bison Books, 2011.

Comer, Krista, *Landscapes of the New West: Gender and Geography in Contemporary Women's Writing*. Chapel Hill: University of North Carolina Press, 1999.

Davis, Mike. *How Cities Won the West: Four Centuries of Urban Change in Western North America*. Albuquerque: University of New Mexico Press, 2008.

Durham, Philip, and Everett L. Jones. *The Western Story: Fact, Fiction, and Myth*. New York: Harcourt Brace Jovanovich, 1975.

Engel, Leonard, ed. *The Big Empty: Essays on Western Landscapes as Narrative*. Albuquerque: University of New Mexico Press, 1994.

Etulain, Richard W. ed. *The American Literary West*. Manhattan, KS: Sunflower University Press, 1980.

Everson, William. *Archetype West*. Berkeley, CA: Oyez, 1976.

Fender, Stephen. *Plotting the Golden West: American Literature and the Rhetoric of the California Trail*. Cambridge: Cambridge University Press, 1981.

Fiedler, Leslie. *The Return of the Vanishing American*. New York: Stein and Day, 1968.

Folsom, James K. *The American Western Novel*. New Haven, CT: Yale University Press, 1968.

Franklin, Wayne, and Michael Steiner, eds. *Mapping American Culture*. Iowa City: University of Iowa Press, 1992.

Fussell, Edwin S. *Frontier: American Literature and the American West*. Princeton, NJ: Princeton University Press, 1965.

Greenfield, Bruce. *Narrating Discovery: The Romantic Explorer in American Literature, 1790–1855*. New York: Columbia University Press, 1992.

Grossman, James R., ed. *The Frontier in American Culture*. Newberry Library and Berkeley: University of California Press, 1994.

Gurian, Jay. *Western American Writing: Tradition and Promise*. Deland, FL: Everett/Edwards, 1975.

Haslam, Gerald, ed. *Western Writing*. Albuquerque: University of New Mexico Press, 1974.

Hazard, Lucy Lockwood. *The Frontier in American Literature*. New York: Thomas Y. Crowell, 1927.

Heyne, Eric, ed. *Desert, Garden, Margin, Range: Literature on the American Frontier*. New York: Twayne, 1992.

Holthaus, Gary, et al., eds. *A Society to Match the Scenery: Personal Visions of the Future of the American West*. Niwot: University Press of Colorado, 1991.

Hyde, Anne Farrar. *An American Vision: Far Western Landscape and National Culture, 1820–1920*. New York: New York University Press, 1990.

Kolodny, Annette. *The Land Before Her: Fantasy and Experience of the American Frontiers, 1630–1860*. Chapel Hill: University of North Carolina Press, 1984.

Kowalewski, Michael. *New Essays on the Literature of the American West*. New York: Cambridge University Press, 1996.

Lee L. L., and Merrill Lewis, eds. *Women, Women Writers, and the West*. Troy, NY: Whitston, 1979.

Lee, Robert Edson, *From West to East: Studies in the Literature of the American West*. Urbana: University of Illinois Press, 1966.

Levin, David. *History as Romantic Art: Bancroft, Prescott, Motley and Parkman*. Stanford: Stanford University Press, 1959.

Love, Glen A. *New Americans: The Westerner and the Modern Experience in the American Novel*. Lewisburg, PA: Bucknell University Press, 1982.

Maguire, James H. "Fiction of the West." In *The Columbia History of the American Novel*. Emory Elliot, ed. New York: Columbia University Press, 1991, 437–464.

Meldrum, Barbara Howard, ed. *Old West-New West: Centennial Essays*: Moscow: University of Idaho Press, 1993.

Mexal, Stephen J. *Ready for Liberalism: The Overland Monthly and the Writing of the Modern American West*. Lincoln: University of Nebraska Press, 2013.

*Under the Sun: Myth and Realism in Western American Literature*. Troy, NY: Whitston, 1985.

Milton, John R. *The Novel of the American West.* Lincoln: University of Nebraska Press, 1980.

Mitchell, Lee Clark. *Witnesses to a Vanishing America: The Nineteenth-Century Response.* Princeton, NJ: Princeton University Press, 1981.

Morris, Gregory, ed. *Talking Up a Storm: Voices of the New West.* Lincoln: University of Nebraska Press, 1995.

Niamias, June. *White Captives: Gender and Ethnicity on the American Frontier.* Chapel Hill: University of North Carolina Press, 1993.

Pearce, Roy Harvey. *Savagism and Civilization: A Study of the Indian and the American Mind.* 1953. Rpt. Berkeley: University of California Press, 1988. Originally published as *The Savages of America: A Study of the Indian and the Idea of Civilization.*

Pilkington, William T., ed. *Critical Essays on the Western American Novel.* Boston, MA: G. K. Hall, 1980.

Prown, Jules David, et al. *Discovered Lands, Invented Pasts: Transforming Visions of the American West.* New Haven, CT: Yale University Press, 1992.

Schlissel, Lillian, Vicki L. Ruiz, and Janice Monk, eds. *Western Women: Their Land, Their Lives.* Albuquerque: University of New Mexico Press, 1988.

Simonson, Harold P. *The Closed Frontier: Studies in American Literary Tragedy.* New York: Holt, Rinehart, and Winston, 1970.

*Writers, Western Regionalism and a Sense of Place.* Fort Worth: Texas Christian University Press, 1989.

Slotkin, Richard. *The Fatal Environment: The Myth of the Frontier in the Age of Industrialization, 1800–1890.* New York: Atheneum, 1985.

*Gunfighter Nation: The Myth of the Frontier in Twentieth-Century America.* New York: Atheneum, 1992.

*Regeneration through Violence: The Mythology of the American Frontier, 1600–1860.* Middletown, CT: Wesleyan University Press, 1973.

Smith, Henry Nash. *Virginland: The American West as Symbol and Myth.* Cambridge, MA: Harvard University Press, 1950.

Sonnichsen, Charles L. *From Hopalong to Hud: Thoughts on Western Fiction.* College Station, TX: Texas A&M University Press, 1978.

Stauffer, Helen Winter, and Susan Rosowski, eds. *Women and Western American Literature.* Troy, NY: Whitston, 1982.

Stegner, Lynn, and Russell Rowland, eds. *West of 98: Living and Writing the New American West.* Austin: University of Texas Press, 2011.

Stegner, Wallace. *The Sound of Mountain Water: The Changing American West.* Garden City, NY: Doubleday and Co., 1969.

*Where the Bluebird Sings to the Lemonade Springs: Living and Writing in the West.* New York: Random House, 1992.

Stegner, Wallace, and Richard W. Etulain. *Conversations with Wallace Stegner on Western History and Literature.* Rev. ed. Salt Lake City: University of Utah Press, 1990.

Steiner. Stan. *The Waning of the West.* New York: St. Martin's Press, 1989.

Taylor, J. Golden, and Thomas J. Lyon, eds. *A Literary History of the American West.* Fort Worth: Texas Christian University Press, 1987.

Truettner, William H., ed. *The West as America: Reinterpreting Images of the Frontier, 1820–1920.* Washington, DC: Smithsonian Institution Press, 1991.

Turner, Frederick. *Beyond Geography: The Western Spirit against the Wilderness.* 1980 rpt. New Brunswick, NJ: Rutgers University Press, 1992.
   *Spirit of Place: The Making of an American Literary Landscape.* Washington, DC: Island Press, 1989.
Udall Stewart L., et al., *Beyond the Mythic West.* Salt Lake City: Peregrine Smith Books, in associations with the Western Governors' Association, 1990.
Whipple, T. K. *Study Out the Land.* Berkeley: University of California Press, 1943.
White, G. Edward. *The Eastern Establishment and the Western Experience: The West of Frederick Remington, Theodore Roosevelt, and Owen Wister.* New Haven, CT: Yale University Press, 1968.
Witschi, Nicholas. *A Companion to the Literature of the American West.* New York: Wiley/Blackwell, 2001.
Worster, Donald. *Unsettled Country: Changing Landscapes of the American West.* Albuquerque: University of New Mexico Press, 1994.

## Native American Literature

Allen, Paula Gunn. *The Sacred Hoop: Recovering the Feminine in American Indian Traditions.* Boston, MA: Beacon, 1986.
Brumble, H. David, III. *American Indian Autobiography.* Berkeley: University of California Press, 1988.
Castro, Michael. *Interpreting the Indian: Twentieth-Century Poets and the Native American.* Albuquerque: University of New Mexico Press, 1983.
Fleck, Richard F., ed. *Critical Perspectives on Native American Fiction.* Washington, DC: Three Continents Press, 1993.
Kroeber, Karl, ed. *American Indian Persistence and Resurgence.* Durham, NC: Duke University Press, 1994.
Krupat, Arnold. *For Those Who Came After: A Study of Native American Autobiography.* Los Angeles: University of California Press, 1985.
   *The Voice in the Margin: Native American Literature and the Canon.* Berkeley: University of California Press, 1989.
Larson, Charles R. *American Indian Fiction.* Albuquerque: University of New Mexico Press, 1978.
Lincoln, Kenneth. *Indi'n Humor: Bicultural Play in Native America.* New York: Oxford University Press, 1993.
   *Native American Renaissance.* Los Angeles: University of California Press, 1983.
Murray, David. *Forked Tongues: Speech, Writing, and Representation in North American Indian Texts.* Bloomington: Indiana University Press, 1991.
Owens, Louis. *Other Destinies: Understanding the Native American Novel.* Norman: University of Oklahoma Press, 1992.
Ramsey, Jarold. *Reading the Fire: Essays in the Traditional Indian Literatures of the Far West.* Lincoln: University of Nebraska Press, 1983.
   eds. *Recovering the Word: Essays on Native American Literature.* Berkeley: University of California Press, 1987.
Tedlock, Dennis. *The Spoken Word and the Work of Interpretation.* Philadelphia: University of Pennsylvania Press, 1983.

Velie, Alan R. *Four American Literary Masters: N. Scott Momaday, James Welch, Leslie Marmon Silko, and Gerald Vizenor*. Norman: University of Oklahoma Press, 1982.

Velie, Alan R., and A. Robert Lee, eds. *Native American Renaissance: Literary Imagination and Achievement*. Norman: University of Oklahoma Press, 2013.

Vizenor, Gerald, ed. *Narrative Chance: Postmodern Discourse on Native American Literatures*. Albuquerque: University of New Mexico Press, 1989.

Wiget, Andrew, ed. *Critical Essays on Native American Literature*. Boston, MA: G. K. Hall & Co., 1985.

*Dictionary of Native American Literature*. Hamden, CT: Garland, 1994.

*Native American Literature*. Boston, MA: Twayne, 1985.

Wong, Hertha Dawn. *Sending My Heart Back across the Years: Tradition and Innovation in Native American Autobiography*. New York: Oxford University Press, 1992.

## Hispanic American Literature

Anaya, Rudolph A., and Francisco Lomeli, eds. *Aztlan: Essays on the Chicano Homeland*. Albuquerque: Academia/El Norte Publications, 1989.

Anzaldúa, Gloria. *Borderlands/La Frontera: The New Mestiza*: San Francisco, CA: Spinsters/Aunt Lute, 1987.

Bruce-Novoa. *Chicano Poetry: A Response to Chaos*. Austin: University of Texas Press, 1982.

*Retrospace: Collected Essays on Chicano Literature, Theory, and History*. Houston, TX: Arte Publico Press, 1990.

Calderon, Hector, and Jose David Saldivar, eds. *Criticism in the Borderlands: Studies in Chicano Literature, Culture, and Ideology*. Durham, NC: Duke University Press, 1991.

Gutierrez, Ramon, and Genaro Padilla, eds. *Recovering the U.S. Hispanic Literary Heritage*. Houston, TX: Arte Publico Press, 1993.

Hernandez, Guillermo E. *Chicano Satire: A Study in Literary Culture*. Austin: University of Texas Press, 1991.

Herrara-Sobek, Maria, ed. *Beyond Stereotypes: The Critical Analysis of Chicana Literature*. Binghamton, NY: Bilingual Press, 1985.

ed. *Reconstructing a Chicano/a Literary Heritage: Hispanic Colonial Literature of the Southwest*. Tucson, University of Arizona Press, 1993.

Herrara-Sobek, Maria, and Helena Maria Viramontes, eds. *Chicana Creativity and Criticism: Charting New Frontiers in American Literature*. Houston, TX: Arte Publico Press, 1988.

Huerta, Jorge A. *Chicano Theater: Themes and Forms*. Ypsilanti, MI: Bilingual Press, 1982.

Jiminez, Francisco, ed. *The Identification and Analysis of Chicano Literature*. Binghamton, NY: Bilingual Press, 1979.

Kanellos, Nicolas. *The History of Hispanic Theatre in the United States: Origins to 1940*. Austin: University of Texas Press, 1990.

Lattin, Vernon E., ed. *Contemporary Chicano Fiction: A Critical Survey*. Binghamton, NY: Bilingual Press, 1986.

Limon, Jose Eduardo. *Mexican Ballads, Chicano Poems: History and Influence in Mexican American Social Poetry*. Berkeley: University of California Press, 1992.

Padilla, Genaro M. *My History, Not Yours: The Formation of Mexican American Autobiography*. Madison: University of Wisconsin Press, 1993.

Pettit, Arthur G. *Images of the Mexican American in Literature and Film*. College Station TX, Texas A & M University Press, 1980.

Promis, Jose, *The Identity of Hispanoamerica: An Interpretation of Colonial Literature*. Trans. Alita Kelley and Alec E. Kelley. Tucson: University of Arizona Press, 1991.

Rocard, Marcienne. Trans. Edward G. Brown Jr. *The Children of the Sun: Mexican-Americans in the Literature of the United States*. Tucson: University of Arizona Press, 1989.

Saldivar, Ramon. *Chicano Narrative: The Dialectics of Difference*. Madison: University of Wisconsin Press, 1990.

Sanchez, Marta Ester. *Contemporary Chicana Poetry: A Critical Approach to an Emerging Literature*. Berkeley: University of California Press, 1985.

Shirley, Carl R., and Paula W. Shirley. *Understanding Chicano Literature*. Columbia: University of South Carolina Press, 1988.

Sommers, Joseph, and Thomas Ybarra-Frausto, eds. *Modern Chicano Writers: A Collection of Critical Essays*. Englewood Cliffs, NJ: Prentice-Hall, 1979.

Tatum, Charles M. *Chicano Literature*. Boston, MA: Twayne, 1982.

Vallejos, Tomas. *Mestizaje: The Transformation of Ancient Indian Religious Thought in Contemporary Chicano Fiction*. Ann Arbor, MI: University Microfilms, 1980.

## Asian American Literature

Cheung, King-Kok. *Articulate Silences: Hisaye Yamamoto, Maxine Hong Kingston, Joy Kogawa*. Ithaca, NY: Cornell University Press, 1993.

Kim, Elaine H. *Asian American Literature: An Introduction to the Writings and Their Social Context*. Philadelphia: Temple University Press, 1982.

Lim, Shirley Geok-lin, and Amy Ling, eds. *Reading the Literatures of Asian America*. Philadelphia, PA: Temple University Press, 1992.

Ling, Amy. *Between Worlds: Women Writers of Chinese Ancestry*. New York: Pergamon, 1990.

Nomura, Gail M., et al., eds. *Frontiers of Asian American Studies: Writing, Research, and Criticism*. Pullman: Washington State University Press, 1989.

Wong, Sau-ling Cynthia. *Reading Asian American Literature: From Necessity to Extravagance*. Princeton, NJ: Princeton University Press, 1993.

## Environmentalist Literature

Abbey, Edward. *The Journey Home: Some Words in Defense of the American West*. New York: E. P. Dutton, 1977.

Buell, Lawrence. *The Environmental Imagination: Thoreau, Nature Writing, and the Formation of American Culture*. Cambridge, MA: Harvard University Press, 1996.

Cooley, John. *Earthly Words: Essays on Contemporary American Nature and Environmental Writers*. Ann Arbor: University of Michigan Press, 1994.

Elkins, Andrew. *Another Place: An Ecocritical Study of Selected Western American Poets*. Fort Worth: Texas Christian University Press, 2002.

Halpern, Daniel, ed. *On Nature: Nature, Landscape, and Natural History*. San Francisco, CA: North Point Press, 1986.

Kolodny, Annette. *The Lay of the Land: Metaphor as Experience and History in American Life and Letters*. Chapel Hill: University of North Carolina Press, 1975.

Marx, Leo. *The Machine in the Garden: Technology and the Pastoral Ideal in America*. New York: Oxford University Press, 1964.

McClintock, James I. *Nature's Kindred Spirits: Aldo Leopold, Joseph Wood Krutch, Edward Abbey, Annie Dillard, Gary Snyder*. Madison: University of Wisconsin Press, 1994.

Nash, Roderick. *Wilderness and the American Mind*, Third Edition. New Haven, CT: Yale University Press, 1982.

Norwood, Vera. *Made from This Earth: American Women and Nature*. Chapel Hill, University of North Carolina Press, 1993.

Paul, Sherman. *For Love of the World: Essays on Nature Writers*. Iowa City: University of Iowa Press, 1992.

Ronald, Ann, ed. *Reader of the Purple Sage: Essays on Western Writers and Environmental Literature*. Reno: University of Nevada Press, 2003.

Servid, Carolyn, ed. *Reflections from the Island's Edge: On Nature, Values, and the Western Word*. St. Paul, MN: Graywolf Press, 1994.

Slovic, Scott. *Seeking Awareness in American Nature Writing: Henry Thoreau, Annie Dillard, Edward Abbey, Wendell Berry, Barry Lopez*. Salt Lake City: University of Utah Press, 1992.

Snyder, Gary. *The Practice of the Wild*. San Francisco, CA: North Point Press, 1990.

Stewart, Frank. *A Natural History of Nature Writing*. Covelo, CA: Island Press, 1994.

Turner, Frederick. *Rediscovering America: John Muir in His Time and Ours*. New York: Viking, 1985.

# INDEX

*Cambridge Companions to ...*

AUTHORS

*Edward Albee* edited by
Stephen J. Bottoms
*Margaret Atwood* edited by
Coral Ann Howells
*W. H. Auden* edited by Stan Smith
*Jane Austen* edited by Edward Copeland
and Juliet McMaster (second edition)
*James Baldwin* edited by Michele Elam
*Beckett* edited by John Pilling
*Bede* edited by Scott DeGregorio
*Aphra Behn* edited by Derek Hughes and
Janet Todd
*Walter Benjamin* edited by David S. Ferris
*William Blake* edited by Morris Eaves
*Boccaccio* edited by Guyda Armstrong,
Rhiannon Daniels, and Stephen J. Milner
*Jorge Luis Borges* edited by
Edwin Williamson
*Brecht* edited by Peter Thomson and
Glendyr Sacks (second edition)
*The Brontës* edited by Heather Glen
*Bunyan* edited by Anne Dunan-Page
*Frances Burney* edited by Peter Sabor
*Byron* edited by Drummond Bone
*Albert Camus* edited by Edward J. Hughes
*Willa Cather* edited by
Marilee Lindemann
*Cervantes* edited by Anthony J. Cascardi
*Chaucer* edited by Piero Boitani and
Jill Mann (second edition)
*Chekhov* edited by Vera Gottlieb and
Paul Allain
*Kate Chopin* edited by Janet Beer
*Caryl Churchill* edited by Elaine Aston
and Elin Diamond
*Cicero* edited by Catherine Steel
*Coleridge* edited by Lucy Newlyn
*Wilkie Collins* edited by
Jenny Bourne Taylor
*Joseph Conrad* edited by J. H. Stape
*Dante* edited by Rachel Jacoff
(second edition)
*Daniel Defoe* edited by John Richetti
*Don DeLillo* edited by John N. Duvall
*Charles Dickens* edited by John O. Jordan
*Emily Dickinson* edited by Wendy Martin
*John Donne* edited by Achsah Guibbory

*H. D.* edited by Nephie J. Christodoulides
and Polina Mackay *Dostoevskii* edited by
W. J. Leatherbarrow
*Theodore Dreiser* edited by Leonard
Cassuto and Claire Virginia Eby
*John Dryden* edited by Steven N. Zwicker
*W. E. B. Du Bois* edited by
Shamoon Zamir
*George Eliot* edited by George Levine
*T. S. Eliot* edited by A. David Moody
*Ralph Ellison* edited by Ross Posnock
*Ralph Waldo Emerson* edited by Joel
Porte and Saundra Morris
*William Faulkner* edited by
Philip M. Weinstein
*Henry Fielding* edited by Claude Rawson
*F. Scott Fitzgerald* edited by Ruth Prigozy
*Flaubert* edited by Timothy Unwin
*E. M. Forster* edited by David Bradshaw
*Benjamin Franklin* edited by
Carla Mulford
*Brian Friel* edited by Anthony Roche
*Robert Frost* edited by Robert Faggen
*Gabriel García Márquez* edited by
Philip Swanson
*Elizabeth Gaskell* edited by Jill L. Matus
*Goethe* edited by Lesley Sharpe
*Günter Grass* edited by Stuart Taberner
*Thomas Hardy* edited by Dale Kramer
*David Hare* edited by Richard Boon
*Nathaniel Hawthorne* edited by
Richard Millington
*Seamus Heaney* edited by
Bernard O'Donoghue
*Ernest Hemingway* edited by
Scott Donaldson
*Homer* edited by Robert Fowler
*Horace* edited by Stephen Harrison
*Ted Hughes* edited by Terry Gifford
*Ibsen* edited by James McFarlane
*Henry James* edited by
Jonathan Freedman
*Samuel Johnson* edited by Greg Clingham
*Ben Jonson* edited by Richard Harp and
Stanley Stewart
*James Joyce* edited by Derek Attridge
(second edition)

*Mario Vargas Llosa* edited by Efrain
Kristal and John King
*Virgil* edited by Charles Martindale
*Voltaire* edited by Nicholas Cronk
*Edith Wharton* edited by Millicent Bell
*Walt Whitman* edited by Ezra Greenspan
*Oscar Wilde* edited by Peter Raby
*Tennessee Williams* edited by
Matthew C. Roudané
*August Wilson* edited by Christopher Bigsby

*Mary Wollstonecraft* edited by
Claudia L. Johnson
*Virginia Woolf* edited by Susan Sellers
(second edition)
*Wordsworth* edited by Stephen Gill
*Wyndham Lewis* edited by
Tyrus Miller
*W. B. Yeats* edited by Marjorie Howes
and John Kelly
*Zola* edited by Brian Nelson

## TOPICS

*The Actress* edited by Maggie B. Gale and
John Stokes
*The African American Novel* edited by
Maryemma Graham
*The African American Slave Narrative*
edited by Audrey A. Fisch
*African American Theatre* by
Harvey Young
*Allegory* edited by Rita Copeland and
Peter Struck
*American Crime Fiction* edited by
Catherine Ross Nickerson
*American Gay and Lesbian Literature*
edited by Scott Herring
*American Modernism* edited by
Walter Kalaidjian
*The American Modernist Novel* edited by
Joshua Miller
*American Poetry since 1945* edited by
Jennifer Ashton
*American Poets* edited by
Mark Richardson
*American Realism and Naturalism* edited
by Donald Pizer
*American Science Fiction* edited by Gerry
Canavan and Eric Carl Link
*American Travel Writing* edited by Alfred
Bendixen and Judith Hamera
*American Women Playwrights* edited by
Brenda Murphy
*Ancient Rhetoric* edited by
Erik Gunderson
*Arthurian Legend* edited by Elizabeth
Archibald and Ad Putter
*Asian American Literature* edited by
Crystal Parikh and Daniel Y. Kim

*Australian Literature* edited by
Elizabeth Webby
*Autobiography* edited by Maria DiBattista
and Emily Wittman
*The Body in Literature* edited by David
Hillman and Ulrika Maude
*British Fiction since 1945* edited by
David James
*British Literature of the French
Revolution* edited by Pamela Clemit
*British Poetry, 1945–2010* edited by
Edward Larrissy
*British Romantic Poetry* edited by James
Chandler and Maureen N. McLane
*British Romanticism* edited by Stuart
Curran (second edition)
*British Theatre, 1730–1830* edited by Jane
Moody and Daniel O'Quinn
*Canadian Literature* edited by
Eva-Marie Kröller
*Children's Literature* edited by M. O.
Grenby and Andrea Immel
*The Classic Russian Novel* edited by
Malcolm V. Jones and Robin Feuer Miller
*Contemporary Irish Poetry* edited by
Matthew Campbell
*Creative Writing* edited by David Morley
and Philip Neilsen
*Crime Fiction* edited by Martin Priestman
*Early Modern Women's Writing* edited by
Laura Lunger Knoppers
*The Eighteenth-Century Novel* edited by
John Richetti
*Eighteenth-Century Poetry* edited by
John Sitter
*Emma* edited by Peter Sabor